Advance Praise for *Perfect Storm*

"Thane Gustafson offers a detailed appraisal of how Russia's complex relations with the West ruptured under Vladimir Putin and a clear-eyed assessment of how they might be restored beyond Putin. This deeply insightful book is a 'must read' for anyone seeking to understand the current Russian challenge and its prospects. And Gustafson proves again why he is one of the most astute and accomplished observers of modern Russia."

—**Fiona Hill**, former presidential adviser on
Russian and European affairs, Senior Fellow
at The Brookings Institution, and author of
There Is Nothing For You Here

"Vladimir Putin's clash with the West, and his embrace of China, is often cast as a story of grand strategy imperial ambition. This wise and timely book by Thane Gustafson, a world expert on the geopolitics of energy, shows that it is a human tragedy too: the failure of a 30-year dream of Russian opening to Western businesses, technologies and ideas of what makes a good society."

—**David Rennie**, Geopolitics editor and columnist, *The Economist*

"Russia's brief opening to the West and how it came undone by war and sanctions is a complex story of social and economic ties that now lie in ruins. Thane Gustafson masterfully explains this period with nuance and depth, and he argues that Russia's future, despite all that has happened, still one day lies with an eventual return to Europe and the West."

—**Tom Nichols**, Staff writer at *The Atlantic* and Professor
Emeritus, U.S. Naval War College

"*Perfect Storm* is an invaluable contribution to our understanding of why the United States and Russia are such bitter foes today despite the great hopes for partnership at the end of the Cold War. Gustafson provides an in-depth exploration of an often-overlooked cause: Americans' and Russians' unrealistic expectations for business cooperation and investment. Unfulfilled hopes, he shows, eventually produced deep mutual resentment, which reinforced Vladimir Putin's geopolitical turn against the West and lay behind the West's 'hurricane' of anti-Russian sanctions since his invasion of Ukraine. Gustafson draws the key lessons from this failed effort at cooperation, which should inform US policy when Russia eventually seeks to restore relations, as Gustafson compellingly argues it will after Putin departs the political scene."

—**Thomas Graham**, distinguished fellow at the Council on Foreign Relations and author of *Getting Russia Right*

BOOKS BY THANE GUSTAFSON

Perfect Storm:
Russia's Failed Opening, War, Sanctions, and the Future

Klimat:
Russia in the Age of Climate Change

The Bridge:
Russian Gas in a Redivided Europe

Wheel of Fortune:
The Battle for Oil and Power in Russia

Russia 2010:
And What It Means for the World (with Daniel Yergin)

Crisis Amid Plenty:
The Politics of Soviet Energy under Brezhnev and Gorbachev

Capitalism Russian-Style

Reform in Soviet Politics:
Lessons of Recent Policies on Environment, Land, and Water

Co-edited Books:
Soldiers and the Soviet State: Civil–Military Relations from Brezhnev to
Gorbachev
(co-edited with Timothy Colton)

Russia at the Crossroads: The 26th Congress of the CPSU
(co-edited with Seweryn Bialer)

Perfect Storm

Perfect Storm

Russia's Failed Economic Opening, the Hurricane of War and Sanctions, and the Uncertain Future

By

THANE GUSTAFSON

OXFORD
UNIVERSITY PRESS

OXFORD
UNIVERSITY PRESS

Oxford University Press is a department of the University of Oxford.
It furthers the University's objective of excellence in research, scholarship,
and education by publishing worldwide. Oxford is a registered trade mark of
Oxford University Press in the UK and in certain other countries.

Published in the United States of America by Oxford University Press
198 Madison Avenue, New York, NY 10016, United States of America.

Library of Congress Cataloging-in-Publication Data
Names: Gustafson, Thane, author.
Title: Perfect storm : Russia's failed economic opening, the hurricane of
war and sanctions, and the uncertain future / by Thane Gustafson.
Description: New York, NY : Oxford University Press, [2025] | Includes
bibliographical references and index.
Identifiers: LCCN 2024039674 (print) | LCCN 2024039675 (ebook) |
ISBN 9780197795682 (hardback) | ISBN 9780197795705 (epub) | ISBN 9780197795712
Subjects: LCSH: Russia (Federation)—Foreign economic relations—Western
countries. | Western countries—Foreign economic relations—Russia
(Federation) | Russia (Federation)—Economic conditions—1991-
Classification: LCC HF1558.2.Z4 G87 2025 (print) | LCC HF1558.2.Z4 (ebook) |
DDC 337.47—dc23/eng/20241203
LC record available at https://lccn.loc.gov/2024039674
LC ebook record available at https://lccn.loc.gov/2024039675

DOI: 10.1093/oso/9780197795682.001.0001

Printed by Sheridan Books, Inc., United States of America

This book is dedicated to my family, Nil, Peri, Farah, and Kenan, with all my love.

Contents

Acknowledgments

This book could not have been written without the help of many good friends and colleagues, who have been constant companions along the way. Over the past three years we have been in practically daily touch, exchanging ideas, sources, and news. I am especially grateful to Simon Blakey, Julian Cooper, Stephen Fortescue, Tom Nichols, Bob Otto, and Philip Vorobyov.

Many thanks to those who read and criticized earlier versions of the manuscript or individual chapters. In addition to those already named, Tom Graham, Jeff Lord, Bruce Parrott, David Rennie, Andrew Seck, Chris Weafer, and Irina Zamarina, all took the time and trouble to contribute valuable corrections and suggestions.

I have benefited from many conversations with friends who have shared their insights from their own research and expertise, notably Harley Balzer on Russian–Chinese relations, Marjorie Mandelstam Balzer on the Siberian Arctic, Angelina Davydova on Russian climate policy, Jackie Kerr on Russian cyber, Jeff Lord on the US sanctions system, John Lough on German–Russian relations, Tatiana Mitrova on Russian energy, the late Peter Reddaway on the security services, Andrew Seck on LNG, Jesse Scott on the European Union, Sergey Vakulenko on Russian oil, and Stephen Wegren on Russian agriculture. Craig Kennedy's path-breaking work on the oil sanctions has been a steady inspiration, as have those of Philip Connolly on the Russian financial system and Julian Cooper on military and civilian technology.

Special thanks to several long-time friends and former colleagues who have related to me their experiences of doing business in Russia, notably Peter Charow, co-founder of the American Chamber of Commerce in Moscow and a long-time senior advisor to BP. Likewise, I am grateful to many former members of the Western business community in Russia who shared their recollections, among them Jacques de Boisseson, Petter Nore, Michel Soublin, and David Tournadre.

I have also enjoyed the fellowship of an informal circle of Russia-watchers, who have dubbed themselves the *kruzhok* ("the circle"), and who correspond by Internet, sharing a common fascination with a country that always surprises. One of great pleasures of participating in the *kruzhok* has been the renewal of ties with many long-time friends, such as Paul Josephson and Peter Rutland.

I would like to pay tribute to the work of the late US-Russia Business Council, to its director Dan Russell and his deputy Randi Levinas, and especially to Anton Chaliy, whose tireless daily reporting was a constant and valuable resource.

My colleagues and students at Georgetown continue to be a source of friendship and inspiration. The Government Department, under its present chairman Anthony Arend as well as its past heads, has been a happy and productive home. Special thanks also to the Georgetown Center for Russian and Eurasian Studies (CERES), led by Michael David-Fox and the CERES team, Lisa Gordinier, and Jessica Miller. The Georgetown School of Foreign Service under Joel Hellman has been a hospitable second base, particularly its program on Science, Technology, and International Affairs (STIA), which is in the capable hands of Joanna Lewis and Theresa Sabonis-Helf. Many thanks to them, as well as to Alan Langlieb, for his always helpful advice.

It is always a special pleasure for a professor to stay in touch with former students and to watch them progress to successful careers and accomplishments. In several cases these have become close friends, in particular Tom Nichols and Phil Vorobyov. Among many others, I would like to mention Matias Burdman, Tina Dolbaia, Nursultan Eldosov, Jonathan Hayes, David Larsen, Andy Lee, Raphael Piliero, Hugh Ramlow, Claire Vogel, and Adam Wozniak. Lastly, I am grateful to Jonas Heering for his kind coaching in the German language and for many friendly conversations over the years.

I remain in close touch with many former teammates at Cambridge Energy Research Associates (CERA), notably Anna Galtsova, Kelly Knight, Laurent Ruseckas, Dina Sholk, Michael Stoppard, and Irina Zamarina. And I am grateful as always to Daniel Yergin and Angela Stent, who made my long association with CERA and Georgetown possible.

The field of Russian studies in the West remains vigorously alive, despite the present low point in Russian–Western relations. I am grateful to the Davis Center at Harvard, my former home, and especially its long-time former director and my friend of many decades, Timothy Colton. In the field of energy, the Oxford Institute of Energy Studies, led by James Henderson, is a unique resource. Its research on Russian energy features notably several valuable recent studies by my former colleague Vitaly Yermakov.

The entire Russian field has been enriched by the latest flow of talented people out of Russia, many of whom are friends and former colleagues. From their new homes in the West, they continue to deepen our common knowledge of Russia, working with research organizations such as the Carnegie Endowment's Russia Eurasia Center in Berlin, the Peterson Institute in Washington, and the Center on Global Energy Policy at Columbia University. Special thanks are due to the Kyiv School of Economics, which maintains an indispensable database on the status of Western companies in Russia. I am also grateful to Tatiana Mitrova and her team of former researchers from Skolkovo, who led for several years a valuable think tank in Belgrade.

Despite the efforts of the present regime, Russia remains surprisingly open as a source of information and commentary, thanks to the Internet and online resources such as Telegram. I am grateful to many Russian friends and colleagues with whom I correspond regularly, although they cannot be named here. I wish them courage and endurance.

Alla Baranovsky, my research assistant for this book, has been an invaluable source of advice and suggestions, as she has painstakingly read successive drafts, patrolled Russian-language sources, tracked down innumerable errors, and debated with me on the best ways to improve the book. This is Alla's second book with me, and in both projects she has been a unique partner. Heartfelt thanks to her.

I am grateful to the editorial team at Oxford University Press, Dave McBride, Emily Benitez, and Mhairi Bennett, for managing this project with unerring skill, and for their patient moral support throughout. Many thanks also to Raja Dharmaraj of Integra, based in my favorite Indian town of Pondicherry, and to the indefatigable and highly capable copyeditor, Bríd Nowlan. To all of them many thanks.

My family, as always, has been my heart's home, my shelter, and my inspiration, and this book is fondly dedicated to them. I am deeply grateful to all of them, and especially to my son Kenan, who graduated this year from Georgetown's School of Foreign Service, and who has been a wise counselor throughout the writing of this book.

September 2024
©Thane Gustafson

Note on Transliteration

Transliteration from Slavic to Latin script is always a challenge, particularly where proper nouns are concerned. Throughout this book I have attempted to follow the guidelines of the US Library of Congress wherever possible. However, for place names the American Association of Geographers has its own conventions, and in most places I have followed those. (Thus: Ob River instead of Ob'.) Finally, if a place or person has been mentioned frequently in the Western media, then I follow the spelling used in the media. (Thus: Mikhelson instead of Mikhel'son.) Unfortunately, the result is a running series of compromises, which will leave no one entirely satisfied.

Introduction

Russia's invasion of Ukraine has brought to a tragic close a thirty-year period of history that began with the collapse of the Soviet Union in the early 1990s and the fall of the Iron Curtain. For three tumultuous decades, Russia was open to the West. The opening set off a vast movement of people, ideas, and money, as Westerners flowed into Russia and Russians came west. But the opening has now been followed by a new closing, driven by the Ukrainian war, the imposition of Western sanctions, and the Russian responses to them. Russian–Western relations today are as hostile as they have ever been.

Who or what is to blame? There is already an abundant literature on the failure of Russian-Western geopolitical relations, the origins and causes of the Ukrainian War, and the parts both sides have played in them. But this book is not about the geopolitics. Instead, it is an attempt to tell the broader story of Russia's flawed opening to the West in its economic, technological, and social dimensions, and the roles these played in its ultimate failure. These are equally essential to an understanding of what happened, and what went wrong. Yet they have received much less attention.

The devil has many guises. But chief among these was the clash of beliefs, the gulf of perceptions and understandings between a triumphant West, flush with its born-again faith in the power of markets and the global liberal order,[1] and a Russia whose decayed system had collapsed from within. The West saw itself as victorious against a defeated enemy, whereas Russians saw themselves as a great people defeated, not by the West, but by a home-grown dictatorship and ideology grown corrupt and weak. Once that system collapsed, Russia had no ready answers or alternative institutions. In that difference of situations and perceptions lay a fertile breeding-ground for devils of every sort. It amounted to nothing less than a confrontation of two civilizations.[2]

Therefore, not surprisingly, the opening of the Russian economy and society was flawed from the beginning. After a brief period of hopeful enthusiasm, the political disorders of the 1990s, the corrupt privatization, and the rise of the "oligarchs"[3] soon produced disillusionment. This was compounded by the manner of the West's entry into Russia, which frequently created misunderstanding and resentment. In parallel, the less savory Russians abroad, such as oligarchs and criminals, stained the reputation of all Russians in Western eyes. The resulting mixture of mutual mistrust and condemnation provided political support and psychological fuel for Putin's growing geopolitical resentment and rage toward the West after the mid-2000s, and for the West's increasingly hostile response. Starting with Russia's occupation of Crimea in 2014 and the first round of Western sanctions that followed, the two narratives of Russia's failed opening—the geopolitical and the socioeconomic—became intertwined and reinforced one another. Vladimir Putin played on both narratives, as it suited him.[4]

The geopolitical story was constantly in the headlines. After an initial period of attempts to build constructive relations, it soon turned sharply negative, as it went from crisis to crisis. The sequence of geopolitical moves and counter-moves took on its own momentum, generating anger and rancor on both sides. In contrast, the economic story was more subtle, less prominently covered in the news (more often in the business section than on the front page), but far-reaching in its consequences. Despite the mixed emotions it aroused, the opening left one overwhelmingly positive legacy— the transformation of Russia into a market economy and an Internet-based society. These revolutionary changes are here to stay.

But the war and the sanctions, together with the Russian responses to them, have now destroyed the economic and business ties between Russia and the West created during the opening. Financial connections have been severed; funds have been frozen; trade has been disrupted; and businesses have withdrawn on both sides. Inside Russia, capital and labor are being diverted to the military; and countless thousands of people, far from the battlefield, are caught in the turmoil. With each round of Western sanctions and Russian counter-sanctions, the mutual alienation of Russia and the West deepens, while the war grinds on. A "flawed" opening has now become "failed."

Will Russia, in any foreseeable future, seek to reopen to the West? In this book I will argue that the historic changes wrought during Russia's thirty-year opening—despite their flaws, despite the war, despite the sanctions— may nevertheless provide a foundation to which Russia and the West can ultimately return.

But for that to happen, two conditions must be met. The first is a change of leadership in Russia—not simply the departure of one leader, but the rise to power of a new generation. The second is a stable end to the Ukrainian war and the beginning of a settlement. Neither condition is likely to be met within less than a decade. That is why my focus is on the longer term, looking to the mid-2030s as the earliest horizon when a new opening of Russia to the West, and a rebuilding of Russian–Western relations, might be possible.

Despite the closing to the West, Russia remains actively connected to the rest of the world. Over the past decade, and especially since the invasion, it has pursued a "pivot to the east," expanding its relations with developing countries, and especially China.[5] Russia in that sense is hardly isolated. The current Russian leadership hails the eastward shift as part of a new era in world economic power, in which the West will play a declining role while the East dominates. Under Putin and Xi Jinping, Russian and Chinese leaders share an ideological vision of multipolar global leadership. But I will argue that the pivot to the East comes with serious liabilities for Russia, which will become increasingly evident as time goes by. Russia's long-term interest lies in a reopening toward the West.

This book consists of three parts. The first describes the opening of Russia between 1992 and 2022, the movement of the West into Russia and that of Russia into the West, and asks, What went right and what went wrong? What was achieved, and what failed? And what was Putin's role? The second part recounts the hurricane of sanctions that followed the Russian invasion of Ukraine, the dismantling of the financial and business relations built over the previous thirty years, followed by the exit of Westerners from Russia and the massive emigration of Russians to the West and to the former Soviet Union, both of which are still ongoing. This part asks, What has been the impact of these events on Russia in the short term, and what will it be over time? The third and final part looks ahead, and explores the conditions under which a reopening to the West might take place.

The opening of Russia was ultimately about people—the politicians and diplomats, the entrepreneurs and managers, the experts and advisors, and the ordinary travelers and consumers—who interacted with one another over the course of thirty years. The reader will find here many portraits of the actual players and their stories. They are in the end the real story of Russia's failed opening—and its possible reopening.

The Flawed Two-Way Opening of Russia

The sudden and unexpected opening of Russia in the 1990s marked the end of seven decades of isolation that had begun in the 1930s with Stalin's creation of the Soviet planned economy and its policy of "autarky," a systematic self-isolation from the West. The arrival of the Westerners in Russia had actually begun under Mikhail Gorbachev, but accelerated manyfold with the end of the Soviet Union, bringing thousands of companies and hundreds of thousands of individuals into close contact with one another.

On many levels, it was a time of extraordinary achievement, perhaps the single most transformative period in Russian history. The consumer sector blossomed, a vigorous retail sector was born, small businesses multiplied, and a whole new tier of market-oriented services and professions came into being. People traveled; money moved; and the world's goods flooded in. Partnerships prospered, friendships formed, and not a few marriages. Several thousand Russian orphans were adopted by Western families. The opening shaped the lives of millions of Russians, as well as those of the Westerners who took part in it.

The impact of the opening on Russian industry was less immediate and colorful than in the consumer sector, but it was no less profound. The energy sector was reorganized and modernized, and a new generation of infrastructure was built to support exports of oil, gas, and coal. The metals industry was extensively updated with new Western plants and technology. Several branches of manufacturing were upgraded. The automotive sector was revamped and the railroads were improved. Agriculture was rebuilt, with the advent of private "agro-holdings" oriented toward world markets. In all of these, Western companies played influential roles, as suppliers of capital, technology, and expertise.

Over the course of thirty years, Russia became a market economy, increasingly open to international trade and investment. The Internet came to Russia, and quickly became the indispensable foundation for commerce, entertainment, and social life. New financial services proliferated, such as mortgages for real estate, stimulated by the mass privatization of housing. Underlying these were significant reforms in institutions, notably the courts, which despite their many imperfections became widely used for business disputes, both among private claimants and between citizens and the government.[6] Much of this was done on Western business models, with active Western participation, and extensive collaboration on both sides.

The Western presence in Russia, however, engendered conflicting emotions. Russians increasingly resented being tutored and hectored by the Westerners and treated like second-class citizens in their own country. They saw themselves as disrespected at home and diminished abroad, in a world that no longer perceived Russia as a great power. Likewise, the Russian presence in the West frequently led to hostility and mistrust, as the West reacted to the excesses of the Russian oligarchs and the proliferation of corrupt finance and organized crime of Russian origin, as well as the ambitions of Russian state-sponsored companies like Gazprom and Rosatom.[7] As disenchantment deepened on both sides, it provided fuel for populist politicians, and above all Putin himself.

In thinking about the two-way opening of Russia, it is difficult to disentangle its influence on Russian public opinion from the impact of the Soviet collapse and the anarchy of the 1990s. Especially outside of Moscow, this was a time of hardship for most Russians, and for today's older generation the memory of the two is inevitably connected. For them, the 1990s were transformative, but often traumatic. For younger Russians, the 1990s are already ancient history. They take the positive changes for granted, but echoes of the negative ones linger on, reinforced by the regime's propaganda machine.

But for both generations, young and old, the opening of Russia changed their lives. It was a unique event, which owed its special character to the extreme differences between Russia and the West after sixty years of the Iron Curtain. When Russia next reopens to the West, however and whenever that happens, it will not happen again in the same way. "No man ever steps into the same river twice," Heraclitus said 2,500 years ago. "For it's not the same river and he's not the same man." Both Russia and the world will have changed. In that changed world, what conditions and circumstances will be necessary before a reopening can take place? We return to this question in the final part of the book.

The Hurricane of Sanctions

Since the beginning of Russia's invasion of Ukraine, Russia has been hit by sanctions from over forty different Western countries; a hurricane of tens of thousands of bans covering everything from financial payments to oil exports; imports into Russia of high technology and key components, both civilian and military; and a wide range of consumer goods and services. Thousands of Russians, both inside and outside of Russia, have been sanctioned and their property frozen or confiscated. The post-invasion sanctions aim to impose overwhelming costs on the Russian economy as a whole—its industry, its military, and its financial system—and to prevent Russia from pursuing its aggression in Ukraine, while punishing the Putin regime that caused it. And although they are explicitly not aimed at the Russian people, the sanctions also ban a wide range of consumer and luxury goods.

The sanctions, combined with the West's support for Ukraine, are in effect an attempt to create a new containment policy, in updated financial and economic dress. But the world has changed, and so has Russia. It is no longer the era of George Kennan, in which a powerful and united West, under the leadership of a United States at the height of its power, sought to contain a militant totalitarian ideology with global pretensions and great-power ambitions. The West is weaker and less united than it was during the Cold War. Russia too is weaker, and is no longer the beacon of revolutionary Marxism-Leninism around the world. Containment in Kennan's sense is neither possible nor relevant. The enemy is no longer the Soviet Union, but Putinism, a perverted blend of vengeful Russian imperialism, kleptocracy, and a distorted reading of history. It is Putinism that must be contained.[8]

Seen from that perspective, the Western sanctions are limited in scope, aimed at defeating one man and his system. So far, they have failed to weaken the Putinist onslaught. But over time, if the West perseveres in them, they will degrade the wealth and competitiveness of the Russian economy and society, undermining the basis of the Putin regime. Yet sanctions are a costly instrument, with damaging side-effects and undesirable long-term consequences for both sides. The longer they are pursued, the more they will lead to a lasting atrophy of Russia's ties to the West, together with its alienation from Western institutions and values. In parallel, the wholesale application of sanctions over an extended period will lead to a degradation of the self-regulating institutions that govern finance, trade, and innovative entrepreneurship in the global economy, and ultimately a decline in the influence of the dollar and the euro.

This is not a favorable outcome for either side. Rather, the proper aim of sanctions must be to prepare the way for a settlement of the Ukrainian conflict and the eventual return of Russia to a constructive relationship with the West, leading to the sanctions' ultimate removal. However, this will not be possible so long as Putin and his circle are in power.

Toward a Reopening of Russia to the West?

As we look into the future, through the present fog of war and sanctions, we may be confident that someday Russia will seek to rebuild constructive relations with the West. A country that extends across eleven time zones, with an educated society and an advanced industrial economy, will not remain an international pariah, nor should the West wish it to be one. Someday, under a new leadership, in the hands of a new generation, Russia will look to re-emerge from its self-inflicted isolation, and the West will need to respond. Speculation about any reopening of Russia may seem premature today. But in human affairs nothing lasts forever. Great periods of conflict are followed by great efforts to rebuild, in new times and under new leaders. These take partly the form of diplomacy, with new agreements and new treaties, and new alliances in the ever-shifting balance of global geopolitics. But they also take the form of new economic relations. Under the driving forces of business, finance, trade, and technology, new opportunities and challenges arise, with new players. New institutions are created. New deals are struck. New bridges are built. So it will be again this time.

But before any reopening of Russia is possible, two things must happen. The first is the departure of Vladimir Putin. He is mortal, whether politically or physically. Within another fifteen years at most, he will be gone from the scene. Putin's departure will open new opportunities, but also new uncertainties. In a worst-case scenario, it could lead to renewed political chaos in Russia, as long pent-up forces are released and Putin's successors fight for power and wealth. Yet the final part of this book will argue that there is also a plausible positive scenario, with more favorable prospects than the first time around. The failures of the first opening will not necessarily be repeated. The worst is not inevitable.

The second precondition, however, is that Putin's chief legacy, the Ukrainian war, must end. Putin's departure will not by itself remove the many underlying causes of the Ukrainian conflict. There will be many years ahead of difficult negotiations with Putin's successors, whoever they are—over reparations and "frozen assets," over weapons and arms control, over deterrence and crisis management, over the boundaries between Russia and Europe—all of which have been casualties of the war. Progress will need to be accompanied by the step-by-step removal of sanctions and the restoration of economic ties between Russia and the West. But Putin's departure will provide the opportunity, if it is seized.

Yet the damage caused by Putin's war will long outlive him. Putin's Russia will not be easily forgiven for its crimes in Ukraine, and Putin's imperial ambitions will leave a lasting legacy of mistrust in the West, especially among Russia's European neighbors. The hopes and naive enthusiasm of the 1990s will not be repeated. It will take a generation or more before constructive relations can be rebuilt, on a different basis and in a changed world. It will truly not be the same river.

But let us first turn back to the beginning, with the arrival of the first Western businesses, and their ultimate symbol, the Golden Arches of McDonald's.

PART I
RUSSIA'S FAILED OPENING

Chapter 1
Through the Cracked Looking-Glass

The West Arrives in Russia

The Arrival of McDonald's

You had to be there. On January 31, 1990, 8,000 Muscovites stood in line for hours for the opening of the first McDonald's in the Soviet Union, on Moscow's Pushkin Square, for their first taste of US-style hamburgers and French fries, served by smiling waitresses (a radical departure from the usual dour take-it-or-leave-it style of Soviet service), complete with ketchup and pickles. By the end of the first day, 30,000 customers had been served. The Golden Arches had arrived, and along with them, the golden era of Western business in Russia. That first day, McDonald's first restaurant on Pushkin Square broke the record for the most hamburgers sold by any McDonald's restaurant anywhere. By the time it exited from Russia, thirty-two years later, McDonald's owned over 800 restaurants with 62,000 employees.

Everything had to be improvised from scratch. George Cohon, the Canadian-born head of McDonald's Russia, created an entire supply chain for the company in Russia. He scoured the landscape, looking for Russian farmers who would agree to grow just the right potatoes for the all-important French fries. "We needed farmers to switch from producing the small, round, traditional Russian potatoes to the longer variety that we required," Cohon recalled.[1] He found Russian providers for beef and buns, but pickles were a special challenge, until Cohon located a farmer who would grow the proper cucumbers and pickle them to McDonald's exacting standards.[2] In the end, everything was sourced locally, making several fortunes for the Russian providers who agreed to take the risk—notably the plucky pickle producer, Anatolii Reviakin, who went on to become the "Pickle King" of Russian processed food.[3]

Cohon made a point of only accepting rubles, and no foreign currency, so as to avoid any suspicion of black-market dealings. But this posed a problem: the ruble was not yet convertible, and it was not possible to repatriate profits. But Cohon thought up a clever way of monetizing McDonald's ruble revenues, by using them to upgrade Soviet office buildings in Moscow to "European Standard," and then leasing them to Western multinationals arriving in Russia—which would then transfer hard currency "offshore" to McDonald's headquarters from their home offices in the West.[4]

The story of McDonald's in Russia illustrates several features that characterized all Western business in Russia over the following years. The first was the uneasy coexistence of business and politics, and the essential importance of partnerships with politically influential Russian players. It had taken Cohon fourteen years, beginning in 1976, to break through the Soviet bureaucracy and build the necessary political support for his vision. The green light ultimately came from Mikhail Gorbachev himself (who later wrote a friendly foreword to Cohon's autobiography). Similarly, the subsequent expansion of McDonald's throughout Russia required the building of elaborate networks with regional political authorities. Where such partnerships did not exist, progress was slow if not impossible, and McDonald's and other early Western businesses could find themselves out in the cold or dispossessed altogether.

Second, Cohon's improvisations underscored a fundamental fact—that the institutional and legal foundations for Western business did not yet exist, and the Soviet foundations had collapsed as well. In the prevailing vacuum, much had to be done informally—"Russian-style"—with a wink and a nod, and occasional subterfuge. Third—and ultimately the most important feature—the arrival of McDonald's, the ultimate symbol of capitalism, aroused both enormous excitement among ordinary citizens, but also envy and resentment, a mix of emotions that characterized the Russian responses to the West over the next thirty years.

In short, the story of McDonald's already carried within it the main themes of the Russian–Western relationship in Russia as it developed over the following three decades, from ordinary citizens to top leaders, and from the capital to the regions. The early excitement over the arrival of McDonald's was soon followed by more mixed emotions on the part of the Russians. We turn to those first.

Excitement and High Expectations, Followed by Resentment and Disappointment

A major theme of this chapter is the deep flaws in the opening, and the negative views that Russians and Westerners developed about one another as a result. Initially, in the early 1990s, there was a "romantic" phase, when the arrival of Western goods and businesses, like McDonald's, was greeted by Russians with heady excitement and high expectations. But disillusionment and resentment soon followed, as Russians became aware that many Westerners viewed Russia with contempt as the "losers" of the Cold War, a defeated country "in receivership," as Zbigniew Brzezinski once put it.[5] The newcomers often knew little about Russia beyond the headlines and tended to exaggerate the chaos of the "Wild East," while underestimating the Russians' underlying capacities and skills. They typically spoke no Russian, apart from a handful with Russian family roots. In Moscow, Western consultants and bankers preached to their Russian clients about transparency and the sanctity of contracts, causing mounting irritation. As Boris Jordan, who came to Moscow for Crédit Suisse and played a key role in Anatoliy Chubais's privatization program, later recalled, "We made every mistake an American makes in a foreign country. We were arrogant. We'd walk in a room and tell everybody how it's supposed to be done."[6] In these respects, the Europeans were not fundamentally different, although they were generally more diplomatic.

Up to a point, the Russians were willing to put up with patronizing lectures—what US diplomat Victoria Nuland memorably dubbed the delivery of "spinach" to the Russians—provided the Westerners also delivered tangible support. On one memorable evening in 1993, at the inaugural meeting of the joint Gore-Chernomyrdin commission (a body set up to develop avenues of cooperation between the US and Russian governments), Larry Summers (then undersecretary of the Treasury for International Affairs) lectured Prime Minister Viktor Chernomyrdin at length on "conditionality," i.e., the conditions under which the International Monetary Fund (IMF) would grant loans.[7] Chernomyrdin was furious. But he was not alone; many Russians shared his feelings, although usually not as colorfully as the Russian/Georgian oligarch Kakha Bendukidze, who one day exploded: "I know you guys would like to come here and teach us heathens how to eat with a fork and knife and just to make sure we brush our teeth the right way."[8] Many Russians, at all levels, felt the same.

The problem was aggravated by the high turnover among the Western expatriates. Each new wave of arrivals went through the same initial phase of elementary learning about Russia, *likbez*, as the Russians call it, a contraction of *likvidatsiia bezgramotnosti*, meaning literally, "liquidation of illiteracy" or "learning the ABC's." As Bob von Rekowski of Fidelity, a Moscow veteran who had seen many expats come and go, commented, "The Russians were sick of being lectured by each new wave of people that didn't do their home-work to be ready for prime time for the Russians . . . We just had endless waves of newbies from the West coming over and the Russians eventually just tired of it."[9]

Relations could be particularly tense in sectors where the Russians were long-established, with histories and conventions of their own. In Siberian oil country, for example, Western expats arrived armed with the latest techniques, especially "fracking" and horizontal drilling, all designed to pro-duce oil "Western style," as fast and profitably as possible. The Russian oil establishment objected that such practices shortened the life of the fields, diminishing their total production, but the brash Westerners dismissed them as unenlightened primitives. Time was money.[10]

Another case of tense relations was the Baltika brewery, which was taken over by Carlsberg in 2008. Baltika had long been a popular brand in Rus-sia, but Carlsberg brought in its own managers and changed the beer's recipe. This caused simmering resentment among the brewery's Russians. As one former senior Carlsberg executive commented, after Carlsberg was removed in 2023 and its previous Russian management restored, "They didn't resent the ownership so much as they resented that Carlsberg was trying to tell them how to work, when they knew better . . . Who are these Danish guys telling them how to do their job?"[11]

The Russians' feelings were not improved by the fact that the Westerners enjoyed fat pay packages and perks, compared to those of their Russian col-leagues. The 1998 financial crisis caused particular resentment, as Russian employees, who were paid in rubles, suffered a 75% devaluation of their buy-ing, while the expatriates, who were paid in dollars, were largely unaffected. As Michael Morgenstern, finance director of the Perestroika joint venture and later a participant in an oil joint venture in Siberia, put it:

My deputy at my company Perestroika, who was a very smart guy and a very fast learner, could quickly do almost everything I could. He resented the fact that I was making a salary much greater than he was. In Siberia, it was even worse because you had all these shoot-from-the hip oil guys from Texas bringing their own housing and their own food into a small town of 15,000 people in which some people were living in cleaned out oil drums for housing. Russians soon found out that there was nothing the foreigners were doing that they couldn't do or learn themselves. The discrepancy in compensation and treatment . . . added onto the overall underlying sense of dissension and disenfranchisement among the Russian population in general.[12]

Over time, these feelings grew, especially as the Russians quickly mastered the skills the Westerners had brought—not least because the Westerners had trained them and then promoted them, precisely in order to replace the expensive expats. As the 1990s went on, the Westerners' perceived value steadily declined, while that of the Russians increased—but not their pay packages.

Proximity was not necessarily the decisive factor. Most Russians outside Moscow and Saint Petersburg never met an actual live Westerner throughout these years, except for brief visitors and temporary workers, and certain popular tourist destinations, such as Novgorod. Even large cities with over a million inhabitants had no resident foreigners.[13] A typical example was Chelyabinsk, a military-industrial center that had been closed in Soviet times. A frequent Western visitor to Chelyabinsk was Anne Garrels, the Moscow correspondent for NPR, who made annual visits there to "see the real Russia" outside of Moscow, and wrote a unique first-person account, called *Putin Country: A Journey into the Real Russia.*[14] By 2000, good times had come to Russia, thanks mainly to high oil prices. In Chelyabinsk, Garrels found, there were Western-style restaurants and franchises of US and European hotel chains such as Holiday Inn and Radisson, which catered to foreign visitors, mostly investors and consultants and sports teams. There were shops offering Western fashions and cosmetics. But they were owned and staffed by Russians, not foreigners. The locals' views and feelings about the West were shaped by the foreign brands that poured into the city, and also increasingly by foreign travel, and above all by the Internet, which became universally available from about 2010, mainly via foreign-made smartphones. Their reactions were highly mixed. They felt the same ambivalence, the same contradictory mixture of appetite for all things Western, combined with an increasingly defensive nationalism, that all Russians felt everywhere.

In the rest of this chapter we illustrate these themes by looking at the main areas of interaction between the Westerners in Russia and their Russian hosts: economics and market reforms, professional services, industry and technology, and the consumer sector. The first question is, What roles did Westerners play in the creation of Russia's market economy?

Prelude: The Influence of the West on the Russian Economic Reforms

The earliest and most far-reaching influence of the West in Russia, but also the most controversial, was its role in Russia's rediscovery of economics and the early efforts to develop the institutions and policies of a market economy. There were two phases. The first was a period of radical reform, which ran from 1992 through 1998. The second was one of consolidation, which began in 1998 and continued up to the eve of the 2022 invasion of Ukraine. During the first phase, the influence of Western individuals and institutions was strong and direct; during the second, this influence faded sharply and by the end became essentially nonexistent.

"Rynok": Russia Rediscovers Economics and the Market

The Soviet command system had been built around a radical rejection of the market and all its institutions, beginning with private property. Money, the lifeblood of a market economy, became a secondary unit of account. Accordingly, the Soviet system had little use for Western-style economics or its practitioners. Under Stalin, as economist Gregory Grossman memorably put it, "The economics disappeared with the economists themselves."[15]

The ideas behind privatization and market economics had begun circulating in the Soviet Union as early as the 1980s, especially in Saint Petersburg, where the declining Soviet economy had performed even more poorly than in the rest of the country. There a group of young economists, led by Anatoliy Chubais, who was subsequently one of the main leaders of Russian privatization, began reading forbidden books on liberal economics and meeting in informal groups among themselves as early as 1980, to study how market economies worked. They established ties with other reform-minded thinkers, notably an economist named Yegor Gaidar in Moscow, who subsequently became prime minister in Yeltsin's first government. Gaidar, whose father was a foreign correspondent for Soviet newspapers, had lived in Yugoslavia as a teenager and was well-read in Western economics, which could be accessed easily in Eastern Europe.[16] These two men, more than any others, became the chief architects of the Russian market revolution.

The early Russian reformers had never experienced a market economy in real life, and it was not until the late 1980s that they traveled in the West and met actual Western counterparts. They were strongly influenced, but at a distance (Gaidar was the rare exception), by East European economists, notably the Hungarian Janos Kornai, and by the early experiments of the East Europeans with market reforms in Hungary and Yugoslavia. Partly because of this East European influence, the thinking of the Russian reformers took an increasingly radical turn. In this they were encouraged by many Western economists. By the 1980s, liberal economists in the West had embraced the view that market reforms, to be successful, needed to be introduced all at once, in a single package. The two central features of this "shock therapy" approach were rapid privatization and the decontrol of prices. Shock therapy had worked well when applied in Poland after 1989, and also in Bolivia. The Saint Petersburg liberals became convinced that it would work in Russia as well.

Westerners played multiple roles in Russia's rediscovery of economics and the development of its marketization program in the 1990s—as advisors to the economic reformers in the government, as models of economic policy, and as sources of emergency funds (and correspondingly as sources of exhortation and pressure).[17] The World Bank, the IMF, and the European Bank for Reconstruction and Development (EBRD) all opened offices in Moscow and dispatched mission after mission to advise the Russian government, extending credits and drawing rights to keep it afloat, while urging it to adopt Western-style macroeconomic policies.[18] Westerners worked in the offices of the Russian market reformers, such as the Privatization Committee, led by Anatoliy Chubais, and they helped to organize some of the early privatization auctions, notably in Nizhnii Novgorod, an early hotbed of market reform (where several of the subsequent leaders of the privatization program, including Sergei Kirienko, today the first deputy head of the Presidential Administration, first got their start). Russia's market economy was fundamentally a Russian creation, but the "visible hand" of the West was present everywhere in the 1990s—largely at the invitation of the reformers—and especially in the fashioning of the privatization program.

Thus, when Western free-market economists arrived in Moscow in 1991, they found a ready audience among the Russian reformers and in President Boris Yeltsin. The failed coup against Gorbachev and the collapse of the Soviet Union had suddenly put Yeltsin in power, and his top priority was to dismantle the Soviet system, including the planned economy, and to prevent it from ever returning. The key to success was thought to be speed, lest the Communists make a comeback. Yeltsin named as prime minister the leader of the economic reformers, Yegor Gaidar, and gave him free rein to implement a radical program based on mass privatization, convertibility of the ruble, and decontrol of prices. Although the Western economists were brought in at Gaidar's invitation to help design the plan and make the case to Yeltsin, the program itself was largely a Russian creation.[19] Yeltsin bought into it, and Russia's shock therapy was under way.

It proved a disaster. The sudden decontrol of prices caused runaway inflation. Money disappeared from circulation, and within months Russia had turned into a barter economy with a dollar-based black market, a resurrection of the Soviet-era shadow economy. The mass privatization campaign, based on vouchers distributed to the population without any restrictions on reselling them, miscarried badly, as speculators bought up vouchers from ordinary citizens for a pittance and sold them on by the bagfull to wholesale purchasing centers in Moscow. Enterprises stopped paying taxes, and the Russian treasury spiraled ever deeper into debt. To make ends meet, it resorted to borrowing through short-term bonds, for which it had to offer increasingly dizzying interest rates, in order to attract money from private Russian banks and foreign punters.

The Russian parliament, the Duma, which was dominated by opposition deputies, then blocked the reformers' program. The reformers were too weak, the conservatives too entrenched, and the Russian state itself too fractured, for the reformers' efforts or the Westerners' exhortations to prevail over the opposition. Yeltsin withdrew his support, and in 1993 the shock therapists were thrown out of office. Gaidar was replaced as prime minister by former Soviet official Viktor Chernomyrdin, the chairman of Gazprom. Over the next five years, Russia careened out of control, as Yeltsin sought to navigate between left and right, and quick-witted opportunists (famously dubbed "oligarchs" by one of them, Boris Berezovsky) seized the commanding heights of the former Soviet economy—chiefly oil and gas—through a series of rigged auctions, with the support of Boris Yeltsin, who needed their support for his 1996 re-election campaign.

As the crisis worsened, the World Bank and the IMF continued to provide credits, but these were soon overwhelmed by the torrents of speculative money, domestic and foreign, that poured into Russian debt. In July 1998 the IMF made its last emergency loan to the Russian government, an infusion of $4.8 billion, but this last desperate measure was unavailing, as speculators rushed to convert their rubles into foreign currency, and the government's reserves collapsed. As John Odling-Smee, then the IMF's top official for the

Former Soviet Union (FSU), wrote in his memoirs, "We and the Russians had shot our bolt."[20] Less than two months later, the Russian government defaulted on its debts, the speculators sold out for pennies on the dollar, and the entire house of cards came tumbling down.[21]

In 1998, Chernomyrdin was replaced as prime minister by Yevgeny Primakov, who had previously served as first deputy chairman of the KGB and director of foreign intelligence. Primakov managed for a brief time to steady the ship of state, but by this time the damage had been done. Shock therapy had done its work all too well: it had completed the destruction of the command economy begun under Gorbachev, but there was nothing to replace it.[22]

Popular opinion blamed the reformers—and also their Western advisors. Anders Aslund, who was one of the Western advisers in those days,[23] recalls seeing posters on Moscow billboards in September 1998 with the text, "Nobody will save Russia except ourselves." Underneath one of them, a wag had scribbled the signature of Michel Camdessus, the head of the IMF.[24]

But then came a surprising turnaround. In 1999 world oil prices hit bottom and started rising, and oil money began flowing into Russia again. The arrival of Vladimir Putin as president in 2000 brought a rapid reconsolidation of power around the Kremlin. And in a landmark decision, he named a reform-minded economist from Saint Petersburg, Aleksey Kudrin, as his minister of finance. These events marked a capital turning point, both in Russia's finances and in its political fortunes.

Kudrin was a different sort of reformer. From the beginning there had been two streams of market-minded economists from Saint Petersburg. There were the "shock therapists" on the one hand, but also a group of more cautious and experienced figures, including Aleksey Kudrin and his younger colleague German Gref, as well as Vladimir Putin himself, who, when Sobchak's health declined, became the de facto mayor of Saint Petersburg. For the next several years, Kudrin and a group of like-minded colleagues managed the finances of the city. Thus, unlike the first wave of reformers, they had hands-on experience in the actual management of government finances. Kudrin and Putin formed a close team. It was Kudrin who first brought Putin to Moscow, and Putin subsequently returned the favor, by not only naming Kudrin deputy prime minister and finance minister, but keeping him in those positions for a decade. He left the Finance Ministry in 2011, following a dispute with then-President Dmitri Medvedev, but after returning to Saint Petersburg as dean of the liberal arts faculty of Saint Petersburg, he was named by Putin as the head of the Chamber of Accounts. In all of these positions he was a strong voice for liberal reform but also conservative financial management. After the 2022 invasion of Ukraine, Kudrin quietly made known his opposition to the war,[25] and shortly afterward left the government. His unique experience, and reputation for honesty and competence, make him one of the few public figures in Russia to qualify as an "elder statesman."

Another key member of the "second wave" was German Gref, today the head of Sberbank, Russia's largest bank, who had come to Moscow with Putin in 1996. He became known chiefly as the author of the 2000 "Gref Program," which provided the blueprint for Putin's economic policies during his first term. It incorporated most of the ideas of the market reformers, but in a sequenced ten-year roadmap aimed at building sound institutional foundations for a market economy, after the catastrophic experiment with shock therapy.[26] The IMF continued to play an influential role in it behind the scenes,[27] but the program also included some unorthodox Western ideas, such as a "flat tax," which up to that time had never been tried before, and only existed in the minds of some conservative economists in California. Gref himself went on to serve from 2000 to 2007 as head of the Ministry of Industry and Energy (as it was then called), which in those years, according to Martin Gilman, who headed the IMF's Russian office at the time, was the "primary institution in the formulation of economic policy" in Putin's first two terms.[28]

The lessons learned in the 1990s have proved lasting. The team centered in the Ministry of Finance and the Russian Central Bank (RCB) today practices the same principles as the "Washington consensus" favored by the World Bank and the IMF—a strong central bank, balanced budgets, careful control of inflation, a convertible ruble, and a modern tax system. The current prime minister, Mikhail Mishustin, is an alumnus of the Russian Tax Service. The present minister of finance, Anton Siluanov, came up under Kudrin in the Ministry of Finance. Elvira Nabiullina, who leads the RCB, initially rose as an associate of German Gref. The managers of the Russian financial system, and especially the RCB, are acknowledged by central bankers around the world as first-rate professionals. (We return to their role in the Russian responses to Western sanctions in Chapter 5.)

After Putin came to power in 2000, the direct influence of the Westerners over Russian economic policy rapidly ended. But the opening of Russia on economic matters continued in other ways, with the Russians solidly in charge. The entire structure of Russian higher education was remodeled around modern economics. Several new private universities, as well as state institutions such as the Russian Presidential Academy of the National Economy (RANEPA) and the Higher School of Economics (VShE, commonly known as the Vyshka) became centers of up-to-date research and policy advocacy on economic matters.[29] A steady stream of young Russians studied and taught economics in the West and went on to work for the Moscow offices of Western banks and consultancies. One example is Sergei Guriev, a young economist who joined the New Economic School, a venture funded by Western philanthropist George Soros, and soon became its rector. The New Economic School played a major role as an educator of a whole generation of young Russian economists. One of its early graduates was Ksenia Yudaeva, who went on to earn a doctorate in economics at MIT, then returned to Russia, eventually to work at Sberbank, and subsequently as first deputy governor of the RCB, where she still serves today as an advisor to the chair, Elvira Nabiullina, the leading figure among the market liberals.[30]

What Western Business Found in Russia, and What It Brought

On the business front, the first Westerners began arriving in Russia in the late 1980s, attracted by Mikhail Gorbachev's *perestroika* and his endorsement of international joint ventures. But by the early 1990s, the Russian economy was practically in ruins, owing to the break-up of the Soviet centrally planned economy. All its underlying weaknesses were suddenly revealed for all to see. The Soviet-era consumer and services sectors, anemic to begin with, had collapsed. The food distribution system had disintegrated. Grocery shelves were empty. Collective farms were disbanding. In industry, whole factories and towns lay idle, especially the closed military-industrial cities,[31] where military orders had ceased. The oil industry had practically fallen apart. The civilian nuclear industry had been plundered. What remained of the Soviet economy was a shambles.

This created attractive opportunities to invest in restoring production, especially of exportable commodities. The Western companies brought capital, both in direct investments and in credit. The World Bank estimates that between 1992 and 2020 the inflow of capital into Russia totaled over $630 billion.[32] This was matched, however, by an even greater outflow of capital from Russia that took place in parallel, as Russian players moved assets abroad. Anders Aslund, after careful review of various estimates, puts the total of Russian private money outside Russia by the mid-2010s at about \$800 billion.[33] This made the input of capital into Russia by the Western companies all the more valuable, and in principle, should have made it all the more welcome.

But the biggest opportunity for the Westerners lay in the fact that, after seven decades of the Soviet system, entire sectors of a modern economy had simply never been built. A market system based on money and contracts required a whole new range of professions, from lawyers and advertisers and real-estate agents to bankers and accountants and consultants. Businesses based on profit required a radical mental rewiring and new market-oriented skills. There was no lack of talented and well-educated Russians, but the Soviet system had had little use for those specialties, and the educational system, which was largely focused on science and engineering, did not offer them.

Western companies filled the void, bringing missing ingredients essential to the post-Soviet market economy—new business models, new skills, new financial products like mortgages and credit cards, venture capital and private equity, efficient management, and commercial problem-solving. An army of Western professionals of all sorts arrived in Russia and set up shop, primarily in Moscow and Saint Petersburg, to the fascinated amazement of the Russians, for whom all of this was wholly new. Their chief role was to serve the Western companies and the emerging Russian private sector, but they also advised the Russian government and private firms on how to do business with the West. These diverse professionals played an important role in acquainting the Russians with the Western business and legal world and its complex rules.

For US companies in Moscow, the American Chamber of Commerce (known as AmCham) played a key role as a source of information and advice, and as a conduit between the companies and the Russian government. Much of the credit for AmCham's early effectiveness goes to Peter Charow, who was its first head from 1994 to 1997 and built up its membership from nothing to 450 companies. AmCham drew on its members to answer requests from the government or the Duma. As Charow, in his oral history for Columbia's Harriman Institute, recalls:

> So if a committee in the state Duma, or a minister or a deputy minister needs to know something about, How do you tax capital markets? How

do you manage the transition from state-sponsored extraction of natural resources to natural resources being extracted by private companies? How do you regulate a pharmaceutical industry? We said, "Let us help you." We would reach out to our member companies. And we started producing this series, that we called White Papers, on whatever topic the government was interested in learning about. We would feed them into the relevant ministries. It was just—I've never heard of anything like this in my life, actually, because basically, I had access to any minister in the cabinet of ministers; I had access to the prime minister, Viktor Chernomyrdin.[34]

Who Were the Westerners?

To a crude approximation, one could divide the flow of Western people and money into Russia into two categories. The first were broadly "self-starters," people who did not belong to large corporations or state bodies, but were rather young professionals like lawyers and bankers, small businessmen, traders and retailers, as well as not a few adventurers, who were attracted by the new opportunities that began opening up under Gorbachev in the late 1980s. They were often junior employees of Western banks and law firms, who went to Moscow as a personal challenge, or sometimes at the order of their bosses. Most of these were Americans, while Europeans were initially less present.

Many were unprepared for the circus they found in Russia, and did not last long. As Thomas Pickering, who served as US ambassador from 1993 to 1996, recalls:

There was a significant number of young Americans of Russian extraction, often with the language, who came back, and some successfully (for a while) started banks and other things. But most of them, like non-Russian speakers and non-Russians, Americans with no Russian antecedents who also came over to start businesses—they were quickly squeezed out.

They would whip up a partner because Russian law required it, but the partner would often turn out, after a year, to be in close cahoots with the local government. The American would suddenly find himself out of the partnership, his investment fully in the hands of the Russian partner operating it for him. Then the American's only option was to pack his bag and go home.[35]

For those early arrivals, Russia was a special challenge, because the Soviet Union had ceased to function, yet the basic institutions of a market economy did not yet exist. As Peter Charow recalls in his oral history:

> It was a partially-formed legal system. Property rights were unclear. Taxation was very unclear. A lot of the tax laws that were written were not well-written, and in many cases they contradicted other tax laws that had been written. If you look at what you might call the business side of doing business, it was navigating your way through this maze of often-conflicting laws and regulations about how your business should operate in the country. There were certainly instances of more aggressive tactics on the part of Russian companies going after Western companies, for whatever reason, because they wanted assets, they wanted the business, they wanted the customer base, what have you. That was certainly part of what was going on there at the time. But I think mostly, for most American companies at that time, it was just trying to figure out how the place worked, and being confronted with all these bureaucrats, who also didn't really know how it worked. It was just complicated.[36]

The survivors were the ones who learned to find solid Russian partners, to build personal relationships, and to take account of Russian rules, written and unwritten. Those who remained soon learned their way about, in particular a handful of fearless souls who found opportunity in the privatization auctions that were held in the early 1990s, at which the people who had bought up blocks of privatization vouchers traded them for shares in newly privatized companies.[37] A lucky few made quick fortunes this way, such as Bill Browder, who founded an investment firm in Moscow called Hermitage Capital.[38]

Others were more classic venture capitalists, who worked with Russian partners to grow new companies based on technologies that were new to Moscow. One of the most important success stories was that of John Boynton, an early backer of Yandex, which became known as the Russian Google. Boynton had studied Russian in high school and made his first trip to Russia in 1983. After graduating from Harvard in 1988, he headed back to Russia. His timing was perfect. In 1990, he met Arkady Volozh, the co-founder of Yandex. This marked the start of a thirty-year partnership. Boynton, who served as chairman of the board of Yandex for twenty-three years, helped it to go public on Nasdaq and to expand into new ventures outside Russia, notably in the United States, up to the eve of the Russian invasion.[39] (See the account of the subsequent fate of Yandex in Chapter 7.)

Those were often stormy years. It was not uncommon for Western businessmen to have bodyguards accompanying them everywhere, especially if one had the misfortune to get into a conflict with a powerful person. Fortunately, the Westerners had a valuable set of friends in the Western community of journalists, such as Chrystia Freeland, today the minister of finance of Canada, who was the Moscow bureau chief for *The Financial Times*. On one famous occasion, Freeland blew the whistle on the attempt by an oligarch to dilute the shareholding of Hermitage Capital in an oil company called Sidanco. The affair made so much international noise that the Russian government vetoed the share issue.[40] On the whole, however, the Western companies preferred to keep a lower profile and avoid such high-profile and potentially dangerous confrontations.

The Retail and Consumer Sectors

It was in the retail and consumer sectors that the impact of the Western companies was most visible to ordinary Russians. We have already seen the story of McDonald's. But McDonald's was just one of thousands of Western companies that came to Russia, most of them in the consumer sector. The number of Western companies expanded like a spring flood in the desert of the Russian consumer world, especially once global oil prices began rising at the end of the 1990s and oil-export revenues poured into Russia, raising the disposable incomes of Russian consumers to unprecedented heights. Western companies sold home furnishings (IKEA), groceries (Auchan), high fashion (Cartier), cosmetics and beauty products (Estee Lauder), digital phones (Nokia) and then smartphones (Apple), and much more. Almost all of these products were imported, although some companies (notably McDonald's, for its trademark fries) set up their own domestic supply chains, contracting with Russian farmers.

One equally path-breaking symbol of the opening of Russia was the arrival of the Swedish furniture retailer IKEA, which opened its first store in the Moscow suburb of Khimki in March 2000, to waiting lines even longer than those around McDonald's. Over the following twenty-two years, IKEA opened a dozen furniture outlets and shopping malls throughout Russia, transforming the shopping habits of middle-class Russians, as they flocked to IKEA to upgrade their apartments to the "European standard." In 2006, IKEA opened a furniture factory and sawmill in Karelia in Russia's Northwest. Its ultimate aim was to source all of the furniture for its global network inside Russia, and like McDonald's, it built supply chains with dozens of Russian suppliers.

IKEA did not have it easy. Practically from the beginning, it faced constant harassment from local authorities, who used land-use regulations and other obstacles to impede construction and delay openings. Any excuse, it seemed, would do, ranging from denying a permit to build a pedestrian bridge across a highway, on the grounds that it would interfere with a local World War II monument, to a 2014 investigation into IKEA's acquisition of a land parcel from a collective farm twenty years earlier. Much of the motivation on the Russian side was to extract bribes or to extort a share in the business.[41] But IKEA's Swedish owners took a firm line against payoffs or concessions, and they fought back. As a result, IKEA was constantly embroiled in battles, and in 2009 called a halt to any further expansion. Yet in the end, IKEA's policy won it several victories and respect, and after the initially rocky years it prospered—up to the invasion.

The Western Roles in Professional Services

The opening of Russia brought a profusion of new service professions, which had never existed in Soviet times. Real estate companies, residential and commercial brokerages, entertainment and media firms, modern hospitality providers, telecoms, advertisers, and law offices all sprang up like mushrooms, especially in Moscow. Some were well-known international names, such as Radisson Hotels, Coldwell Banker, LeBoeuf Lamb, Hines, and Sprint. Many more were local creations founded by Western entrepreneurs, which served the new Russian private sector. Some of these became favorite landmarks among the expats, such as Uncle Gilly's and Starlight Diner. An English-language newspaper, *The Moscow Times*, soon appeared in hotel lobbies and Western offices and on the foreigners' breakfast tables.[42]

Westerners, primarily American, transformed the entertainment industry, bringing new movies and movie theaters, FM radio, and independent TV and print media. With the end of the Soviet Union, the state-controlled entertainment industry had collapsed. A young American, Paul Heth, had the idea of creating an American-style movie theater. In partnership with

Kodak, he built a flashy 600-seat theater called Kino Mir, complete with pop-corn, Coca-Cola, and stereo sound. On opening day, he showed *The Rock*, with Sean Connery. It was a huge hit. As Heth recalls, "The lines were out the door to get into the theater. The first year they had one million visi-tors and were the highest grossing movie theater in the world. At one point, they grossed 50 per-cent of all movie revenues in Russia."[43] Kodak Kino Mir spread rapidly throughout Russia, growing to more than 200 theaters, and in the process it helped to kick-start a revival of the Russian movie industry.

With the rise of Russian private property, a whole new financial industry arrived in Russia, and founded financial centers and exchanges, investment firms and private equity companies. One of these, Baring Vostok, had a spec-tacular run, investing in a wide range of new private companies, including mineral water (Borjomi), shipping (Volga Tanker), and the emerging Rus-sian Internet (Vympelcom). The epic of Baring Vostok came to an untimely end, when its founder, Michael Calvey, was arrested on fabricated charges in 2019 and given a suspended five-year sentence. In March 2023 he was finally able to leave Russia.[44] In retrospect, this was a preview of a scenario that became all too common after the Russian invasion.

The US government also played a key role in bringing modern finance to Russia. Through the US-Russian Investment Fund and its successor, the Delta private-equity fund, it trained many Russians, some of whom later became leading figures in the Russian financial sector. The head of the US-Russia Fund and Delta, a US private-equity expert named Patricia Cloherty, recalls,

> We launched 55 new companies—the first mortgage bank, the first credit card issuing bank, the first bottled water company, etc., all managed by Russian entrepreneurs. In 2001, we launched The Center for Entrepreneur-ship, to teach skills like managing cash flow, hiring and rewarding key people, and so on. Fifty-two of the companies were sold for extraordinary returns ... My staff of 33 was Russian, except for two or three, and virtually all were multilingual.[45]

Delta's most famous "alumnus" is Kirill Dmitriev, who now leads the Russian Direct Investment Fund, Russia's sovereign-wealth fund.[46] Dmitriev is a tal-ented investment banker, who joined Delta with degrees from Stanford and Harvard and a prior career at Goldman Sachs and McKinsey. In 2011 he was named by Putin to be the first head of the Russian Direct Investment Fund

(RDIF), a vehicle designed to attract foreign investment to Russia. With his extensive background in the United States and in US companies, Dmitriev is emblematic of Russia's opening to the West—but also of its reclosing. In February 2022 Dmitriev and the RDIF were sanctioned by the US and Canada.[47]

The Western Roles in the Banking Sector

In contrast to financial advisories and equity funds, Western banks played only modest roles in the development of the private Russian banking, whether as investors or advisors. A handful of Western banks, mainly Citi, Unicredit, and Raiffeisenbank, created retail networks, but these remained small. Unlike the early joint ventures that led to the creation of the MICEX and the RTS, there were no significant partnerships with the Russian banks themselves. The sixty-odd Western banks that eventually opened offices in Russia mostly served the foreign community.

The main reason for the modest presence of foreign banks was the systematic opposition of the emerging Russian commercial banks throughout the 1990s. Fearing competition from the foreigners, the new private bankers lobbied the Duma to pass legislation in 1992 barring the licensing of foreign banks in Russia. Only two foreign banks, the French Crédit Lyonnais and the Franco-German alliance BNP/Dresdner, slipped under the bar, because they were already licensed before the law was passed.[48] But even they had only an insignificant presence: in January 1999, out of the top twenty banks in Russia, only one (BNP/Dresdner) made the list, in thirteenth position, but with only one branch.[49] It was only in the 2000s that the bar was gradually lifted and the foreign banks were able to obtain licenses and develop retail branches, but by then they had missed out on the biggest opportunities, and their role remained small.

Yet the modest direct presence of the foreign banks understates the actual importance of Western financial advice, especially that of international financial institutions, in the development of the Russian banking system. Their biggest contribution was in the development of a strong and independent central bank. The IMF and other financial bodies strongly supported the RCB in its efforts to modernize its operations and establish its independence, especially in the RCB's battle for independent inflation-targeting.[50] In contrast to the controversial role played by the IMF in the design of shock therapy and Russian privatization, the World Bank's contribution to the strengthening of the RCB was crucial.[51] As Juliet Johnson writes, "With the aid of international financial institutions, over the next few years the RCB introduced credit auctions, developed the treasury bill market, improved the payments system, enforced more stringent reserve requirements on commercial banks, achieved positive real interest rates, and introduced a 'ruble corridor' to attempt to stabilize the exchange rate."[52] It was an impressive achievement.

Of equal importance was the role of training programs. In the early 1990s, few of the new Russian bankers had any background in economics or finance, and in the provinces, most of them were former engineers. Inside the RCB, over half the staff consisted of older veterans of the Soviet State Bank. But this changed quickly over the 1990s. European banks, notably the Bank of England and the Bundesbank, played particularly active roles, establishing training centers both in Russia and in Europe, with funding from bodies such as the EU's TACIS.[53] All told, these programs trained thousands of Russian bankers.

Relations between the Russian bankers and their Western advisors were not necessarily easy, but there does not seem to have been the same level of resentment as in some other sectors. The fact that the big Western banks were initially barred from operating in Russia limited the scope for competition and hostility. Much of the new Russian banking sector started as a blank slate, and the new Russian bankers were more receptive to the mentorship of the Westerners than others in more established sectors.

A special case of Western mentorship was with the emerging "oligarchs," notably Mikhail Khodorkovsky and his partners at Menatep Bank, one of the first private banks in Russia. In the late 1980s, the new Russian go-go bankers were rank beginners. "We didn't know anything," one of Menatep's early founders remembers. A Geneva-based global-trust company, Valmet, which had a wealthy clientele that included the ruling family of Dubai, took charge of instructing them in the basics of capitalist business practices, from standard banking to offshore shell firms and acquisitions. They had to start from the ground up. Christian Michel, one of Valmet's senior partners, recalled, "I taught them what a credit card was, and how to use a checkbook." But the Russians were fast learners. By 1995 Khodorkovsky and Valmet were in West Siberia—with funding from the World Bank—to evaluate two of the oil properties that Khodorkovsky would shortly acquire in the notorious "shares for loans" auctions. Over the following years, Valmet acted as a key advisor not only to Khodorkovsky's Menatep Bank but also to other oligarchs, such as Boris Berezovsky (AvtoVAZ) and Vitaly Malkin (Rossiiskii Kredit), as they expanded abroad.[54]

Most of the new Russian bankers were quite young, including those inside the RCB, where the older Soviet-era veterans were quickly weeded out. They were on the whole receptive to Western tutorship. In addition, the two financial crashes of 1998 and 2008–9 helped to persuade the Russians the hard way of the soundness of Western methods, and once the "Wild East" phase of Russian banking had passed, the Russian bankers began to see their foreign colleagues as fellow members of a transnational community, and looked to them as role models. A leading example was Sberbank, Russia's largest bank.

The Team that Gref Built: The Modernization and Expansion of Sberbank

Sberbank is far and away Russia's largest bank—over 60% of Russians keep their savings there—but by the beginning of Putin's second term, it had remained largely unchanged from its Soviet days. In 2007 Putin appointed German Gref to head the bank. We have already met Gref, as one of the "second wave" of Russian economic reformers from Saint Petersburg. During Putin's first two terms, he had served as minister of economic development, during which time he remained an effective advocate for Russia's continued opening and economic reform.[55] When he first arrived at Sberbank in 2007, Gref was viewed with suspicion by old-line conservatives, who saw him as one of the Saint Petersburg radicals (unfairly, since Gref had played no active part in the shock therapy phase of reforms). When Putin appointed him to the head of Sberbank in 2007, he was received coldly by the shareholders, who associated him with Gaidar and Chubais. "You destroyed the country with your policies," said one of them acidly at the first shareholders' meeting over which Gref presided, reported *Kommersant* at the time. "Are you now planning to do the same thing with Sberbank?"[56]

But as Gref took charge, he won over his critics. He began by purging Sberbank of the problem loans that had accumulated like barnacles since the collapse of the Soviet Union.[57] Sberbank became consistently profitable, even as the rest of the Russian banks were losing money.[58] Gref actively sought out Western investors, and by 2017 Western shareholders, drawn by Sberbank's superior performance, owned 45.5% of Sberbank's shares (while the RCB owned the other half).[59]

Ten years on, Gref was praised for having turned a sleepy Soviet savings bank into the most modern and entrepreneurial bank in Russia.[60] Along the way, he changed the bank's name from Sberbank to the hipper-sounding "Sber." He computerized the retail network, so that within five years Sberbank customers were doing their banking online instead of in line. As time went on, Gref's plans for modernizing the bank grew steadily more ambitious. Starting around 2015, he built a new team of young digital specialists, many of them trained in the West or in Western companies. To lead it, he hired a senior official from Citi, an Israeli American named David Rafalovsky, who had previously been the chief technology officer for Citi Global Functions. Before he took the job in December 2017, after twenty years at Citigroup in New York, Rafalovsky had never been to Moscow. But he proved highly effective in translating Western experience into Sber: within two years, it was conducting 80% of its transactions on its digital platform. One of its first partners was the city of Moscow, with which Sber created a joint venture. Sber was regularly cited at international conferences for its widespread adoption of digital services, one of the biggest in the world.

Gref's ambition was to expand the Russian "cloud," turning Sber into a "metaverse," offering a wide menu of advanced digital services. In 2019 he concluded an agreement with Nvidia.[61] Using Nvidia software, Sber-Cloud's centers would provide big-data services, machine-learning, and AI to support Sberbank's "cloud for rent" platform, called SberCloud. Developed in-house by its Sber-Tekh division, it began operation in 2021.[62] On the eve of the invasion, Sber was the only Russian bank able to compete successfully with the Russian telecom giants, which up to that time had had the field to themselves. (In 2021 Rostelekom ranked first in revenues from cloud services; SberCloud was second, just ahead of MTS.)

But following the 2022 invasion, Gref's high-tech ambitions came crashing to the ground. Within days, Sberbank and Gref were sanctioned. The foreign investors quickly sold out. In June 2022, Sberbank was expelled from SWIFT, the international financial messaging system. Rafalovsky left Russia immediately,[63] followed by most of the technology team. Internet service providers withdrew, sometimes leaving existing service contracts hanging.

Sberbank was excluded from access to App Store, Google Play, and Apple iPhone technology, and it had to scale back its plans for Sberbank Online, its online consumer banking service. Sberbank's Russian cloud collapsed overnight: it had been about to install Russian-made "Baikal-S" servers for a network of regional data centers, but had to suspend the project for lack of imported processors, which had been under development with Taiwan's TSMC, the world's leading producer of advanced chips.[64] Today Sberbank remains the centerpiece of the government's plans to digitalize Russia's economy and its government services, but it is difficult to imagine how it will be able to play this role effectively, given its lost access to foreign IT providers and personnel. (For more on Gref and the Sberbank story, see Chapter 7.)

But let us return now to the 1990s and the roles of the Westerners in the development of financial services. A capital innovation was the arrival of credit cards, and especially American Express.

American Express, Aleksey Maslov, and the Arrival of the AMEX Credit Card

From the 1950s on, American Express had built a worldwide network of local offices, whose main business was express shipping, but also the issuance of "travelers' checks," which a traveler could buy at home and carry abroad, to be converted into local currencies at, of course, the friendly American Express office. In the late 1950s, American Express branched out into international credit cards. In Russia, American Express opened an office in Moscow in 1958, closely followed by Diner's Club, catering to foreign tourists in the Soviet Union. In the 1980s, a handful of Soviet officials and privileged travelers were issued the first VISA payment cards for use abroad. By the end of the Soviet Union, about 800 of these Gold Cards had been issued.[65]

The rise of private commercial banks after 1991 brought an explosion in the availability and use of credit and payment cards in Russia. There was intense competition among the Russian banks, and they were joined in the fray by Western companies, including American Express. In 1993 a young graduate of MGIMO, the prestigious Moscow State Institute of International Relations, Aleksey Maslov, took a job with American Express, handling travelers' checks for Russia and the FSU. When American Express opened its first bank in Russia, Maslov was put in charge of negotiating correspondent accounts. Over an eighteen-year career, he rose to become head of AMEX Russia, replacing the initial expat managers. By the time he left AMEX in 2011, he was one of Russia's leading experts on SWIFT and other international payment vehicles. He became the founder and head of the Russian SWIFT Association, which on the eve of the invasion counted 400 Russian subscribers. Maslov stands as a typical example of the young Russians who started out with foreign companies and are still members of the Russian financial elite today.[66]

But in the early 1990s credit cards were still a novelty for most Russians. Today every self-respecting Russian owns debit and credit cards, and these have completely transformed the country's shopping and banking habits. But such a development would not have been possible without the most revolutionary development of all—the Internet. Here too the Westerners played significant early roles.

The Internet Comes to Russia

The single most important part of the tidal wave that poured into Russia in the 1990s was the Internet and the telecommunications that support it. Apart from the end of the Soviet system itself, nothing has so transformed Russia as the mass adoption of cellular telephony and the Internet. A modern market economy would simply be impossible without them, particularly for conducting all the modern services discussed earlier, whether organizing financial and real estate markets, restaurants, and a whole range of conveniences, down to reserving a haircut. By the end of the 2000s the Internet had become the indispensable platform for Russian business, commerce, and social life. Today nearly all Russians are connected to it, mostly on smartphones but also on all sorts of other devices, and they spend several hours a day on it, playing games, watching movies, buying goods and services online, cruising the world,[67] and even, for a brief time in the 2010s, crowdsourcing for political demonstrations. Private businesses use the Internet, as do government agencies and officials—including Putin—and of course, the security apparatus, as well as the underworld of cybercrime.

Russia already had strong skills in computer science, especially in software, going back to Soviet times. Russia's early forays into computer networks date from the 1960s and 1970s, primarily the work of scientists in state research institutes, who used it for scientific communications among themselves. In the mid-1980s, a group of programmers at the Kurchatov Institute, Russia's leading research institute for nuclear applications, decided to create a computer network called Relcom to link together scientists in Moscow and Saint Petersburg with an e-mail connection.[68] Relcom was immediately popular among the Soviet technical elite. By 1990, on the eve of the Soviet collapse, it connected 70 cities, and was used by more than 400 organizations, mostly universities and research institutes, and some high schools, as well as—sign of the times under Gorbachev—the first "cooperatives" (i.e., private businesses) and embryonic commodity exchanges, as well as Russia's first independent wire agency, Interfax. By the time of the failed coup of August 1991, in which a group of Soviet die-hards attempted to overthrow Gorbachev, the network had thousands of subscribers inside Russia, and it played a major role in communicating news of the coup in real time from Russia to the outside world.

But progress in networking was held back by the lack of support infrastructure and equipment, especially the decrepit Soviet telecommunications system, as well as outdated data protocols. The isolation of the Soviet citizenry from the rapidly evolving computer and telecoms technologies in the outside world was extreme, even for the most elite institutions. To connect with the rest of the country, the Kurchatov team relied on the ancient copper-wire analog system that was still the basis of the Soviet intercity and international telephone network. In the late 1980s, the Soviet Union had only 150 international voice lines. To extend the Relcom network as far as a Finnish university in Helsinki, its creators had to borrow the use of the institute's only direct international connection, the director's own personal line.

Early Soviet experimentation with digital communications was also limited by the lack of computer hardware. At that time, Western computer and telecoms technology was subject to export controls, and there were not yet any Western IT or computer companies present in Russia. The first "server" available to Relcom was a first-generation IBM 286 personal computer. The early enthusiasts, ever resourceful, partly offset the deficit by using programmable microcalculators, which were widely available,[69] but these were hardly more than a stopgap.

Two Western companies played major roles in the modernization of the Russian telecoms system. The first, in the late 1980s, was Sprint International. Working through its European office, Sprint persuaded the Soviet authorities to devote one of their voice lines to a new high-tech protocol that enabled high-speed data communication, the essential foundation, for example, for communications between airlines and financial trading. In the early 1990s, Sprint and Moscow Central Telegraph formed a joint venture, which was so successful that even before the end of the Soviet Union it managed virtually all of the country's international data traffic.

But the Sprint protocol was still based on the primitive Soviet infrastructure. The real revolutionary leap forward came with the arrival of cellular telephony, based on a completely new digital fiber-optic system that replaced the outmoded analog copper-wire system. A US telecom company, US West—one of the seven "Baby Bells" born from the break-up of AT&T—opened an office in Moscow in January 1991, to lead a consortium of European telecom companies, working with the still-Soviet Ministry of Communications, to create an optical fiber system.

The key event that opened the way for the new system was the failed coup of August 1991. US West's partner, Vladimir Bulgak, who was the last Soviet minister of communications, brought his ministry over to the Yeltsin side.[70] Bulgak thus became the first Russian minister of telecoms. Over the following five years, working partly with US West and partly with other European players, Bulgak obtained $520 million in credits from Denmark and Japan and contracted with Danish and Japanese companies to install a brand-new system of digital fiber-optic trunklines that connected Russia through a modern network with the rest of the world, one line running east-west from Saint Petersburg to Vladivostok (with connections to Copenhagen and Tokyo) and one north-south (which linked up with Istanbul). The first five years of the 1990s were transformative. By the time Bulgak was done, Russia's international connections had ballooned from 2,000 analog lines in 1990 to 66,000 digital lines in 1995.[71]

In Moscow, the modernization of the trunkline system, combined with the rapid proliferation of private companies after 1990, touched off a boom in private-sector entrepreneurship in digital telecommunications. As Bulgak later recalled, demand grew so fast that the new lines were used at capacity within five years, instead of the fifteen that his team had originally imagined. Although phone rates and access tariffs were high, Russia's emerging private businesses were increasingly able to afford them, especially for international trade. They were also quick to perceive the potential profits to be made from the Internet inside Russia; thus as early as 1992 one of Russia's first investment funds, Rinako, bought a stake in Relcom. Other Internet service providers soon appeared, and they began to show tidy revenues from advertising, a field new to Russia. By the second half of the 1990s there were enough users and advertisers in the capital to support Russia's first search engine (Rambler.ru), the first news service (National News Service, launched by *Kommersant*), the first website of a political party (Yabloko), and the first blog, *Vecherniy Internet* (the *Evening Internet*, which actually originated in Israel). New players entered the picture, some of them co-funded by Western philanthropists such as George Soros.[72]

US West, which had stayed in Moscow throughout the failed coup, expanded its activity as well. Between 1991 and 1995, it co-founded twelve cellular companies in Russia, co-owned with Rostelecom and the telephone provider Electrosviaz. Its joint venture with Rostelecom installed the first automatic international gateway calling between Russia and the rest of the world. US West's holding company in Russia held assets in Russian subsidiaries, but also provided assistance in training their Russian staff in such skills as frequency acquisition, technology marketing, financing, and business. As Fred Ledbetter, who was US West's man in Moscow in those years, recalls, "Many of our employees rose through telecoms to manage companies like Microsoft and Google in Russia. It was excellent on-the-job training for their careers."[73] In retrospect, US West played a historic role in the Russian telecoms revolution, first by persuading Russian officials of the importance of cellular telephony and second, equally importantly, in helping to train a whole generation of Russian telecom professionals.

Indeed, from this point on, Russian players began taking the lead roles. Three new companies, Vympelkom, MTS, and Megafon, quickly seized the lead in developing the IT market in Moscow and Saint Petersburg. They had very different biographies, and Western companies and investors played different roles in them. Vympelkom was an offshoot of the Soviet military-industrial complex, a rare instance of successful military conversion to a civilian business. It was the creation of Dmitrii Zimin, a senior manager of Vympel, a leading military design bureau. Zimin, through a chance encounter with an American businessman, formed a Russian-American joint venture that led to Russia's first private telephone company, Beeline. Zimin, though already nearing retirement age at the time, proved to be an energetic and resourceful entrepreneur, who used his connections in the military sector to smooth the way for the new company. Founded in 1992, Vympelkom (under the spelling VimpelCom) became the first Russian company listed on the New York Stock Exchange, in 1996. The following year, thanks to the capital raised on Wall Street, VimpelCom rolled out Russia's first 2G GSM (Global System for Mobile Communications) network in Moscow and the surrounding Moscow Oblast; by 2001 it was setting up second-generation GSM networks throughout Russia's regions.

In contrast, Vympelkom's two main competitors, Megafon and MTS (Moscow Telephone Systems), were founded primarily by foreign companies and focused on different locations.[74] Megafon had its early roots in Saint Petersburg, where it was founded in 1993. It was the creation of Aleksandr Malyshev, then head of the data computing center at the Leningrad intercity telephone station. A group of Scandinavian companies supplied early capital, equipment, and business know-how, and in 1995 Megafon (then called North West GSM) launched the first GSM service in Russia. For the rest of the decade, Megafon concentrated on Saint Petersburg and the Russian Northwest, but in 2002 it expanded into Moscow, challenging VimpelCom on its home territory. The two companies have been rivals ever since, jockeying for the top two positions in the Moscow market.[75]

Russia's new generation of digital arteries based on fiber-optics would have been of little use if Russians had lacked the income to use it. But the tide of oil money that flowed into Russia after 2000 put money in people's pockets as never before in Russian history. One of the main things people used it for was to buy computers, and above all, mobile phones. Russian businesses saw the opportunity, and between 2000 and 2010 private mobile phone companies and Internet service providers sprang up in profusion. After 2010, despite a slowdown in the economy and in real incomes, Russians remained avid buyers of smartphones. Even during the pandemic, although sales slumped, Russians still bought 31 million smartphones in 2020, spending about $7.6 billion on them.[76] Today, Russian Internet usage is still mainly via mobile phones. One-quarter of Russian Internet users use mobiles exclusively; among older users (age fifty-five and above) the proportion is over one-third. But even among those who have access to other devices, three-quarters do most of their surfing on their mobiles.

However, the Russian telecoms system and the Internet had one major weakness: they remained almost entirely dependent on imported technology and services. This became a liability after February 2022, as the Russian companies came under sanctions and Western suppliers and providers withdrew. (See Chapter 4 for the impact of sanctions on the Russian IT sector.)

Western Roles in Russian Heavy Industry: Opportunity, Ambivalence, and Resistance

Western companies also played innovative roles in several branches of heavy industry. The big Western corporations were somewhat slower to arrive in Russia than the service and consumer firms. Few of them had worked in the Soviet Union before. Like McDonald's, they needed time to establish connections and partners, and they also required offices. But they benefited from the fact that by the time they arrived, the way had already been prepared by the Western service firms in law, real estate, IT, banking, and finance. The industrial companies had more money to spend than the earlier arrivals; they were after bigger game and had longer horizons, but they also had more at risk.

They met a mixed reception from the Russians. One reason is that unlike the foreign companies in the consumer and services sectors, the industrial corporations found the ground already occupied by powerful and well-connected Russian incumbents. They encountered a mix of acceptance and resistance, depending on the Russian companies' stability and state of need, and also on what the foreigners had to offer. The legacy Russian companies were typically not prepared to concede to the Western companies the same degree of latitude and control that the newcomers found in the "soft" sectors, where they frequently started from a blank slate and initially faced no competition. In addition, in some sectors, such as metals and machine-building, there were fierce internal battles going on among the Russians for ownership and control, in which the Westerners were barely more than spectators, and indeed sometimes found themselves the prize.

The Western companies made their greatest contribution in the transportation sector, which spanned both manufacturing and infrastructure. Renault spearheaded the development of a new Lada passenger car with advanced digital components, and several other Western auto manufacturers, such as VW and Stellantis (the maker of Jeep and Ram as well as several European brands such as Peugeot and Fiat) did likewise. Timken and other bearing specialists helped Russian companies make roller bearings to modernize the antiquated Russian railcar stock.

The German company Siemens was a particularly prominent player in Russia's transportation sector. Siemens had been present in Russia since the nineteenth century, and for much of the prewar Soviet period. As early as

1991, Siemens created the joint venture (JV) Interturbo with Leningrad-skii Metallicheskii Zavod (LMZ) in Saint Petersburg, to make turbines for export. By 1995 Siemens had over 3,000 employees in Russia in all fields. In 2000 LMZ became part of a conglomerate called Silovye Mashiny, owned by the powerful oligarch Aleksey Mordashov. In 2011 Siemens restructured its JV into a partnership with Silovye Mashiny, called Siemens Gas Tur-bine Technologies, and it increased its stake to become majority owner of the new JV. It built a new plant in Saint Petersburg for an additional $368 million, which began production in 2014.[77] Siemens also partnered with a Russian railroad group to adapt next-generation trains at a major new plant; its Moscow to Saint Petersburg high-speed train, the Sapsan (Pere-grine Falcon), became the star of the renovated Russian rail system. Siemens likewise worked with a Russian company to develop the Lastochka, another high-speed train.[78] But in 2022, following the Russian invasion, it all came tumbling down, as Siemens withdrew from Russia, which caused significant disruption in Russia's production of gas turbines for the energy sector (see Chapter 6).

Western *presence* did not necessarily mean *domination*. The steel sector, for example, was rebuilt from its obsolete Soviet foundations by three lead-ing entrepreneurs, Viktor Rashnikov of MMK, Vladimir Lisin of NLMK, and Igor Ziuzin of Mechel. Their story is a useful reminder that oligarchs, as such people are often called, come in all shapes and sizes. All three came up from the shop floor; another, Aleksey Mordashov of Severstal, also rose through the ranks of the steel plant in his hometown of Cherepovets. Still others, such as Aleksandr Abramov of Evraz, started out as traders in met-als. Unlike the case of aluminum, which required imported bauxite and thus depended on foreign intermediaries who tried to seize control (see the story of aluminum in Chapter 2), the battle for ownership of the steel industry mostly involved Russian contenders who had their feet solidly planted inside their home enterprises. Once in power, they guarded their domains jealously to prevent inroads by foreign companies, and while they shopped abroad for foreign technology to modernize their plants, they did not allow for-eign managers or shareholders to dominate, even in the few instances when they formed joint ventures with them. "On tap but not on top," was their motto.[79]

But the industrial sector in which the Western companies played the greatest role—indeed, in some cases the dominant role—was energy.

The Saga of the Western Companies in Energy

In this section we look at three contrasting cases from the energy sector that illustrate the theme of opportunity, ambivalence, and resistance—the role of Total[80] in building a new LNG business with a Russian private-sector start-up; the roller-coaster epic of BP in the creation and subsequent loss of TNK-BP; and finally, for contrast, the resurrection of the Russian civilian nuclear industry under Rosatom, by the Russians' own efforts and without any Western participation. The result was three very different degrees of influence and impact by the Western companies, which then played out in different ways after the imposition of sanctions.

Roughnecks, Roustabouts, and Wizards: The First Western Oilmen in Russia

I was fortunate to be a witness to the early arrival of the Westerners in the Russian oil industry. "Early on a winter morning in Calgary, Alberta" (I wrote in 1990),

> I joined a planeload of Canadian drillers on their way to north Russia. Our chartered Boeing 737 had never been built to fly so far—its main virtue was that it was cheap—and we made five refueling stops as we lumbered our way across the Canadian north and over Iceland. We finally landed in Usinsk, an isolated oil town in the Russian Northwest. This is the daily life of the itinerant roughnecks and roustabouts, the foot soldiers of the oil business, who like migrating birds fly across half the globe to work their shifts, typically one month on and on month off, in remote places with even remoter languages and customs.[81]

The Canadians were there as part of an early partnership between the local oil enterprise and an Alberta company, Gulf Canada. As early as 1988, as Gorbachev's *perestroika* reforms began prying open the closed Soviet world, Western oilmen began arriving in small groups, drawn by the prospect of forming joint ventures, which Gorbachev had first authorized in 1987 as a means of attracting foreign technology. The oil industry in Alberta was still recovering from the oil price collapse of 1986, and there were plenty of underemployed Canadian oil workers and companies looking for new opportunities.

It was a voyage of discovery on both sides. "To the Albertans, northern Russia looked like familiar territory: instead of *muskeg* the Russians called it *tundra*, but it was the same swampy stuff, oppressively hot in summer but properly frigid in winter. The Russians played a decent game of ice hockey, held their liquor pretty well by Alberta standards, and the mosquitoes were Canadian-size."[82] But there the similarities ended. The Russians, the Albertans soon recognized, were men who knew their oil, but the way they went about producing it was completely different, and finding common ground turned out to be far more difficult than either side imagined.

The Russians' attitudes toward the foreign oilmen were ambivalent. Until recently, the Soviet Union had been the world's leading oil producer, largely on the basis of its own homegrown science and technology, working in some of the most challenging conditions on the planet. But the Westerners perceived the Russian industry as backward and inefficient, and they did not bother to hide their opinion, often behaving as though they were in a defeated country. To this the Russian oil generals and the hard-bitten oilworkers did not take kindly, but their needs were so pressing that they accepted the foreigners' presence and put up with their tutelage. But there was constant jostling for control, particularly over money. The Russians were unaccustomed to thinking in terms of finance and profit, and they found the Western companies penny-pinchingly frugal. As one early Western oilman put it to me, "The financial piece of the pie was like talking to them in Greek. All they saw was the technical and the bureaucratic. Their rationale was, 'We are as good technically as you are, and it's our company. All we need is money. Give us the money.' And we would say no."[83]

The Western majors, when they arrived in Russia, found the going even tougher. The larger the Western company, the more wary were the established Russian companies, which were fearful of ceding control. Consequently, the Westerners found their best opportunities at the periphery, where there were fewer entrenched interests, and there was frequently strong support from regional governors. Thus the governor of the Komi Republic in the Russian Northwest, Iurii Spiridonov, served as a guardian angel for Conoco's Polar Lights project, one of the earliest Western big-company projects. At the other end of the country, on far-off Sakhalin Island, a succession of local governors smoothed the way for ExxonMobil and Shell. But the single most successful virgin Western project in Russia, one that combined the advantages of strong political support, an entrepreneurial Russian partner, a technology that was new to Russia, and a convenient maritime location at the periphery, was that of the French company Total, and its partnership with a Russian start-up Novatek. Together they pioneered Russia's second major investment in LNG, which was the first Russian LNG project to involve and be led by a Russian company from its inception.[84]

The Story of Yamal LNG: Total's Christophe de Margerie and Novatek

On the evening of October 20, 2014, Christophe de Margerie, the colorful and popular CEO of the French oil company Total—his affectionate nickname in the company was Beeg Moustache, from his bushy white upper lip—was returning to Paris from a lightning twenty-four-hour trip to Moscow. As his company jet gained speed for takeoff, a drunken airport worker unexpectedly drove a snowplow onto the runway, directly in the path of Margerie's plane. It careened into a nearby building and burst into flames. Everyone on board was killed.[85]

But despite Margerie's untimely death, Total continued without missing a beat. Margerie had already opened the way, by creating the strategic partnership with Novatek and a new industry, Russian LNG.

The rise of Novatek as a leading independent gas producer, and more recently as the leading player in Russian LNG, is closely tied to its founder, Leonid Mikhelson, who started out as a builder of gas pipelines. When Gorbachev's reforms began in the late 1980s, Mikhelson was the head of a pipeline construction trust in Kuybyshev (now Samara): "My father was the head of the Kuybyshevtruboprovodstroy, the largest construction unit in the Gazprom system. He took me everywhere with him, wherever the company built pipelines. I used to go to gas and oil fields before I went to school." He quickly realized the opportunities presented by privatization, but since there was no money to be made from pipe-building in those chaotic years, in the mid-1990s Mikhelson went north to Siberia and went looking for gas instead.

At that time licenses to even relatively large gas prospects could be had virtually for the asking, particularly from local geological groups. Because there was so much gas in the ground, and because there were as yet no pipes connecting it to the main pipeline system, the gas was virtually worthless, and licenses could be had for pennies—provided one had political support. So Mikhelson teamed up with the deputy governor of the province and put him on his company's board.

The innovative business concept developed by Mikhelson rested on the fact that independents like him, unlike Gazprom, were allowed to sell their gas at unregulated prices, which enabled him to sell at an attractive profit to factories and municipalities along the main pipeline routes. In addition, he kept tight managerial control over his contractors and his own operations and consequently was a low-cost producer. In the early 2000s, Mikhelson also began carving out a profitable niche as a producer and exporter of gas condensate, a light fraction similar to gasoline, which he exported. Pretty soon, Mikhelson was making real money, and he started to think about his next move.

It was also at about this time that Mikhelson found a powerful ally in the person of Gennady Timchenko, an early associate of Vladimir Putin from Saint Petersburg days. Timchenko became a shareholder in Novatek, and opened the door to the Kremlin for Mikhelson.

Novatek's success in developing and selling condensate attracted the interest of Total and its CEO Margerie. Up to this time, Total had had little luck in Russia, apart from a small JV in the Russian Northwest (Nenets Okrug), and it was looking for a project and a partner. By then, Mikhelson was the largest independent gas producer in Russia, and the two companies began talking about developing LNG. It was about this time that he renamed his company Novatek ("new technology").

In 2011, with Putin looking on, Margerie and Mikhelson signed an agreement under which Total acquired a 12% interest in Novatek. As part of the agreement Total also bought a 20% stake in Novatek's subsidiary, Yamal LNG, to develop the South Tambey field on the Yamal Peninsula, which held 1.25 trillion cubic meters of gas reserves and was strategically located on the northeast coast of the peninsula. The innovation of Mikhelson and his French partners was the vision that LNG from South Tambey could be exported both east and west—west to Europe during the winter and east to Asia during the summer via the Northern Sea Route, with the assistance of nuclear-powered icebreakers. The latter was a daring concept, since it depended on the availability of ice-breaking tankers, and ultimately on the melting of the Arctic sea ice.

But thanks to the partnership between Novatek and Total[86] and the strong support of the Russian government—which provided tax breaks and financed the development of a new port on the Yamal Peninsula—progress was rapid. Three years after Margerie's untimely death, the first tanker from the Total-Novatek alliance sailed for Asia with LNG from Yamal, via the

Arctic Northern Sea Route. At a ceremony attended by Vladimir Putin, it was christened the *Christophe Margerie*; painted on its bow was a large white moustache.[87] Today this first project is producing at its full capacity of 21 million metric tons per year (mpta) and has so far been little affected by sanctions.

What was Total's special contribution? Acting as the general manager, Total recruited a wide variety of international providers. Technip, the general contractor for engineering, procurement, and construction (EPC), was French. The three main shipbuilders were South Korean, while a fourth, Mitsui OSK, was Japanese. The supplier of the gas-turbine compressors needed to liquefy the gas, Baker Hughes, was American, and the provider of the cryogenic technology, Linde, was German. Italy's Saipem and a Turkish partner worked on the concrete gravity-based platforms. The builders of the platforms were Chinese. In short, the Yamal project was the very symbol of Russia's dependence on foreign technology for new ventures. This has proved a source of vulnerability since the Russian invasion of Ukraine.[88]

Novatek, with the help of Chinese contractors, managed to complete the first of three planned LNG platforms, despite the departure of foreign suppliers.[89] But in early 2024, in response to the US threat of secondary sanctions, foreign shareholders withdrew from Arctic LNG-2, the successor project to Yamal LNG,[90] canceling their financing commitments and offtake contracts for the project, forcing Novatek to suspend its supply agreements and declare *force majeure*. Following a brief start-up of production from the first train of the project in early 2024, Novatek suspended production from Arctic LNG-2, owing to the sanctions and a lack of buyers. But the key bottleneck is the lack of tankers. South Korean shipbuilders have withdrawn from a contract to help build fifteen tankers at Rosneft's new *Zvezda* shipyard, leaving ten still unbuilt. The South Korean shipbuilders have also stopped work on six more, under construction in South Korea, leaving them in various stages of non-completion.

Meanwhile, the West's financial sanctions have also had an impact. Russia's VEB.RF, the development bank that was supposed to be the owner/lessor of the new tankers, has been hit by US sanctions, blocking foreign contractors from doing business with it.[91] Financial sanctions have impeded settlement of payments from buyers.

Russia's long-term plan calls for export of 100 mtpa of LNG by 2030, from a series of projects that will include seven liquefaction sites around the country, in addition to the Yamal Peninsula. But the supply of ice-worthy LNG tankers will continue to bedevil progress. In round numbers, 100 mtpa of LNG require 100 tankers; Russia at this moment has only 33, not all ice-class. The prospects for contracting with foreign shipyards for additional tankers are dim; there is currently a worldwide boom in LNG develop-ment, and shipyard order books for tanker construction are full everywhere. Meanwhile, Russia's own capabilities for tanker construction are making lit-tle progress. As Andrei Klepach, chief economist for VEB.RF, said at the 2024 Petersburg Gas Conference, "The infrastructure for building LNG tankers in Russia will not appear before 2030."[92] Consequently, Russia's access to East Asia via the Northern Sea Route remains limited. For the time being, Novatek has been exporting LNG to Europe. But this is only a short-term solution, since the EU, increasingly confident of obtaining LNG from other sources, looks likely to ban Russian LNG before long, along with all remaining pipeline imports of Russian gas.

We turn next to the case of BP, which developed far and away the most profitable and influential of the Western investments in the Russian oil economy.

The Odyssey of BP in Russia and the Battle for Control

BP's twenty-five-year odyssey in Russia, from 1997 to 2022, was driven by the aim of its entrepreneurial CEO, John Browne, to "hunt for elephants." Russia appeared to have whole herds of them. But how to bag them? In 1997, Browne signed a deal with a Russian oligarch, Vladimir Potanin, for a 10% share in a West Siberian company called Sidanco, which controlled Russia's largest Soviet-era oilfield, Samotlor. Ahead of any of the Western majors, Browne and BP recognized the potential "Soviet dividend" to be had from such legacy fields. But almost immediately BP found itself embroiled in a bat-tle between two rival groups of oligarchs, Vladimir Potanin's Interros Group versus Mikhail Fridman and Petr Aven of Alfa Group. Browne had certainly found elephants in Russia, but they turned out to be wild bulls. To save its investment, BP went to war with both. The result was a draw: in 2003, after nearly five years of warfare, it concluded an alliance with its former enemies. Together they formed a new company, called TNK-BP, in which BP took a 50% stake; but more important, it also took operating control, with primary responsibility for finance, technology, and management. It stands as the only case in which a Western major was able to gain control of a large Russian oil company.

The results, over the next five years, were highly successful. Between 2003 and 2008 TNK-BP became the single most innovative and profitable of all the Russian oil companies. BP brought in over 300 foreign technical experts who modernized production at Samotlor, using an arsenal of techniques familiar in the West—horizontal drilling, "fracking," advanced waterflooding, and seismic visualization. However, BP was unable to move TNK-BP into exploration or new-field investment, owing to the resistance of its Russian partners. It effectively became a "Russian brownfield company," quite different from BP's approach in the rest of the world. While the adventure lasted, it proved uniquely profitable. But by 2008 the remaining potential of Samotlor had been largely exhausted, and the profits from TNK-BP declined. This led to another war between TNK-BP and its Russian partners. The latter had tolerated BP's control so long as it brought profits; but as those faded, the marriage was finished. In 2008, as rancor mounted, the CEO of TNK-BP, Bob Dudley, fled Russia in fear for his life.[93]

By this time, the wind had shifted against foreign investors in so-called strategic industries, and once-privatized oil assets were being reabsorbed by the state. In the oil sector, this meant the state-owned company Rosneft, headed by a close associate of Vladimir Putin, Igor Sechin. In 2012, Rosneft took over TNK-BP. But BP managed to salvage its 50% stake, trading it for a 20% share of Rosneft and a $17 billion cash settlement. Again, this was a unique achievement; no other foreign company had gained such a large share of a major Russian oil company, let alone the Russian state champion. But its role and its influence were largely reduced to those of a passive investor. BP's epic role in the opening of Russia was over.

In hindsight, where did the Western presence have the most impact on the Russian hydrocarbons industry? Much of the attention of the Western media focused on the big oil companies such as Shell, ExxonMobil, and Total, and their efforts to launch large new projects in virgin territory, such as Sakhalin Island or the Yamal Peninsula. But an equally important contribution came from the Western oil service companies and contractors, which brought new technologies to Russia. Working day to day on the ground, they trained large numbers of Russian oil workers, who are the backbone of the industry today, now that the Westerners have mostly departed.

Chief among the foreign service providers was the French–American company Schlumberger, which owed much of its success to its systematic effort to "look Russian, hire Russian, and act Russian," as it did with local nationals elsewhere in the world. One of the ways it remained under the radar as a foreign company was by quietly buying up small Russian geophysical start-ups and operating them as Schlumberger subsidiaries under their former Russian names. By 2005, out of Schlumberger's 4,500 employees in Russia, 95% were Russian. It had a joint program with Russia's leading oil and gas university, the Gubkin Institute, and in 2006 it opened the first of several training centers in Russia. Over the following fifteen years it trained thousands of Russians in its culture and techniques, ultimately moving several hundred of them into its international business worldwide, some of whom have subsequently returned to Russia as executives in Russian oil companies and the government. Over the last twenty years, Schlumberger's presence in Russia has doubled to 9,000 employees, mostly Russian personnel trained in its own centers.

Schlumberger's chief rivals in Russia, Baker Hughes and Halliburton, withdrew in 2023 following the imposition of US sanctions, and sold their Russian operations to local management.[94] But Schlumberger (now known as SLB) has no plans to leave Russia, although its CEO, Olivier Le Peuch, insists "it has banned any shipments and support of technology," and it is making no new investments in Russia. But if the Russian oil industry today is now able to fly on its own, it is in no small measure thanks to the contribution of the Western oil-service companies during Russia's opening and their continuing legacy today, above all that of Schlumberger.[95]

The Contrast: Russian Nuclear Power

The Russian nuclear industry stands out as a rare—indeed unique—case of a high-technology sector that has not only recovered from the end of the Soviet era and the chaos that followed, but has developed an effective export strategy. On the eve of the 2022 invasion, Russia's nuclear industry was thriving, thanks mainly to its international business. According to Aleksey Likhachev, CEO of Rosatom, Russia's nuclear monopoly, Russia in 2022 was at work on thirty-three nuclear power units in a dozen different countries, including China, India, Belarus, Turkey, Hungary, and Egypt.[96] It sold nearly $12 billion worth of products abroad in 2022, a 30% increase from the year before, and its foreign order book stood at over $200 billion.[97] Rosatom is actively courting new customers, mostly in the developing world; it offers a "full service" package that covers construction and operation, as well as the supply and reprocessing of nuclear fuel. The Russian government actively supports Rosatom with low-interest financing.

In addition to building and operating new powerplants, Rosatom, through its fuels subsidiary Tenex, exports enriched uranium to numerous countries around the world, including the United States and Europe. In Europe, Rosatom also provides fuel-cycle services to five EU countries that operate Russian-built powerplants. Even though the revenues are not comparable (only about $1 billion per year), the fuel exports are key politically, since Russia holds nearly half of the world's uranium enrichment capacity.[98] Because of this dependence, the West hesitated to sanction Russia's nuclear-fuels industry. Finally, in May 2024, the United States banned imports of Russian enriched uranium from Russia (although it provided waivers for imports under existing contracts).[99] The EU has yet to follow suit. But with that exception, Rosatom is able to operate freely abroad, one of the few sectors in the Russian economy to do so.

Rosatom's present commercial success is a remarkable story of near-death and rebirth. The Russian civilian nuclear power program was born out of the Soviet nuclear weapons program. But the end of the Soviet Union in 1991 was a disaster for the nuclear industry. Over the next fifteen years, it largely disintegrated. Key assets were plundered by outsiders, and what remained mostly stopped working. The industry's three major foreign projects, in China, India, and Iran, all legacy projects left over from the Soviet era, fell far behind schedule. There was a massive loss of skills, as experienced workers left for other jobs. By 2005, the Russian civilian nuclear program had virtually stopped.

But in that year Putin named a politician, Sergei Kirienko, to head the nuclear program. Kirienko had had a mixed career up to that time—including a disastrous five-month stint as prime minister that coincided with Russia's 1998 financial meltdown—but he turned out to be a talented manager.[100] He regathered Rosatom's wandering assets under one roof, and after seeing off the predators, he brought the industry's unruly suppliers and contractors to heel. Over the next eleven years, he built Rosatom into a powerhouse. In 2018, Putin rewarded him with a secret medal[101] and a top job, as Number 2 in the Kremlin's Presidential Administration, where he is today.

The secrecy was no accident. When Rosatom was created in 2007, it inherited both the civilian powerplants and the military weapons program, which is organized as a division within Rosatom, the "nuclear weapons complex" known as YOK.[102] Kirienko made vigorous efforts to disentangle the military face of Rosatom from the civilian, but the separation proved easier to achieve on paper than in reality. Today, the civilian and the military parts of Rosatom remain closely connected, as are many parts of the nuclear supply chain, beginning with the mining of uranium, which serves both military and civilian customers inside Russia. YOK is headed by a first deputy general director, Oleg Shubin, who has spent his entire career in the military nuclear division.[103]

Because of these military origins, Rosatom's supply chain, which runs from uranium mining to powerplant construction and operation, depends very little on the outside. As a direct descendant of the Soviet nuclear program, it was built from the beginning to be self-contained, with a minimum of reliance on imported designs and components. That remains the case today. (Indeed, as Russia's leading high-tech company, Rosatom is increasingly being given the mission of filling sanctions-related gaps in other Russian industries.) As a consequence, Western companies played virtually no role in the rebirth of Russian civilian nuclear power in the 2000s.

Rosatom's domestic market looks increasingly unattractive. As its nuclear fleet ages, the older generation of nuclear reactors, the graphite-cooled RBMKs, is gradually being removed from service, but it is not being replaced quickly enough with new models to maintain capacity, since Russia has ample gas available to expand its gas-fired capacity instead. As a result, since 2020 the share of nuclear power in Russia's electricity supply has been declining,[104] and by some estimates, Russia's nuclear capacity at home could diminish by as much as one-third by the mid-2030s.[105] Despite its overall independence from foreign technology, Rosatom has also been hampered by the withdrawal of some of its previous Western partners, notably for the production of gas turbines, which are used in nuclear powerplants and were previously supplied by Siemens's joint venture with "Silovye Mashiny" for Rosatom's domestic projects.[106]

That leaves the export market. Rosatom is involved in over a third of the new reactors being built around the world, including Turkey, Hungary, India, Iran, Egypt, and lately Bangladesh. At the same time, Rosatom is actively marketing powerplants throughout the Global South, with over two dozen memorandums of understanding signed in Africa and Latin America. Russia's future international market in nuclear power may be at risk, as China looms on the horizon as an increasingly powerful competitor. Nevertheless, for the present Rosatom remains a powerful symbol of Russia's capacity for revival.

Conclusions: Thirty Years of Russia's Opening

In the story of Russia's opening to the West, five themes stand out. The first is that the opening was the product of two separate driving forces, the implosion of the Soviet system and the rise of neoliberal globalization in the West, driven above all by the United States. The two were not unconnected: the early Russian market reformers were motivated by the increasingly manifest failure of the Soviet command economy in contrast to the success of the West, and they looked to Western models for alternatives. But when the actual collapse arrived, most Russians were unprepared and had no answers. Russia briefly became an ideological and political vacuum, into which the Westerners arrived like conquerors, bringing the true neoliberal faith.

Second, the pattern of the opening, precisely because of the speed with which it happened and the chaos out of which it was born, was incomplete and uneven. (One observer aptly called it a "shambolic integration."[107]) The consequence was a patchwork: some sectors opened wide and were transformed; others remained largely closed and unchanged. Entire new sectors, which had not existed or had been underdeveloped in Soviet times, were born open to the world. In contrast, some large traditional legacy industries, hastily reassembled into state-controlled monopolies, resisted foreign influences and repelled efforts by foreigners to control them. Where Soviet-era elites remained in power, such as in most of heavy industry, only limited opening took place, with oil and LNG as the main exceptions. In contrast, in services and consumer goods, Westerners played decisive roles, before giving way to a new generation of Russian managers and owners, many of whom the Westerners had trained, and an increasing number of whom, as time went on, were educated in the West.

Third, there were from the start immense cultural and political differences between the Russians and the incoming Westerners, which produced conflicting approaches to business. The traditional Soviet work culture was all about hierarchy, concealment, and the apportionment of blame, whereas Western work cultures promoted transparency and communication, based in particular on tight financial reporting, and governed by strict laws. Russian managers relied heavily on informal ties with circles of friends and colleagues (so-called *krugovye poruki*), in ways that were often illegal in the West. The management practices and technologies brought in by Western companies were frequently unsettling to the Russians. Making legally earned profit the sole acceptable criterion of performance amounted to shining a raw spotlight on a world of extralegal but long-accepted Russian customs, the whole point of which was to prevent higher-ups from finding out what was going on (or to assist them in raking off rents).[108] Even the communications technologies brought in by Western managers were disruptive. Satellite telephony and the Internet, in particular, upended the traditional command structure in which the *vertushka* (dial phone) on the general director's desk, in multiple handsets, was a symbol of his power. The fact that it was foreigners who brashly challenged this familiar world only made the experience all the more irritating. These differences reinforced ambivalence and mistrust on both sides.

Fourth, both sides had unrealistic expectations. Russians expected lavish support, both in the form of state loans and private investment, and they were disappointed when it did not materialize. The Russian liberal reformers were lastingly bitter over their experience with the international financial institutions and the Western governments. Twenty years later, Petr Aven reflected:

> For us, the Gaidar team, the absence of real assistance from the West was shocking . . . We thought that we, the first pro-Western government in decades, would have access to diverse economic support: IMF loans, written-off debts, and so on. But all we had after a year was $1 billion, and with great effort, a rescheduling of foreign debt. That was it.[109]

In actual fact, the US Government and various philanthropic foundations provided abundant funding for a wide variety of programs in Russia, but as often as not these were aimed at supporting non-governmental organizations and building civil society along Western lines. The Agency for International Development (AID) alone allocated hundreds of millions of dollars to projects in Russia. The Department of Energy spent similar amounts supporting Russian scientists in former military research institutes, part of an international effort to promote their conversion to civilian purposes and to lessen the danger of nuclear proliferation.[110] These programs, because of their source and their aims, also tended to arouse suspicion and misunderstanding in Russia.

Fifth, the opening created hostages to political fortune. In particular, the willingness of Russian companies and state institutions to depend on Western technology, supply chains, and financial ties was, in retrospect, remarkable. The prime example is the Russian Central Bank (RCB), which parked half of its foreign reserves (indeed, most of its non-gold reserves) outside of Russia, seeing them as safer and more productive there than inside the country, an astonishingly optimistic wager on continued good relations. The larger Russian companies financed their investments with massive borrowing on foreign capital markets, to offset the weakness of Russia's underdeveloped banking system. Russian manufacturers (including some in the defense sector) grew dependent on external supply chains and foreign service providers, preferring them to domestic ones for their greater efficiency, convenience, and speed.

The Russians did not appear to realize at first that the new global technologies they embraced with such enthusiasm were based on physical structures—"pipes and plumbing," as a recent book puts it—that mostly ran to the United States.[111] The undersea cables that supported the Internet belonged to the private US companies that built them. The global financial networks, based overwhelmingly on the US dollar, were connected to US banks. The ultimate example is SWIFT, which despite its official location in Belgium, has its servers in northern Virginia. This concentration in the United States subsequently made Russia vulnerable to the potential power of US sanctions.

The initial Russian acceptance of dependence was fed by the early optimism bred by the Soviet collapse and the apparent disappearance of barriers. The embryonic Russian middle class, like fresh converts, became for a time true believers in the globalized world and international capitalism (or at least what they understood them to be), and the actions of Russian businessmen and bureaucrats alike suggested that they believed Russia's opening was there to stay.

The illusion of permanence ran both ways. The Westerners who came into Russia were likewise true believers—in profit, to be sure, but more than that. For many of them, the opening of Russia was part of a new era of peace and commerce and opportunity, based on liberal principles. But as both sides invested in retail networks, JVs, equity stakes, consultancies, and local offices, they were creating risk on a grand scale. The later severing has been all the more painful.

But the West's entry into Russia is only half of the story. We turn now to the other face of the opening, the emergence of Russians into the West.

Chapter 2
Black and White

The Russians in the West

The flow of Russians into the West between 1991 and 2022 was quite different from that of the West into Russia. The Russians in the West consisted of four main groups: Russian banks, large industrial corporations, oligarchs and other magnates, and finally tens of thousands of ordinary individuals. Whereas most of the Westerners in Russia belonged to the private sector (the main exceptions being the Moscow offices of the international financial institutions and the Western embassies), the Russians in the West were a mixture. The oligarchs and the individuals were mostly private (or, shall we say, recently privatized), but the Russian banks and corporations were more often state-owned or state-controlled, and their presence in the West was at least partly the product of state strategies. Finally, there was Russian organized crime, which belonged to both categories.

The impact of the Russians on Western opinion was also quite different. Whereas Russian public opinion responded to the presence of the West with a complex mixture of admiration and imitation, but also growing resentment and rejection, the reaction of Western opinion to the Russians in the West was largely negative from the first, and worsened over time—something that the Russians abroad perceived and resented. Thus, in different ways both currents—the West into Russia and the Russians into the West—led to a climate of mutual mistrust and hostility, which reinforced the simultaneous deterioration of geopolitical relations, setting the stage for the sanctions that followed in 2014 and after.

The contrast between Russia and China is striking. The opening of China to the global economy under Deng Xiaoping stimulated a flood of Chinese students and entrepreneurs abroad, studying in Western universities, working in foreign companies, and creating businesses overseas. In contrast, far fewer Russian students and entrepreneurs ventured out of Russia. The Chinese who studied and worked in the West tended to return to China; in Russia far fewer returned (although those who did contributed an important leaven of skills, as we saw in the preceding chapter). China under Deng responded to global opportunities with enthusiasm and creative energy, and the result was a wholesale transformation of China's economy, notably through the creation of thousands of high-tech start-ups, clustered around entire new cities. The dominant Russian reaction, on the contrary, was to limit its ties with the West, while clinging to its signature resource-based profile. As a leading expert on both Russia and China, Harley Balzer, put it in a landmark article in 2008, China's integration with the outside world was "thick," while that of Russia was "thin."[1]

In this chapter we look more closely at Russia's post-Soviet emergence into the West, to try to understand these differences and their consequences. We begin with the Soviet antecedents, the network of "official" Russians who worked at the interface between Russia and the West during the Cold War.

Soviet Antecedents: The Thin Red Line of Official Specialists

In Soviet times, foreign travel was the ultimate perk, a sign of one's trusted standing in the state *nomenklatura*. Thousands of Russians worked in the West, in positions both official and unofficial. They were not all members of the elite. One of them was Lieutenant-Colonel Vladimir Putin of the KGB. As a mid-level officer of modest origins, he was posted to Dresden in East Germany, where his main job appears to have been to oversee the network of Soviet agents in West Germany.[2] He did not amass a fortune there—that came later—and when he returned to Russia in 1991, the best trophy he could manage was a German washing machine strapped to the top of his German-made Trabant.[3] As the Soviet system was dismantled, many people like Putin likewise returned home.

The Soviet command economy had been built by Joseph Stalin to be autarkic, that is, self-sufficient and insulated from the outside world. But the insulation was never total, and at various times the Soviet planners had turned to the West for investments in lagging sectors, such as modern chemistry and automobiles. But these projects were mostly built on a "turnkey" basis; they were tightly controlled by Soviet state ministries; and they involved little movement of people, except during actual construction.[4] In those days, apart from Soviet officials and a few privileged members of the *nomenklatura*, few Russians traveled abroad.

But as the Soviet economy began to weaken, it became increasingly dependent on trade with the outside world, above all with the West. This required more specialists to run it. Then as now, most of the upper levels were graduates of MGIMO, Moscow's prestigious State Institute of International Affairs, which trained diplomats, foreign-trade experts, and spies. One of the trade experts was Vladimir Potanin, who was later to become one of the richest men in Russia, but who as a young graduate of MGIMO started out in the Soviet Ministry of Foreign Trade. Thus, in the final decades of the Soviet period, there was a "thin red line" of Russians specializing in trade and banking, as well as commercial and technology espionage.[5] Their careers were built at the interface between the West and the closed Soviet economy—which was less an Iron Curtain than a semi-permeable membrane across which they diffused back and forth, as they went about their business.

Over time, the Soviet Union's foreign trade expanded, especially as Soviet agriculture began to fail, leading the Soviets to steadily increase grain imports. This led to important roles for Soviet foreign-trade professionals, such as Nikolai Belousov, the head of the Soviet grain-trading agency, Eksportkhleb, then part of the Soviet Ministry of Foreign Trade. Despite the "eksport" in its name, beginning in the 1960s it was importing more grain than it exported, and from 1972, after the catastrophic crop failure of that year,[6] it made larger and larger imports of grain every year. Belousov had come up through the ministry's grain division and was an experienced trader. In 1972 he achieved notoriety for engineering the "Great Grain Robbery," in which he negotiated a series of one-on-one grain deals with US trading companies, carefully keeping each one in the dark about his simultaneous conversations with the others. As the Americans belatedly compared notes, they realized that they had sold him more than the entire US wheat harvest. Belousov was able to outwit the Americans quite simply because he was familiar with the structure of the US commodity-trading community, and especially its fixation on secrecy—whereas the Americans had had up to that time only episodic contact with the Soviet side.[7] As Belousov's colleague Evgenii Bannikov later recalled, "We had a full and clear picture regarding grain supplies situation worldwide and could at any time recommend the most appropriate purchasing strategy depending upon our local requirements at any moment."[8]

Soviet foreign trade also needed a network of banks with offices abroad, and these too employed career specialists, sometimes with KGB backgrounds. For example, Aleksandr Medvedev and Andrey Akimov, based in various Soviet-owned banks in Vienna and Zurich, oversaw financial settlements and trade credits, in support of foreign trade. The Soviet banks in Europe also had a dark side, as they provided funding for left-wing organizations around the world, including radicals and terrorist groups. As the Soviet Union began to crack in the 1980s, they acted as financial intermediaries for the Communist Party and the KGB, which, as they perceived the handwriting on the wall, began moving their assets abroad, out of harm's way.

After the fall of the Soviet Union, some of these Soviet-era professionals went on to second careers in the newly privatized former branches of the state ministries in the post-Soviet world. In the 1990s, both Medvedev and Akimov returned to Moscow, where Medvedev headed Gazprom Export until 2014, while Akimov took over Gazprombank, where he remains today.

The network of Soviet officials in the West naturally included the KGB (then in charge of foreign intelligence) and the GRU (military intelligence), and many of these remained active following the Soviet collapse, notably in Europe, where they recruited a new generation of agents (though using much the same old methods as well as some new ones) to rebuild the Russian intelligence system, particularly focusing on new financial companies. One of these was Wirecard, once the toast of the European fintech sector. In 2023 Wirecard was exposed as a fraud, after it was revealed that €1.9 billion in cash from its Asian operations did not exist. Shortly afterward, the group collapsed. A subsequent investigation disclosed that the group's COO, Austrian Jan Marsalek, was a GRU agent. Over the course of a decade, Marsalek had become one of the GRU's most valuable assets.[9] Wirecard itself had been used as a front to finance Russian undercover operations. When Wirecard disappeared, a GRU officer arranged Marsalek's escape to Russia, where he was last reported as having stolen the identity of an orthodox priest.[10] The GRU's network, however, remains as active as ever; indeed, Russian foreign-intelligence operations are reported to have increased sharply since the invasion.[11]

Russian Banks and Financial Ties: The Increased Roles of Money

Russia's abrupt transition to a market economy implied an increased role for money in all three of its classical functions: as an instrument of economic policy, as a vehicle for transactions and credit, and as a store of value. But for Russian money to play these roles, it required international channels, above all to support its liberalized trade and investment with the outside world. Beginning in the late 1980s, even before the end of the Soviet Union, Russia began joining the Western financial system. To handle cross-border transactions, it became a member of SWIFT, the international interbank messaging system,[12] as well as settlement networks such as Euroclear and ClearStream and Target2.[13] Russian banks established direct correspondent relationships with Western counterparts. These became indispensable vehicles for Russian trade, but also provided the means by which the new private fortunes could be exported outside of the country later on. Thus, the Western financial system played an essential role in all three functions, but above all as a "store of value," as Russian private money sought the security of the West as a refuge. The Russian government itself used the Western financial system as a safe haven for its reserves and assets.[14] On the eve of the invasion, the Reserve Bank of Russia held over $650 billion in gold and foreign exchange; half of the latter was parked abroad, including some €180 billion in accounts managed by Euroclear.[15]

Vladimir Putin, when he became president at the end of 1999, was initially a strong promoter of Russia's membership in international financial bodies. One of his chief motives was to halt the export of capital by Russian organized crime, from drug trafficking and other criminal activities. In 2003, Russia joined the Financial Action Task Force (FATF), the Paris-based global money-laundering and terrorist finance watchdog, and in the early years the Russian government was a constructive member, sometimes in collaboration with the US Justice Department.[16]

Russia's membership in SWIFT was a game-changer. The first Russian bank to join SWIFT was the Soviet Bank for External Trade (Vneshekonom-bank), in 1989.[17] At the time, foreign trade was still a state monopoly, and Russia's initial interactions with SWIFT were conducted out of Vneshekonombank's offices in Moscow. But the end of the Soviet foreign-trade monopoly, and the rapid rise of Russian private banks and traders, soon caused the traffic with SWIFT to outgrow this awkward envelope. In 1992, SWIFT joined three private Russian banks in a joint venture (JV) called "SOVAM-Teleport," to handle the rapidly expanding Russian traffic.[18] By 1994 this had led to the creation of RosSwift, the Association of Russian SWIFT Users, a self-governing body. Over the next few years SWIFT's Russian membership exploded. By 2021, on the eve of the invasion, 400

Russian banks belonged to SWIFT, the second-largest number after the United States, and it had become the indispensable communications service for practically all of Russia's international as well as domestic financial transactions.[19]

In the second half of the 1990s, several state-owned Russian banks opened offices in Europe. They specialized in different functions. Sberbank, Russia's largest savings bank, was the only one to focus on retail banking; it acquired a network of retail outlets in Eastern Europe, and created an online savings bank in Germany, called Sberbank Direct. By 2020 Sberbank Europe had 800,000 customers, 187 retail outlets, and 3,800 employees, with assets of €13 billion.[20] Gazprombank, in contrast, had only twenty-eight local offices in Europe, one in each of the member-states of the EU; their main mission was not to provide retail services, but to handle Gazprom's gas export revenues. VTB, the state-owned descendant of Vneshtorgbank, had only two European offices, an investment bank in Frankfurt called Direktbank, part of VTB Bank (Europe),[21] which specialized in corporate loans and investment banking, rather than retail banking,[22] and an investment firm in London, called VTB Capital.

But these three were not alone. By the mid-2010s, most of Russia's major private banks had opened offices and set up subsidiaries throughout Europe. These new financial channels gave Russia vital access to Western capital markets, which played a key role of providing capital and credit, enabling Russian corporations to offset the weakness of Russia's domestic banks and the low level of savings by the population. Over the following twenty years, Russian corporations borrowed heavily on Western credit markets to support their investments, both via banks and non-bank channels.[23] Between 1999 and 2008, the combination of borrowing via commercial banks and direct issuance of bonds exploded from $26 billion to $245 billion, an amount three-and-a-half times greater than foreign direct investment into Russia by Western firms.[24]

Russia's expanding financial ties with the West ran well beyond banks to include non-bank sectors and services. One of the most spectacular examples was civil aviation, where the Russian airline companies shifted to Western-made aircraft, which they acquired by leasing instead of buying. Leasing was a recent invention, practically a symbol of the spread of financial instruments in the globalized economy. But it had rapidly become the dominant commercial model throughout the world. Whereas in 1970 leases did not yet exist, by the beginning of the 2020s over 50% of all commercial aircraft worldwide were acquired by leases rather than by purchase. For a rental of $1 million a month per plane, an airline could build an entire fleet without spending a penny in capital costs. Russia was a clear candidate. Leasing offered a ready means of replacing obsolete Russian airplanes with up-to-date and efficient Western models. Russia's newly created private airlines, such as Pobeda, became overnight competitors of the state-owned airline Aeroflot, thanks to leasing. But Aeroflot soon caught on. By the eve of the invasion, Russia had leased over 400 foreign aircraft, with Aeroflot accounting for about half.[25] Today, Russian airlines operate about 540 foreign-made aircraft, but only about 150 Russian-made ones.[26]

This created a whole new form of dependence, which had never existed in Soviet times, with clear benefits but also a high potential level of risk—on both sides. For the lessors—many of them based in Ireland to take advantage of Ireland's generous tax laws—there was the risk that in case of trouble Russia could simply impound the planes. But there was also the risk to the Russians, that the lessor would then no longer supply spare parts or provide maintenance. Each side held the other hostage, which proved disastrous for the Western lessors after the invasion. By mid-2023, some $10 billion in leased aircraft were tied up in Russia, leaving Western insurance companies holding the bill.[27] While the Western lawyers quarreled over who was liable, the Russians found a simple solution, by buying up the leased planes that they had initially seized following the invasion. Since by this time these had aged, the Russians were able to acquire them cheaply. However, this did not solve the problem of developing a new generation of Russian airliners.[28]

The Great Transition: The First "New Russians" Come West

The chaos and anarchy of the Russian 1990s led to a change in the numbers and kinds of Russians who came abroad. In the free-for-all that followed the end of the Soviet Union, a new generation of players emerged. Some of them began as complete outsiders, "accidental people" who had not been part of the Soviet *nomenklatura,* and amassed their first fortunes through guile, grit, and luck. But more often the Russian new rich came from privileged backgrounds—former Soviet officials or members of the Soviet intelligentsia.[29] Some among the new winners were scions of established Soviet managers, who discovered new opportunities in previously neglected corners of the Soviet system, such as Leonid Mikhelson, whom we have aready met as the founder of Novatek and the pioneer of Russian LNG, who was the son of a Soviet-era pipeline builder.

But regardless of their origins, before long they were reaching out beyond Russian borders to become international players. An iconic example is Oleg Deripaska, who rose from obscurity to become the king of Russian aluminum, and went on to create an aluminum empire in the West.

Thriving on Chaos: The Story of Oleg Deripaska

Oleg Deripaska grew up in a small town in south Russia, the son of a widowed engineer, and was raised by his grandparents. His talent in mathematics won him a coveted scholarship in the physics department of Moscow State University (MGU), a feat all the more remarkable for the fact that Deripaska was born to a Jewish family, and Jews were subject to tight quotas in university admissions. MGU, located in Lenin Hills above the Moscow River in an imposing Stalin-era wedding-cake structure that dominated the Moscow skyline before the advent of today's gleaming high-rises, was the most prestigious university in the Soviet Union. Oleg became fascinated by theoretical quantum physics, a field that at the time had no practical applications and offered few job prospects outside of academia. His studies were interrupted by the military draft, which was unusual, suggesting a lack of *blat* ("pull"), since most of his better-connected classmates probably managed to avoid service. He spent two years in the Strategic Missile Forces, in far-off East Siberia near Lake Baikal.[30] By the time he returned to MGU in 1989, Gorbachev's *perestroika* was already well on its way to shattering the Soviet system. Research stipends and grants had disappeared. "We had no money," Deripaska later recalled. "It was an urgent and practical question every day. How do I earn money to buy food and keep studying?"[31]

By the time he graduated in 1993, Deripaska was already twenty-five, significantly older than most of his fellow students. An academic career was out of the question, so Deripaska teamed up with a group of friends, ex-draftees like himself, and founded a "cooperative," an innovation of the Gorbachev era that allowed ordinary people to create private start-ups. They dubbed their business the Military Investment and Trade Company (VTK), and like everybody else in that wild era, they went "into the market" (*na rynok* in the phrase of the day), which mostly meant arbitraging between low Soviet prices and the world market, especially in commodities. This path quickly led Deripaska and his fellow students to aluminum.

Their timing was impeccable: the aluminum industry had just been privatized, and it was falling apart. With the end of the state monopoly over foreign trade—one of Gorbachev's most radical reforms in the late 1980s—the traditional ties that had bound the Russian aluminum producers in Siberia, via intermediaries in the state foreign-trade company, Raznoimport, to buyers in London, had shattered. Suddenly, the Russian producers had no one to sell to, and as stocks of finished aluminum piled up unsold in company warehouses, their increasingly desperate Soviet managers faced bills to pay and workforces to support. Cash had practically ceased to exist, and Russia turned overnight into a barter economy. Anyone who could somehow acquire a shipment of aluminum at low official state prices, and get it to the border, was guaranteed an overnight fortune. But that was the last thing that the traditional Soviet managers, who were typically engineers, knew how to do. They were stuck.

Into this picture came the traders. These were mostly people who had stumbled into commodities by chance and connections. The key to their business was the fact that the Russian aluminum producers depended on two essential raw materials, bauxite and alumina, which had to be imported. These were then taken to East Siberia and smelted into aluminum metal, using the abundant hydropower resources of the region. The traders brought the producers an offer they could not refuse, a trading arrangement called tolling: the trader supplied the raw materials the producer turned into the finished product the trader then exported, with both sides taking a cut of the profits (which were conveniently tax-free).[32]

One of the best at this game was an engaging hustler from Tashkent named Lev Chernoy. Like the other new entrants in this period, he got into the aluminum business by accident. As Chernoy told the story, "I had been selling goods to the managers of an alumina plant in northern Kazakhstan. But they, like every other business in the FSU, had no cash. So they were paying me in alumina. The alumina would be processed at an aluminum plant in Krasnoyarsk, in Russian Siberia. The aluminum plant didn't have money to pay either, so it paid me in aluminum." At that point, Chernoy needed a connection in the West, so he turned to a leading international trader named David Reuben, the founder of a London-based company called Trans-World Group (TWG). The two men, after a quick trip to Krasnoyarsk, struck a deal:

TWG would provide alumina and working capital; Chernoy would return with finished aluminum for export.

For the producers, tolling meant survival. But for the traders, who had the producers at their mercy, it meant mastery. Before long, the Russian traders, backed by even bigger traders in London, had taken over the East Siberian smelters, squeezing out, by means fair or foul, the Soviet-era managers. Within a short time, TWG and Chernoy had acquired a whole collection of smelters.

But now they needed a trusted figure on location to run them. At this point, Chernoy turned to Oleg Deripaska, who had become one of his trading partners and was considered both able and reliable. Chernoy put him on the board of directors of one of Russia's largest aluminum smelters, SayanskAZ, as the representative of TWG. Thus at the age of twenty-five, Deripaska, whose previous acquaintance with East Siberia was limited to his brief service as a lowly conscript in the rocket forces, was effectively the boss. He found himself overnight one of the most powerful figures in the economy of the region.

But Chernoy and TWG were in for a surprise. Within another two years, Deripaska had learned from them everything he needed to know about the tolling business, and he abruptly turned the tables on his sponsors, and canceled their export contracts. By this time, Russia's economy had begun to stabilize, money had started to circulate again, and the era of barter trade was fading. Deripaska, now no longer a hostage to foreign traders, started building his own empire, scooping up one smelter after another, using the standard techniques of the day—share dilutions and engineered bankruptcies, with the help of local politicians and "authorities," i.e., crime bosses. By 2005 he was the richest man in Russia.[33]

Up to this point, Deripaska had made his career solely inside Russia, but he soon became part of Russia's growing presence in the West, as he sought to create a reliable supply chain for his aluminum business. This led him to Guinea in West Africa, the world's largest producer of bauxite, the essential raw material for finished aluminum, where Deripaska's company, Rusal, soon became one of the largest investors. As his empire grew, Deripaska himself became increasingly international in his outlook, and his role inside Russia changed accordingly. In 2017 his holding company En+ (which held RusAl) went public on the London Stock Exchange. But in April 2018 Deripaska's international ambitions ran into a roadblock, when he was sanctioned by the US Treasury Department. This led to a major conflict over sanctions policy, discussed in Chapter 4. Despite this, Deripaska remained a voice inside Russian business circles for closer relations with the West, which eventually got him into trouble. When Russia invaded Ukraine in February 2022, Deripaska, alone among the leading members of the Russian elite, spoke out in public against it.[34] For this he was rapped sharply on the knuckles by Putin, and he has since become more discrete.

The story of Deripaska illustrates the rough-and-tumble origins of many of the successful Russians who went on to build business empires in the West. But how typical were they? A variation on the story of Russian metals was the steel industry. Following the emergence of private steel companies and their successful modernization by Russian entrepreneurs, recounted in the last chapter, the leading Russian companies developed a vigorous export business, chiefly in Europe and the United States. In a few cases, they went through a heady phase of foreign acquisitions, buying up steel companies all over the world. The extreme case was Aleksey Mordashov, the owner of Severstal, who had a ten-year odyssey investing in the United States, beginning with his purchase of a bankrupt plant in Michigan in 2003. He followed that up with further acquisitions, and by 2008 he was the fourth-largest steel producer in the United States.[35]

But the overseas investments of the Russian steel magnates were never as far-reaching or successful as those of Deripaska and aluminum. The US steel industry abruptly turned into a money-loser after the 2008–9 financial crisis, and although Mordashov insisted that "America is the future" and resisted giving up on his dream,[36] between 2010 and 2014 he sold all his US properties and retreated back to the Russian domestic market.[37] Two other leading Russian steelmakers, Evraz and Severstal, had also gone through an "American" period, but the financial crisis of 2008–9 likewise forced them to retreat back to the domestic market. In sum, the role of the Russian steel industry in the West remained limited.

Lifestyles of the Russians in the West

A handful of self-made men played key roles in Russia's emergence into the West, but how typical were they? In actual fact, most of the Russians who came into the West after the Soviet collapse came from the Soviet manage-rial class. In the halcyon days before 2022, they invested in the West, they kept their families in London, they vacationed on the Côte d'Azur, and they sent their children to Swiss schools. But most of them retained close ties to Russia, and the Ukrainian war and the sanctions have led to a life crisis for many of them. But here we are getting ahead of our story. Let us look first at how the Russians in the West lived and worked up to the time of the invasion.

Three Different Russian Cities: London, Amsterdam, and Limassol

As Russians came into the West in the 1990s, they settled in different places and were drawn by different things. For some it was a cosmopolitan atmo-sphere and indulgent regulators; for others it was sunshine and low taxes, with many other motives in between. Russian communities already existed in New York City and Tel-Aviv. But the new wave of Russians headed pri-marily for Europe. In this section we look at three cities, each with its own Russian story—London, Amsterdam, and Limassol, Cyprus.

The Rise of "Londongrad"

In 1999, a Russian citizen named Roman Abramovich, the owner of a newly privatized oil company called Sibneft (acquired under the controversial loans-for-shares program established by a Yeltsin decree), bought a 424-acre estate in West Sussex for £12 million from an Australian media mogul.[38] Four years later, Abramovich bought the Chelsea football club, a Premier League champion, and over the next two decades divided his life between Russia and the West.[39] The news caused a sensation in the British media. The "new Russians" had arrived.

But Abramovich was far from the first. The new Russians began com-ing to Britain in the mid-1990s, shortly after the fall of the Soviet Union. The initial trickle soon became a flow, as Russians reacted to the default of 1998 and the financial crisis that followed. By the mid-2000s, overex-cited media accounts put the number of Russians in Britain at more than 250,000, of whom some 700 were said to have "fabulous fortunes," while another 500 were mere millionaires.[40] In reality, the actual number was not nearly so large—about 80,000 is a more probable estimate[41]—but what is not in doubt is the impact of the Russians on London real estate and related businesses. The Russians quickly learned their way around, thanks partly to help from firms like Sotheby's, which opened an office in Moscow in 2001, mainly to serve Russians planning to move to the West. As one British realtor commented, "They now arrive with everything in place—solicitors, finance, and if they like something, they make quick decisions."[42] Sotheby's was not alone, as British specialists of all kinds—lawyers, bankers, and real estate agents—sprang to serve the new arrivals. A whole Russian community began to form, with Russian restaurants, a Russian-language newspaper,[43] and social clubs. The British media began referring to London as "Londongrad."

Abramovich himself had started from nothing at the beginning of the 1990s, parlaying connections from his north Russian hometown of Ukhta into a modest oil-products-trading operation. By 1992, through his trading company AVK, the twenty-five-year-old Abramovich was moving tank cars of oil products, chiefly diesel, from the Ukhta refinery to export points on the Baltic. Within a year, however, he had formed close ties with a leading upstream producer, Noiabrskneftegaz, and had become one of the top traders of crude oil out of West Siberia.[44] In 1995, Abramovich and his then-partner, Boris Berezovsky, acquired Sibneft in the notoriously rigged "Shares for Loans" auctions, for which Abramovich later cheerfully admitted in a London court that they had paid millions of dollars in bribes for political favors and protection fees.[45]

But Abramovich and Londongrad were only the tip of a fast-growing but largely invisible iceberg of Russian property abroad, which soon extended to havens all over the world, where Russians could conceal themselves and their fortunes behind layers of anonymous fronts and shell companies.[46] Some of this early flow consisted of offshore assets of the KGB, the Communist Party, and other Soviet state bodies, but these were soon dwarfed by the tide of individuals big and small, the early winners of the Russian "wheel of fortune," who followed Abramovich's example and moved their new assets abroad. The richest among them soon began spending their money on a grand scale, buying private jets, yachts, and mansions, or, like Abramovich, sports clubs. Yachts were a special favorite; every oligarch, it seemed, had to have one, and as with real estate, specialized agencies soon sprang up to serve them.[47]

The Many Russian Islands of Cyprus

Cyprus is yet another story. Starting in the 1990s, a large population of Russians settled there, drawn by the Mediterranean climate, low taxes, easy-going lifestyle, and widespread use of the Russian language.[48] Cyprus's Russian population on the eve of the invasion numbered up to 50,000, and it came to be known as "Moscow on the Med." For the wealthy, Cyprus's membership in the EU opened the prospect of gaining EU citizenship. Until 2020, Cyprus offered a "Golden Passport," under which anyone who invested €300,000 in Cyprus and remained as a resident property-owner for five years could then apply for Cypriot citizenship and an EU passport. But in that year, an investigation by Al-Jazeera revealed that the Golden Pass-port program had granted citizenships to hundreds of ineligible Russian applicants. The program had been highly profitable for the government of Cyprus. Over the thirteen years of its existence, it had generated over €9 billion (or about $8.7 billion), which had helped to rescue the government from the fallout following a financial crisis in 2013. However, the Cypriot government responded to the 2020 scandal by shutting down the Golden Passport program, and it has since canceled retroactively the citizenship of several hundred Russians with suspicious backgrounds. Since then, wealthy foreign investors can only obtain permanent residencies.[49]

But apart from the very wealthy, the bulk of the Russian population in Cyprus is actually highly diverse. "They consist of several different islands," comments one long-time Russian resident. "There are the geeks—the IT professionals. Then along the shoreline of Limassol you will find the head-quarters of hundreds of Russian offshore companies. It is also an island of lawyers, because Cyprus, conveniently, operates under British law. And finally, Cyprus has a large population of Russian divorced wives, cast off by their husbands back in Russia, and who spend their time shopping and sunbathing."[50]

These different communities mostly live their separate lives, but up to the 2022 invasion they all had one thing in common: they were all con-nected to the Russian economy back home, through a network of banks that were mostly owned by Russian shareholders and managed correspondent accounts in Russia. Many local Russians kept their funds there; at their peak in 2012, Russian deposits in Cypriot banks totaled some $20 billion.[51]

Well before the invasion, the Russian banks and companies in Cyprus had come under scrutiny by the US Treasury and the European Cen-tral Bank, on well-founded suspicions that they were active conduits for money-laundering. After the Russian annexation of Crimea and the first round of Western sanctions, this attention redoubled. In 2016, RCB, a subsidiary of VTB, showed up in the Panama Papers as a source of unsecured loans to close Putin associates.[52]

Since the invasion, the Russians in Cyprus have fallen on harder times. Tourism from Russia has ended, direct flights between Cyprus and Russia have been banned, and money transfers are not allowed. On orders from the EU, the RCB has closed its retail business and has been placed under administration by the government of Cyprus.[53] The Cypriot government, under pressure from the EU, has tightened oversight of Russian companies, to curb sanctions evasion via the island, In response, many Russian companies are leaving Cyprus, either for FSU countries such as Kazakhstan, or the newly created "special administrative zones" inside Russia, which offer low taxes as an inducement (see Chapter 5).[54]

Amsterdam: The Russian "Letterbox City"

An equally important hub for Russian activity was Amsterdam. But whereas "Londongrad" and Cyprus had large populations of ordinary Russians, in Amsterdam the Russian presence mostly consisted of the offices of companies and banks, clustered in the high-rises of the city's financial district, Zuidas. Because of the Netherlands generous tax laws and indulgent regulators, Amsterdam was an attractive spot, and many Russian companies located their international headquarters there. But one would have looked in vain for secretaries and office spaces, because most of them were there only as "letterboxes." The Russians were not alone in this: many multinationals, including US firms, used the famous "Dutch sandwich" to move profits through the Netherlands to tax havens around the world.

For a long time, the Dutch government ignored the mounting evidence that the Russian companies in Zuidas, with the complicity of some banks, were active conduits for money-laundering.[55] The most notorious was the Amsterdam Trade Bank (ATB), a subsidiary of Alfa Bank. On the surface, it engaged in legitimate banking; thus on the eve of the invasion, it had some 23,000 Dutch and German retail customers, and its main public activity was trade finance for companies in the former Soviet Union. But ATB had a bad reputation. Over the years, it had been involved in several scandals, in which investigative journalists claimed that ATB was laundering money for various Russian interests.

In the second half of the 2010s, under pressure from the EU Commission, the Netherlands began to tighten up its tax rules. This was partly the result of a general backlash in Brussels against the excesses of the multinationals, but the "Russian letterboxes" came under particular scrutiny following the Russian annexation of Crimea and the first round of sanctions. In 2017, ATB was raided by the Dutch financial watchdog, the Financial Information and Investigative Service (FIOD). In April 2022, after ATB was sanctioned by the US Office of Foreign Assets Control (OFAC) and Microsoft stopped servicing its e-mail accounts, it was declared bankrupt by the Amsterdam District Court, and was closed.[56]

The largest single Russian player in Amsterdam was Gazprom. Prior to the 2022 invasion, Gazprom operated sixteen subsidiaries in Amsterdam employing several thousand people, ranging from mailbox companies to providers of technical assistance to Gazprom projects around the world. Some of these were the legal owners of Gazprom properties elsewhere, such as the pipeline from Russia to Turkey across the Black Sea. The Amsterdam office of Gazprom's global trading arm, Gazprom Marketing and Trading (GMT) was the conduit for Gazprom export sales to the UK, France, and the Netherlands. Altogether, Gazprom's subsidiaries in Amsterdam were a major vehicle for the transfer of profits and dividends from Gazprom's global gas trade back to Russia.[57]

Serving the Russian letterboxes in Amsterdam was a profusion of Dutch service companies, such as law firms, trust offices, and notaries.[58] Normally such companies go about their business unnoticed, but in August 2022, the Netherlands adopted a law prohibiting them from working for Russian clients. The Dutch service companies promptly went out the door, and the Russian companies found themselves paralyzed, unable to leave the Netherlands even when sanctioned. According to a pair of Dutch investigative reporters:

> Even notaries have self-sanctioned, with the result that Russian companies that need to move are unable to do so, because there is no one to execute the documents. Same thing with accountants, with the result that the Russian companies are unable to publish their annual financial statements, as required by the Russian tax authorities. Many joint ventures (such as between US auto companies and Russian partners), which were registered in Amsterdam, were similarly affected.[59]

In short, the Russian entry into the West led to a wide variety of Russian communities, mostly in Europe, with different populations drawn by different things—whether an open society and a favorable business environment in Londongrad, permissive treatment of global businesses in Amsterdam, or a picturesque mini-Russian island in Cyprus, and there were others, such as Tel Aviv and New York. But what they all had in common was continuing ties with Russia, which remained the ultimate source of their business and assets. This was not yet an "émigre" community—that came later, after the 2022 invasion, which forced many of the Russians established in the West to make a historic choice—to stay in the West or return to Russia—while their numbers were soon dwarfed by a tidal wave of new Russian arrivals.

The Russian oligarchs have been especially affected. Since the 1990s, a whole new tier of global businesses had sprung up to handle their money and their property. But the invasion has caused much of the oligarchs' Western world to weaken or dissolve, and many have returned to Russia. We turn to that story now.

The Russian "Oligarchs" and the Global Wealth Management Industry

In addition to London, Switzerland, with its tradition of banking secrecy, was a favorite haven for money leaving Russia, and it remains so to this day. But much of the new Russian money quickly moved on to even more anonymous destinations, such as the British Virgin Islands and the Cayman Islands, and ultimately to the United States and the UK, protected by permissive laws and multiple layers of shell companies.[60] Since the invasion, however, those conduits have been disrupted. As of 2023, according to the Swiss government, some $50 billion of Russian money, belonging to over 7,500 wealthy Russians (including such Putin intimates as the cellist Sergei Roldugin), lie frozen in Swiss banks, though still protected by many layers of discretion.[61]

As the Russians flooded out of Russia into places like "Londongrad," they transformed luxury markets wherever they went, bidding up the prices of mansions in Belgravia, country homes, beachfront properties, private planes, and yachts. But beyond such trophy items, what they needed above all was safety and anonymity, and protection from prying eyes, state regulation, and taxation. Beginning in the 1990s, the growth of international financial networks, connected via the Internet, made it possible to move assets easily from one haven to another, and to hide beneficiaries behind layers of fronts. This called for a new set of skills, combining trust law, knowledge of markets, data handling, and diplomacy and coincided with the rise of a new profession—wealth management. Starting in the 2000s, new curricula appeared in global financial centers, offering two-year programs leading to a master's degree. Within a decade, there were over 20,000 certified wealth professionals worldwide, available to protect the assets of the One Percent.[62] Many of the advisors and their clients, though far from all, were Russian.

How did the Russian oligarchs and their wealth advisors invest their money outside Russia? For obvious reasons, details are scarce, since the whole point is to maintain secrecy. One of the few such funds to operate in the open is LetterOne Holdings, a Luxembourg-based investment fund created by the Russian founders of Alfa Bank, Mikhail Fridman and Petr Aven (a former Russian minister of foreign trade under Yeltsin).[63] LetterOne invests widely in Western businesses.[64] It is not itself under sanctions, but since the invasion, it has been required to sever all ties with its Russian shareholders,[65] although it is otherwise free to continue its activities. However, two of its founding partners, Fridman and Aven, were sanctioned by both the EU and the United States, as were their partners in Russia.[66] Fridman found himself surrounded by ever-tighter constraints, including limits on his personal spending, and in October 2023 he returned to Moscow. As he commented at the time, "It looks like our attempt to build business outside of Russia was actually useless, just because of the simple fact that we are originally from there."[67] However, the story did not end there. In April 2024 the EU's top court annulled the inclusion of Fridman and Aven on the EU's sanctions list, on the grounds that there was insufficient evidence that the two men had backed Russia's war against Ukraine.[68] This ruling may open the way for hundreds of wealthy Russians to bring suit to annul EU sanctions.[69]

Fridman and Aven paid a high price for the relative openness with which they operated in LetterOne, which made them a visible target. The same is not true of the other Russian oligarchs, many of whom have remained in Russia. The secret funds managed by wealth professionals on their behalf presumably follow much the same investment strategies as LetterOne, that is, acquiring diversified portfolios of Western assets for their clients, but with fewer publicly traded companies and more private properties such as real estate, thus ensuring greater secrecy.[70]

One of the few examples of such secret operations to come to the surface is a trove of over 50,000 leaked e-mails and documents, which shed a bright light on the overseas investments of two of Putin's oldest and closest allies, Boris and Arkadii Rotenberg, and their families.[71] The Rotenbergs have long used the standard techniques of international wealth management to keep their foreign assets hidden and safe. The first requirement is to have a trusted manager. In the case of the Rotenbergs, according to an investigation by the Organized Crime and Corruption Report Project (OCCRP), that key role was reportedly played by a Moscow-born lawyer named Maxim Viktorov, who headed a management company and law firm in London and is known chiefly for his passion for antique Italian violins (in 2009, he paid a record $3.9 million at Sotheby's for a rare eighteenth-century instrument), directed a team that moves the Rotenbergs' assets judiciously from one haven to another, constantly throwing investigators off the trail. Ownership is regularly reassigned to various third parties who are not under Western sanctions.[72]

These techniques have become more difficult to use as more wealthy Russians have come under sanctions since the Russian invasion—and under the increasingly intense focus of Western governments.[73] Boris Rotenberg's son Roman, for example, was included on Western sanctions lists in 2022, forcing his wealth manager to transfer his overseas assets, such as his stake in a large arena in Finland, to less visible front-men. Until recently, there was little effort by Western authorities to track this kind of evasion. That has begun to change, but assets can be easily moved, and there are plenty of would-be havens waiting in line, as well as older ones such as Cyprus and Monaco, which manage other properties of the Rotenbergs.

The Coming of the Russian "Mafias"

Finally, no account of the Russian contributions to the West over the last thirty years would be complete without mention of Russian organized crime and its expansion abroad. Even as the Soviet Union collapsed and the borders opened, the Soviet criminal world (often called the *vory*, or thieves[74]) was quickly alert to the new opportunities outside Russia. Russian criminals—who included other former Soviet nationalities such as Chechens and Georgians—seized upon the resources hemorrhaging from the shattered Soviet system and opened up transit routes to the outside world, initially to Eastern Europe and the Baltic republics, and then to other locations, both deeper inside Europe and close by, such as Cyprus and Israel. Drugs flowed out of Afghanistan through Central Asia and western Russia into Europe; natural gas passed through Ukraine via Ukrainian intermediaries, some of whom had roots in Russian organized crime;[75] money was laundered through complicit banks in Latvia; and women were trafficked via Moldova.

Russian criminals had been living in the United States since Soviet times.[76] The first *vory* began arriving there via the Soviet Jewish emigration of the late Brezhnev period (although few of them were actually Jewish). As more came in the 1990s, they became an increasingly visible element on the US scene, blending into existing Russian communities, particularly Brighton Beach in New York City, where they soon became known for elaborate scams and frauds, some of which have become legend.[77]

The arrival of Russian criminals in Europe and the United States set off a wave of alarm throughout the West. Sensational media stories painted a lurid picture of a massive invasion of Russian organized crime, a theme amplified by a steady stream of Hollywood movies in which the Russian underworld provided plentiful bad guys for action-packed films. Law-enforcement authorities and politicians described the Russians as a dire new threat. As a senior FBI official in charge of fighting Russian organized crime commented in early 1999, "It's a growth industry, and we're still losing."[78]

But more recent studies have put the matter into less feverish perspective. The West's leading expert on Russian crime, Mark Galeotti, in a carefully researched book, *The Vory*, concludes flatly that the supposed Russian tsunami of organized crime into the West, based on "a globalized, universal criminal class able to migrate to wherever a new opportunity seems to be emerging is . . . a myth."[79] As Galeotti observes, it is unusual for gangs to migrate to new places where they lack contacts and experience. The only exceptions are when there are no local competitors or when new markets appear, as was briefly the case in Eastern Europe. On the whole the early movement of Russian criminals into the West was not highly organized— consisting not of wolf packs or many-tentacled octopuses, as Galeotti puts it, but rather viruses, "without any plan or central mind, but simply infecting those hosts which offered the right conditions and which lacked antibodies." However, the West quickly *did* develop antibodies. The early Russian *vory* in the West soon faced a backlash from governments and local rivals, and were forced out.

Meanwhile, the criminal world inside Russia was also changing. The violent street gangs of the 1990s were giving way to more sophisticated players, who moved upstairs to the executive suites, put on suits, improved their manners, and offered new high-end products, such as money-laundering, currency conversion, modern business practices, and security, serving other criminal groups, businesses, and politicians. In contrast to the traditional *vory* who came out of the Soviet prisons, they were the smoother *avtoritety*, the bosses. They became "the criminals behind the criminals," often in partnership with the state's security services. By the 2000s, they had become the new face of Russian organized crime abroad, and they proved far more successful than the first generation of rough-edged street criminals, particularly in creating partnerships with other criminal groups around the world.[80] In the United States, in particular, Russian organized crime had little involvement in the traditional activities of organized crime, such as drug trafficking, gambling, and loan sharking. Rather, they specialized in more sophisticated schemes such as health care fraud, insurance scams, stock frauds, antiquities swindles, forgery, and gasoline-tax evasion.[81]

A notorious example of the "new Russian criminal" was Viktor Bout, a graduate of the Moscow Institute of Foreign Languages, who served as a military translator, and then turned an early private air-freight business into the world's largest arms-trafficking operation, earning him the nickname "Merchant of Death." Clearly supported behind the scenes by elements of the Russian security elite, Bout proved adept at creating multiple fronts all over the world, and it was not until 2008 that a US sting operation caught up with him in Thailand. Extradited to the United States, Bout spent a decade in US prisons, until he was released in 2022 in a prisoner exchange against US basketball player Brittney Griner.[82]

There were many parallels between the Russian oligarchs and the criminal *avtoritety*, and indeed some overlap between the two. The sources of their fortunes were often similarly murky and their methods equally secretive. What they both sought in the West was more often personal security, in response to the dangerous and unpredictable environment inside Russia, rather than profits, which were generally greater at home. And like the oligarchs, the new Russian criminals were above all businessmen, whose main motive was creating legitimate fronts to launder their revenues, such as real estate and tourism. The opportunities they found, and the techniques they used to exploit them, were those created by globalization—international supply chains, free and anonymous movement of capital, and a porous legal environment. There is, in the end, no hard line separating the two groups.

The ultimate example of this phenomenon was the "hybrid" oligarch–international criminal Evgenii Prigozhin, who was a pure product of the early Putin entourage from Saint Petersburg. A self-made entrepreneur of humble origins who created a chain of local restaurants, Prigozhin became Putin's caterer when the latter was deputy mayor. He parlayed that early connection into a large fortune, and ultimately a private army, called Wagner, that reached overseas into Africa and provided the muscle for his growing illicit trade empire.[83] Prigozhin became a convenient instrument for Putin, notably by supplying much-needed manpower for the Ukrainian war, but also for Russia's expanding foreign-policy ambitions in Africa. Prigozhin's subsequent rebellion underscored the vulnerabilities of Putin's quasi-private, quasi-state system of power, but his fiery death—most likely at Putin's instigation, after Prigozhin initiated a march on Moscow—does not spell the end of Wagner's presence in Africa, only its likely takeover by Putin's security services.[84]

The oligarchs and the *avtoritety* were similar in yet another way—their negative impact on Western opinion. Both groups are choice targets for sanctions, because of their unpopularity in the West and the vulnerability of their more visible assets, such as their yachts and mansions. (It is no accident that the branch of the US Treasury that administers sanctions is part of the same unit that oversees international money laundering and organized crime.) The unfortunate result has been to tarnish the reputations of all Russians in the West, including those with legitimate businesses and ordinary citizens.

Big Russia Arrives in the West: The Saga of Gazprom in Western Europe

Another face of Russia's emergence into the West was the state-led corporations, of which the largest and best-known was the Russian gas giant, Gazprom.

Russia had been exporting gas to Europe since the 1970s, but until the early 1990s the Soviet gas industry had no direct presence there.

When Gazprom became a semi-private company under an entrepreneurial chairman, Viktor Chernomyrdin, it began moving into the European mid-stream, at a time when the European gas industry itself was undergoing revolutionary changes. The result transformed the German gas industry.

Gazprom's entry into Western Europe began with a rebellion and a coup, the first in Germany and the second in Russia. Until the end of the 1980s, the Soviets simply dropped off gas at the border, where it was picked up by European shippers. In West Germany, a company called Ruhrgas controlled the only gas transmission system, and as a monopoly middleman, it charged high transit tariffs. Its customers grew increasingly restive. In 1989, BASF, Germany's chemical giant, decided to approach Gazprom in search of a better deal.

The second coup was in Moscow. In the fall of 1991, the Soviet minister of gas, Victor Chernomyrdin (who subsequently became prime minister under Yeltsin), by a skillful maneuver engineered the conversion of his ministry to an autonomous corporation, called Gazprom. At the same time, he swooped down on a long-coveted prize, the gas-export arm of the Soviet foreign-trade ministry. Renamed Gazeksport, it became part of Gazprom, and the commercial engine of a revamped and more entrepreneurial company.[85]

Gazprom under Chernomyrdin had reasons of its own to be dissatisfied with Ruhrgas. Under the traditional arrangement, it had no access to the German domestic market. In the Russians' view, this meant they were sacrificing most of their gas's value to the middleman, namely Ruhrgas. In 1990, Gazprom and BASF's gas subsidiary, Wintershall, agreed to create a JV, to be called Wingas, to deliver and market gas inside Germany.

This was a potential game-changer, but there was only one problem. BASF did not own a pipeline, it had no gas customers, and there had never been gas-on-gas-competition in the German industry. The two conspirators agreed to do something that had never been done before in Europe: to build an entire new pipeline from scratch. Since they had no customers, they built the new line on speculation, effectively on a wish and a prayer, while touring local gas distributors in Germany to sign them up as buyers. It took five years of fierce battles, but by the mid-1990s they had breached Ruhrgas's monopoly, and Gazprom had won a place as a major player inside Germany.[86] From Wingas's headquarters in northern Germany, the two partners, Wintershall and Gazprom, now securely ensconced in the German gas market, worked side-by-side for what turned out to be nearly thirty years. Wintershall's oil subsidiary, Dea, became an investor in the ill-fated NordStream 2 pipeline. The partnership was soon expanded to Russia, where Dea joined in exploring two shale-oil plays in West Siberia. Gazprom also soon repaired its relations with Ruhrgas, and continued shipping through the Ruhrgas pipeline system as well.

But Gazprom's ambitions did not stop at Germany. It then went on to establish a network of subsidiaries, shippers, traders, and banks throughout Western Europe and the UK, and even as far as Singapore.[87] Gazprom's expansion into Western Europe coincided with the liberalization of the European gas trade and the rise of trading hubs. Gazprom Germany consisted of more than forty entities operating in more than twenty countries in Europe, Asia, and North America. In the first half of the 2000s Gazprom began trading gas on hubs in Britain, Belgium, and the Netherlands, and shipping gas directly to European end users. In the UK, its ambitions soon aroused mistrust and opposition, as Russian–British relations soured. In 2006, Gazprom's attempt to acquire a UK gas distributor, Centrica, was rejected by the British government. But on the continent, Gazprom remained a welcome partner and continued to expand its trading activity, especially through the Dutch gas hub, the Title Transfer Facility.

In 2003 Wintershall and Gazprom founded a JV, Achimgaz, in Urengoy, at that time the largest gas field in Siberia, and a new site for Gazprom. This was intended to bring advanced technology to bear on the field's deepest horizon, which was rich in both gas and liquids. The two partners jointly committed $700 million for the first phase, and each took a 50% stake.[88] Wintershall invested $90 million up front.[89] The two partners spoke optimistically of the field producing for forty-three years and yielding over $10 billion. As the then-CEO of Wintershall, Reinier Zwitserloot, said proudly, "Just as we did once before, we are taking on the role of pioneers."

The following year, in 2004, BASF and Gazprom deepened their partnership further. Gazprom increased its stake in Wingas to 50% minus one share; in exchange it gave Wintershall a 35% stake in a new field, Yuzhno-Russkoye, in the northern part of West Siberia. This gas field was also rich in liquids, and required advanced technology. At the same time, as part of the new deal, BASF and Gazprom began discussing a new northern European gas pipeline, to bring the gas from Yuzhno-Russkoye to Germany, which ultimately became the ill-fated NordStream.

For Gazprom, the invasion of Ukraine was disastrous. Within a year, its gas exports to Europe had collapsed, except for smaller flows through

Ukraine and Turkey.[90] But Gazprom itself was not sanctioned, nor was its main bank, Gazprombank, which is still active in Western Europe. Gazprombank is the main remaining conduit for Russian foreign banking transactions, and as a result many Russian companies have switched their accounts to it, and carry on the same activities as before.

The rise and fall of Gazprom in Europe began with high ambitions and daring execution, which led to the building of a major new player in one of the most strategic sectors of the European economy. It became the very symbol of the optimistic belief in Europe that good business would reinforce good political relations. All that remains of it today is the ruins.[91]

Conclusions and Reflections on the Russians in the West

The thirty-year odyssey of the Russians in the West actually consisted of five separate stories, which were only partly connected to one another: the integration of the Russian financial system with the world of international money, the arrival of the oligarchs and other magnates, the activity of Russians in money-laundering and other illicit transactions, the westward expansion of Russian state-controlled industrial corporations and banks, and finally the outward movement of hundreds of thousands of individuals. What overall observations can one distill from these separate stories?

The first story, the integration of Russia into the world financial system, was the most successful and transformative. From a system that was largely closed to the outside world, Russia quickly developed an elaborate web of financial connections, which enabled Russian banks and companies to exchange information, process transfers and payments, and borrow money. The symbol of this transformation was Russia's membership in the SWIFT messaging system, and its active participation in international settlement platforms such as Euroclear and Clearstream. Of equal importance was the RCB's policy of keeping a large part of its reserves abroad. In parallel, many Russian banks, both state-owned and private, also branched out into the West. The result was the creation of a dense network of financial ties, which provided the essential structure for Russia's entire opening to the West.

The second and third stories—the arrival of the oligarchs and the Russian involvement in illicit activities—were overwhelmingly negative. They were part of the vast hemorrhage of capital out of Russia that started in the 1980s and continued, with only minor breaks, up to 2022, and that bled Russia of much of the value of its legacy resource endowment. The flight of capital continues today, although on a reduced scale.

The fourth story, the westward expansion of Russian state-controlled corporations and banks, is mixed. On the one hand, the major companies involved—Gazprom, Rosatom, and Sberbank—had been extensively reorganized following the Soviet collapse, and under new leadership they were newly infused with entrepreneurial energy and ambition. Their expansion into the West opened up major new sources of income for them at a time when domestic earnings were uncertain. But their great liability was the ever-presence of the state behind them, and their hybrid identity as commercial businesses and agents of state power, which brought mistrust and pushback as geopolitical relations worsened. The Russian opening also brought private Russian companies into the West, such as LUKOil, Yandex, MMK, and RusAl. These tended to be more straightforwardly commercial, and Western reactions to them varied, depending on the strategic sensitivity of their product or business.

The last story is that of the outward migration of hundreds of thousands of individuals, Russia's fourth mass emigration in modern times. The new Russian communities have impacted markets such as real estate in all the places where they are concentrated, such as London and Cyprus, but also New York and Tel-Aviv, as well as smaller clusters such as Amsterdam, Zug in Switzerland, and Silicon Valley. The lasting consequence has been the creation of a new Russian diaspora in the West, composed in the main of highly educated and skilled people. This flow of Russians into the West has expanded manyfold since the Russian invasion of Ukraine, with new destinations such as Germany, Slovakia, and Poland. The result is a vast loss of talent for Russia, and a great gain for the West.

Coda

Reflections on Russia's Failed Two-Way Opening

Three words sum up the legacy of the two-way opening of Russia—*motives, beliefs,* and *emotions*.

Contrasting Motives: The Westerners in Russia, and the Russians in the West, were driven by a wide variety of motives. Both sides saw opportunity, but there was one fundamental difference. For many of the Westerners in Russia, there was a sense of mission, to "re-form" Russia, whether as a democracy, a civil society, a country of laws, or as place to do business. This point should not be overstated: many Westerners came to Russia simply to make money. But that is precisely the point: On the whole, the Westerners in Russia believed in the neoliberal narrative of "civilized globalization," and together with the Russian "liberals," they sought to transplant it into Russia, if to their own advantage. In contrast, most of the Russians in the West had no such larger ambitions or illusions. They took a more skeptical view of the Western neoliberal story. Their motives for coming to the West were more narrowly short-term and opportunistic, whether to expand Russia's export earnings or to hide and protect their assets abroad. They took advantage of the convenient features of the West—both the best and sometimes also the worst—but they did not aspire to change it.

Shared Optimism: By and large, both the Westerners in Russia and the Russians in the West shared a common belief that Russia's opening was lasting, that the neoliberal order had come to stay, and that good relations would endure. They built strategies and structures on those assumptions, whether it was the RCB parking reserves abroad or Gazprom building a gas network in Europe, or the Western majors investing in Russian energy and telecommunications. The Russians allowed themselves to become dependent on Western technology and capital; the Westerners gambled on the protection of the Russian government. In retrospect, both sides underestimated how vulnerable they would prove to be to geopolitical risk.

The overoptimism was not that of the Westerners alone. The ultimate example was the RCB's decision to keep half of Russia's foreign-exchange reserves outside the country. The RCB's willingness to accept the risks involved reflected its belief that Russia's participation in the global financial system was "here to stay" (although combined no doubt with the RCB's perception of the high risks associated with keeping them in Russia).

Negative Emotions: In contrast to the optimism that pervaded much of the activity of companies and individuals within them, at least until the mid-2010s, many aspects of the two-way opening engendered negative emotions, ranging from mistrust and suspicion (primarily in the West) to disappointment and disillusionment (mainly in Russia). These emotions bred growing hostility and rejection, which interacted with the downward trend in geopolitical relations that began as early as 2005 and deepened in the mid-2010s, with the Russian annexation of Crimea and the first rounds of Western sanctions.[1] The common consequence was that the opening of Russia, despite its historic transformative impact on Russian society and the economy, proved to be flawed and fragile.

In the next part of this book, we take up the sequel—the mass imposition of Western sanctions and the Russian responses to them, the two-way exodus of business on both sides, and Russia's return to isolation from the West. But first, we turn to the role of Putin himself.

PART II
PERFECT STORM

Sanctions and Responses

Chapter 3
Putin and the Opening of Russia

What were Putin's roles in the opening of Russia before the Ukrainian war? This question has two parts: What was Putin's understanding of an "open market economy," and what policies did he pursue to promote it? What was his attitude toward the opening of Russia, the arrival of Westerners in Russia, and the movement of Russians and Russian capital into the West, up to the time of the invasion?

Putin's positions on both questions are a complex dance, in which his moves shift depending on his audience and the circumstances. As always with Putin, it is difficult to tell his inner thoughts from his tactics. But over time, there is a clear evolution. Putin's public attitudes toward the key features of a market economy—privatization, protection of property rights, "liberal" economic policy, and open international trade—began as strongly positive during his first two terms but became increasingly negative during the following two. In parallel, his policies toward the presence and investment of Western businesses in Russia, and toward the various roles of Russians in the West, went from relatively supportive (or tacitly permissive, depending on the case) between 2000 and the mid-2010s, to increasingly restrictive thereafter. In both cases, Putin's economic positions and policies mirrored the evolution of his geopolitics. After 2013 and the occupation of Crimea, his economic views and policies were dominated overwhelmingly by his hostility toward the United States and by his obsession with Ukraine.[1]

1990s to Mid-2010s: Putin the "Pro-Market Liberal"

During his first two terms and even up to the mid-2010s, Putin was consistently supportive in public of the phrases "market economy" and "private property." From the beginning it was never clear exactly what he understood by them, yet there is a clear timeline to his pronouncements. Initially, he was perhaps not too different from most Russians, for whom a market economy boiled down to the word *rynok* (the Russian word for "market"), which was hardly more than an extension of the gray "informal" economy of the Soviet era. He was not one of the Saint Petersburg market reformers, and he was reportedly uncomfortable about their "shock therapy" policy, feeling that "it was asking too much of a population in desperate straits."[2] He played no part in the Gaidar market reforms or the Chubais-led privatizations of the 1990s. Although he was exposed to economic theory in various settings, it is fair to say that he learned about market economics mainly "in the school of life," as the Russian saying goes, in the swirling environment of 1990s Saint Petersburg.[3]

In the chaos of the Saint Petersburg of those days, the term "market economy" was hardly more than a euphemism for violence and crime. The notorious head of the Tambov gang, Vladimir Kumarin, launched a war for control of the fuel market in the city, and by 1996, the year Putin left for Moscow, Kumarin was so powerful that he had come to be known as the Night Governor of Saint Petersburg. Putin had no choice but to deal with him—although a few years later had his revenge by swooping down on Kumarin and throwing him into Moscow's Matrosskaya Tishina prison, where he still sits today.[4]

By the time he became president in 2000, Putin's public views on the market economy had evolved into a more coherent set of positions. He strongly supported German Gref's liberal reform program and appointed him to head the Ministry of Industry and Energy, which in those years was the most powerful body in economic policy. Putin's annual speeches (*poslaniia*) to the Federal Assembly, the combined session of both houses of parliament, in 2002 and 2003, consisted of a ringing affirmation of market principles, economic liberalization, open trade, privatization, and protection of property rights.[5] He vowed that there would be no tampering with private property and no renationalizations; instead, he promised to extend private property even further, notably with a new Land Code to accelerate privatization of housing and farmland.

In international policy, Putin laid out an equally reform-minded liberal agenda. He called for liberalization of trade, a new Customs Code, and Russian membership in the World Trade Organization. He acknowledged that capital flight was a major problem, but he opposed restrictions on capital movements and currency convertibility. "Capital flight will cease," he said, "when conditions are right inside the country. We should not keep capital captive." It was up to Russia to make itself a more attractive place to invest and do business. Instead, Russia offered only high risks, a bad financial system, and poor protection of property and contracts. The total capitalization of the Russian stock market, Putin observed, was only $50 billion, less than one-fifth of that of Finland. The fault lay, he said, in the deeply rooted "status rent" mentality of Russians, who get more excited about the division of revenues than in looking to what creates them in the first place.

Putin was especially critical of Russia's bad courts, which, as he said, were "not fast, not fair, and not just." During his first two terms, he made determined efforts to reform the legal system and the judiciary, with new criminal and labor and procedural codes, new rules on the selection of judges, and the creation of a new tier of courts, the "justices of the peace." The system of commercial courts (*arbitrazh* courts) was expanded and streamlined. While implementation typically fell well short of his stated goals, especially in politically sensitive cases, and "shadow justice" (as Putin called it) remained the norm, the judicial reforms enjoyed substantial support, as evidenced by the growing use of courts by the population. The *arbitrazh* courts, in particular, came to be widely used by private-sector plaintiffs to bring suit against the state for redress in such matters as taxation.[6] Business welcomed measures such as the abolition of the tax police. By the end of Putin's first term in 2004, concludes a leading expert on Russian business practice, "the laws and codes needed for a market economy to function smoothly were in place."[7]

But by the end of Putin's second term, his enthusiasm for liberal reforms had visibly begun to fade. In November 2008, in his last *poslanie* before he turned over the presidency to Dmitry Medvedev for a four-year term, Putin's tone had already changed. He hardly mentioned the words, "market," "privatization," or "property," and while he continued to praise Russia's open economy, it was to urge Russian producers to push harder to develop export markets, lest they be shut out by faster-moving competitors. He had apparently lost interest in applying for membership in the World Trade Organization.[8] His only mention of liberal economics was all but mocking: Quoting the economist Vasilii Leont'ev, who said that a free-enterprise system could be compared to a giant computer that solves problems automatically, Putin quipped, "But anyone who has had anything to do with computers knows that sometimes they break down and cannot operate without supervision."[9]

Yet at other times and before other audiences, Putin's public stance toward the market economy and private property remained supportive. As late as 2011, as he was about to resume the presidency for his third term, Putin declared to a meeting of business leaders, drawing on the government's response to global crisis of 2008–9:

> We supported the private entrepreneur, we backed you up, gave you loans, helped you refinance from Western banks, put up collateral . . . But we did not proceed towards nationalization of our economy. This is a fundamental choice of the government: We don't want to create a system of state capitalism—we want to create a system of socially-oriented market economy . . . including using the tools of privatization.[10]

Still, in the very phrasing of his remarks lay the key to the contradictions at the heart of Putin's view of a market economy. For Putin, property rights are conditional; the state protects them only as a reward for loyalty and service. And Putin has always seen his primary mission as that of protecting the Russian state.

Capitalism and markets, in other words, cannot be allowed to operate without control. But control has two aspects. On the one hand, control means maintaining macroeconomic stability and flexibility. This Putin achieved by consistently supporting the economic "liberals"—the *finansisty*—in his macroeconomic, fiscal, and budgetary bodies, chiefly the ministries of finance and economy, and above all the Russian Central Bank.

But control also means control over rents and favors, using especially oil and gas revenues, which began flooding into Russia shortly after Putin's accession.[11] These are ultimately the keys to Putin's power over the various elites that make up his system. The two forms of control clearly overlap: control over taxes and spending, credits and subsidies, inflation rates, and the value of the ruble, are all essential instruments of economic policy, as they balance the allocation of resources between social welfare and investment, and between civilian and military. Yet at the same time, they are also the keys to the informal system of power.

Putin's determination to control rents and power became more conspicuous with each passing term. At first, he appeared content to let private capital live by its own market rules, provided it stayed out of politics. His attack on Mikhail Khodorkovsky, the founder of Yukos, showed this rule at work: Khodorkovsky had stepped over the bounds and meddled in politics, and was accordingly punished. But Putin's next move, when he seized Khodorkovsky's company Yukos and folded it into Rosneft, showed Putin's broader aim, to control the "commanding heights" of the economy, by placing them under state-owned entities. Several other privately owned oil companies, such as Bashneft, were also absorbed into Rosneft, even though their owners were loyal to Putin. (We return to the Yukos Affair below.)

In 2007, Putin took one important further step, with the creation of so-called state corporations, or *goskorporatsii*. Despite their name, they are in reality a novel form of property, based on the legal shell of a non-profit "non-state organization," or NGO. There are six of these, of which the two most important are Rostekh, the military-industrial conglomerate, and Rosatom, the nuclear power agency. They are endowed with state funds, but they are not the property of the government, and they lie outside its control. Their assets, once donated to them, become their legal property, as do any companies transferred to them. The president—Putin himself— appoints their CEOs and supervisory boards. They are accountable not to government ministries, but to individual officials and the administration of the president, and they are exempt from oversight by the State Audit Chamber and from all government interference. In short, they are essentially the property of the president and his closest associates. Aleksey Kudrin, Putin's former ally and finance minister but now estranged from the Kremlin, called state corporations a covert form of privatization.[12] Somewhat defensively, Putin justified the creation of state corporations in key industries such as the aviation and shipbuilding industries, by saying. "We're not nationalizing anything. We're simply consolidating under one roof companies that were already state-owned." He promised that "once we've made them competitive, we'll sell some of their shares on the open market."[13]

In contrast, controlling the market economy at the local level poses challenges that Putin has never managed to solve, despite a quarter-century of unsuccessful attempts. His core problem from the beginning has been the lack of a *vertikal'*, a reliable system of control to replace the defunct apparatus of the Communist Party of the Soviet Union (CPSU), which formerly spanned all institutions and all levels. The Party apparatus was a remarkable creation: It transmitted orders, it spotted and promoted talent, and it stood for a coherent official ideology that justified the whole structure.[14] Putin has never managed to replace it. Over the years he has tried everything: He has promoted Kremlin-approved political parties and youth groups, official competitions to spot promising prospects, a substitute *nomenklatura* managed by the Presidential Administration, and an official Kremlin party grouping the stalwart and the ambitious—nothing has worked satisfactorily. The very prevalence in high positions today of the *deti*, the children of Putin's KGB network and other early associates from Saint Petersburg, underscores the point: as the old guard ages, Putin keeps them on hand behind the scenes by hiring their children.

The greatest failure of all has been Putin's reliance on the security services. The Federal Security Service (FSB)—the renamed KGB—in particular was Putin's first answer, and it remained his chief instrument throughout his first two terms. He initially saw it as a new *vertikal'*, a reliable substitute for the CPSU apparatus. He drew heavily on friends and relations from the Leningrad KGB to staff his personal guard and to lead his state corporations, and to control the bureaucracy at the regional and local levels. But the FSB turned out to be an unsatisfactory solution, especially as an instrument of control over an unruly market economy. It was riven by factional rivalries; its values promoted distrust and concealment instead of transparency; and above all it was deeply corrupt. Nevertheless, to this day the security services remain Putin's default solution to the control problem at the local level, because he has no other. His main response has been to play the various services against one another, but this is no more than a palliative, and only creates new problems.[15]

Finding and promoting new talent is a special problem as the old guard ages. The closest Putin has come to reproducing the CPSU cadres system is to use province governorships as test beds to try out promising younger officials, using the Presidential Administration as a substitute for the Central Committee apparat. Candidates are selected after participating in a newly created institution, the School of Governors. If they perform well as governors, they are promoted to ministerial positions in Moscow or to the Presidential Administration. Thus, in the personnel changes that followed Putin's re-election in the spring of 2024, four governors were promoted to minister.[16] (Putin has also spoken of using the occupied eastern provinces of Ukraine in a similar role, but that new route has not yet led to any promotions.) This system has produced new talent, but in too few numbers to solve the overall problem of aging cadres.

This problem of enforcing control at the local level runs through the entire Putin era, and it helps us to understand patterns in Putin's behavior that are otherwise baffling. It cannot be said that Putin is unaware of the problem. He addresses it repeatedly in speeches and interviews, and in his annual live call-in shows.[17] Take, for example, Putin's responses to the bitter complaints of businessmen about corruption at regional and local levels, and the systematic predation upon the private sector by the corrupt bureaucracy and judiciary, above all by the state security apparatus. In his 2015 address to the Federal Assembly, Putin complained that despite the Kremlin's efforts to curtail the powers of local bureaucrats and so-called law-enforcement bodies, those powers kept growing back. "A whole army of inspectors interferes with honest businesses," he said. Putin tallied the damage: in 2014 security agencies opened so-called economic crime investigations against 200,000 entrepreneurs, as a result of which 83% lost some or all of their business while only 15% received any kind of verdict. Putin acknowledged that security officials—called the *siloviki*—used investigations simply as a tool to steal businesses. The victims, he said, "were pressured, robbed, and then released."[18]

Yet Putin has appeared strangely powerless to deal with the problem. During his April 2016 call-in show, one entrepreneur complained that the state still treated business as a "cash cow," and wondered when the *siloviki* would stop "feeding" on private business. Putin responded lamely, conceding only that a certain "bureaucratic mentality" prompted officials to abuse their position with business. But during his press conference the following year, Putin came close to admitting that he was unable to stop the *siloviki's* business extortion practices. Reminded by a member of the audience of then-President Medvedev's 2008 exhortation to stop giving nightmares to business, Putin conceded that not much had changed. He related an incident in which FSB head Alexander Bortnikov had investigated a group of FSB officers suspected of extorting businesses. A court convicted the officers, but Bortnikov said that their successors picked right up with the same practices.[19] The passing years have brought no improvement. A decade later, in his 2019 address Putin again called for an end to the bureaucratic and legal harassment of business.[20] After a hiatus of five years, Putin returned to this theme once more in his 2024 address to the Federal Assembly. Noting that he had said it before and was saying it yet again, Putin restated that "no one, including government officials or law enforcement bodies, is allowed to harass business or to misuse the law for selfish purposes." [21] It is almost certainly not the last time he will say this, but no doubt to equally little effect.

Putin's self-professed helplessness in defending private business is not entirely feigned; it is a reflection of a system in which the power of presidential decrees and orders weakens the moment they leave his desk. Many presidential decrees are no more than dead letters, and are systematically ignored even by his own ministers, let alone the rest of the government hierarchy.[22] On the one hand, this is a sign of Russia's perennially disordered government. But it also reflects Putin's lack of resolve in combatting the problem, his weakened commitment to reform and the defense of private business, and his growing willingness over time, in his search for control, to accommodate corruption, repression, and opportunism.

Yet Putin appears increasingly hostile toward private capital. In his annual "State of the Federation" speech in February 2024, Putin blasted "those who call themselves the elite, who have performed no services to society, and who consider themselves a kind of caste with special rights and privileges. I especially have in mind those who in earlier years filled their pockets thanks to all kinds of goings-on in the economy of the 1990s—they are not an elite." Instead, Putin praised those who have served Russia in the "special military operation" in Ukraine—"they are the genuine real elite," he said—and he proposed a series of measures to give them preference in appointments to state positions and business. From there to advancing their ambitions to become a new generation of "deserving" owners is but a step. The battle over "deprivatization," meaning in practice a wholesale replacement of the old business elite by a new one oriented to state service inside the country—may only have begun.[23]

We turn now to the second question: What were Putin's attitudes toward foreign investment and presence in the Russian economy, and how did his policies toward them evolve?

Putin and Foreign Investment and Presence in Russia

Putin's attitudes toward foreign companies and their presence in Russia were likewise shaped by his early experience in the St. Petersburg government, where for five years (1991–1996) he was responsible for foreign economic relations.[24] There was strong interest in Russia from foreign investors, but most of it was concentrated on acquiring property for renovation, acquiring commodities for export, or developing retail outlets in Russia, not in modernizing factories or transferring technology. At the historic Smolnyi Palace, by now the seat of the Saint Petersburg mayoralty, the city government formed the Committee for Foreign Economic Relations (known as KVS), that was responsible for registering companies involving foreign partners. Over the next five years, it registered over 9,000 companies. Its chairman was Deputy Mayor Putin.

Dealing with foreigners in Saint Petersburg in those early days was primarily about doing deals, in which Putin played the role of facilitator, particularly in relations with German businessmen, thanks to his knowledge of German and his years in Dresden. In some of these agreements, Putin's committee, KVS, was itself a co-founder and minority shareholder. Some of those deals ended badly, however, notably an ill-fated "resources for food" contract, which almost cost Putin his job. From this early experience, Putin took away two lessons: foreign investment brought benefits, but foreign businessmen were not to be trusted, any more than domestic ones.[25] As he wrote at the time, in a signed article that appeared shortly before his departure for Moscow in 1996, "We need foreign resources, Western experience, new ecological technology. We don't need to be afraid of attracting large-scale Western capital. Business is egotistic by its very nature, but we can lay down strict legal limits."[26]

As Putin arrived in Moscow in 1996, the arrival of foreigners was already at the flood, and it accelerated further in the second half of the 1990s, catalyzing the revolution in services and trade described in Chapter 1. Putin did not initially play a direct role in this process. His first major intervention was the arrest of Mikhail Khodorkovsky, mentioned earlier.

There were many reasons why Khodorkovsky was singled out, not least his provocative behavior, his public defiance of Putin, and his obvious political ambitions. But the precipitating factor in Khodorkovsky's arrest was the prospect that Yukos was about to merge with a US oil major.

Khodorkovsky had been negotiating with Chevron since the summer of 2002. By the fall of 2003, an agreement was in place, and there remained only the matter of the two companies' respective shares in the combined company. At a key meeting in Saint Petersburg between Khodorkovsky and Chevron's CEO Dave O'Reilly, O'Reilly offered Yukos 37.6% of the merged company, but Khodorkovsky held out for 43%. The two men were unable to bridge the gap, and the deal broke down.

Meanwhile, unbeknown to Chevron, Khodorkovsky had also proposed a stake in Yukos to ExxonMobil, and following the failure of the Chevron deal, the negotiations with ExxonMobil intensified. In October, Lee Raymond, the CEO of ExxonMobil, met with Vladimir Putin in New York to brief him on the talks with Yukos. According to one account, Raymond made plain his ambition to go beyond a merger and ultimately take control of Yukos.[27] To Putin, Raymond's plan apparently came as a surprise, and he returned to Moscow seething with anger, determined to head off any takeover.

When Raymond arrived in Moscow one week later to meet with Khodor-kovsky to close the deal, Khodorkovsky was forced to leave hurriedly in the middle of their meeting, when his wife called him to say that armed police were raiding the homes of Yukos executives all over Moscow, and that several of them were under arrest.[28]

Time had run out for Khodorkovsky. Three weeks later, armed troops from the FSB's crack Alfa brigade swarmed aboard his private plane at a refueling stop in Novosibirsk and took him, handcuffed and hooded, to Moscow. He spent the next decade in prison, before being exiled to the West, where he lives today. Over the following four years, Yukos was systemati-cally dismantled, and its assets were absorbed by Rosneft, the state-owned oil company.[29]

The dramatic arrest of Khodorkovsky and the destruction of Yukos marked a symbolic turning point in Putin's handling of the oil industry and foreign investment in it. The Yukos Affair demonstrated where Putin drew the line on the participation of Western companies in Russia's most strategic sector. Foreigners were welcome, indeed sought after—but West-ern ownership and control were not. After the Yukos Affair, other Western energy projects went forward with Putin's support—such as production-sharing agreements (PSAs) with ExxonMobil and Shell at Sakhalin (to which Putin gave personal support when he attended a joint conference on PSAs on Sakhalin Island in 2000), as well as joint ventures between Total and Novatek and between Gazprom and Wintershall (both strongly sup-ported by Putin)—but in these relationships foreign majority stakes and control were not allowed. The only exception was BP's 50-50 joint owner-ship of TNK-BP, which, however, proved highly unstable (as Putin himself had warned BP it would), and it ended in absorption by Rosneft.

Over time, Putin drew the line on foreign participation in oil ever tighter, and by the time of the Crimean takeover in 2014, the foreign stakeholders were being squeezed out. Following the 2022 invasion, only BP and Total remain, but as passive investors, unable to export their dividends. (although Total continues to export its share of LNG from the Yamal LNG project).[30]

The same rules did not necessarily apply to less sensitive sectors, such as automotive and aviation, and even natural gas and LNG, where Putin continued to play the role of promoter and enabler. In those areas, even as Russia's geopolitical relations with the West darkened, Putin's interest in attracting foreign investment remained strong. As late as the mid-2010s, Putin frequently acted as an informal Russian ambassador and promoter of

Western investment, occasionally traveling to foreign capitals such as Paris and Berlin to meet with the heads of companies of interest. Most of the major projects by large Western companies were preceded by personal meetings between their CEOs and Putin in the Kremlin, and when the time came, they were graced by Putin's presence at their projects' inaugurations, such as the opening of VW's plant in Kaluga in 2009 (see Chapter 7).

Putin's relations with foreign investors were frequently built around personal friendships with foreign leaders. Italy's Silvio Berlusconi was a special favorite. Beginning with their first meeting in 2000, the two men became close friends, and their relationship flowered into joint ventures in both countries. Most of their business conversations were about gas, but they soon extended to other sectors as well. In 2004 Putin and Berlusconi presided together at the inauguration of the Stinol factory in Lipetsk, a joint venture with the Italian company Merloni, which made refrigerators, washing machines, and other household appliances. At the ceremony, with Berlusconi standing next to him, Putin emphasized the importance of Italy's business presence in Russia, not just for capital but also for transfer of skills and techniques. As Putin said, "We need not just money, but also new technologies, new ideas, and specialists with high production skills."[31]

By 2008, Russia's business relations with Italy had blossomed further. When Putin visited Berlusconi in Italy that year, he pointed to a wide range of joint projects, "in airplane construction, in transportation, in space, communications, and IT."[32] By far the largest was Eni, Italy's national oil and gas company, which had acquired gas assets in Russia, and there was discussion of Gazprom investing jointly with Eni in Libya. The two men even discussed the possibility of Aeroflot making a bid for Italy's loss-ridden national airline Alitalia, although in the end nothing came of this.[33]

Putin's attitudes toward French business leaders were similarly warm, especially with the CEO of Total, Christophe de Margerie. Putin held several meetings with Margerie, both in Russia and in Paris, and presided over the signing of the alliance with Novatek. Following Margerie's death in a plane crash, described earlier, Putin was present at the launch of the LNG tanker named after him. French companies were the fifth-largest contingent of foreign companies in Russia, after the United States, Germany, the UK, and Japan.[34] Putin made several trips to Paris, notably in 2007, when he came to court the CEO of Renault, Carlos Ghosn, and the leaders of the French government (described in Chapter 6).

But by far the most consequential relationship between Putin and a European leader was with Chancellor Gerhard Schroeder of Germany and the creation of the multiple joint ventures between Gazprom and BASF/Wintershall.[35] Putin presided personally at all the key moments. At the official signing of the memorandum of understanding on NordStream-1 in 2002, in a ceremony at the annual Hannover Trade Fair held together with Schroeder, Putin praised the BASF–Gazprom partnership as a historic development. "This is not a one-time event," he said. "In essence, it marks a step toward the mutual penetration of the two economies."[36] By the time of the actual signing ceremony two years later in Tomsk, Angela Merkel had replaced Schroeder at Putin's side, but although their personal relationship was not warm, Putin was ebullient. Hailing the deal as a "first in contemporary history," Putin said, "It is the best example of the fact that Russia and Russian companies are ready for a deep and all-embracing collaboration."[37]

Putin's attitudes toward US investors were more mixed and underwent the sharpest change of his relations with any country. When he first came to power, his stance appeared quite positive. His visit to Texas in November 2001, two months after 9/11, marked the high point of Putin's public good feelings toward the United States. In a forty-five-minute speech at the Baker Institute, Putin praised the United States and went out of his way to call for warm US–Russian relations. He sounded like a virtual salesman for Russia, highlighting its ongoing economic and judicial reforms, which he said made Russia an attractive place for US business to invest, as several companies were already doing.[38]

But by 2007, Putin's view of the United States had changed completely. At the Munich Security Conference in February of that year, Putin delivered a bitter diatribe against the United States, and after that, he returned there only once, to attend the annual meeting of the UN General Assembly in 2015. Nevertheless, he remained broadly supportive of the role of US companies in Russia, which outnumbered by far those of any other foreign country, including several in strategic manufacturing. Boeing, which was present in both the aviation and titanium industries in Russia, was a leading example. At the 2007 Saint Petersburg Economic Forum, only a few months after his Munich speech, Putin singled out Boeing's research center in Moscow as a source of innovation for the company's new airplanes, accounting for as much as one-third of Boeing's designs.[39] Putin's consistent support for Boeing's ambitious plans in Russia continued right up to the February 2022 invasion of Ukraine.[40]

Yet overall, as Putin's geopolitical attitudes toward the West became more hostile, his earlier enthusiasm for Western presence and investment in Russia waned as well. In his 2011 speech to the RSPP, quoted earlier, his one brief mention of foreign investment in Russia was anything but enthusiastic: "When we invite in foreign resources," he said, "we must defend effectively our economic interests." Clearly influenced by the 2008–9 subprime financial crisis, Putin called for a "new financial architecture," by which he meant a diversification away from the monopoly of the dollar and the transformation of Russia into a leading financial center. Already by this time, Putin was stressing import substitution as the basis for government policy.

Since the 2022 invasion of Ukraine, Putin's stance toward Western investment and presence in Russia has oscillated between verbal support for the remaining Western businesses and de facto assent to the confiscation of them (as we shall see in Chapter 5). At the 2023 Saint Petersburg Forum, he vigorously denied that there was any policy to "kick anyone out of our market; on the contrary . . . each of our partners had the right to choose." But at the same time he praised the energy with which Russian entrepreneurs had filled the empty space left by departing Western businesses, especially in the retail sector, and had replaced Western brands with Russian ones. "At first," Putin said, "our entrepreneurs were very worried about the departure of Western companies." But that phase had quickly passed. On the contrary, Putin said, now they were pressing him not to allow the "straying" Western businesses back into Russia. But Putin insisted he rejected such a punitive approach. "If foreign producers wish to return to our market, we're not closing the doors to anyone . . . And to those who stay with us, we consider them to be Russian companies, and we will treat them as our own."[41] His positions remain an unpredictable dance, reflecting his own ambivalence.

Meanwhile, what about Putin's positions on Russian capital and business outside Russia?

Putin and the Russians in the West

By the time of Putin's arrival in Moscow in 1996, the exodus of Russians to various havens in the West was already well under way. Capital was streaming out of Russia, partly as investment, but more often as simple capital flight. But thanks to the turnaround in oil prices that began in 1999, virtually at

the moment that Putin became prime minister, far more capital was flowing in than out, and until the subprimes crisis of 2008–9, capital flight was
not a top-priority concern for Putin. On the contrary, some of the biggest
exporters of Russian capital were members of his own circle of favored oligarchs. When he mentioned the loss of capital, he portrayed it as testimony
to Russia's unattractiveness as a place to invest. In June 2002, speaking at the
4th Congress of the Chamber of Commerce and Industry, Putin said:

> It would be a good thing for entrepreneurs, together with the government,
> to think about creating favorable investment conditions and how to return
> to Russia the funds previously withdrawn to offshore. The state should not
> grab everyone by the sleeve, asking where these funds came from, if it was
> unable to create normal conditions for investment.[42]

In contrast, Putin has been enthusiastically in favor of overseas investments
by Russian state-owned companies. The largest Russian investment in the
West, as we saw in Chapter 2, was that of Gazprom. Putin supported its ambitions wholeheartedly. With the building of Gazprom's gas export system and
its far-flung retail network in Europe, both Putin's geopolitical aims and
Gazprom's profit motives meshed seamlessly. The same was true later on,
when Sergey Kirienko, with Putin's strong support, rebuilt Rosatom around
its foreign business.

But by the time of Russia's annexation of Crimea, as East–West tensions
worsened over Ukraine, Putin's attitudes toward Russia's export of private
capital to the West had begun to change. As the first Western financial sanctions struck, Putin backed the efforts of the *finansisty* to limit capital exports,
and he called on Russian private capital, in increasingly strong terms, to
return to the homeland. In his annual *poslanie* in February 2023, he lashed
out at the oligarchs who had moved out of Russia. Russians facing Western sanctions, he said, deserved no sympathy. "Some people want to live
out their days in a foreign mansion with their blocked accounts . . . But
for the West those people are alien. They are second-class citizens . . . You
have another choice: to be with your country."[43] Returning to the theme
of "swallowing dust," Putin added, "Once, as a joke—many of you may
remember—addressing representatives of Russian business, I said: 'You will
get tired of swallowing dust, running around the courts and the offices of
Western officials to save your money.' That's exactly how it turned out."

Conclusion

In sum, Putin's positions and policies on the market economy and foreign investment have gone through two phases. In the first phase, from the early 1990s to midway through his first term, Putin was broadly favorable to both, and his public views echoed those of the market liberals. The first symbolic turning point was the Yukos Affair of 2003. Thereafter, following the brief liberal interlude of Dmitry Medvedev's one-term presidency, Putin in his second two terms turned increasingly conservative, in parallel with his more hostile geopolitical views toward the West. His liberal reforms ceased, and he promoted statist policies. The second turning point was the occupation of Crimea and the first Western sanctions. As the geopolitical atmosphere worsened outside Russia, Putin's policies toward the private sector and foreign presence inside the country grew steadily more restrictive.

In a revealing moment during his visit to Houston in 2001, during his speech at the Baker Institute, Putin turned toward James Baker and recalled with a smile that he had first met him in Saint Petersburg in 1992, "when I was a modest city bureaucrat, and he was a big boss."[44] At that time, Putin's influence did not reach beyond Saint Petersburg, but by the time of his Houston speech in 2001, it was Putin who had become "the big boss," and his actions from then on were increasingly decisive in shaping Russia's opening to the West—and its reclosing. They remain so today.

Twenty years later, as Putin made ready to invade Ukraine, was he prepared for the sanctions that would follow, the interruption of Russia's financial and trade ties to the West, and the end of Western investment in Russia? His behavior suggests that, where the United States was concerned, he anticipated how Washington would react, but discounted its reach. In contrast, the EU's strongly negative reaction appears to have taken him by surprise. His calculation was apparently that with a quick conquest of Ukraine, he could present the West, and especially Europe, with a fait accompli, and he was prepared to weather the brief squall that would follow. But in both his military strategy and his economics, he miscalculated.

Part II of this book addresses the sanctions that followed the invasion of Ukraine, Russia's responses to them, and Putin's continuing roles.

Putin the International traveler

Putin has been a frequent world traveler during his two-and-a-half decades as president.[45] In the years up to 2020, he averaged twenty to twenty-five foreign trips a year, although since then the number has shrunk to a half-dozen or fewer. Thus, Putin's foreign travels mirror the state of the world, his shifting priorities, and the history of his presidency. Revealingly, Ukraine was near the top of the list with twenty-one visits, a reminder of Putin's tangled relations with that republic during his first decade and a half in power. His last trip there was in July 2013, for obvious reasons, when he met with then-President Viktor Yanukovych. Interestingly, Putin has never traveled to the independent Baltic Republics.

While most of Putin's foreign travels have been to attend diplomatic events and summits, or to consolidate relations with the FSU (Belarus and Kazakhstan top the list overall), they have typically been combined with meetings with business leaders to pitch trade ties and investment opportunities in Russia. Western Europe was a frequent destination, especially France and Germany, with Turkey, Italy, and Finland close behind. But since 2019 Putin has made no further trips to Western Europe, with the exception of Turkey in 2024.[46] His last trip to Paris was in 2019, and to Berlin in 2020.

Putin's travels as international pitchman for Western investment were focused above all on Western Europe. Putin made a total of forty-six visits to France, Germany, and Italy, many of them combined with meetings with business leaders. France, Germany, and Italy alone accounted for 725 businesses in Russia. In contrast, Putin made only seven visits to the United States, and all on official diplomatic occasions, even though the 769 US companies were by far the largest Western contingent in Russia.[47]

China is almost the opposite story. Putin made his first trip there in 2000, to meet with then-President Jiang Zemin, and over the following decade he visited China nearly every year. But since 2014 the frequency of his visits has doubled, and they have been increasingly focused on economic relations. All told, Putin has made twenty-one visits to China.[48] India is not nearly as frequent a destination, and the rest of south and southeast Asia hardly figures, except for international conferences. In short, to judge from Putin's travels, Russia's "pivot to the east" remains largely confined to China, with India a distant second.

Chapter 4
The Hurricane of Western Sanctions

What is life like in a pariah state that's been cut off from the outside world? To find answers, Russia's popular YouTube host, Aleksey Pivovarov, traveled to Teheran shortly after the start of the Russian invasion of Ukraine and filmed a documentary on "life under sanctions" in Iran.[1] Not surprisingly, it went viral in Russia (with over 8.6 million views as of April 2022), where ordinary Russians in all walks of life were anxiously asking themselves, How will we live under sanctions? How long will they last?

Pivovarov took his viewers on a stroll through Teheran, visiting stores and talking to people. He showed how Iranians had adapted. He held up a can of Coca-Cola, but explained that it was made in Iran and had nothing to do with the Western company. A look-alike of Danone yoghurt was sold under the name Danette. Apple and Samsung smartphones were for sale everywhere, imported by middlemen from Turkey. There were uncensored social media; Iranians kept up with the Internet via virtual personal networks (VPNs); and Telegram was wildly popular (as it is in Russia).[2]

Pivovarov's overall message to his fellow Russians was reassuring: Iranians have learned to live with sanctions, and Russians can too. "Everything can be done illegally," said Pivovarov. "Iran is a country of risky schemes." Moreover, Iranians did not believe that the sanctions would last, and they lived their lives in the expectation that sanctions would be lifted soon, as they briefly were in 2015–16. The question, said Pivovarov, is not how long you can live with sanctions, but rather, For what? "Everyone needs to answer this question for themselves, as Iranians have been doing for decades, and as we need to do in Russia."

But in actual fact the two cases are not comparable. The sanctions against Iran are aimed at a narrow band of sectors and groups in a relatively small economy. In contrast, since the beginning of Russia's invasion of Ukraine, the country has been hit by sanctions from over forty different Western countries, a hurricane of tens of thousands of documents.

Nothing on this scale, against so large a country and one so integrated into the world economy, has ever been attempted before.[3] The sanctions imposed since February 2022, in their sweep, scope, and complexity, go far beyond those imposed on Iran and Cuba, as well as those on Russia in 2014–15 in the wake of the Crimean and Donbas occupations. Unlike the partial sanctions adopted then, the post-invasion sanctions are aimed at imposing overwhelming costs on the Russian economy as a whole—its industry, its military, its energy sector, and its financial system—and preventing it from pursuing its aggression in Ukraine, while punishing the Putin regime. And although they are explicitly not aimed at the Russian people, a wide range of consumer and luxury goods is also banned.

This chapter describes the machinery of the Russia sanctions of the three main sanctioning powers, the United States, the European Union, and the United Kingdom. My key proposition is that if the sanctions are maintained and vigorously enforced, they will have increasingly severe long-term impacts on the Russian economy, causing its gradual degradation.[4] As Aleksandra Prokopenko, a former deputy director of the RCB, writes, in a nice phrase, "Putin's military adventure in Ukraine and the sanctions have not made a breach in Russia's economic fortress, but they put a time bomb under its foundations."[5]

But the machinery of sanctions has serious weaknesses and vulnerabilities, which have lessened their effectiveness so far, making them difficult to enforce and easy to evade. In addition, the sanctions have significant costs for those who impose them, and these too will grow over time. Lastly, the sanctions will be hard to maintain, if the initial unity of the sanctioning powers erodes, as it already shows signs of doing.

Yet the dilemma for the West is that, despite the sanctions' defects, it has no choice but to persevere with them, while improving and strengthening them wherever possible. Today as in the past, and so long as peace remains out of reach, economic sanctions are the West's only alternative to an expanded war.

The sanctions systems of the United States, the EU, and the UK are very different, reflecting their very different policymaking structures. What they have in common is their complexity, which is compounded by the circumstances of the Russian invasion: The post-invasion sanctions were adopted in haste, driven by emotion, and largely improvised. The result is a confusing tangle of inconsistencies, exceptions, and walk-backs. Since then, despite efforts to introduce greater coherence (witness the greater care with which the oil sanctions were developed, discussed below), these fundamental problems remain. Over time, the challenges of managing this disorderly system will only grow. Meanwhile, the Russians have taken vigorous actions to offset or evade them, as we shall see in the next chapter.

These difficulties are inherent in the nature of sanctions. Sanctions are economic instruments, deployed to serve political objectives, and as such they are effective only insofar as there is clarity over those objectives. That is presently not the case. US spokespeople, in particular, have sometimes given the impression that the objective is nothing less than the destruction of the entire Russian economy. When the United States began its latest round of sanctions following the Ukrainian invasion, White House officials described them in sweeping terms. Daleep Singh, then a deputy head of the National Security Council, exclaimed on *60 Minutes* that "the Russian economy is in free fall ... our best projections are that it is going to be half its size."[6]

President Biden too trumpeted the radical aims of the sanctions. In March 2022, when he announced the US ban on Russian oil imports, he asserted that the sanctions had already caused the Russian economy "to crater." That same month, Biden tweeted that, thanks to the West's unprecedented sanctions, "the ruble was almost immediately reduced to rubble," and that "soon Russia would not even rank among the top twenty economies of the world."[7]

The language of the EU Commission has been far less sweeping. When Ursula von der Leyen, president of the commission, briefed the European Parliament on the European Council's initial sanctions packages in March 2022, she listed three limited objectives: to drain Putin's financial resources for the war, to put pressure on elites close to Putin, and to "bite hard" into the Russian economy.[8] One year later the EU's senior diplomat on sanctions, David O'Sullivan, stated essentially the same three limited objectives: to deprive Russia of military technology on the battlefield, to cut the flow of resources needed to wage war, and to impose costs on Russian industry.[9] Both put restoring Europe's energy independence at the top of their list. But the positions of the various member states vary widely, from barely veiled opposition to the sanctions (in the case of Hungary) to radical calls for a total trade embargo on Russia (notably by Poland). In short, there is no deep unity on objectives, either within the EU, or across the Atlantic.

Equally missing from the West's sanctions is clarity over their implementation and, above all, their eventual termination. The sanctioning powers have made impressive efforts to collaborate with one another and to coordinate their sanctions policies, and so far they have kept a common front. But maintaining that unity will become increasingly difficult over time, since the sanctions regime is a hostage to the larger politics of the Ukrainian war.

There is as yet no indication how the sanctions might be used in actual nego-tiations, and how they might eventually be dismantled. Despite occasional informal statements by US policymakers on what the Russians would be expected to do to obtain relief, there is no official US position, and the same is true of the EU[10] and UK sanctions.[11] There is no apparent endgame. Indeed, with each new Russian atrocity on the Ukrainian battlefield, the Western urge to punish only grows, new sanctions are adopted, and the hurricane gains in intensity.

Yet the longer the sanctions regime remains open-ended, the more the regime itself becomes a cause of discord and an obstacle to eventual political solutions. We return to that subject in the final chapter of this book. But first, a quick recap on the sanctions themselves.

Brief History of Sanctions

Economic blockades have been used for centuries. Traditionally they were used as instruments of war, as part of military hostilities. But after the First World War they came to be perceived as alternatives to war, as a safer means of gaining victories without having to fight. Woodrow Wilson in 1919 gave the most eloquent description of the aim of economic sanctions, as "some-thing more tremendous than war." The threat of sanctions, he wrote, is "an absolute isolation . . . that brings a nation to its senses just as suffocation removes from the individual all inclinations to fight." Sanctions, he contin-ued, are a "peaceful, silent, and deadly remedy," which removes the need for force. The impact of sanctions was not only economic, in Wilson's view, but mental and moral, "when a nation knows that it is sent to coventry and despised."[12]

Economic sanctions became increasingly popular after the Second World War. They were invoked against Cuba, North Korea, Rhodesia, South Africa, Libya, and above all against Iran.

But, as Wilson himself recognized, economic sanctions were blunt instru-ments, which struck entire civilian populations and economies, causing lasting hardship. Beginning in the 1990s, this led to a search for something better. The "financialization" of the global economy made it possible to cre-ate a new model of sanctions, using financial levers aimed at the elites of targeted countries instead of their people. These so-called smart sanctions were advertised as "surgical" and "tunable," since they could be focused on specific sectors and ratcheted up or down by executive order, in exchange for concessions by the targeted side. Smart sanctions were notably used with considerable success in persuading Iran to accept restrictions on its nuclear enrichment program and to agree to promote greater transparency.[13]

"Smart sanctions" were also the main Western response to the Russian annexation of Crimea and its support for pro-Russian secessionists in the Ukrainian Donbas in 2014–15. They were explicitly designed to strike at key individuals in Putin's entourage and specific parts of the Russian economy. In the energy sector, for example, sanctions banned Western investment and technology for Arctic offshore projects and for "shale oil" (sometimes called "tight oil"), which has driven the recent boom in US oil production. These were intended to constrain Russia's future oil capacity. But there was no attempt to embargo current Russian oil exports, and the gas industry remained exempt. In the financial sector, certain banks that were considered close to the Putin circle were sanctioned—but Russia's access to the global financial messaging system, the so-called SWIFT network, was not. The explicit intent of the post-Crimean sanctions was to put selective pressure on the Putin leadership and to create leverage for negotiation, while limiting the impact on the Russian economy and population as a whole.[14]

But the sanctions imposed since February 2022 go far beyond the Crimea/Donbas sanctions of 2014–15. In place of "limited" and "surgical" sanctions, the latest US and EU sanctions are aimed at the entire Russian economy, not just at its means of prosecuting the war, by weakening its ability to raise capital or to conduct basic financial operations with the outside world. The oil sanctions this time are far broader; they ban the entire range of oilfield technology and impose restrictions on Russian oil exports.

In short, the doctrine of "smart sanctions" has been laid aside (even if the tools are the same, such as financial sanctions against individuals and entities). If the earlier sanctions could be called limited warfare, the present all-out offensive represents a return to broad sanctions, but this time aimed at a far larger and immediate set of targets than any attempted before.

Expansion and Complexity: "Self-Sanctioning" and Deterrence

At the present rate, there will soon not be much left to sanction. The list of sanctioned goods and services, organizations, and personalities continues to expand. The only major exceptions are basic foods, medical supplies, and "humanitarian" items, plus certain key commodities regarded as "strategic" for the West's own needs.[15] Even in the latter categories, the net of sanctions is tightening steadily.

The category of "luxury goods" banned by the EU illustrates the point. It covers twenty-two separate categories, many of which are only loosely connected to one's idea of "luxury." They include sporting goods and apparel, games of all kinds, musical instruments, household appliances (including ceiling fans and burglar alarms), and practically all clothing. (Russian smokers will be glad to know, however, that while cigars and cigarillos are banned, cigarettes are not.[16]) The list of "luxury goods" administered by the US Department of Commerce is equally wide-ranging.[17]

So long and complex are the sanctions lists that many companies have reacted by pre-emptively suspending all dealings with Russia, except where an item or an entity has been explicitly exempted. There are, in effect, two concentric circles of sanctions: an inner one, which is the zone of explicit bans; and an outer one, which one might call the "shadow of fear and uncertainty," where companies refrain from doing business with Russia, to be on the safe side and avoid legal trouble or damage to their reputations and brands, and to avoid the costs of monitoring their compliance.

The phenomenon of self-sanctioning, however, can lead to "oversanctioning," with awkward diplomatic consequences. This has been a constant concern for Treasury officials, who have given multiple warnings to banks and companies not to "overcomply." Self-sanctioning has been particularly widespread in the financial sector, as many banks have simply refused to process transactions with Russian banks, even those that have not been sanctioned. This led Treasury Undersecretary for Terrorism and Financial Intelligence Brian Nelson to criticize Western banks in early 2023 for "indiscriminately cutting off access for entire categories of customers."[18]

Yet this deterrent effect is central to the sanctions. Their effectiveness depends on maintaining an atmosphere of apprehensive uncertainty on the part of companies and their legal advisors, both in the countries directly targeted and in third countries. But that in turn depends on enforcement. If enforcement is perceived to be lax or spotty, then apprehension declines, and the zone of fear and uncertainty shrinks. This point is especially important in the case of the EU, since the actual monitoring and enforcement of the EU's sanctions is the responsibility of the member states. In several of the latter, where enforcement has been poor, many companies have continued to do business with Russia, particularly in the gray zone of trade, which is especially difficult to track. In those countries, the deterrence effect is weakened by poor enforcement.

Of the three major sanctioning powers, it is the United States that has historically been the most devoted user of sanctions as a key instrument of its foreign policy. It is also the United States that led the development of "smart sanctions" based on financial tools. But the EU has emerged since February 2022 as a surprisingly vigorous sanctioner as well, and it too has made increasing use of financial weapons. Overall, despite the very different decision-making machineries on both sides of the Atlantic, and an earlier history of conflicts over sanctions, there has been convergence, as the sanctioners work together to reconcile their different approaches. But how solid is the overall system? What are its vulnerabilities? How easily can it be tuned or eased, if and when future circumstances call for it? These are the subjects of the rest of this chapter. Then, in the next chapter, we will turn to the responses of the Russians.

The US Sanctions System

In the United States, there are four main federal agencies responsible for imposing and monitoring the different kinds of sanctions.[19] They differ from one another in their aims, their targets, their history, their skills, and one might add, their culture. The oldest, which dates back to the Cold War, is the system of export controls administered mainly by the Department of Commerce, through its Bureau of Industry and Security (BIS). The original mission of the Commerce Department in those days was to prevent the export of "dual-use" technologies that might benefit the Soviet military.[20] After a brief pause at the end of the Cold War, the export-control function was revived in the mid-2010s, and today it is still located in Commerce.

Unlike *export controls*, which regulate what products and processes can be exported, *sanctions* apply to the people and organizations that finance or trade in them.[21] The State Department, jointly with the Treasury Department, is the agency primarily responsible for deciding sanctions on persons (so-called Specially Designated Nationals, or SDNs) and companies, although the other agencies may do so as well in their areas of expertise.[22]

The Justice Department is the enforcer, the agency that seizes sanctioned assets from suspected violators and brings them to trial. It leads an interagency task force called KleptoCapture, which is the newest of the US sanctions agencies, having been established only in 2022, specifically in response to the Russian invasion of Ukraine.[23] It works jointly with the FBI.

But by far the most active and powerful part of the US sanctions system is the Treasury Department, and especially OFAC. As of early 2023, OFAC oversaw nearly 15,000 sanctions on individuals and organizations, over 2,500 of which originate from OFAC itself.[24] Yet it is a small organization, with only about 300 employees, responsible for the entire range of financial sanctions, as well as an assortment of financial crimes.[25] (Its former chief, Andrea Gacki, aptly described it as "small but mighty."[26]) In contrast, BIS in Commerce, with a much narrower remit, has nearly 600 employees.[27] In recent years, OFAC has struggled with staff shortages and attrition, as experienced OFAC officials migrate to other government posts or better-paying private-sector jobs, notably in the fast-growing sanctions compliance industry.[28]

The division of functions among the various federal agencies poses constant challenges. At the top of the system, there is an Office of the Sanctions Coordinator, which reports to the secretary of state. Despite its name, it is not responsible for coordinating sanctions within the government, but instead represents US sanctions policy internationally (although the heads of the other US sanctioning agencies are frequent foreign travelers as well). This body, created under President Obama, was abolished under Trump but revived under Biden. It reports directly to the White House.[29] In practice, much of the day-to-day coordination of sanctions in the US government is managed "horizontally" by the agencies themselves, through frequent interagency meetings and the publication of joint updates.[30]

The Rise of OFAC and the Doctrine of "Smart Sanctions"

The rise of the Treasury Department and OFAC is a relatively recent phenomenon. As late as the 1980s, Treasury was still a minor player in US sanctions policy toward the Soviet Union. The flow of money was a secondary concern, reflecting the fact that in those days the USSR was largely self-isolated from the world economy. While funding for Soviet-front organizations and terrorists, for example, in Germany (where Putin worked in the 1980s) did figure on the US government's radar screen, it was mainly the province of the intelligence agencies.

The rise of the Treasury Department to its present prominence in the US sanctions system reflects the growing importance of financial flows in an increasingly globalized world economy, as well as the advent of international computerized networks for the management of payments and information. As financial flows became more powerful, and more traceable, they required expanded financial skills, particularly greater capacity to monitor international financial flows. But in those days OFAC had fewer than twenty-five employees, and even as late as the turn of the century OFAC still had fewer than 100.[31]

The decisive event in the evolution of US sanctions policy was 9/11, which launched the United States into an all-out war against international terrorism. The key to impeding the flow of funds to terrorist groups was to stop them at their source, mainly by focusing on the profits from the drug trade and the associated laundering of drug revenues. But in the new century this flow increasingly passed through the international banking system, as well as parallel networks, such as Western Union (which handled remittances from migrant labor) and associated businesses like insurance companies. Financial sanctions and Treasury's role in overseeing them grew rapidly, and by 2010 they had become the centerpiece of US sanctions policy.

Treasury's role in sanctions today is also the result of 9/11 for another reason: In 2001 the Bush White House responded to the shock of the terrorist attack by creating a Department of Homeland Security, into which it grouped most of the law-enforcement agencies—"the guns and badges"—of the federal government, including the Secret Service and the Bureau of Tobacco and Firearms. These had been the province of the Treasury Department practically since the founding of the republic, and on the eve of 9/11, Treasury controlled some 40% of all law-enforcement personnel in the federal government. Suddenly these were lost to the new agency, and a much-diminished Treasury Department was forced to redefine its architecture and its mission.[32] Financial intelligence and sanctions, which had been secondary activities in Treasury prior to 9/11, were the answer. Today's Treasury is no longer just a "cop," but a financial detective.

More recently, since the mid-2010s, there has been a shift from the primary US focus in the post-9/11 sanctions on private-sector actors (such as money-launderers and terrorists) to state actors. This is particularly evident in the case of the sanctions against Russia.

Following the fall of the Soviet Union, Russians had become major players in international money laundering and the drug trade. During the 1990s, the wide-open atmosphere that followed the end of the Soviet system had catalyzed the creation of hundreds of fly-by-night Russian banks, most of which were devoted to moving assets and rents out of Russia through elaborate money-laundering schemes. Ironically, during Putin's first two terms (2000–2008) the US Treasury and the Kremlin found themselves on the same side. Following his election in 2000, Putin gave high priority to cleaning up the banking system, and the Russian government cooperated with international efforts to control money laundering. To lead this effort Putin appointed one of his closest associates from Saint Petersburg, Viktor Zubkov, the head of the Kremlin's powerful Rosfinmonitoring, which tracked Russian financial transactions inside and outside the country.[33] Zubkov worked with US officials at the time, and Treasury officials made frequent visits to Moscow.[34] In 2003 Russia joined the Financial Action Task Force (known as FATForce), the international group created to monitor and control money laundering.[35] Thus, for the first few years, Russia played, at least nominally, a positive role.

But the Crimean occupation in 2014 brought a sharp change. For the first time since the Cold War, the US Government responded with sanctions against both companies and government organizations, this time covering energy and finance as well as personalities. Though broad, they were nevertheless focused on specific targets. Thus, the energy sanctions did not attempt to embargo oil and gas exports. Instead, they applied only to specific energy technologies, such as arctic offshore exploration and deep deposits such as shale oil. Thus, as mentioned earlier, the Crimean sanctions marked the high point of the doctrine of "smart sanctions."

Treasury played the lead role, but the advent of the Trump Administration caused the exit of Treasury's "smart-sanctions" team, who relocated to a Washington think tank, where they kept up a steady flow of position papers advocating a tougher use of targeted sanctions against Russia and closer cooperation with the EU.[36] With the election of Joe Biden as president, several of them returned to the government (including NSC), just in time for the Russian invasion of 2022.[37]

Three years into the Russian invasion, the hurricane of US sanctions continues to expand steadily, with Treasury's OFAC in the lead role, in coordination with the State Department. They have issued wave after wave of sanctions, and the momentum keeps building. In September 2023, OFAC and State jointly announced blocking sanctions on over 150 additional entities and individuals, targeting a wide range of Russian manufacturers, as well as several notorious Turkish companies that were acting as middleman suppliers to the Russian military.[38] In February 2024, following the death of Russian opposition figure Aleksey Navalny, Treasury and State responded with the most extensive package of sanctions yet imposed, targeting over 500 entities and individuals, ranging from prison officials to Russia's coal giant SUEK and steel producer Mechel, as well as Russia's National Payment Card System.[39] On May 1, 2024, nearly 300 additional entities, this time targeting international suppliers of military equipment and technology, were added.[40] The following month, Treasury unveiled a massive expansion of its list of secondary sanctions aimed at foreign banks that do business with Russian companies.[41] The pressure on Russian and third-country banks continues to increase, with the US Treasury Department leading the charge. As deputy Treasury secretary Wally Adeyemo explains, "By raising the stakes for banks supporting sensitive trade with Russia . . . our coalition is pouring sand into the gears of Russia's military logistics."[42]

The EU Sanctions System

The Russian invasion of Ukraine in February 2022 has also brought a transformation of the European Union's sanctions regime, all the more remarkable for the fact that Russia was a close trading partner. In 2021, Russia was the EU's fifth-largest market, while the EU was Russia's largest. Accordingly, the EU sanctions system has been greatly expanded; for example, it now includes legal advisory services, and above all, new financial expertise.

The EU sanctions system, like that of the United States, reflects its history and its evolution. The EU originated as a trade alliance with limited powers, but over time its scope has expanded to cover the entire range of policy issues facing its members, including finance, security, and diplomacy. In the process, two new decision-making bodies have gradually come to the fore, the European Council and the European Parliament, in effect the EU's executive branch and legislature, which share powers with the original European Commission.[43] The individual member states have a strong voice in all three, and especially within the Council, where key decisions require unanimity.

The result is a system of extraordinary complexity,[44] in which policy is made through an elaborate process of negotiation, both within and among all three bodies, together with representatives of the member states.

In addition, the European Court of Justice stands guard over the entire structure, to make sure that all decisions conform to the treaties that govern the EU's authority.

A brief description will give the flavor. Officially, proposals for sanctions come from the High Representative of the Union for Foreign Affairs and Security Policy, until recently Josep Borrell, a former politician from Spain,[45] but before that, they go through an elaborate process of negotiation and vetting. Proposals can originate from a wide variety of sources, including experts from the member states, and are gathered together by the Sanctions Committee of the Foreign Relations Counsellors Working Party, known as RELEX.[46] They are then reviewed by a committee of representatives of the ambassadors of the member states, called COREPER, before being forwarded to the Foreign Affairs Council of the Council of Ministers. The Council of Ministers, a sub-group of the European Council, then adopts new sanctions decisions by unanimity, whereupon they are announced by the High Representative.

The challenge in a system of such complexity is maintaining unity. One measure of this point is the steadily increasing amount of time it is taking for the member nations of the EU to negotiate each new package of sanctions and to bring dissenting member states on board. The eleventh package took several weeks, the twelfth several months. The thirteenth package appeared likely to take longer still, when the tragic death of Russian opposition leader Aleksey Navalny cut short the Council's deliberations and enabled a shortened version to be waved through, together with the mandatory six-month extension of the existing sanctions, on the second anniversary of the Russian invasion. A fourteenth package then followed at the end of June 2024.

The Growing Role of Financial Sanctions in the EU

The European Commission historically focused mainly on trade, over which it had an exclusive mandate (or, in EU parlance, "competence"), while financial questions were the prerogative of the member states, although even there they played a minor role compared to trade. It is only relatively recently that financial issues have emerged as a leading area of the Commission's activity, including sanctions. In this respect, the evolution of the EU system parallels that of the United States with the rise of OFAC. The main financial directorate-general in Brussels, called FISMA, was only created in its present form in 2015; with about 350 employees, it is one of the smallest in the Commission.[47] Yet FISMA is responsible for the entire range of the Commission's financial policies; and only one of its five divisions, the division covering financial crime, is directly responsible for sanctions matters. Thus, FISMA's financial sanctions team, like that of OFAC in the United States, is understaffed for the many jobs it has to do. However, FISMA is not responsible for carrying out sanctions once adopted. That is primarily the job of the member states, while FISMA oversees the process and lends a hand where needed. As Mairead McGuinness, the commissioner who oversaw FISMA through 2024, explained,

> I am responsible for implementing what's already on the table . . . We don't have a strong centralized mechanism in place, so we're working with the member-states. Some have huge capacity, but others need support, so we're giving them support. We're increasing our focus on preventing circumvention.[48]

As an example, FISMA has focused on non-performing loans to Russian banks in Ireland, which have been a particular problem since the Russian invasion. Dublin had been a popular location for private Russian banks and had become a hub for borrowing by Russian companies through so-called "special-purpose vehicles," non-bank financial firms that acted as "secretaries" between lenders and borrowers. But after February 2022, the Russian banks and firms abruptly vanished, leaving the lenders with a raft of non-performing loans. In response, FISMA has helped to implement financial sanctions on the delinquent Russian banks.[49]

At the same time, trade remains a key part of the Commission's work on sanctions against Russia. These are the responsibility of the Directorate General for Trade (DG-Trade), which has its own sanctions division, under a deputy director-general who covers trade enforcement.[50]

Europe's Growing Diplomatic Service, and the Special Envoy for Sanctions

Another expanding role for the European Commission is diplomacy, reflecting the EU's increasing activity in foreign affairs. The growing place of diplomacy in the EU's agenda prompted the creation in 2010 of a new structure, the European External Action Service (EEAS), which functions as the EU's diplomatic corps, covering both foreign policy and defense.[51] At the top, it brings together officials from the Commission, the Council Secretariat, and diplomats from the member states. Its head is the public "face" of the EU's sanctions policy; he announces new EU sanctions when they are approved by the Council and is officially responsible for them.[52]

The creation of the EEAS was meant to combine the Commission's traditional focus on trade with its increasing involvement in finance, and to bring both to bear in the Commission's dealings with third countries. To lead this effort and to give it political heft, the Commission recruited one of its most respected statesmen, David O'Sullivan, inviting him out of retirement to take the job of Chief Operating Officer. O'Sullivan, over a thirty-year career in the Commission, symbolized to a unique degree the combination of skills the new body required. He had occupied practically every top job in the EU power structure, including Secretary-General of the Commission, Director-General for Trade, and Director-General of External Relations. O'Sullivan had also served as the EU's Ambassador to the United States from 2014 to 2019. There he had the opportunity to observe the US sanctions machinery in action, especially OFAC.[53] He was known on both sides of the Atlantic as a consummate diplomat.

However, O'Sullivan's background had been solely in trade policy, which was consistent with the EU's "exclusive competence." But his new role in EEAS touches on both financial matters and trade. Accordingly, O'Sullivan was also named an "advisor" to Commissioner McGuinness in FISMA, to ensure close contact with the Commission's financial team. This in turn required coordination with representatives of the member states, the main implementors of the financial sanctions, thus adding further to the demands of the position. As O'Sullivan commented, only half-humorously, "When I look at my own career [in the Commission], I think the most solid thing I did was actually trade . . . where the Commission is the exclusive negotiator, and you don't have bothersome member-states getting in your hair."[54] Commenting on the EEAS's own role in bringing together the disparate parts of the EU foreign-affairs apparatus, O'Sullivan added philosophically, "It combines the schizophrenia of the various Commission bodies into one head."[55]

The Russian invasion, and the hurricane of EU sanctions that immediately followed, brought even more complexity—with a new package of EU sanctions coming nearly every two months—but also led to increased efforts to provide more coordinated leadership.[56] In some respects, the Commission was ready. As the former EEAS sanctions chief, Sandra de Waele, describes it:

> Normally, there are two stages in the decision-making: there is a "political" stage, which usually takes weeks, but has been highly compressed in the case of the latest Russia sanctions. A lot of the internal thinking had already been done even before the invasion, as the Russian build-up and the threat grew, so as to be able to respond quickly. The first six packages were essentially already ready to go.[57]

The chief lesson of the first year of sanctions was that tougher enforcement was needed, especially in dealing with third-party countries like Turkey, the United Arab Emirates (UAE), and the countries of the FSU, which are not parties to the EU sanctions regime, in order to counter increasingly widespread evasion by Russia.

In response, in January 2023 the Commission created a new office, the International Special Envoy for the Implementation of EU Sanctions. The function of this office is above all diplomatic. The first special envoy is again David O'Sullivan, who thus combines the functions of head of the EU's diplomatic service with that of the EU's top ambassador on sanctions.[58] "My role now," O'Sullivan commented, "is to ensure that the sanctions are effectively implemented and not circumvented by third countries." Since his appointment, O'Sullivan has been spending much of his time traveling, with high-level visits to the Middle East, Central Asia, and East Asia, focusing particularly on countries that are not party to the sanctions.[59] As commissioner McGuinness, confirms, "O'Sullivan's role is precisely to talk with third countries."[60] These visits are typically done jointly with the relevant US officials.

The Weak Spot of the EU Sanctions System: The Member-States

The member-states are responsible for implementing the EU's sanctions. The European Council sets the overall framework, but it is the member states, through their own national laws, that carry it out, whether by freezing assets, applying trade restrictions, investigating and prosecuting breaches—or granting exemptions and derogations. This decentralized system gives the member states considerable latitude, which unfortunately in practice produces wide disparities both in the laws themselves and in their enforcement. It can happen, for example, that a company may find itself targeted in some member states but not in others.

Enforcement, in particular, has been the weak spot of the EU sanctions.[61] Some member states are vigorous enforcers, others are more lax. As a group, they do a poor job of communicating with one another and reporting back to Brussels; there are few published decisions on breaches and prosecutions, and there is no centralized platform on which to find them.[62] This has been a particular problem, for example, in locating the frozen reserves of the RCB held by individual member states.

Because of uneven enforcement by the member states, some European companies have simply ignored the sanctions and continued their operations in Russia, despite earlier pledges to stop. For example, the Finnish company Tikkurila and the Dutch firm AkzoNobel, two of Europe's largest producers of paints and coatings, have actually expanded their production and sales in Russia, even though their products are under sanctions. But so far there has been no prosecution by the Finnish or Dutch authorities.[63]

When an investigation by a member-state leads to an actual arrest, it makes the headlines. In a much-publicized case in the Netherlands, the Dutch Fiscal Information and Investigation Service, alerted by a bank, swooped down on a fifty-five-year-old individual, Dmitri K., the founder of a company that was supplying Russia with microchips by exporting them through an unsanctioned third country. The actual final customer, according to the Dutch investigators, was the purchasing manager of a Russian IT company, named SpetsPromSviaz, that supplies Rostec, the Russian military-industrial conglomerate.[64] But Dmitri K. is clearly only the tip of a large iceberg.

The Commission has attempted to address the problem of loose enforcement in two ways, first by coordinating the actions of the member states, through working groups such as a "Freeze and Seize" task force, designed to coordinate criminal law measures, and the EU Sanctions Whistleblower Tool, which allows anyone to report anonymously violations of EU decision. Second, the Commission has raised the stakes, by making the violation of EU sanctions a criminal offense. It remains to be seen how effective these moves will be.

The UK's System of Sanctions

The United Kingdom is the third major source of Russia sanctions. As in the United States, different aspects of the UK sanctions system are under separate agencies. Thus, the Foreign Office is responsible for "designations" of sanctioned companies and individuals. But the main body responsible for sanctions in the UK is the Office of Financial Sanctions Implementation, known as OFSI, located under the Treasury. OFSI is a recent creation: It was established in 2016 by then-chancellor George Osborne, in response to criticism from some British MPs that the government had made only weak efforts to respond to Russia's annexation of Crimea and intervention in the Ukrainian Donbas.[65] At first, the new office grew slowly; on the eve of the invasion, it still had only forty-five employees. But Britain's exit from the EU compelled the government to play a more active role, since it was no longer subordinated to the Commission. OFSI is now responsible both for devising new sanctions and for implementing them. Today it numbers over 135 employees, and its headcount is growing steadily.[66]

The British role in sanctions is potentially very important, not only because large numbers of Russians live in the UK, but also because the global marine insurance industry, which is a critical instrument in the application of the oil embargo and price cap (discussed below), is concentrated in London. While OFSI has so far played no significant role in overseeing the insurance industry's activities in the Russian oil trade, that may be about to change. Under expanded powers granted by Parliament in May 2024, the UK added a large Russian insurer, Ingosstrakh, to its sanctions list. Ingossttrakh, which is part-owned by the Italian insurance giant Generali, has played a major role in insuring Russia's "ghost tankers."[67] But it remains to be seen whether this augurs a more proactive stance on the part of OFSI toward the London-based insurance industry.

To date, OFSI has done little to enforce its sanctions. While the UK has followed the pattern of the US Treasury and the EU in issuing periodic lists of sanctions, OFSI in its entire history, has imposed only two criminal penalties for sanctions violations, and none since the Ukrainian invasion. One reason is that it lacks investigative powers, and it can only examine cases that have been reported to it.[68] It devotes far more attention to the issuance of "licenses," that is, exceptions and exemptions granted to otherwise sanctioned Russian entities, on the grounds of exceptional circumstances.

OFSI has been criticized for being overly generous with its licenses, particularly where the UK's large resident "oligarch" population is concerned.[69]

The sanctions machineries of the other Western G7 powers are smaller than those of the three main sanctioners. Canada's, for example, is still in the "low double digits,"[70] and consequently these countries tend the follow the lead of the United States and the EU.

Comparisons of the US, EU, and UK Systems

As the previous sections have shown, the three main sanctions systems—US, EU, and UK—have very different origins and functions. The US system originated during the Cold War and traditionally consisted mainly of export controls motivated by security concerns. The EU system arose later and focused primarily on trade. The UK system is the most recent arrival, driven by the UK's separation from the EU. Overall, the United States has historically made more frequent use of sanctions than the EU and has been more aggressive in their implementation. Compared to the other two, the UK system is smaller, and until recently, much of its activity consisted of processing licenses and granting exemptions. Since the invasion, however, it has increasingly aligned itself with the United States and EU.

The US and EU sanctions systems share some key weaknesses. They were both put together incrementally, from crisis to crisis; they have grown by accretion; and they are riddled with exceptions and exemptions. They are both governed by larger political currents and constraints, which makes them unpredictable, and are exposed to uncertainties, as governments change and new leaders take over. The US and EU sanctions agencies are both handicapped by staff shortages and high turnover. Consequently, they are both weak on monitoring and enforcement, which causes them to delegate as much as possible of the job of ensuring compliance to the private sector.[71] Both systems have tended to evolve toward financial sanctions as their main instrument, which has brought a corresponding increase in the influence of the departments that handle finance. But as the financial markets themselves evolve and generate new products and technologies, such as cryptocurrencies and artificial intelligence (AI), the sanctioning agencies on both sides of the Atlantic face similar challenges in updating their skills.[72]

However, it is the differences between the two systems that are ultimately the most important in shaping their effectiveness. The biggest one is the United States' vigorous use of *extraterritorial* and *secondary* sanctions, which until recently were barred by the EU. An extraterritorial sanction is one that applies to any person or company that deals with a sanctioned entity, even if that person or company is located in a third country. For example, an extraterritorial sanction by the United States against a Russian exporter could be applied to a Turkish bank that deals with it. The concept of secondary sanctions adds a further twist: any company or person that violates a US sanction can itself be sanctioned and added to the SDN list, thus shutting off that entity from access to the United States and all dollar-denominated operations.[73]

The EU has traditionally considered that extraterritorial sanctions (and a fortiori secondary sanctions) are contrary to international law. This led to a famous showdown in 1980, when the Reagan Administration invoked extraterritorial sanctions (although ultimately unsuccessfully) against the Soviet Union's plan to build a gas pipeline from Siberia to Europe. The EU denounced the US sanctions and European companies ignored them.[74] Another famous case occurred in the mid-1990s, when the United States imposed extraterritorial sanctions on Cuba, Libya, and Iran. The EU fought back by bringing its case before the World Trade Organization, and forced Washington to retreat.

But beginning with the Obama Administration, the United States has made more and more frequent use of secondary sanctions. In earlier years the EU objected strongly. However, the Russian invasion of Ukraine in 2022 has caused the EU to move quietly closer to US sanctions policy on several fronts, and notably on extraterritorial and secondary sanctions. Officially, the EU position remains unchanged. In June 2022, Sandra de Waele, who then headed the sanctions division of the EEAS, said flatly, "We think the US extraterritorial sanctions are illegal." The EU sanctions, in contrast, "do not have extraterritorial effect."[75] In April 2023, David O'Sullivan, on a visit to Kazakhstan, stated explicitly: "I want to be very clear: our sanctions do not target third countries."[76] The same was presumably even more true of secondary sanctions. Yet barely two months later, in the EU's eleventh package of sanctions, adopted in June 2023, the EU included secondary sanctions on eight Chinese companies, of which four were already on the US sanctions lists. This did not escape the media's notice. As Henry Foy of the *Financial Times* noted, "The move takes the EU into new territory of targeting third countries."[77] However, as a general practice, the EU still prefers to deal with third countries through diplomacy rather than coercion.[78]

The second major difference between the US and EU sanctions systems is the role of enforcement, although here it is important to distinguish between the threat and the reality. The US system is quick to pull the trigger, singling out violators and threatening them with fines or worse, but most such cases so far have led to settlements rather than prosecution. The EU system, at least at the Commission level, tends to prefer diplomacy. This reflects the fact that implementation, and especially enforcement, are in the hands of the member states. However, since the sanctions machinery of the latter remains under-developed, it is perhaps no accident that when senior US sanctions officials visit Europe to urge tougher enforcement, they spend more time in the member states than in Brussels. Belgium's role is particularly significant, because two of the key financial institutions, SWIFT and Euroclear, are based there, and are subject to Belgian laws (for more on this, see below).

Third, the three systems also differ in their flexibility. Most of the US sanctions administered by OFAC consist of "executive orders" under the president's emergency powers, which can be modified or rescinded at the stroke of the president's pen.[79] This makes the current US system, on the whole, potentially more tunable (a key feature of the smart sanctions doctrine), which makes it better suited as an instrument of pressure or as a bargaining chip. In contrast, the systems administered by Commerce and State are based on acts of law (the Arms Export Control Act in the case of Commerce), which makes them inflexible. The EU system is also inflexible, since it requires elaborate coordination and unanimous decisions among the member states, which makes it cumbersome and increases its vulnerability to disagreements and defections.

Finally, there is a fundamental difference in the "institutional bias" of the US and the EU sanctions machineries: the US system (particularly OFAC) is biased toward *escalation* (tradition of frequent use, pressures from Congress and the media, etc.); the EU system is biased toward *de-escalation* (the unanimity rule in the European Council, the six-month review requirement, the potential for disagreements among the member states, the reliance on more-or-less enthusiastic member states for actual enforcement, etc.). The tension between the two biases creates the potential for conflict between the United States and the EU.

This brings us to the vital subject of collaboration and cooperation. Despite their differences, are the similarities and shared goals of the two systems sufficient to make collaboration and cooperation possible, especially over time?

Collaboration and Coordination

Given the differences between the US and EU systems, it is no surprise that there has been, over the years, a history of conflict. That makes it all the more remarkable that, in the first three years since the Russian invasion, the United States and the EU have made impressive efforts to coordinate their policies and to collaborate in implementing them.

As the clouds darkened over Ukraine in the fall of 2021, the US and EU sanctions teams met to prepare for the worst. In late 2021, Björn Seibert, the *chef de cabinet* of Commission president von der Leyen, led an EU team to Washington that worked closely with Jake Sullivan, the US national security advisor. "The two sides underwent weeks of intensive technical work in secure rooms, attempting to mesh their trade and sanctions systems," even though "many European countries, including France and Germany, were skeptical of the US's increasingly dire warnings that Russia was planning an all-out invasion."[80] At about the same time, then-OFAC director Andrea Gacki was sent to Europe, with the same mission of coordinating advance preparations.[81] When the invasion occurred, the Council's working group of permanent representatives gathered immediately.

However, more typically the lists of sanctioned personalities, companies, and goods show a large measure of improvisation, as the various sanctioning agencies scramble to answer the politicians' calls for ever more measures and ever more exceptions. Both sides provide constant clarifications and modifications, and have occasionally had to backtrack, to correct overhasty decisions.

Both sides have been working to do a better job of coordination. The latest effort is the creation of a Sanctions Coordinators Forum, chaired by Finance Commissioner McGuinness. Its first meeting, in February 2023, "gathered all EU Member States and a broad coalition of international allies and like-minded partners—the US, the UK, Japan, Canada, Australia, New Zealand, Norway, Switzerland and, importantly, Ukraine."[82] This is welcome, but the larger the group, the more potential there is for disagreement and delay. These vulnerabilities, naturally, can be exploited by the target country.

Another collaborative group is the so-called Russian Elites, Proxies, and Oligarchs (REPO) Task Force, which brings together not only the United States and the EU, but also most of the members of the G7. (The United States is represented by the Treasury and Justice Departments.) REPO has several missions, mostly related to improving joint tracking of Russian financial assets. Its main target, in Treasury's words, is Russian "proxy networks" that "attempt to use global financial centers to store and access wealth."[83] In plain speech, this means primarily the Russian oligarchs, as discussed in Chapter 2. In addition, REPO has lately been charged with tracking down the Russian "sovereign assets" (meaning mainly those belonging to the RCB and the Ministry of Finance) that have been blocked inside the G7 countries.[84]

Shared Weaknesses of the Sanctions Machineries

Political Uncertainty: The greatest single weakness of the US/UK and EU sanctions systems is their vulnerability to political developments that are today unforeseeable, and above all to the future course of the Ukrainian conflict and of relations with Russia. Certain features of each system contribute to this uncertainty. In the EU, as already mentioned, it is the presence of mandatory "sundown clauses"; in the United States, it is the constant possibility of action by Congress, which can tie the hands of the executive agencies in unpredictable ways and restrict the ability of the president to "tune" the system through executive orders.

An additional source of political uncertainty is changes in leadership. In the EU, the commissioners change every five years, after each parliamentary election. The new parliament chooses a new Commission, beginning with the chair, and the parliament then vets all the other commissioners. There is typically extensive turnover at this stage.[85]

In the United States, there is even more political uncertainty. So-called Schedule C officials, beginning with assistant secretaries, are political appointees, and they typically change with each new presidential administration. A change of party in the White House could bring a weakening of the political commitment to the Ukrainian cause, and some of the US panoply of sanctions, notably those stemming from executive orders of the president, could disappear overnight.

Political uncertainty is compounded by a high rate of turnover. All of the senior figures at Treasury and State have changed jobs over the last two years; some have moved within the government, while others have left for the private sector. At Treasury, as noted above, the cadre of long-standing officials who had played key roles in the development of the "smart" financial sanctions, has mostly moved on, and valuable experience has been lost.

Both the US and EU sanctions systems have a shortage of specialized expertise. Where the Russia sanctions are concerned, there are no Russia experts in senior positions, to say nothing of specialists on the Russian economy or energy. The senior ranks at both Treasury and State are dominated by lawyers, who are highly skilled but have only general knowledge of Russia.

Absence of "Off-Ramps": The second major weakness of both systems is the absence of any clear criteria by which the sanctions might be dismantled or scaled down. In this respect the US system is potentially more flexible, because of the president's discretionary powers over executive orders, but it is no less politically fraught. In the EU, the wide range of views among the member states over the conditions that would lead to dismantling or scaling down sanctions mean that rescinding any part of the sanctions structure by unanimity would require at the very least a difficult and protracted renegotiation, with the ever-present possibility of defection by one or another of the member states. The greater likelihood is that parts of the EU sanctions could simply disappear for lack of a unanimous vote to renew them.

Spotty and Unpredictable Enforcement: Enforcement has been the weakest part of the sanctions regime for all the sanctioners. In part this is due to short-handed staffs. Despite the best efforts of the sanctioning agencies to keep their "customers" fully and currently informed, notably through the use of websites to post regular announcements and answer FAQs, there are not enough hours in the day and not enough people to answer the constant flood of inquiries that come from companies and banks, who complain that the agencies are unresponsive, when in reality they are simply undermanned and overburdened.

As a result, the United States and EU rely heavily on the private sector for compliance and have so far approached actual prosecution with a light hand.[86] In the United States, the three main agencies in charge of sanctions implementation (Treasury, Commerce, and Justice) take the position that generally they will not seek prosecution of companies that "voluntarily self-disclose potentially criminal violations."[87] In the EU, the Council of Europe in November 2022 adopted a measure "criminalizing" sanctions violations,[88] but there have been few actual prosecutions to date.[89] Prosecution, in any case, would be the responsibility of the member states.

Instead of prosecutions, the sanctions system relies on investigations and threats. An investigation forces a targeted company to spend large sums on legal fees, both as a pre-emptive measure (to avoid an investigation in the first place through rigorous compliance) and during actual investigations, which can end in costly settlements. According to one prominent sanctions attorney, "foreign banks have paid billions in settlements to OFAC."

One problem with the enforcement system is that actions against suspected violators can take a long time to process. As an example, it took nearly seven years for Commerce and Treasury settle a case against Microsoft for violations in 2016–17, involving the selling of software to two sanctioned Russian entities, Glavgosekspertiza and United Shipbuilding.[90] Similarly, on the EU side, it took equally long for a German court to impose a €1.3 million fine on a company that had sold equipment to build the Crimean Bridge linking Crimea to the Russian mainland in 2016.[91]

Outright smuggling of military-related technology is a clear criminal offense, but even in that category there have not been many actual arrests and prosecutions. One of the few reported cases to date was the break-up in December 2022 of a Russian smuggling ring that ran a collection of shell companies in the New York area.[92]

The major sanctioning governments have grown increasingly frustrated with the inefficiencies and leaks in the sanctions system and have vowed to tighten enforcement. As a result, both Washington and Brussels have been focusing more on sanctions implementation, not only against Russia, but also against "third countries," notably Turkey and the UAE, where middlemen have built thriving businesses re-exporting goods to Russia, especially from Europe.[93] Several countries of the FSU, such as Armenia, Kazakhstan, and Georgia, have also become important conduits for re-exports to Russia. Exports from the EU to various countries in the FSU have increased by nearly half; most of that increased traffic is destined for Russia.[94]

Since there are over 7,500 products under sanction by the EU alone, it is clearly impossible to stop more than a small fraction of them. Consequently, the EU Commission has narrowed its focus to a short list of forty-five products that are found in actual weapons on the battlefield, and it concentrates on persuading third countries to stop passing them on to Russia. So far, says David O'Sullivan, there has been only mixed success; ironically, the most cooperative have been the FSU countries, particularly Kazakhstan, while non-FSU countries such as Turkey (a NATO member) and the UAE, have been the most reticent. David O'Sullivan is philosophical: "Once you have sanctions you have circumvention, and there's no point in trying to pretend that you won't, or that you can shut down all circumvention." The incentive to cheat is simply too great.[95] Andrew Adams, the head of the US Department of Justice's KleptoCapture team, puts it similarly: "It's like water on the sidewalk, it will find cracks. Our job is to identify those cracks and fill them as quickly as possible."[96]

Given the vulnerabilities and weaknesses in the sanctions systems, there are few clear successes to point to, despite the ongoing efforts of the sanctioners. The three outstanding illustrations are the sanctions relating to oil, to financial transactions, and to weapons. We begin with oil.

Sanctions in Action: The Oil Embargo and the Price Cap

Since the Russian government's budget, and the Russian economy generally, rely so heavily on exports of hydrocarbons, the prime target for the application of sanctions is Russian oil and gas exports, and especially oil. This has been the single most prominent area of sanctions since the beginning of the Russian invasion, but it has also been the most challenging. The story of the oil sanctions illustrates both of the main themes of this chapter—the challenge of competing objectives and the difficulties of monitoring and enforcement.[97]

The global oil market is like an immense bathtub, in which over 100 million barrels of crude oil and products are traded daily, traveling from hundreds of supply points to thousands of destinations. Within this system, oil of many different grades—thick and thin, "sweet" and "sour"—move in all directions. It is the ultimate illustration of a market system in action, in which oil supply and demand are coordinated by prices, in an elaborate and unceasing dance. Remarkably, the dance is largely self-regulating, as hundreds of thousands of players respond to its signals.

In designing a system of oil sanctions, the essential puzzle to solve is how to serve two aims at once: both to curtail Russia's oil revenues—to punish the aggressor and to limit its capacity to finance its war—without cutting its volume of exports and thus squeezing world oil supply, setting off a spiral of high prices. An additional challenge is that any system of sanctions carries with it the risk of distorting the self-regulated market system through excessive state intervention. How have the sanctioning powers reconciled these competing issues?

The EU led off first. In June 2022 the European Council approved a comprehensive embargo on Russian maritime imports into the EU, together with associated maritime transportation services, a category that includes shipping and trading, finance, flagging, and most importantly, insurance.

The ban on services applied to third countries as well. The embargo went into effect in December 2022 (for crude oil) and February 2023 (for refined products). To overcome the objections of some member states, Hungary in particular, the EU "temporarily" exempted imports by pipeline, and thanks to this carve-out, the Council was able to muster unanimous consent.

The US government, concerned about the impact on world supplies and prices, reacted cautiously. US policymakers were aware that Russian exporters relied heavily on EU marine service providers, who control most marine services worldwide. They feared that without access to EU-based services, Russia would not be able to keep its oil exports whole, and world oil supply would be squeezed.

The US proposed instead a price cap on Russian oil exports, which would allow Russian oil to retain access to transportation services, provided it was sold below a certain price level—a "price cap." This initiative was the brainchild of US Treasury Secretary Janet Yellen and a group of advisors in Treasury.[98] Even though the oil sanctions are trade matters, it is Treasury that has played the lead role throughout. Treasury's leaders designed the system and have traveled the world to promote it, and Treasury's OFAC has continued to oversee it, issuing regular guidance and dealing directly with market participants.

The US price-cap proposal was put before the G7 powers in September 2022. The G7, ever since Russia was expelled from it in 2014 after its occupation of Crimea, is essentially the coalition of Western powers allied against the Russian invasion.[99] India and China, notably, are not part of it. Even though the US proposal required unanimous approval by the G7 members, it was adopted remarkably quickly, in December 2022. The cap was set at $60 a barrel.

The resulting EU/G7 system consists of two parts: first a ban on imports of Russian oil to all coalition countries and second, a ban on the use of any coalition marine transportation services for carrying Russian oil, unless they comply with the cap.

The warhead in the EU/G7 price-cap measure is insurance. For a Russian tanker to obtain (and then renew[100]) insurance services from a reputable provider, its cargo must be acquired for less than the price cap. In other words, the price cap is not a ban on Russian oil exports; on the contrary, it is a measure designed to keep Russian oil exports flowing, but at a lower price. Thus the price cap is, in theory, an elegant way of meeting both of the objectives of the sanctioning powers—to limit Russian oil revenues, while not disrupting the world oil market.[101]

The embargo and the price cap took nearly a year to put in place. Initially, all was confusion. Some established oil traders and shippers, as well as service providers such as insurance companies, reacted by refusing to buy or ship Russian oil at all.[102] Such de-risking by traders and shippers raised the danger that the global oil market could be disrupted, precisely what the US government wanted to avoid.[103] In the spring of 2023, US Treasury officials met with two leading traders, Trafigura and Vitol, to urge them to resume taking Russian oil, and they shortly did so. In the meantime, new players, many of them with Russian connections, stepped in to fill the gap.[104] Between those two groups, there is now no longer any shortage of traders or shippers available to buy Russian oil.[105]

The immediate result of the EU's embargo was a drastic decline of Russian maritime flows into Europe, where nearly three-quarters of Russian maritime oil exports had previously gone. Russia responded by rerouting its maritime oil exports to other destinations, mainly to India. The volumes were roughly the same, but the result was a sharp decline in net profits to the Russians. Russian exports now had to travel longer distances, which implied higher costs.[106] And since India was now the main buyer, the Indians suddenly had bargaining power; as a result, the Russian were obliged to sell their oil at a discount, which at times exceeded $35 a barrel. Overall, in its first year alone, the embargo deprived the Russian treasury of $40–$50 billion in revenue.[107]

The oil price cap, in contrast, remained largely untested until the fall of 2023: until then world oil prices were well below $60, and therefore the price cap was only theoretical, since all buyers could meet it.[108] It was only when oil prices rose above $60, as they began to do in the fall of 2023, that the equation changed, and the price cap was tested for the first time.

We will take up the Russian responses to the oil sanctions in the next chapter. But first, since the price-cap system rests heavily on the willingness of the mainstream shipping and insurance industries to cooperate, we need to take a look at how they are structured and how they operate.

In the Crosshairs of the Oil Sanctions: The Maritime Insurance Industry

At the center of the maritime oil shipping industry sits a remarkable private club called the Intergovernmental Group for Protection and Indemnity, or IGP&I. It is based on a convention created several decades ago to decide the question, "Who is ultimately liable for oil spills?" To cover the billions of dollars potentially at risk, the shipowners formed P&I (Protection and Indemnity) clubs, to self-insure among themselves. P&I insurance is required, for example, before a ship buyer can obtain a "mortgage," i.e., a loan to buy a ship, from established lenders. Over the years the role of P&I insurance—and the clubs behind it—has grown into a vast private regulatory system that governs ship traffic—including particularly oil tankers—going in and out of all the ports of the world. As one member of a P&I club, North Standard, explains,

> All shipowners who use their vessel for business or transportation, or for transporting passengers, workers, or cargo across international seas, must carry P&I insurance. To enter ports around the world, the master must provide a "certificate of entry" given by the shipowners' respective P&I club, demonstrating their insurance to the port authorities.[109]

The IG system covers 90% of the world's shipping with P&I insurance; for oil tankers, it covers 95% of the global market for spill liability. Most legitimate (so-called mainstream) shipowners belong to these clubs. But problems arise when a ship ages, say, beyond fifteen years. At that point the original owner sells it; and many of the new owners are "cowboys," who buy the ships on the cheap. One of the main ways the Russians have worked around the oil sanctions, as we shall see in more detail in the next chapter, is by building up a massive "shadow fleet" of such "gray" tankers, acquired on the second-hand market.[110]

But the weak point in the Russian evasion strategy is precisely insurance.[111] Mainstream insurers belonging to the P&I clubs will not cover the shadow tankers. The Russian government has attempted to find insurers outside the P&I system (so-called non-IG insurance), and to provide reinsurance through the RCB, which has guaranteed $9 billion to cover non-IG insurers.[112] This is a less than satisfactory arrangement, however, since non-IG insurance is risky, and may not pay out in case of an accident or a spill. Port authorities in many destination countries are reluctant to accept shadow tankers that do not carry mainstream insurance.

Thus the IG insurers are the key players in the implementation of the embargo and the price cap. But enforcement could be problematic. Under EU rules, insurers must obtain attestations from their clients that the Russian crude shipped on the insured tankers complies with the price cap. But as reported by Bloomberg, "If an attestation were to be falsified, the insurers are not considered in breach of sanctions as long as they can prove they acted in good faith."[113] This creates an opening for fraud, and there have been numerous reports of P&I shippers carrying Russian oil under false attestations.

Consequently, there are now two streams of maritime traffic carrying Russian oil at prices above the price cap.[114] Oil shipped on shadow tankers not belonging to the EU/G7 countries trades openly at "screen prices," that is, at the prevailing market price, since countries that do not subscribe to the price cap can import Russian oil freely at market prices. However, the owners of shadow tankers carrying such oil are typically unable to obtain insurance and other services from reputable providers.

The other stream consists of Russian oil shipped on mainstream tankers, but with false attestations. So far, the combination of shadow tankers and attestation fraud has enabled the Russians to keep maritime export volumes reasonably close to their pre-invasion levels of about 6 million barrels a day. We examine these Russian responses more closely, and the Western efforts to counter them, in the next chapter.

The Oil Sanctions in Perspective

The story of the oil embargo and the price cap is important for what it tells us about the functioning of the sanctions machinery itself, and especially the ability of the Western allies to cooperate, even though their objectives may differ.

On the level of policymaking, the performance has been impressive. In a matter of months, the sanctioning powers set up two totally different systems—a regional embargo and a global price cap. They did so with a minimum of discord, working through joint working groups such as the G7/EU Maritime Advisory committee, a newly formed body that makes recommendations on topics such as insurance verification. But as time has passed, the oil sanctions have begun to show the same weaknesses as the rest of the sanctions regime. The most serious one is that they do not cover the whole market, since many oil buyers have refused to cooperate. The prime case is the UAE, which has become the main transshipment hub for exports of Russian crude oil and refined products to the rest of the world. The UAE has declined to join the price cap consortium, which leaves it free to accept whatever cargoes it likes at whatever prices it pleases. But that has become a hole through the EU's embargo, since crude and products that leave the UAE's port of Fujairah near Dubai are no longer legally Russian, and can therefore be re-exported into Europe.[115]

The oil story also illustrates the side-effects of the sanctions. The shipping of oil has been until now a largely privately regulated system. But sanctions are imposed by states. The more the sanctions system grows in scale and complexity, the more private players are under pressure to conform to state-imposed mandates, and indeed to play regulatory roles to which they may be poorly suited; this is particularly the case with the insurance industry. In short, the oil sanctions carry with them the risk of disrupting what has long been a key part of the liberal regime governing the global economy.

Some of the creators of the price-cap system had a premonition of what they would be up against. Ben Harris, one of its architects, said, "We're coming to this with a lot of humility and we're just asking that everyone else can adopt the same level of uncertainty. These are really opaque markets, the data's not great on it. Let's just acknowledge that from the outset when we're making conclusions."[116] But these words of caution were the exception. For the most part, the oil sanctions were greeted with enthusiasm as the chief means by which Russia's budget would be driven into deficit and its financial ability to wage war would be weakened. Yet, as we shall see in the next chapter, Russia's efforts to defeat the oil sanctions have been resourceful and at least in the short term, effective.

The oil sanctions have attracted more public attention than any of the other sanctions. But it is the financial sanctions that may be the most powerful in the long run. We turn to those next.

Financial Sanctions: More Effective than Oil

The financial sanctions have been the most effective part of the Western sanctions arsenal. Russia's twenty largest banks have been sanctioned and excluded from the SWIFT international messaging network and the Euroclear settlement system. They are also barred from accessing US banks or conducting dollar-denominated transactions with any bank that has US operations. Only three banks in Russia (other than very small ones) are still able to conduct international transfers and payments. Two of those

(Raiffeisen and Unicredit) are foreign and are under growing pressure from the EU to shut down their Russian operations, which would leave only Gazprombank.[117] The Moscow Exchange and its National Clearance Center (NCC) have also been sanctioned, and their foreign assets are blocked in Luxembourg. And although some 300 Russian banks remain connected to SWIFT and the European clearance systems, they are smaller banks and conduct mainly domestic business.

As the Western powers have tightened their enforcement of secondary financial sanctions since the end of 2023, Russian banks and companies are finding it increasingly difficult to process foreign transactions. "The number of foreign banks that are willing to deal with us is steadily shrinking," complains Andrei Kostin, the head of VTB. "As soon as a good is coming in or out of Russia, 'stop' signs light up, regardless of the bank or country or the sanctions status of the Russian party, especially with so-called 'friendly countries' . . . Delays in settlements are increasing, commissions are going up, and more and more documentation is required, especially for critically important goods like electronics, computers, and high-precision machine tools." Often, Kostin says, when a settlement is denied, no explanation is given.[118]

In June 2024, in response to the latest round of US sanctions, the Moscow Exchange halted trading in dollars and euros. Anyone wishing to exchange rubles for dollars and euros in Russia, for example, to purchase foreign currency for payments, now has to shop bank by bank, an awkward arrangement that is both opaque and costly. As Janis Kluge, an analyst at the German government's think tank SWP, put it nicely, "Imagine a medieval town where the central market shuts down. There will still be farmers looking to sell food and villagers looking to buy, they just have to meet in some corners all over town. This is what is to happen in Russia."[119] The likely result will be an increasing resort to barter.

Russia's access to capital has likewise been shut off. Russian companies have lost access to Western credit markets and are unable to use debt to finance their investments, as they did previously. International credit cards and cash cards, mainly Mastercard and VISA, are unusable inside Russia or by Russians traveling abroad. Private investors with assets outside Russia are unable to sell them and repatriate the proceeds, because of the sanctions on the NCC.[120] Above all, half of Russia's sovereign foreign-exchange reserves, which were located outside the country on the eve of the invasion, have been blocked abroad and cannot be accessed by the RCB.

The shut-down of much of Russia's external financial network is especially significant because of the country's heavy dependence on external sources of revenue and capital. Since the 1990s, Russian companies had come to rely on outside sources for credit and investment, since domestic savings were modest and the domestic banking system was small. Finally, the whole external system relied on the dollar, and to a lesser extent the euro, as a medium of payment and as a store of value. The Russian dependence on the Western financial system became its greatest source of vulnerability.

The Russian government has attempted to turn to China as an alternative source of credit and financial services. But so far this "pivot to the East" has not worked very well. We return to this problem in Chapter 7.

We turn now to the Western sanctions on the Russia military and military industry. These have understandably been the most controversial aspect of the sanctions. In the short run, they have arguably been the least effective part; but in the longer run their grip could become increasingly powerful, less because of their impact on today's weapons than on the capacity of the Russian technological system to create new ones.

The Impact of Western Sanctions on Military Industry

The impact of Western sanctions on the Russian military industry can be divided into three tiers: first, the near-term effects on Russia's access to the current generation of weapons and the machines needed to make them; second, the mid-range effects on design and production in both military and civilian sectors; and third, the longer-range impact on Russia's entire military-industrial system, ranging from high-precision machine tools to advanced microelectronics. In the latter sector, military industry overlaps with civilian production, particularly in IT, such as chips, servers, and data centers, and ultimately the Russian "cloud." We consider first the impact of sanctions on Russian microelectronics, then look at the broader picture of military-industrial innovation.

In the first tier, that of near-term impact, Western sanctions are unfortunately already too late. The current generation of Russian weapons, as findings from the Ukrainian battlefield show, depends on older Western chips and other components that are widely available on "gray" markets, or are covered by licensing agreements that were concluded before the Crimean sanctions in 2014. In both cases, however, Russian weapons producers are increasingly limited to obsolete designs using these simpler products. This is meager comfort, to be sure, since such weapons, though not leading-edge, can be devastating on the battlefield or as part of a scorched-earth strategy. (The Iranian-produced drones being used in Ukraine, though hardly advanced in their control systems, demonstrate the point.)

Western sanctions will have little effect in stopping this flow: there are simply too many sources of supply and too many channels. The Western powers, using both primary and secondary sanctions, will be able to stamp out individual illicit traders and jobbers, but such efforts are unlikely to have more than marginal effects on the overall traffic in this category, as new players, like dragon's teeth, will constantly appear.

In the second category, however, Western sanctions are already having a substantial impact. The current Russian microelectronics industry has good design capabilities, but only weak fabrication capacity. During the brief heyday described above, Russian chip designers began turning to foreign "fabs," while Russian companies underinvested in their own production facilities. The post-invasion sanctions have abruptly interrupted this supply chain, cutting the access of Russian designers to foreign foundries like Samsung or TSMC. As a result, Russian designs such as Elbrus and Baikal were left in the lurch, having lost access to production abroad, while having only limited production capacity at home.[121]

In this second tier, then, Western sanctions stand a good chance of being effective in coming years. Russian policymakers have responded to the cutoff with an emergency program to increase fabrication capacity by strengthening the connections between Russian "fabless" designers and "semi-fab" producers. But increasing fabrication will take large-scale investment—and time. They now have a captive domestic market, inasmuch as their customers, both private and state, will be increasingly barred from buying foreign products. But considering the length of time it took Asian fabs to tool up in places like Taiwan and South Korea, progress in Russian fabrication will be at least a decade away.

Finally, in the third category, that of long-term impact, the Western sanctions could be decisive. There are only a handful of US and Asian designers and producers capable of developing the necessary architecture, advanced lithographic equipment, and chip designs for the next generation of semiconductor systems—and even fewer that are able to combine them into actual mass production—and the Russians have neither design nor production capacity below 90 nanometers of separation. No amount of crash government programs will enable them to overcome a gap that took decades of misguided government policy to create. (On this point, see the more detailed discussion of the reasons for the Russian lag in microelectronics in the next chapter.)

Outside the IT sector, Western sanctions on military production have generally had less impact. A striking example is machine tools, which are essential to the production of weapons. According to Julian Cooper, a leading expert on Russian manufacturing technologies, the machine-tool sector has adapted successfully to sanctions, unlike the microelectronics sector, for several reasons.[122] The Soviet Union had built a strong machine-tool industry, and despite the Soviet collapse and the disappearance of military orders in the 1990s and 2000s, it came into the 2010s reasonably intact. With the revival of military spending from the mid-2010s, the machine-tool sector recovered quickly, helped by the rise of several new companies, notably STAN, created by former defense industrialist turned private entrepreneur Sergei Nedoroslev, who assembled several Soviet-era plants into a sizable conglomerate. Despite relying where necessary on imported machinery, especially for advanced types such as numerically controlled cutting tools, Nedoroslev, whose top priority was the defense industry, promoted home-grown manufacture and the displacement of imports.

Following the Russian takeover of Crimea and the first round of Western sanctions in 2014, the machine-tool industry accelerated its efforts to replace imports with Russian-made models. Nedoroslev's STAN, in particular, was helped by the growing power of Rostekh, the military-industry conglomerate led by Putin's close ally Sergei Chemezov. When STAN ran into financial trouble, Chemezov's Rostekh bailed it out, and subsequently took over the company. In parallel, the machine-tool industry drew on stocks of uninstalled machines. Thanks to measures such as these, by the time of the post-2022 sanctions, the Russian machine-tool industry was well prepared.

In addition, Russia has reached out to foreign middlemen who supply machine tools, especially from China. These are not necessarily the latest models, but they do not have to be. According to a recent investigation, a Chinese broker based in Shenzhen buys up second-hand machine tools made by the Japanese company Tsugami, of which there are over 100,000 in use in China alone.[123] Similar middlemen are based in the UAE and Turkey.

Concluding Thoughts on The Long-Term Effectiveness of the Sanctions

Broadly, the effectiveness of the Western sanctions against Russia has varied by sector, according to the degree of Russia's prior dependence on foreign channels on the eve of the invasion, the availability of ready alternatives, and the extent to which Russian policymakers had prepared in advance. On the whole, the sanctions have had their greatest near-term impact in the financial sector, a variable impact in the case of oil exports, and the least in dual-use technologies. In all three areas, however, the long-term effects will grow over time—if they are maintained.

When do economic sanctions "work"? On this point there is a large literature, much of it by former practitioners, based on experience with earlier sanctions. One of the designers of the doctrine of "smart sanctions," former Acting Undersecretary of the Treasury Adam Szubin, summed up the three conditions required for success: (1) a broad and stable multilateral coalition; (2) clear policy objectives, including precise criteria and procedures for the sanctions' eventual removal; and (3) adequate staffing and capability to gain intelligence and maintain cooperation between government and the private sector.[124]

The Western sanctions imposed on Russia since the 2022 invasion have so far met the first criterion reasonably well, but not the other two. As we have seen in this chapter, the machinery of sanctions developed by the major powers suffers from severe weaknesses. The sanctions are complex, inconsistent, and unpredictable. They are served up in incremental doses in response to the political pressures of the moment and the emotions aroused by the war. There is no clear way of removing them in exchange for concessions.

The Russians have been resourceful in devising ingenious ways to beat the sanctions, through workarounds, "parallel imports," "shadow fleets," "gray markets," front companies and back offices, false reports, and many other maneuvers. After an initial few months of disarray in early 2022, the Russian economy has adapted to the onslaught of sanctions, and is currently actually prospering. (Chapter 5 explores the Russian responses in more detail.)

As a result, the sanctions' record to date is not encouraging. They have not isolated Russia from the non-Western world; they have not crippled its economy; and above all, they have not impeded Russia's will or ability to prosecute the war in Ukraine. Russia is simply too large, its economy is too highly developed in many of the key sectors, and it is too well connected to global trade flows. This is precisely what experienced practitioners might have predicted.

Moreover, the sanctions are all too easy to beat. They create irresistible opportunities for arbitrage by intermediaries, who take advantage of the convoluted supply chains that lead from producers to Russian buyers, passing through networks of middlemen in countries that either reject the sanctions or apply them, as the Russian expression goes, "by looking through their fingers." The result is higher costs and uncertainties for the Russians, but no significant loss of capacity, at least for current goods and technologies.[125]

The sanctions are high-cost instruments in other ways. They are costly to administer and enforce, not only for government agencies but also for the private sector, which bears the expense of employing lawyers and consultants to self-monitor its compliance. Thus, the sanctions inflict losses on the countries that use them, in terms of lost profits and productivity, and the mounting pressure on third countries by the sanctioning powers provokes resentment on the part of unaligned countries. Lastly, the effort to maintain unity among the sanctioners, without which no success is even remotely possible, requires constant expenditure of diplomatic effort and political capital.

Given these obstacles, there is a temptation to double down, leading to steadily larger sanctions. But the overuse of sanctions damages the reputations of the sanctioners as reliable suppliers, disrupts the self-regulatory networks on which the global economy depends, and weakens the dominance of the dollar and the euro as the reference currencies for world trade and finance. The Russians' efforts to adapt to the sanctions are likewise causing collateral damage to the world economy, by altering oil markets, disrupting established trading flows, and destabilizing insurance regimes.

Those in charge of the West's sanctions are well aware of these "collateral costs." The US Treasury Department itself has voiced disquiet over the dangers of overusing sanctions as instruments of foreign policy. As early as 2016, following the first round of US sanctions in response to Russia's occupation of Crimea, then-Secretary of the Treasury Jack Lew warned against what he called "overreach": "The more we condition the use of the dollar and our financial system on adherence to US foreign policy, the more the risk of migration to other currencies and other financial systems in the medium term grows. Such outcomes would not be in the best interests of the United States."[126] It is already clear that Lew's warning is coming true. Russia's pivot to the East and the growing use of the renminbi in Russian–Chinese trade in response to sanctions are accelerating a shift away from the dollar and the euro, although central banks have been slower to follow.[127] These effects will last long after the Ukrainian war is over.

The Other Side of the Coin: The Longer-Term Effects of the Sanctions on Russia

Yet that is not the end of the story. Over time, the sanctions will exert a growing drag on the Russian economy, the early signs of which can already be seen. Russia has been shut out of Western capital markets and is no longer able to borrow abroad on any meaningful scale. The profits from its energy exports have declined, particularly those from gas. As a result, its investment in infrastructure and civilian sectors has shrunk, as the government devotes a growing share of its revenues to the war. Its access to Western expertise to develop leading-edge technologies has been blocked. Its companies are unable to access Western services and spare parts, except at lower quality and higher prices. And its ability to process payments for imports through efficient channels, and to receive the proceeds from exports, is severely diminished.

The RCB agrees with this assessment. In September 2022, an internal RCB document listed a number of impacts:

> declines in the value of Russian securities and bank capital, as well as US$300 billion in Russia's foreign exchange reserves frozen as part of sanctions. The Moscow Exchange Index is now about 20% below its February levels . . . . 80% of banking sector assets were directly affected by sanctions, while financial sector entities also suffered from being cut off from SWIFT and from losing access to foreign equipment and software. Instruments such as derivatives, hedging, Eurobonds, and IPOs had "practically disappeared."[128]

For the moment, the long-term effects of sanctions have been masked by four things. First, thanks to high oil prices, at least until late 2024, Russia has enjoyed record export revenues. Second, existing inventories enabled Russian manufacturers to maintain supply chains for a time, and offset the loss of banned components. Third, the growth of parallel imports from third countries has sustained consumption of foreign consumer goods, limiting the

impact on living standards and public opinion. Lastly, Russian financial policymakers, and especially the RCB and Finance Ministry, have been creative
in developing new sources of budget revenue while maintaining macroeconomic stability.[129] As a result, the Russian government is on a "high," during
which it appears able to finance all objectives at once, while maintaining the
appearance of normality in everyday living standards and welfare.

But the present high cannot last indefinitely. It is the longer-term impact of
sanctions on the modernization of the Russian economy that ultimately matters most. The loss of access to Western capital markets means that Russian
companies will be less able to invest in new infrastructure and technology.
Controls on advanced technology will hamper innovation. Building higher-
cost value chains to work around sanctions will drag down productivity.
The overall result over the long term will be a loss of competitiveness and
growth.

These long-term effects are not due to the sanctions alone. The sanctions
hit pre-existing vulnerabilities, notably the reliance on foreign technologies,
on foreign capital and credit, and on revenues from commodity exports.
These weaknesses have now been compounded by the side-effects of the
war, most strikingly the mass exit of skilled manpower, which has aggravated Russia's shortage of people and skills. The civilian sector has been
particularly hard-hit by the demand for skilled manpower from the military
industry.[130]

During the prosperous years of 2000–13, when oil-export revenues were
high, the government chose to devote them to modernizing key state-owned
industries, primarily in the commodities sector, but neglected the broader
task of upgrading the urban infrastructure inherited from Soviet times, such
as heating systems and local electrical grids. These choices now haunt the
population. During the long Russian winters, there have been widespread
power outages and failures of heat supply, the result of long neglect and
underinvestment.[131] According to the Russian Ministry of Construction,
between 45% and 60% of all utility systems need repair, and more than $100
billion will be needed to modernize communal networks over the coming
decade. Yet even as military spending balloons, investment in communal
infrastructure has stagnated. The epidemic of burst steam pipes, ruptured
sewage systems, and power outages will only grow worse over time.[132]

In short, one cannot consider the sanctions in isolation. Russia's pre-
existing weaknesses, magnified by the war, aggravate their effects, and the
longer the sanctions are sustained and the war goes on, the more their impact
will grow.

The Hardest Part: The Lifting of Sanctions

The single most difficult part about the Russian sanctions will be the ending of them. Until now the entire focus of the sanctions regime has been on their creation and enforcement; virtually no attention has been paid to their termination. Officials responsible for the sanctions regime are all but silent on what would happen if Russia actually fulfilled their demands. What if Moscow actually withdrew from Ukraine, or returned Crimea?

The acts of Congress that are the legal foundation for the US sanctions do address the question of termination, but only in exceedingly hypothetical language. For example, CAATSA, which underlies most of the present Russia sanctions, provides that:

> The President should call on the Government of the Russian Federation: (a) to withdraw all of its forces from the territories of Georgia, Ukraine, and Moldova; (b) to return control of the borders of those territories to their respective governments; and (c) to cease all efforts to undermine the popularly elected governments of those countries.[133]

But CAATSA is silent on how the US government should respond if the Russian government actually began taking steps to meet those demands. It provides only that if the president wishes to remove a specific sanction, he must submit a request to the appropriate congressional committee, which then holds hearings. But there is no suggestion that CAATSA itself might be repealed if Russia met the required conditions.

US sanctions laws are almost never repealed. Presidents do have the authority to rescind executive orders, but these pertain only to specific sanctions. As for the underlying laws themselves, as sanctions expert Richard Nephew observes, "Some sanctions regimes are old enough that they have become ossified and have become a permanent part of the policy landscape. Even once the process of sanctions removal has begun, many remain as 'residual sanctions.'"[134] In some cases, "fossilized" might be the better term. The ultimate example is the famous Jackson-Vanick Amendment to the Trade Law of 1974, which sanctioned the Soviet Union for restricting the emigration of Jewish citizens. It remained on the books for nearly forty years, and was not repealed until 2012, long after the Soviet Union had ceased to exist.

The EU sanctions regime has the opposite problem. The various categories of EU sanctions must be renewed periodically by the Council, at intervals varying between six and twelve months. Each renewal requires unanimity among the member states, which opens the way to protracted negotiations or even, potentially, the elimination of part of the structure. Thus, whereas the US regime is prone to ossification, the EU regime is subject to decay.

On the few occasions when sanctions have been eased or terminated, particularly in the case of multinational sanctions, the process has been anything but smooth. Simply getting the sanctioning parties together and reaching agreement is difficult enough. While sanctions may satisfy the immediate urge to "punish Russia," the removal of them is more tentative and ambiguous. Residual sanctions may remain in force, even as others are being lifted. The response from the business sector may be halting and tentative. Many actors may continue to self-sanction. The release of frozen assets may be delayed, despite explicit comfort letters provided to financial institutions. Termination will most likely turn out to be the hardest and most prolonged part of the sanctions regime.

How to Improve the Sanctions Regime

But for the present the key question is, How to improve the effectiveness of the sanctions regime, while limiting their costs? The first answer is to toughen enforcement. The single most powerful lever in the hands of the sanctioning powers is the deterrence effect on suppliers, shippers, and lenders. Self-sanctioning by companies is ultimately the sanctioners' best ally, but it requires constant reinforcement through investigations and actual prosecutions, singling out the occasional offender *pour encourager les autres.*

The second answer is to distinguish more clearly between what is important and what is not. There is an understandable tendency to go after the most visible targets, "because the light is better." But are the yachts and villas of the oligarchs, for example, really worth the time and effort that are given to them? By the same token, the sanctioners need to be mindful of the risk of inflicting collateral damage on bystanders. For example, blocking the use of the Mir debit card by Russians abroad simply traps many people who are trying to escape from the war.[135] Limits on entry visas into Europe raise the same question.

In contrast, the most effective sanctions are those that constrain Russia's financial flows and limit its ability to conduct financial operations. The

THE HURRICANE OF WESTERN SANCTIONS 139

remaining available conduits for payments to and from Russia should be closed wherever possible. Thus, Gazprombank should be sanctioned and its role in processing gas payments should be stopped. Raiffeisenbank should be summoned to complete its exit from Russia. De-SWIFTING the last Russian members should continue, and payments via Euroclear should be systematically blocked. Financial pressures on third-country targets should be increased; for example, Indian banks should be reminded of the potential costs to them of financing refineries that process Russian oil.

In the end, the effectiveness of sanctions is limited by broader trends in the global economy and in technology. A recent article in the Carnegie Endowment's online Russia series puts it nicely:

> The factors driving Russia's adaptation—the ubiquity of digital technology, globalized supply chains, and geopolitical fragmentation—are not mere loopholes to be closed. They are enduring, structural features of today's world. Russia's adaptation to export controls may be unexpected, but it is less reflective of any weakness of the sanctions themselves than of the new realities of the global technology marketplace and the implications of geopolitical fragmentation.[136]

Economic sanctions are high-cost instruments with limited impact. They are difficult to apply and enforce. Yet the West has little choice but to persevere with them, while improving them wherever possible, until the right conditions for their removal are met. As Mairead McGuinness, the outgoing EU commissioner for finance, says, "Sanctions are the only weapon we have." Other than war itself.

Chapter 5
Dancing in the Rain

The Russian Responses to Sanctions

Nabiullina's Dilemma

It quickly became a standing joke on social media in Moscow. Question: Do you want to know whether Russian interest rates are going to move up or down? Answer: Watch to see what kind of brooch the chair of the Russian Central Bank (RCB), Elvira Nabiullina, is wearing at her next press conference. A red bird meant one thing, a white pigeon another. On one occasion, Nabiullina wore a miniature Nevalyashka doll, a favorite Russian toy that pops back up when pushed over. Nabiullina, amused by the game, dismissed all guesses with a smile. But after the Russian invasion, the game stopped: today Nabiullina dresses mainly in black, and the brooches are gone.

Nabiullina's public comments on the outlook for the economy, in this and other venues, have been so consistently dark that they sparked rumors in late February 2022, which were quickly picked up by the Western media, that she had attempted to resign from the RCB, but that Putin had blocked her from doing so. Nabiullina vehemently denies the story, and there has been no independent confirmation of it. But Nabiullina and her team at the RCB are clearly deeply unhappy about the implications of the invasion and sanctions for the future of the Russia economy. In May 2023, Alexander Morozov, the head of the RCB's research department, spelled out on the bank's website what the term "structural transformation," frequently used by government spokesmen, actually means: "Technological regression in many sectors"—in a word, he concluded, it would bring "reverse industrialization."[1] Every sentence compounded the gloom, as Morozov went on to predict a lower share of imports and exports, an increasingly closed economy, and declining GDP.

Nabiullina's past career suggests why she and the other *finansisty* stay on the job. Throughout, she has served two causes. The first, beginning with her doctorate at Moscow State University under a prominent market reformer of the Gorbachev era, is the development of a modern market economy in Russia. But at the same time, Nabiullina has always been a devoted servant of the Russian state, having spent nearly a decade as minister of the economy before she moved to the RCB. One might call her the ultimate "market technocrat."

Nabiullina symbolizes the dilemma of the generation of economic reformers who have led financial, monetary, and fiscal policy under Putin. As a group, they are exceptionally able. Nabiullina herself, after guiding Russia through the "Great Recession" of 2008–9, was hailed as "Banker of the Year" by Western financial media and is highly regarded by fellow central bankers around the world.

But the invasion and sanctions present the Russian financial technocrats with acute moral and political dilemmas. The future welfare of 145 million Russians, they tell themselves, is at stake. This view is reportedly shared by the staff of the RCB as a whole: out of some 50,000 employees, only about 50 have left. The watchword is, "Serve the country, and stay out of politics." The conclusion is clear: Nabiullina is not about to resign.[2]

Yet as time goes on, her position, and that of the liberal *finansisty* as a group, is becoming increasingly difficult to sustain. So far, the liberals have kept the upper hand, thanks to support from Putin. But there is growing opposition to them by "patriotic" conservatives and state-owned businesses, and even some of the *finansisty* themselves, who favor a return to hands-on state planning and more determined countermeasures against sanctions. Later on in this chapter, we shall see why.

But first, we need to look at the overall picture of Russia's responses to the sanctions, and the politics surrounding them. That is the subject of this chapter.

Russia's Responses to Sanctions: Adaptation, Evasion, Retaliations, and Substitutions

Russia's responses to the Western sanctions have been of four sorts: macroeconomic and financial adaptations, evasion and workarounds, import substitutions, and retaliations. Each one is led by a different set of players in the Russian government and the business sector. The first and most important response, *adaptation* has been financial; this is largely the province of the financial and fiscal team, of which the two most important are the RCB and the Ministry of Finance. So far, it has been creative and successful. The second response, the zone of *evasion and workarounds* is mainly that of the economy at large, consisting of companies, traders, and individuals who have responded to sanctions by developing parallel imports and exports via both legal and illicit channels, chiefly through "friendly" third countries. These too have been largely successful.[3]

The third response, *import substitutions* are government initiatives, mainly led by the Ministry of Economic Development, aimed at replacing imported goods, services, and technologies, with Russian-made equivalents or Chinese-made alternatives. The Ministry of Finance and the RCB are attempting to substitute other currencies, such as the Chinese renminbi, for the dollar and the euro. The state's efforts to promote substitutions of Russian-made equivalents for Western technology, however, face many obstacles, and have little success to show for them to date, and the effort to replace the dollar and euro with the renminbi has been slow going.

The fourth and final response, *retaliations*, is expanding, as the Russian government responds to seizures of frozen Russian assets by the G7 allies.

The main proposition of this chapter is that the first two responses have enabled Russia to adapt to the Western sanctions in the short term, while the third and fourth responses have been less successful to date. In particular, the Russian government has failed to deter the G7 from seizing a portion of the frozen sovereign assets of the RCB.

Over time, as the West expands and tightens its sanctions, the Russians will continue to refine their responses. The dance of "sanction and respond" will undoubtedly play on so long as the sanctions remain.

Responses to Financial Sanctions: The RCB Goes to Work

Within days after Russia invaded Ukraine, Russia was hit by an unprecedented storm of economic sanctions from the West, discussed in the last chapter. At the center of the storm was a small team of Russian officials, led by the RCB and its chief Elvira Nabiullina, the minister of finance Anton Siluanov, and the heads of the main state-owned banks, notably German Gref, the chairman of Sberbank, Russia's largest bank. That team is still in place today.

Most of the Russian monetary and fiscal team consists of alumni and protégés of the financial advisors Putin brought with him from Saint

Petersburg in the early 2000s, who have been in charge of Russian financial and monetary policy throughout Putin's rule. The current finance minister, Anton Siluanov, came up through the finance ministry, as did Prime Minister Mikhail Mushustin, who is an expert on taxes.

Even before the invasion, *the finansisty* had been alarmed by the signs of an escalation of the war in Ukraine and the prospect of expanded Western sanctions. In January 2022, one month before the invasion began, they met with Putin at his private residence at Novo-Ogarevo. German Gref, one of the early members of the Saint Petersburg team, led off with a joint position paper, based on elaborate stress tests, warning of the potentially disastrous consequences for the economy if the conflict with Ukraine were to escalate further. According to eyewitnesses, Putin refused to listen. But he kept his plans to himself. Up to the last minute, the *finansisty* had no inkling that war was about to begin. Like the rest of Russia, they learned about it from watching state television.[4]

For the first few weeks after February 2022, as Russia came under the Western sanctions, the entire country panicked. The ruble lost half of its value overnight, plunging from 70 to the dollar to over 140. Inflation immediately jumped to 18%. Consumers went into shock.[5] Anyone who could get their hands on foreign exchange rushed to get it out of the country or hide it under their mattresses. According to Andrei Kostin, chairman of VTB, Russia's second-largest bank, in the first two weeks after the invasion, depositors pulled $26 billion out of VTB alone—the other Russian banks experienced much the same.[6] The Moscow stock market cratered. Storefronts shuttered. The economy seemed about to slam to a halt.

But after the initial shock, the government's team of *finansisty* in the RCB and the Ministry of Finance responded quickly, in three main directions:

- First, "circle the wagons," to deal with the immediate economic repercussions of the sanctions, chiefly by imposing capital controls to shut off the mass exodus of foreign capital and by raising interest rates to rescue the falling ruble and bring down inflation.
- Second, "head off the worst," through measures to protect current production, by lowering taxes on businesses and allowing parallel "gray" imports to replace sanctioned goods (especially spare parts and components), while closing an eye to the illegal use of foreign brands and patents.

- Third, "make life easier for industry," by declaring a moratorium on bankruptcies, decriminalizing debts, increasing state spending on key sectors (notably the arms industry) and relaxing restrictions on imports of foreign technology (at least where these were still possible).

Much of this list of measures came straight out of textbook macroeconomic doctrine, such as the use of interest rates to "target" inflation and allowing the currency to "float," subject only to supply and demand. The ghost of John Maynard Keynes hovered over the corridors of the Ministry of Finance, as it increased emergency spending to stimulate the faltering economy. Putin's financial team had first put this menu to work in responding to the Crimean sanctions after 2014.[7] By now, they were old hands at sanctions management.

By the beginning of May, these emergency measures had succeeded in reversing the initial free fall. In response to higher interest rates, the ruble quickly rallied. The government further bolstered it by blocking citizens and companies from using rubles internally to buy or export foreign exchange. The public mood in Russia improved markedly. By late spring, according to the Levada Center, Russian consumers had recovered from the initial shock of the sanctions and had already begun to find ways of adapting to them in their everyday lives.[8] By the time of the annual International Economic Forum in June 2022, the government proclaimed that the situation was under control.

Thus, in responding to the immediate emergency the Russian financial team demonstrated a high degree of professional competence and tactical skill—just as they had in responding to previous financial crises. They kept the boat from sinking. But even as they baled, they sounded like a crew of Cassandras, warning of doom. Aleksandr Morozov, RCB chief of research and forecasting, wrote that the sanctions would make Russia increasingly closed off from the rest of the world.[9] German Gref of Sberbank predicted that GDP would fall by 7% in 2022 and 10% in 2023, relative to 2021, and that it would take until the end of the decade before GDP recovered to the 2021 level. Compounding the gloom, Nabiullina lamented that the impact of the Russia sanctions would last "for a long time, if not forever."[10]

Indeed, the dance had only begun. Thanks to high oil and gas prices, Russian export revenues ballooned throughout 2022.[11] As foreign exchange flooded in and the balance of trade soared to record levels, the ruble rose with it. But now Russia faced the opposite problem—a surfeit of foreign exchange that it could not spend, because of sanctions, and a ruble that was too high, making its exports less competitive and endangering the Russian budget.[12] The RCB was forced to reverse course by lowering interest rates again and relaxing foreign-exchange controls. Indeed, it urged citizens to draw down their dollars and euros and take them abroad. And so it went, throughout the summer months and into the fall of 2022, as Russia's economic team danced from one foot to the other in response to shifting events and fluctuating energy prices, oscillating between inflation and recession. The devil's dance indeed.

In the spring of 2023, yet another phase began. Energy prices began to decline, taking Russia's hydrocarbon revenues down with them. The West's oil embargo cut the profit margins on Russian oil exports, as the Russians were forced to ship oil over longer distances and pay more for shipping and insurance (see below). Russian imports began to recover. All of this put downward pressure on the ruble, which went from a high of 70 to the dollar in May to over 100 by August, igniting inflation. Once again, the RCB was forced to dance, this time by sharply raising interest rates.

But by this time Nabiullina and her team were no longer dancing alone. An increasingly restive coalition of industrial exporters and opposition deputies demanded that the Ministry of Finance intervene directly in the exchange rate to raise the ruble, while Russian nationalists have mounted increasingly virulent attacks on the RCB and its chair, Nabiullina. In November 2023, a leading opposition economist, Sergei Glaz'ev, blamed the RCB's management for $1 trillion in capital flight, "Only weak-minded people and those aligned with foreign-exchange speculators can believe that you can target inflation with a floating ruble."[13] A prominent nationalist TV commentator, Vladimir Solov'ev, echoed him, "The whole world is laughing at us now."

The Kremlin has attempted to take the middle ground. A rising star on Putin's team, Maksim Oreshkin, has edged closer to a more interventionist policy.[14] Whereas earlier he aligned with the liberals, Oreshkin has switched sides. Personable and articulate, he appears to enjoy Putin's favor, and he now argues for a more interventionist stance in financial policy and a more aggressive industrial policy, based on state subsidies and credits, financed by government debt. In August 2023, when the ruble weakened to above 100 to the dollar, Oreshkin, in a public debate with Nabiullina, blamed the RCB's "excessively soft" policy, which was encouraging a mass exit of foreign currency out of the country. Oreshkin said, "the country needs a high ruble."[15] Putin, increasingly concerned by inflation as the March 2024 presidential election approached, watched this debate nervously, drumming his fingers.

The Politics of the Dancing Ruble

Throughout these ad hoc adjustments—which will no doubt continue in the same fashion in the future as the underlying causes gyrate unpredictably— the RCB, as before, has relied primarily on two tools, interest rates and occasional restrictions on foreign-exchange movements, while letting the economy respond accordingly. Nabiullina and the RCB have stuck firmly to their policy of non-intervention.[16] For Nabiullina, this is a deeply held belief. As early as June 2022, at the annual meeting of the influential Russian Union of Industrial Producers (RSPP), Nabiullina spoke out against inter- vening in currency markets to drive down the ruble "artificially," by tying it to the value of other foreign currencies. That would result, she argued, in binding Russia to the monetary policies of other powers. She has restated her position on many public occasions since. "A floating-rate currency is a great benefit," she said in July 2023, "because it enables us to absorb exter- nal shocks and changes."[17] She vowed that the RCB would continue to stand guard over the ruble, using its control over interest rates to prevent excessive fluctuations.

But pressure on Nabiullina continues to mount. A perennially difficult issue is capital controls. As the ruble has weakened, Russians have rushed to protect their assets by converting them into foreign currency and mov- ing them out of the country. The government's financial players have been divided over how to respond. Finance Minister Anton Siluanov has joined the conservative side by calling for tougher restrictions, while Nabiullina has vigorously opposed them, arguing that capital controls will only hinder for- eign trade and make Russia more isolated from the global economy. "We must not create difficulties for our economic actors," she said, "who have managed, despite great difficulty, in finding ways of settling foreign-trade accounts." She remains adamant that Russia's best weapon is the manage- ment of interest rates. "Mandatory repatriation and sale of foreign currency will not stabilize the ruble."[18] Nabiullina so far continues to enjoy Putin's support, but hers appears to be an increasingly lonely voice, as even some fellow *finansisty* have begun to criticize her for being "too liberal" (meaning, clearly, too market-oriented).[19] Over time, as Russia increasingly moves to a wartime footing, pressures are growing for compulsory repatriation of export earnings and a partial restoration of a state foreign-trade monopoly, accompanied by tighter controls. The interventionists look increasingly likely to win the battle for Putin's ear.

The Dance over the RCB's Frozen Reserves

The Russian government has been less successful in loosening the West's vise around Russian funds frozen in the West. These are of two sorts: the blocked non-sovereign assets of individuals and companies and the government's sovereign funds, chiefly those of the RCB.

According to the RCB, the blocked non-sovereign Russian assets of Russian companies and some 5 million individuals total over 5.7 trillion rubles, or about $70 billion. The Russian government has been trying to persuade the European Commission to agree to swap them against blocked Western assets held in restricted, "C-type," accounts.[20] So far, the Commission has turned a deaf ear to the idea.

Russia's frozen sovereign assets are far larger, and the battle over them is correspondingly more intense. Russia's purchases of euros and euro-denominated securities were mostly kept in Europe with two securities depositories, Euroclear in Belgium and ClearStream in Luxembourg.[21] By the time of the invasion, these amounted to nearly half of Russia's foreign-exchange reserves. In retrospect, this was a major miscalculation. Before the invasion, the EU had been a more than willing partner in helping Russia to move from the dollar to the euro. The EU's decision to join the US financial sanctions seems to have taken Moscow by surprise.

An increasingly controversial question is what to do with these assets. The United States urged seizing the entire amount, to devote it to the reconstruction of Ukraine.[22] The EU, and Germany in particular, opposed a total confiscation, fearing creating a legal precedent, but it agreed to a more limited measure, the seizure of the profits from them. In 2023, Euroclear earned €4.4 billion in interest, coupon payments, and postponed redemptions. These profits will continue to accrue to Euroclear and the other holders of frozen sovereign reserves, but starting in 2025 the profits will be made available as backing for a new Extraordinary Revenue Acceleration Fund which will administer a system of loans to Ukraine to fund reconstruction and to buy weapons for Ukraine. The total amount of the loans, backed by the frozen profits, could be as much as $50 billion.[23] At this writing, however, the United States and the EU are still struggling over a series of legal issues, and the plan's fate is unclear.

The Russian government, not surprisingly, has adamantly opposed all of these variants, and has threatened to retaliate by seizing Western assets in Russia.[24]

Fox-Trotting around SWIFT

The dance over the financial sanctions continues. The Russian government has been campaigning to restore membership in SWIFT to key banks, but so far without success. Its top candidate for reinstatement has been the Russian Agricultural Bank (Rosselkhozbank), which handles settlements for Russian agricultural exports. The fact that Rosselkhozbank has been de-SWIFTed means that it has become much more difficult for Russia to get paid in dollars and euros for its agricultural exports. Yet so far the Western powers have resisted re-SWIFTing the Agricultural Bank—in contrast to their hands-off policy on Gazprombank, which has been sanctioned by the US but not by the EU. The reason for the difference is that Gazprombank is the only remaining large Russian bank able to process energy transactions between Russia and the West—in other words, the West *needs* Gazprombank—whereas in the case of the Rosselkhozbank the West perceives it as a bargaining chip to guarantee safe passage for Ukrainian agricultural exports. So far negotiations are at an impasse, and Rosselkhozbank remains sanctioned.

Failing to regain access to SWIFT, the sanctioned Russian banks have resorted to second-best solutions, such as using smaller, unsanctioned domestic banks to conduct their international operations. However, this is hardly more than a Band-Aid, since these banks lack foreign experience and connections.[25] The Russian government is promoting an all-Russian alternative, called the System for Transfer of Financial Messages (SPFS), as a substitute for SWIFT. But it is used mainly for domestic transactions, plus some settlements with so-called friendly powers.

In short, the Russians' responses to the financial sanctions have so far been confined mainly to short-run macroeconomic adjustments, while more proactive measures to deal with blocked assets and sanctioned banks have fallen short. So far, these short-term adjustments have succeeded in restoring balance. But whether they will continue to do so will depend above all on energy prices and the effectiveness of the Russian responses to the oil sanctions, since oil revenues are now the main remaining source of capital.[26] We return to that subject now, to expand on the discussion of the oil sanctions in Chapter 4.

Dancing on the Energy Front: Russian Responses to the Oil Embargo and the Price Cap

The second most important set of Russian responses to sanctions is on the energy front. The entire Russian economy, society, and political system depend heavily on commodity exports, and especially oil and, to a lesser extent natural gas. In 2019, the last "normal" year before the COVID-19 pandemic and the invasion, Russia earned $325 billion from energy exports, three-quarters of which was from oil alone.[27] Oil and gas exports together provided 39% of the Russian federal budget.[28] While the West's financial sanctions aim to squeeze the Russian economy as a whole by shutting off its access to global financial markets, the energy sanctions try to reduce the flow of revenues to the Russian state.[29] Thus, the energy sanctions and the financial sanctions work in tandem.

The West's oil sanctions, as we saw in the last chapter, take two main forms: the EU's oil embargo and the G7's oil-price cap. These combine two objectives: to cut Russia's energy-export revenues, while simultaneously limiting disruptions to the world economy from energy supply shortages and higher prices. The Russians are the opposite partners in the dance. Their responses have consisted of three main strategies. The first has been to offset the EU's oil embargo by finding new buyers outside Europe, chiefly India, and using third-country export hubs, particularly the United Arab Emirates (UAE). The second has been to defeat the G7/EU price cap by acquiring a fleet of so-called ghost tankers, as well as by fraudulent reporting of sale prices. The third strategy has been to join forces with OPEC+, and especially the Saudis, to restrict global oil production and thus to push up oil prices, keeping them above the price cap. At the same time, however, the Russians have refrained from "weaponizing" oil through large-scale cuts. In the next three sections, we look at each of these Russian responses.

Ghosts and Frauds

As we saw in the last chapter, one of Russia's main responses to the West's oil embargo and price cap has been to acquire a large fleet of second-hand tankers. The main challenge has been to find enough of them to serve the longer routes from Russia to Asia, now that European destinations are largely closed. The export route from Russia's Baltic ports to India and China runs either through the Suez Canal or around Africa, which adds to the transportation distance and the time required for a round trip. This in turn increases the number of tankers the Russians need. But there are too few of them available on the second-hand market to enable Russia to meet its oil export needs quickly at any reasonable cost, and Russia's acquisition program has caused the prices of second-hand tankers to soar. Craig Kennedy (introduced in the last chapter) estimates that this strategy could end up costing over $20 billion and would require several more years to carry out,[30] calling into question its cost-effectiveness. There are signs that Russian policymakers have performed the same calculation: after peaking in early 2023, Russia's purchases of shadow tankers have fallen off sharply, leaving its tanker capacity well below its current export needs.[31]

The other problem with the shadow tanker strategy, as we saw in the last chapter, is insurance. The average age of the shadow tankers bought by the Russians is eighteen years—too old to be recertified by international insurers. The Russians have therefore turned to untested alternative providers, which poses the risk of uncovered environmental liabilities. These in turn could cause Russian shadow tankers to be denied access to ports or passage through territorial waters such as the Danish Straits.

Lacking sufficient tanker capacity of their own, the Russians still rely on mainstream shippers, which leads to the second strategy, submitting fraudulent reports to the shippers on the price at which a cargo was sold, by forging attestation papers to show that it was priced below the cap. At first, such fraudulent reports were only used for cargoes shipped out of the eastern port of Kozmino, which receives oil through the ESPO pipeline from West Siberia. Because of its high quality, it has been selling at more than $70 a barrel, well above the $60 price cap.[32]

As noted in the last chapter, the price cap remained inactive so long as oil prices elsewhere were below $60 a barrel. But by early 2024 oil prices had risen to close to $80, and the price cap came into play, particularly on exports from Russia's Baltic ports. Russian sellers have been evading it, however, by claiming that they are indeed selling oil below the $60 price cap, but that the difference between $60 and the reported sell price is due to the increased costs of "services," which include insurance—even though much of the revenue from those services actually accrues to the Russian producers and traders. This form of fraud has become widespread, even for oil carried by mainstream carriers.

To deter mainstream tanker operators from carrying oil priced above the cap, the sanctioning powers have toughened enforcement, to ensure that the mainstream fleet carries only compliant cargoes. To achieve this, one measure under discussion is to develop a "white-list" of approved traders, who would certify that a shipper's cargoes have been sold under the price cap. Shippers in violation would lose their insurance and loans, in effect, they would be expelled from the IG system.[33] In parallel, enforcement against shadow tankers has been tightened, notably by banning uninsured tankers from the territorial waters of transit countries.

An Unexpected Hole in the Russian Strategy

As the Western powers pondered the challenges of enforcing the oil sanctions, they discovered an unexpected hole in the Russian strategy. Tankers typically fly "flags of convenience," that is, they are registered in countries that offer attractive terms and loose oversight. But flagging services, it turns out, are mostly outsourced to US companies—and this provides a lever that the US sanctioners can use to ban the tankers involved. Beginning in October 2023, Treasury's OFAC began sanctioning shippers whose tankers were flagged in countries that used US intermediaries. Between October 2023 and February 2024, OFAC sanctioned fifty tankers, fourteen of which belonged to the Russian shipping company Sovcomflot.[34] In parallel, OFAC also designated a number of "shadow traders," based in Hong Kong and the UAE. In response, about half of the designated tankers immediately stopped operating,[35] and a number of mainstream shippers, notably Greek tanker owners, abruptly withdrew from the Russian oil trade.[36]

As a result, by early 2024 Russian oil was once again trading at a discount, while shipping costs had increased, cutting into Russia's net oil profits. In January, Aleksandr Novak, the Russian deputy prime minister in charge of the economy and energy policy, conceded that "The current spike [in the discount] is associated with the sanctions package that came out at the end of last year," although he put a brave face on it by predicting that the supply chain would improve and the discount would soon narrow again.[37] But the Russians appear to face an unpalatable choice: either to cut back on their oil exports (to fit the size of their shadow fleet), or to sell at lower prices (to meet the price cap and thus use mainstream tankers). Both courses would threaten their oil-export revenues.

These challenges have put the spotlight on a key figure, Aleksandr Novak, until recently minister for energy and environment and now the deputy prime minister for the economy, who is in charge of managing the Russian responses to the oil sanctions.

Aleksandr Novak, Mastermind of Oil Sanctions

Aleksandr Novak was an unusual choice for energy minister when Putin first appointed him in 2012, shortly after Putin's return to the presidency. He did not come from Putin's Saint Petersburg crowd, but from the mining town of Noril'sk in the remote Siberian province of Krasnoyarsk, where his family moved from Ukraine when he was a child. He had no background in energy; his degree was in metallurgy and economics, earned at the local finance institute in Noril'sk, which he attended at night while working by day on the shop floor of the Noril'sk Nickel combine. He had never been abroad and spoke no English or other foreign languages.

But Novak is clearly a man of unusual abilities. By age twenty-nine, he was vice-president of Noril'sk Nickel; in his early thirties he was mayor of the town of Noril'sk; and by age thirty-six he was deputy governor of Krasnoyarsk. The following year, in 2008, he was promoted to Moscow as deputy minister of finance, where he served under Putin's long-time finance minister Aleksey Kudrin and became acquainted with the present prime minister, Mikhail Mushustin, who also came out of the Finance Ministry. (Thus, one might call Novak an honorary *finansist*.) Novak was named energy minister four years later, and in 2020, Putin made him deputy prime minister, in overall charge of energy and environment. It has been a lightning rise from modest origins.[38]

At 6 feet 3 inches, Novak cuts an imposing figure (among other achievements, he played center on his high-school basketball team). He is an effective public speaker, and as energy minister, he earned a reputation as a skilled manager and diplomat. In energy policy he occupied a middle ground: On the one hand, he echoed Russia's traditional defense of its hydrocarbon resources and exports, especially natural gas and LNG, but also coal. Yet he has also paid attention to the emerging problem of climate change, and he was one of the first senior Russians to accept the "peak oil demand" narrative. He supports "green" energy technologies such as hydrogen and renewables, and as deputy prime minister he has intervened to push back proposals to cut subsidies for renewables.[39]

But it is the 2022 invasion that has put Novak in the limelight, as the main coordinator of Russia's responses to the oil sanctions. Since 2015 he had been lead negotiator in talks with Saudi Arabia (described below), and he has been the main advocate of limiting oil production within the framework of the alliance with OPEC+, a position that Putin supported over the objections of Igor Sechin, the head of Rosneft.

Novak is seconded by a team of energy experts, notably his deputy Pavel Sorokin, whose experience includes Western training as a consultant for Morgan Stanley. Although his early background was in equity research, Sorokin during his decade in the energy ministry has become responsible for a wide range of energy issues as Novak's key aide. In particular, he was Novak's main "sherpa" in the negotiations with the Saudis, with whom he is said to have excellent relations. As Novak does not speak English, Sorokin has acted as Novak's personal interpreter, and has been present at all the negotiations.[40] By all accounts, they are an effective team.

The Russian-Saudi Axis

A major feature of the Russian response to the oil sanctions has been the consolidation of Russia's partnership with Saudi Arabia within the framework of OPEC+, the expanded cartel that now counts twenty-three members, including Russia. All the members share an interest in keeping oil prices stable, and accordingly since 2016 they have collaborated in making periodic adjustments in production, while strengthening OPEC's capacity to monitor market trends and enforce its decisions. In 2019 they signed a Charter of Cooperation to formalize the new alliance. Since then they have repeatedly raised or cut production, as market conditions dictate. In 2023, Russia and Saudi Arabia between them cut 2 million barrels a day in production.[41]

The cuts initially helped to restore oil prices after the pandemic and was a welcome boost to both countries' revenues. It has been, on the whole, a successful alliance.[42]

That said, it is not a comfortable or stable one. Russia's acquisition of a large tanker fleet and its rerouting of crude flows to India and China have driven up the costs of transportation and services for all exporters, and this has cut into the margins of the other OPEC+ members. In addition, since the Russian government badly needs oil revenues to help balance its war budget, it will have a growing incentive to avoid further production cuts, leaving the Saudis with the dilemma of whether to soldier on alone—or to retaliate by boosting production to preserve their own revenues.[43] Saudi Arabia has shouldered much of the burden of the production cuts to date, but the Saudis will not be willing to play the role of de facto swing producer indefinitely. Recent production cuts have been less effective at keeping oil prices high, chiefly because of the rise of new suppliers from outside OPEC+, as well as increased production from Russia.[44] A more fundamental long-term problem is that despite the expansion of OPEC's membership, its share of global oil production is declining, and its overall leverage is tending to weaken. As a result, there are growing strains within the OPEC+ group, which could threaten the Russia–Saudi alliance.[45]

The Rising UAE Connection

The oil sanctions, and the Russian responses to them, are reshaping global oil markets and flows.[46] The impact has been particularly marked in the world of traders and global oil trading. The traditional center of trading for Russian oil was Geneva. But since the invasion, and the imposition of sanctions by Switzerland, most of the established Russian traders have moved to Dubai. The UAE has not joined the Russia sanctions, and consequently Russian oil can move freely in and out of the UAE, particularly the refined-products port of Fujairah, near Dubai, and many oil traders have moved there.

One of the most prominent of these oil traders is a veteran operator named Murtaza Lakhani, whose multiple companies have traded oil for Russia's Rosneft for over a decade. Born in Pakistan but raised in the UK and Canada, Lakhani earned his spurs with Glencore, a leading global trading company. As one of Rosneft's top allies, Lakhani is reportedly close to Rosneft's chairman Igor Sechin, who celebrated New Year's Eve aboard Lakhani's yacht in Dubai. Lakhani is said to have been one of the chief architects of Russia's shift in export destinations from Europe to India.[47] He is not under sanctions, although the US Department of Justice has launched an investigation of his relationship with Sechin.[48]

But Lakhani is far from alone. Over 104 buyers of Russian oil are now established in Dubai, including eight out of the top twenty traders, such as Litasco, LUKoil's trading arm. Many of these are previously unknown players, operating specifically to handle Russian oil, notably from Rosneft, through discrete front-owners who are not nominally Russian nationals, but who are presumably connected to them. This large community of traders handled nearly one-third of all Russian oil exports in 2023, most of which never actually lands in the UAE, but goes directly from Russian ports to Asia, Africa, and South America—everywhere, indeed, except Europe and North America.

There is one major exception, however. Russian refined products imported and stored in Fujairah are considered Emirati oil and are re-exported to Europe. This has become one of the main loopholes in the EU's oil embargo. In 2023 such transit volumes of Russian refined products accounted for about one-fourth of all imports passing through Fujairah, fluctuating around 100 thousand barrels per day.[49]

The result has been an influx of wealth into Dubai and the UAE, mainly benefiting the banks that process payments for oil trades. The booming trading business has, in turn, touched off a mass in-migration of oil specialists of all kinds, including traders, bankers, and lawyers, who benefit from Dubai's cosmopolitan atmosphere, absence of personal income taxes, and what the *Financial Times* delicately calls "light-touch regulation." As a result, Dubai has become the world oil-trading capital, displacing the position traditionally held by Geneva.

At least as important as the actual oil flows and tanker traffic are the financial flows. To buy tankers, one needs money; and to move money, one needs channels that are not sanctioned. The UAE is a logical hub for both. Until recently, the most likely source of finance for buying tankers was the export profits of the Russian oil companies, operating through their trading arms. These are increasingly located in Dubai, the financial capital of the UAE. This money probably never returned to Russia.

This leakage attracted the scrutiny of the Russian Ministry of Finance, and particularly that of the veteran deputy minister Aleksey Sazanov, who keeps watch over the tax revenues from the oil companies. As suspicion grew inside the Ministry of Finance that the Russian oil companies were keeping a portion of their export revenues offshore, the government responded by changing the basis by which the export price was calculated, thus increasing the tax take from oil.

However, this has left the oil companies with smaller offshore revenues with which to finance (among other good causes) the continued purchase of oil tankers. The government has turned to VTB, one of the largest state-owned banks, for help in financing such acquisitions.

The ultimate owners of the shadow tankers are mostly Russian, but they operate through brokers and discrete front companies, many of which are also conveniently located in the UAE. The UAE does not impose sanctions on Russian banks, which can therefore maintain offices and correspondent accounts in Dubai. Any payments to brokers and operators can be settled through them as well. In short, the UAE has become a full-service hub for the purchase and operation of Russia's shadow tanker fleet.

The major sanctioning powers have not been inattentive, and there have been several visits to Dubai by high-level delegations from Washington and Brussels, seeking to discourage the UAE oil-trade conduit. But here too the sanctioners have kept to a light touch, not wishing to disrupt what has become a major new artery of global oil flows, and desiring to maintain good relations with an increasingly important player in Middle Eastern geopolitics. At this moment the Russian oil trade through the UAE is still growing.

Russian Responses in Non-Energy Trade

The last set of Russian responses discussed in this chapter is non-energy trade. This category poses two distinct sets of challenges. The first concerns intellectual property in civilian trade. The second concerns technology, particularly so-called dual-use technologies with military applications.

We begin with intellectual property. As the Russian economy opened to the West, it became part of the vast web of international agreements governing trademarks, licensing, royalties, and taxation. In August 2012, after nineteen years as an applicant, Russia joined the World Trade Organization, and promised to abide by its elaborate rules, including those concerning intellectual property. Initially, it largely did so,[50] but since the invasion Russia, on Putin's orders, has increasingly ignored the rules governing intellectual property, through so-called parallel imports and gray imports.

Parallel Imports and Gray Imports

In one of the earliest responses to the Western sanctions, in March 2022, Putin signed a law authorizing the import of Western brands that had either been banned or had left the Russian market voluntarily.[51] This law on so-called parallel imports allowed sanctioned products to be imported and sold in Russia without the permission of the brand or patent owner. It thus amounted to a suspension of intellectual property rights.[52] A Russian importer would pay import duty to the government, but no royalty to the foreign brand owner. Since such goods were now considered legal on the Russian market, however, many shadow middlemen leapt to seize the opportunity to import them without bothering to declare them—or to pay the import duty either. These are known as gray imports.

Both categories quickly ballooned. By May 2022, when the list of goods authorized for parallel imports was published, it covered some ninety products, ranging from matches and watches to metals and nuclear reactors, as well as cosmetics and clothing. It also included key manufacturers of digital products, such as Intel.[53] It was estimated that the list accounted for some $100–$120 billion a year, or roughly half of Russia's total imports.[54]

The main avenue through which Western sanctioned and self-sanctioned goods continue to flow to Russia is through third countries that do not participate in the sanctions regime. Turkey plays a major role. Even though it is a member of NATO, Turkey under prime minister Erdoğan has taken a neutral position between Russia and the EU in trade matters and continues to provide a large part of Russia's parallel-import network, despite diplomatic efforts on the part of the sanctioning powers to dissuade it. This has led to a thriving community of middlemen based in Istanbul, who handle the re-export of Western goods, mainly coming from Europe and going to Russia either directly or indirectly via FSU countries such as Georgia or Armenia.

One example of the Turkish connection is Russian logistics company Novelco, which is based in Moscow but has a subsidiary in Turkey called Smart Trading. It is the creation of a Russian entrepreneur, Grigory Grigorev, a life-long specialist in cargo transportation. Grigorev, unlike most people in this business, is not shy about what he does. He has organized seminars in Moscow to publicize the best ways to take advantage of opportunities in parallel trade, and he is active on LinkedIn, promoting his events and his company's services.[55] Since one of his specialties is importing semiconductors, in April 2023 both Grigorev and Novelco were placed on the US list of banned entities by the State Department and Treasury's OFAC.[56] But from their base in Istanbul they continue to prosper.

The re-export business through Turkey is so large and diverse that it is practically hopeless to go after specific items, especially since it is always possible to conceal the ultimate destination by shipping through additional third countries. After high-level visits from US and EU officials in early 2023 (described in the preceding chapter), the Turkish government agreed to cooperate by enlisting the Turkish customs to patrol the flow.[57] But the traffic is far too great, and the Turkish customs too understaffed, to have had much effect. Going after the middlemen instead may be a more promising avenue, as well as persuading Turkish banks not to accept the Russian MIR card in payment, as the US has attempted to do.[58] But these countermeasures are unlikely to work unless they are accompanied by actual prosecutions, which so far neither the sanctioning powers nor the Turkish authorities have been willing to resort to (especially since, in the case of Turkey, the Turks import significant amounts of Russian natural gas, on which the economy depends).

Turkey is increasingly caught in the middle of the sanctions war between Russia and the West. As the Ukrainian conflict entered its third year, the Western powers increased pressure on Turkish banks and middlemen to cooperate. In response to an executive order in December 2023, issued by the Biden Administration to toughen secondary sanctions, many Turkish banks immediately cut ties with Russian banks, closing Russian correspondent accounts and stopping settlements.[59] Some even sent back to Russia payments that had already been received, on the grounds that they were for "prohibited goods." As a Russian broker complained, "Right now not a single payment from Russia is being accepted—in lira, in rubles, no matter." Several Russian companies found their Turkish accounts closed, and Russian individuals reported difficulties obtaining bank cards. Amid loud complaints from Moscow, in February 2024 Putin visited Ankara to seek to reverse the cuts, but he was only partly successful.[60]

Parallel imports also include substitute items produced by Chinese companies (although often these are the same products, long produced in China for sale under Western brands). These too have grown rapidly. But they have caused some uneasiness among Russian policymakers, lest the Chinese imports, like cuckoos, take over the Russian nest. "Let's not go overboard with parallel imports," warned Denis Manturov, the then-minister of industry and trade in charge of import regulation, shortly after the publication of the parallel-import decree, "Don't forget that our biggest competitors are in Asia."[61] Instead, Manturov advocated a longer-range policy, allowing Russian manufacturers to keep importing Western brands temporarily, while pushing to replace them with Russian-made items. Manturov's stance reflects the view of many Russian businessmen, who complain that parallel imports from China are inadequate substitutes for Western imports.[62]

Nevertheless, the Western sanctions are not without effect. Parallel and gray imports are inefficient methods, compared to conventional direct imports. They require longer routes, they pose problems of reliability and quality control, and they involve roundabout payment schemes. In short, they do impose costs on Russia. The question, as with all sanctions, is whether the gains outweigh the cost for the sanctioners, especially in terms of lost goodwill with the West's trading partners.

As far as the Western powers are concerned, however, the more immediate issue is the flow of high-technology goods with potential military applications. We turn to those now.

Dual-Use Technologies

Dual-use technologies are those that can be used in both military and civilian applications. They are not necessarily high-tech; for example, two dual-use products targeted by Western sanctions are cotton cellulose and nitrocellulose, which are used to produce gunpowder and rocket propellants. But the single most important category is electronics. One of the most eye-opening results of the Ukrainian war has been the revelation of the role of foreign electronics in Russian weaponry in the field. Several Western think tanks, notably the UK's Royal United Services Institute (RUSI), working together with Reuters and the Ukrainian military, have examined thousands of captured or downed Russian weapons.[63] The findings are startling: every single one contains microelectronic components from leading Western and Asian firms, many of them supplied since the imposition of the first round of sanctions following Russia's occupation of Crimea in 2014. The study provided dramatic evidence of the continuing Russian dependence on foreign microelectronics. Since then, several subsequent investigations have shown that this has not changed since the 2022 invasion. Russia continues to have wide access to imported electronics with military applications, especially in the area of semiconductors.[64] This has led to charges that the sanctions on industrial imports, particularly electronics, have failed.[65]

In reality, the picture is more complicated. Semiconductors and computer components are a catch-all category that covers many different sectors. "Chips" range from those produced by dozens of manufacturers worldwide and used in millions of smart phones, to the most advanced "two-nanometer" circuits produced by only one fabrication unit in Taiwan. But what they all have in common is that almost none are mass-produced in Russia. On the eve of the invasion, Russia depended on imports and had only begun forming partnerships with high-end foreign producers. But as discussed in Chapter 4 on sanctions, every category of dual-use electronics, whether military-related or civilian, has been banned under the Western sanctions, and all of the previous partnerships have been dissolved or suspended.

But why is the Russian microelectronics industry, and semiconductors in particular, so dependent on Western suppliers? To understand this, we need to look briefly at the past.

A Long History of Backwardness, Followed by a Brief Heyday

The Russian microelectronics industry is minuscule compared to those of Europe and Asia, and its capabilities have long lagged far behind those of the world leaders. The reasons for this go back to the Soviet period. The nascent Soviet IT industry was largely closed to the outside world. When the first transistors and integrated microcircuits sparked the computer revolution in the West from the 1960s through the 1980s, the Soviet Union remained on the sidelines. While the Soviets had world-class skills in physics, the bureaucrats who ran its military-industrial system restricted their IT experts to copying Western designs and products, which were acquired—despite Western export controls—by a worldwide network of spies (and the occasional turncoat). Thus, dependence on foreign technology was etched into the Soviet microelectronics industry from the start.[66]

But for a crucial quarter-century after the break-up of the Soviet Union, Russia benefited from the era of good feelings that followed the end of the Cold War. The United States relaxed its export controls, applying them only to technologies with direct military uses. This reflected the optimism of the age: trade and innovation would generate growth and wealth, which would trump geopolitics. This view was widely applied to microelectronics as well.

Meanwhile, however, another fundamental development, outside Russia, was transforming the prevailing business models and trade patterns of the microelectronics industry. This was the so-called fabless revolution. As historian Chris Miller recounts,[67] until the early 1990s most producers of semiconductors and processors combined both design and fabrication. But then a new player in Taiwan, TSMC, pioneered a model under which it would no longer design its own chips; instead, it would manufacture other companies' designs under contract. (Such companies are called fabs, while companies that only design chips are called fabless.) This model turned chip designers into TSMC's loyal customers and, thanks to this network, TSMC has built a commanding position in chip-making. TSMC now holds a virtual global monopoly, producing over 90% of the advanced chips in the world.

For Russia's chip companies, the fab revolution represented a golden opportunity. By signing manufacturing contracts with TSMC, the Russian companies could bypass their own weaknesses in fabrication, importing leading-edge microprocessors and servers, which in turn would open the way for modern data centers—leading to a Russian cloud. Russia would continue to depend as before on foreign architecture and chip-making machinery, but the fab/fabless model would enable its chip designers to move forward quickly from design to mass production. During this period, the Russian companies established working relations with leading chip manufacturers, especially TSMC.[68]

Dependence Deepens

The new openness of the Russian economy, and the eased access to manufacturers, only deepened the dependence of the Russian microelectronics sector. This happened for several reasons. First, the newly privatized Russian economy chronically underinvested in its own microelectronics industry. According to the Russian government, China invests $280 billion a year in computer-related electronics, the United States around $50 billion, but Russia, on the eve of the invasion, only $1 billion.[69] As a result, the entire Russian technological chain, from the manufacture of silicon chips through microprocessors to servers and data centers—not to mention finished computers and smartphones—remained weak.

The second cause was Russian customers' rejection of Russian products. For over two decades, Russia became part of the global supply chain in microelectronics and computers, as well as consumer products based on them, such as smartphones. Given a choice, both Russian companies and consumers preferred the foreign items, which were now widely available. Civilians were not alone; as the recent revelations from the Ukrainian battlefield show, this was also true of the military.

Lastly, the government as a whole paid little attention to the problem. It was only from the mid-2010s, as the geopolitical atmosphere turned increasingly cold, that the leadership became concerned about Russia's dependence in microelectronics. Government ministries began churning out ambitious plans to displace foreign products, chiefly by requiring Russian-made technology in state contracts. But these programs had little success; they were unpopular with both the Russian electronics companies and their customers, and even state agencies largely side-stepped the government's orders. At this stage, the government did not yet push very hard in practice, and Russian companies in both the civilian and military sectors continued to rely on imported components.

Then came February 2022 and the Russian invasion. TSMC and the leading fabs abruptly severed all connections with Russian companies. The Russians were forced into the gray market, working through front companies and covert intermediaries that bought chips from US producers and passed them on to Russian buyers. As the profusion of Western components found in Russian weapons in Ukraine has shown, such channels continue to supply the Russian military.

Yet for military applications, Russia is not without resources of its own. Many of the microchips used in Russian weapons are not the most advanced design; but what matters most is that they be robust and reliable. Russia is able to produce many of these itself. In addition, it imports microelectronics for use in weapons from Belarus, which also supplies radiation-hardened chips for Russia's nuclear and space programs.[70] But imports from the West remain crucial. A good example is the fast-moving frontier of ultra-small transistors.

The Next Frontier: Ultra-Small Transistors

To handle the torrents of data generated by modern IT, companies and governments need ever more advanced computers with millions of transistors packed ever more closely together. The separation between two transistors is measured in nanometers, or billionths of a meter. State-of-the-art chips today are on the verge of reaching separations of only 2 or 3 nanometers, compared to several hundred a mere decade ago. These will be the basis of the next generation of smartphones, servers, and other applications. But there are presently only two companies in the world that are capable of working at such super-small widths—TSMC and Samsung—and they in turn depend on the small handful of partners that supply them with architecture, photolithography, and production machinery.

The Russian chip companies are so far limited to much greater widths. Mikron, Russia's most advanced microelectronics company (co-owned by the giant military-industrial conglomerate Rostekh), can produce small quantities of chips in the 90–180 nanometer range.[71] But its main product is a processor with a 250-nanometer node, for use in bank cards and passports.[72] Russia's newest producer, Akvarius, is similarly handicapped.

A width of 22 nanometers turns out to be a crucial Rubicon. Crossing it requires a completely new design concept—three-dimensional chips called FinFET, coupled with extreme ultraviolet photolithography, plus a new manufacturing fab to match. TSMC, thanks to massive investment starting a decade ago, successfully crossed the 22-nanometer divide, with Samsung right behind, to reach today's 2- and 3-nanometer chips. This is the cutting-edge technology that will enable the fifth generation of applications, known as 5G. But without licenses to these new processes, and with no access to the fabs that will produce them, the Russians are stuck.

But for how long? In 2023 Apple began using TSMC's 3-nanometer chip in its new iPhones and Macs, and a 2-nanometer chip is on the way.[73] The latest chips will be incorporated in millions of new phones and laptops all over the world, which the Russians will be able to buy through networks of parallel imports. Game over? Not at all. By that time, the race will have moved on—but Russian technology, including the military sector, will still be a decade or more behind.

Dual Technologies: Front Companies and Fraudulent Routes

Russian front companies have sprung up in key locations around the world, specializing in purchasing semiconductors and other electronic components on the open market, then reselling and shipping them to Russia. Most of these items are well-known brands. According to Russian customs data, microchips from Analog Devices and Texas Instruments microchips, as well as hundreds of millions of dollars of products from Intel and other US-based companies, have continued to flow to Russia virtually without interruption since the 2022 invasion.[74] Most of these come from the US companies' outsourced production in China and Malaysia,[75] and are transshipped through countries such as Morocco and Turkey. A network of Russian intermediaries then distributes them to Russian buyers, including by e-commerce.[76] Despite increased efforts by the sanctioning powers to toughen monitoring and enforcement, the picture has not changed.

Most of these clearinghouses are located in China, Hong Kong, India, and Turkey. According to a report by the US Director of National Intelligence in July 2023, China has become a major source of dual-use technologies with potential military applications. But cases have also come to light involving NATO/EU members such as Lithuania, Germany, and the Netherlands.[77] Some of the latter take the form of ghost trade, that is, items supposedly transiting through FSU countries such as Kazakhstan, Kyrgyzstan, and Armenia, which disappear in the direction of Russia without ever reaching their nominal destinations.[78] According to an investigation by the *Financial Times*, the volume of such ghost trade in the top forty-five most sensitive dual-use goods tripled between 2022 and 2023, and on the present trend is likely to exceed $200 million in 2024.[79]

Another fast-growing center of dual-use traffic is Hong Kong. Here the Russian response to sanctions was virtually instantaneous. In the first nine months of 2022 following the invasion, thirty-five companies were newly registered in Hong Kong as doing business with Russia, twice the number as over the same period in 2021.[80] One example is a company called Pixel Devices, which was founded in 2017 in Saint Petersburg.[81]

But Pixel is only the shipper. According to a review of Russian customs data by Riga-based Verstka, Russian companies, operating through
intermediaries like Pixel, imported over $500 million in dual-use technolo-
gies, mainly semiconductors and microprocessors, in the first half of 2023.
The five leading Russian buyers belonged either to Rostekh, the Russian
military-industrial conglomerate, or Glonass, the state-owned space satellite
company.[82]

The UAE, mentioned earlier as a growing hub for the Russian oil trade,
is also an emerging crossroads for traffic in dual-use electronics, notably
semiconductors and navigation devices. Between February 2022 and June
2023, the EU's exports of dual-use components to the UAE reached $1.8 bil-
lion, half again as much as in the same period the year before. Most of these
items then went on to Russia. The EU, departing from its traditional doctrine on third-party sanctions, has recently sanctioned several UAE-based
companies for supporting the Russian military. But the key to improved
enforcement is information, which the UAE has been reluctant to provide. In
September 2023, EU Commission President Ursula von der Leyen met with
UAE President Sheikh Mohammed bin Zayed in Abu Dhabi to urge the Emirates to share more of their trade data. Although von der Leyen described
the talks as "excellent," other Western officials called bin Zayed's response
"disappointing."[83] In this as in other respects, the UAE has been careful
not to endanger its profitable role as a middleman between Europe and
Russia.[84]

Through these means, by the end of 2023, most Russian industrial companies had found short-term ways of obtaining imported equipment and parts,
including dual-use microelectronics of military importance. Yet the sanctions and self-sanctions on microelectronics, like those on oil, do impose
costs and create problems for the Russian buyers. For example, the gray flow
contains many defective chips. The leading foreign fabs, above all TSMC,
made their reputation by working hard to increasing the "yield," that is,
the percentage of non-defective chips that come off their assembly lines.
But barred from direct access to manufacturers such as TSMC, Russian
designer/manufacturers complain that many of the chips they buy on the
gray market are defective.[85]

Yet the real problem with the gray market and illicit purchases goes
deeper. They are necessarily limited to yesterday's technologies.[86] But for the
Russian IT industry to overcome its backwardness, it requires direct access
to the companies that are at the leading edge today, driving the continuing

headlong revolution in IT. The sanctions have abruptly interrupted that access, and although this is not a problem for the weapons systems presently used in Ukraine, in longer-term perspective, the sanctions, if vigorously enforced, will have a cumulative effect over time on the Russian economy as a whole.

How are Russian policymakers addressing that challenge?

Longer-Range Responses to Sanctions

In parallel with the short-range measures described above, Russian policy-makers have also attempted to develop longer-range policies to weaken the impact of sanctions. The two main ones are "import substitution," to replace imported technologies with Russian-made ones, and "de-dollarization," to develop trade in currencies other than the dollar and the euro. Russia is making progress in moving away from the dollar and the euro, mainly toward the Chinese renminbi. In contrast, it has made little headway with import substitution. But if pursued over the longer term, these two policies will reorient Russia's economy fundamentally, away from the dependence on the West that was the central feature of Russia's thirty-year opening, and toward an economy more oriented toward the East.

Import Substitution

Replacing imported products and components with domestic ones has been on the agenda of the Russian government since about 2012 (when Putin returned to the Kremlin for his third term), but it was not until the occupation of Crimea in 2013 and the first Western sanctions the following year, that the substitution policy (*importozameshchenie*) became a top priority, especially in the defense sector. Since then, it has steadily increased in importance, especially since the 2022 invasion.

There are two ways of reading the results to date. On the one hand, in several sectors the early attention to import substitution helped domestic producers to adapt quickly to the 2022 sanctions. This was particularly the case in the machine-tool industry, which had been at the top of the government's list from the beginning, because of its vital importance for military industry.[87]

In other sectors the import-substitution program has been less successful. One reason is internal opposition by Russian companies. In the private
sector, where civilian production predominates and companies must compete on cost and consumer acceptance, there has been strong resistance to
the government's attempts to impose domestic quotas. In a recent survey by
the Russian Higher School of Economics, over half of companies surveyed
complain that import substitution is "complicated," meaning delays, higher
costs, and problems with reliability. This is especially the case in six leading sectors, including computers, electronics, and optical equipment, where
70% of respondents answered "complicated." In those sectors, the level of
dependence on foreign imports remains high. A recent survey by the Bank
of Finland comes to the same conclusion.[88]

In contrast, government offices and state-owned companies that rely
on procurement contracts face particularly heavy pressure to switch to
Russian-made products. A leading example is software. As late as 2020 it
was estimated that only 7% of the Russian software market, even for government business, consisted of Russian products; the rest was imported. As
official pressure has grown, state-owned companies are reluctantly making
the switch, most notably VTB, a state-owned bank, and RZhD, the railroad
monopoly. But even when the software is Russian, these companies typically
continue to run on Western operating systems such as Microsoft Windows.

Microsoft software and services play such a crucial role in the Russian
IT sector that when Microsoft CEO Brad Smith announced in March 2022
that it was suspending new sales and services to Russia,[89] there was a wave
of anxiety among Russian users, who feared that they would be stranded.
Microsoft initially said it would continue to support existing contracts, but
not sell updates or new licenses. In July 2022 it announced it would no longer
provide technical support of any kind,[90] and in September it barred Russian
users from downloading updates for its widely used Windows 11 system,
including security patches to protect users from hacks. But Russians soon
found ways to adapt, such as creating fake US IP addresses, which gave
them easy access to all of Microsoft's services.[91] Perhaps for this reason,
in the spring of 2024, Microsoft reversed itself, and reopened access to its
Windows and Microsoft Office services, as well as its cloud services, to Russian users.[92] Thus, at this moment the status of Microsoft in the Russian IT
market remains unclear.[93]

The biggest single form of import substitution has not actually been substitution at all, but replacement of Western substitution by third-country

products, notably from China and Turkey, as already noted. This has caused some controversy among Russian players. At an industrial forum in Tatarstan, the director of a defense plant, upon hearing of another company's plans to "replace" imports with Chinese equipment and software, exclaimed, "We call this import substitution, but we just bring in (*tashchim*) stuff from elsewhere. It's not import substitution, nothing of the kind."[94] Such feelings are widespread, especially among IT specialists.

The one major civilian sector in which import substitution has been an unquestioned success is the oil industry. This is due to three things, acting together. The first was an early start. In the 1990s the oil industry had declined badly, but privatization brought an influx of new capital and management skills from abroad. Second, until the invasion foreign personnel were strongly present, especially in the upstream, where they brought advanced technology and modern management skills. But unlike in most other sectors, the foreign oil companies, especially those in oil services, made a point of training Russian nationals in state-of-the-art techniques, partly with a view to moving them outside Russia to staff their own global operations. As a result, the Russian companies today have a plentiful supply of skilled professionals. Third, the oil industry enjoyed high profits from exports, thanks to which it was able to invest in modernizing older fields and developing new ones. For all these reasons, Russian oil production has never faltered under the sanctions, and no special government import-substitution programs have been needed.[95]

An important exception is IT for the energy sector, where there has been only slow progress in replacing foreign software in its internal management and operations, following the abrupt departure of SAP, Oracle, and Microsoft. In this area, movement has been slow and "painful," despite the crusading efforts of the minister of Digital Technology, Maksut Shadaev, who wields state orders and tenders as levers over the energy companies.[96] Other industrial sectors, such as automobiles and metallurgy, report the same thing. At a conference in May 2024, Aleksey Mordashov, CEO of steelmaker Severstal', said, "We see various attempts, various projects in Russia . . . but systems that could replace SAP don't exist yet." He estimated that it would take at least five years and billions of dollars before an adequate Russian substitute would be available. Yet in the meantime, he said, "we are cut off from the vendor and can't do updates."[97]

The Mishustin government has vowed to increase the pressure on Russian companies to use home-grown products. The top official in charge of import-substitution policy is a rising star, Denis Manturov, who was recently promoted to first deputy prime minister. Manturov is an interesting example of the new generation of technocrats now rising to influential positions.

An economist by training, with a doctorate from Moscow State University, Denis Manturov then earned a degree in aviation engineering, and went into the helicopter business, selling Russian-made helicopters to India and China. From there he became the chairman of Oboronprom, the main state company in charge of aviation technology and air-defense systems. He brings to his present job two decades of experience in Russian military industry, both as a private-sector entrepreneur and a government official. Manturov's father-in-law, Evgenii Kisel, introduced him to Sergei Chemezov, the powerful head of the Rostekh military-industrial conglomerate and one of Putin's closest associates, having served with him in East Germany. In 2018 Oboronprom was taken over by Rostekh. Suddenly Manturov was on his way, and he has been Chemezov's close ally ever since. His recent promotion to deputy prime minister suggests that import substitution has now moved to the top of the government's agenda.

"De-dollarization"

Another front in Russia's effort to diversify has been de-dollarization. Confronted with successive waves of Western financial sanctions, Russia has responded with policies to lessen its dependence on Western currencies, chiefly the dollar and the euro, and to increase the share of non-Western currencies. With each phase in the steadily deteriorating relationship with the West, the Russian effort has increased. It now covers reserves, trade settlements, and debt.[98]

Reserves: The policy of lessening dependence on the dollar actually began as early as 2008, following the sub-prime financial crisis of that year. The RCB began increasing its purchases of gold, a policy it has continued since. Then, in response to US post-Crimean sanctions in 2014, Russia began a more active policy of cutting its dollar-denominated reserves. At that time, an astonishing one-third of Russian reserves was held in the United States, mostly in the form of US Treasuries. But in that year the RCB began selling off US Treasuries and buying "cash dollars" (which were held in Russia), euros, and more gold. In 2015, for the first time, it bought Chinese renminbi.

The next round of US sanctions, in response to CAATSA in 2018, led to further sell-offs of US Treasuries and increased the RCB's move into euros and renminbi. By the time of the Ukrainian invasion in 2022, Russia had sharply cut the share of dollars in its reserves.[99]

Payments and Trade Settlements: In this category as well, Russia began moving away from the dollar a decade before the invasion, following the first round of US sanctions in 2014. In that year, the RCB launched the Russian interbank messaging system SPFS, intended as an alternative to the dollar-based SWIFT system. By 2020 some 400 institutions had joined it, mostly Russian but also 23 foreign banks. On the eve of the invasion, the SPFS accounted for over a fifth of Russia's domestic interbank traffic.

The Chinese government proved a willing partner in this effort. Beginning in 2014, Russia and China established direct ties for clearing payments in local currencies. In 2015 came the first direct credit line in renminbi, as VTB and Sberbank partnered with the China Development Bank to establish a 6 billion yuan[100] credit line to support Russian imports from China. Russian businesses have steadily increased the share of their trade in renminbi, and by 2023 the renminbi displaced the dollar as the most-traded currency in Russia. Renminbi deposits in Russian banks now exceed those in dollars, lending in renminbi is growing rapidly, and debt is steadily being converted from dollars and euros.[101]

Trade settlements with India, which is now the leading importer of Russian oil, have been more problematic. Russia has built up a large surplus of rupees, which it cannot easily spend. It would like India to pay in renminbi, which Russia needs, but the Indian government has refused. For the moment, India pays for most of its Russian oil with a combination of UAE dirhams and dollars, which does not particularly satisfy either side.[102]

Debt: Russian efforts to move away from the dollar in borrowing also began well before the invasion, although here they were only partially successful. The shift was particularly pronounced in corporate debt. Russian corporations had traditionally borrowed mainly in dollars, but after peaking in 2015, the share of the dollar in corporate debt declined from 70% to 50%, mainly to the benefit of the euro. In contrast, Russian banks have been generally reluctant to borrow in Chinese renminbi.[103]

After 2022, Russian efforts to move away from the dollar accelerated in all categories, and the dollar has now been joined by the euro as an "unfriendly" currency.

Conclusions

Russia's responses to the Western sanctions have been vigorous, creative, and on the whole effective in restabilizing the economy and restoring growth after the initial disarray of the first few months after the invasion. The financial team, led by the RCB and the Ministry of Finance, has used a combination of interest rates and occasional capital controls to prevent a meltdown of the ruble and to limit capital flight. Russian energy companies have reoriented the country's oil trade away from Europe, while acquiring a large fleet of "shadow tankers" and promoting creative reporting (let us call it that) for coping with the price cap. The military industry and security services have developed worldwide networks of middlemen to keep factories supplied with dual-use components, at least for current technologies that are widely available on world markets.[104] And thanks to the Kremlin's policy on "parallel imports," plus vigorous if illegal gray imports by the private sector, Russian consumers have mostly been able to obtain whatever they want, if generally at higher prices. These responses have enabled the Putin regime to continue to prosecute its war in Ukraine while insulating the population and the economy from its direct effects. All in all, it has been a successful effort—at least for the near term.

Yet over time the effectiveness of these measures tends to decline. One example is civilian aviation. Keeping Russia's civilian fleet flying has forced the creation of ingenious new supply chains. Advanced parts arrive in Russia in passengers' suitcases, sent by small suppliers who have sprung up since the invasion, mainly in Dubai and the UAE. But this route is expensive and undependable. S7, a major private airline, reports that imports of foreign parts for its fleet have declined from $100 million a year before the war to less than $20 million today.[105] As Sergei Chemezov, the head of Rostec and a close Putin ally, told Putin in a meeting in August 2023, "From 2025 on, we will start losing all our foreign planes, because they will need full maintenance overhauls."[106]

To replace Russia's fleet of foreign airliners, the government in June 2022 announced a sweeping plan, under the Russian military-industrial-conglomerate Rostec, to manufacture over a thousand civilian airplanes using only Russian-made parts. In January 2024, it allocated $3 billion to help finance the program, although the target was scaled down to just over 600 planes. As of 2024, however, none of them had actually been built.[107]

Russia has been helped in responding to the sanctions by two things. First, a handful of third countries, chiefly Turkey, the UAE, and several FSU countries, have helped Russia to evade the sanctions on trade, including in dual-use goods with military applications. Above all, China has played a key role. Chinese banks have extended trade credits (in renminbi) to Russian borrowers. Chinese middlemen, based mainly in Hong Kong, supply dual-use components to Russian counterparts, and China sells some directly. China has also increased its imports of Russian fossil fuels. Support from China has been more measured than might have been expected from the "no limits" pronouncements coming from the top leaders, but such as it is, it has been vital to Russia, and it is likely to keep increasing.[108] (We return to this subject in Chapter 7.)

Second, the ability of the Russians to respond to sanctions has been helped by weaknesses in the sanctions regime. In the case of the oil sanctions, the chief problem has been the conflicting objectives of the sanctioners and consequent inconsistencies in the sanctions, both in their design and in their implementation. The West has been concerned not to disrupt global oil markets or to provoke price spikes, and therefore the energy sanctions leave deliberate loopholes. The trade sanctions feature major exceptions for goods related to food, health, or "humanitarian" needs. Enforcement has been spotty, mostly confined to bans and warnings, with only a handful of actual prosecutions. This is partly due to understaffing. But the main constraint is the hesitation of the Western powers to apply secondary sanctions and resort to more vigorous enforcement against third countries, where the result would be increased resentment and loss of international support for the sanctions policy generally. The Russians have been able to take advantage of these weaknesses.

The West's efforts to control the trade in dual-use goods have been complicated by the rise of new financial instruments that facilitate invisible payment across borders. The main one is cryptocurrency, chiefly "stablecoin," traded on digital platforms such as Tether, a privately held company registered in the British Virgin Islands. Russian buyers pay in rubles, which are then converted into "tether" by middlemen and paid to suppliers in local currencies. So far there has been little success in limiting this channel; as Deputy Treasury Secretary Wally Adeyemo told a committee of Congress in April 2024, new congressional authority is needed for new tools, especially to bolster secondary sanctions against foreign digital asset providers, "since unlike banks, foreign cryptocurrency exchanges and some money services businesses do not have or depend on correspondent accounts for all of their transactions."[109]

The Russian responses to sanctions did not begin in 2022. There had been close to a decade of "doomsday prepping" (in the nice phrase of political economist Daniel McDowell), following the first round of US sanctions in 2014.[110] As a result, the Russians had gained considerable experience in dealing with sanctions, and although the scale and sweep of the post-invasion sanctions posed new challenges, they have largely adapted to them. Much the same team of *finansisty* is in charge today as was then. This continuity, both in the policies and in the people in charge of them, has helped to make the Russian responses more effective the second time around.

Not surprisingly, the Western sanctions have angered the Russians, from ordinary consumers to the top levels of government, beginning with Putin himself. This has led to retaliation in some sectors, notably in gas exports to Europe and grain and fertilizer exports through Ukraine. The Kremlin has effectively destroyed its gas market in the EU, while the fate of the grain and fertilizer exports is as yet unknown.

But the Russians, after some internal debate, decided not to weaponize oil exports, and have found ways to live with them instead. As Craig Kennedy has argued, the downsides of weaponizing oil exports would be considerable for the Russians, given their dependence on oil-export revenues. But the politics of the oil sanctions remain unstable. The West may yet find ways of making the price cap more effective. And it cannot be ruled out that Putin will lash out against the West over oil, as he did with gas.

Three years into the hurricane of sanctions, most Russian policymakers are claiming victory. Yet their optimism does not run deep. This is particularly the case among the *finansisty*, who continue to support the basic features of a liberal market economy. The main issue for them is the increasing dominance of the state in the allocation of resources through subsidies and investment. Their unease was on clear display at the 2023 Saint Petersburg Economic Forum. RCB chair Nabiullina (wearing no brooch) was outspoken as always, warning about government overreach in a crisis atmosphere. "This temptation can lead to the suppression of private initiative." She added, "If decision making is concentrated in the state hands rather in the private sector about where to direct financial resources and which industries to develop, . . . this is a big risk." Finance Minister Anton Siluanov agreed: "We give money to state-owned enterprises, and they create a business that interferes with commercial business . . . It is necessary to reduce subsidies." He concluded, "We need to change the logic."[111] For the conservatives, however, this is precisely the point: the state needs to take even more control. This debate is gaining in intensity.

The war is compounding the effects of the sanctions by drawing an ever-increasing share of the economy's resources into the military-industrial sector and putting growing pressure on the Russian budget. This is leading to tensions among the *finansisty* themselves. The Ministries of Finance and Economics, which are responsible for producing the budget, are under pressure to "balance between the cabbage and the goat," as the Russian saying goes, by making dutifully optimistic assertions that the economy can support the steady increase in military funding, while keeping the rest of the economy in reasonable balance. Accordingly, the official budget for 2024, drawn up largely by those two ministries, was based on a $85 oil price, 2.3% GDP growth, and a 90-ruble dollar. But the RCB under Nabiullina remains bearish as usual, projecting only a $60 oil barrel (in other words, the level of the price cap) and GDP growth of only 0.5–1.5%.[112] Prime Minister Mishustin hovers uncomfortably in-between. For the time being, the government is resorting to stop-gap measures such as raising taxes on all exporters, to generate extra revenue for the budget.[113] But over time, these tensions are likely to grow, as the costs of the war, both direct and indirect, keep mounting, and the balancing act of the *finansisty* grows steadily more difficult. In response, the government is likely to increase taxes on consumers and on corporate profits.

Overall, Russia's economic policymakers recognize that the success of their early responses is unlikely to last. So long as the war continues, and sanctions remain in force, their drag on the economy will grow. In the next chapters, we turn to a more detailed look at the longer-term effects and their consequences, beginning with the ongoing exodus of the Western companies from Russia.

Chapter 6
The Great Western Quasi-Exodus

The Russian invasion of Ukraine on February 24, 2022, was followed by a flurry of announcements from Western companies in Russia, pledging to stop operations, launch no new projects, make no new investments, and—for many of them—to exit from Russia. Many of these pledges preceded the actual imposition of sanctions and were prompted by the companies' desire not to appear supportive of the aggressor. But three years on, only a small minority have actually left. According to the Kyiv School of Economics (KSE), out of nearly 4,000 foreign companies present in Russia at the time of the invasion, only about 425 are gone.[1] Over 3,500 remain, although most have curtailed their activities, their revenues have declined, and there is a continuing slow stream of departures. This chapter attempts to explain this pattern, before going on to analyze the consequences of this "quasi-exodus" for the Western investors and the Russian economy, as well as the long-term prospects for a return by Western businesses and investment, if and when Russia reopens to the West. We begin with the story of Renault.

The Great Escape: Renault in Russia

On the eve of the invasion, a joint venture of the French carmaker Renault-Nissan and AvtoVAZ had become the largest producer of automobiles in Russia. Renault's entry into Russia was the brainchild of Carlos Ghosn, the French Lebanese CEO of Renault and Nissan. At Putin's invitation, Ghosn launched the French company on a fifteen-year, multibillion-dollar odyssey that ended only with Putin's invasion of Ukraine. The troubles that Renault encountered in Russia, and its achievements, are a vivid example of the role of foreign companies and the subsequent impact of the Western departures on Russian industry and technology.

At the beginning of the 2000s the global auto industry was ripe for a revolution. It was a mature technology, based on traditional components and materials—mainly still steel and aluminum—and largely unchanged in the previous half-century. But at the turn of the century new materials (such as plastics and other synthetics) and high-tech digital components (notably semiconductors and information technology) began creating the basis for a new industry. Car people began to speak of "analog" cars versus "digital cars," the latter featuring innovations such as anti-lock brakes, traction control, airbags, and advanced power steering. Today, a digital car contains over fifty computer-controlled systems, which have become so familiar that we take them for granted. But it isn't only the cars that have gone digital: factory production lines (e.g., automation and robotics) and supply systems (e.g., "just-in-time") are likewise new.

This trend had two revolutionary implications. First, it resulted in cheaper and more efficient cars, ideally suited to a fast-growing mass market in developing countries. Second, there was less and less need for skilled high-paid labor; this too favored developing countries, where cheap unskilled labor was abundant. But the developing countries could not yet produce the advanced components themselves. This called for a complete rethink of the entire value chain, an international division of labor between high-tech suppliers and low-tech assemblers.

The first auto executive to grasp the revolutionary implications of this trend for the auto industry—and to act on it—was Carlos Ghosn, then already one of the most famous businessmen in the world, a celebrity of near rock-star status. Ghosn was unquestionably a business genius, with a charismatic personality and a powerful vision perfectly attuned to the glory years of globalization in the early 2000s. His business strategy for Renault, which stemmed from his observations as the head of Nissan in Japan and his prior experience with Michelin in Latin America, can be depicted as a "spoke and wheel": using European (mainly French) technology ("the spoke") to make advanced components, which were then shipped to plants all over the developing world for assembly ("the wheel"), using cheap local labor and "just in time" production techniques modeled on the Japanese electronics industry. The Ghosn model was first tried out successfully in Romania (where Renault had acquired the local automaker Dacia), then expanded to plants in Turkey and throughout the developing world, and finally to Russia.[2]

Russia seemed the perfect candidate for the new business model. In the early 2000s the Russian auto industry had all but disappeared. It had suffered from all the classic ailments of Soviet-legacy industry, combined with the baneful effects of Russia's "Wild East capitalism" of the 1990s: antiquated models and production lines, corrupt contractors and suppliers, technological backwardness, financial incompetence, and bloated and inefficient workforces. The arch-symbol of the sector's collapse was AvtoVAZ, Russia's largest automaker, which had once been a showpiece of détente in the 1960s, when it was co-founded with Italy's FIAT, but which by the 1990s had become a ruin. In short, it seemed tailor-made for Ghosn's vision.

One can also imagine Ghosn's immense appeal for Putin. What Renault had done for itself and for Nissan it could now do for AvtoVAZ, producing quickly a new line of affordable cars for Russian consumers. In 2007, Putin came to Paris to personally court Ghosn and the French government.[3] Renault agreed to take a 24% stake in AvtoVAZ and to supply the technology needed to modernize the plant. Ghosn's ambitions seemed limitless: in 2009, he trumpeted that Renault would be producing 1.4 million cars in Russia by 2017, and that Russia would be his largest market.

But Renault's first experience in Russia was a failure. No sooner had the partnership been concluded than the sub-prime financial crisis of 2008–9 hit the world. AvtoVAZ's sales, instead of increasing, fell by half. As a minority shareholder, Renault was powerless. When Putin offered Ghosn an increased stake in exchange for a fresh injection of capital, Ghosn insisted on total control. Putin agreed, and in 2012, Renault took a 51% stake in AvtoVAZ. Ghosn became chairman, and Renault had a majority on the board.

It was now up to Renault to show what it could do. Ghosn hired a tough Swedish auto executive named Bo Andersson to run AvtoVAZ. Andersson was no newcomer to Russia; he had caught Ghosn's eye when he turned around Russia's truck maker GAZ and made it profitable. As the new CEO of AvtoVAZ, Andersson promptly laid off 30,000 employees, purged AvtoVAZ's corrupt network of suppliers, and set up a new supply system based on imports of advanced components from abroad, chiefly from France and Romania. The initial results were highly successful. But Andersson's two-fisted tactics brought demonstrations at AvtoVAZ and threats of reprisals from Russian suppliers. And once again events intervened: Russia's actions in Ukraine in 2013–14 provoked Western sanctions, and the ruble plummeted, making reliance on imported parts unprofitable. AvtoVAZ's sales cratered, and in 2016 Andersson was dismissed.

From this point on, Renault tempered its approach (or, as its last CEO delicately put it, "*nous avons arrondi les angles*"—"we've softened the sharp edges"). The next CEO was a Frenchman, brought in from Renault's successful Romanian operation, Dacia, where presumably he had learned to deal with socialist sensitivities. In response to pressure from his Russian partner, the military-industrial giant Rostec, he began turning to domestic suppliers, although Renault continued to rely on foreign imports for digital components.[4] Between 2016 and 2021, the company finally became consistently profitable.

Then came the invasion of Ukraine. Renault responded instantly, selling its factories to its Russian partners for the symbolic sum of 2 rubles and an option to return within six years.[5] Practically overnight, it was gone. It had been a wild ride. Through nearly fifteen years of effort and expense, Renault Russia had lived through three economic crises, countless conflicts and misadventures, and ended up with net losses of over $2 billion.[6] Yet it had also achieved the seemingly impossible, working with its Russian partners to turn a Soviet-era relic into a modern and efficient showcase.[7]

The story of Renault was spectacular. But how typical was it? We turn now to the broader picture of the Western quasi-exodus.

The Western Quasi-Exodus: Hundreds Have Left, Thousands Remain

The several thousand Western companies that had come to Russia over the preceding three decades ran the gamut in size, from large corporations to small family concerns, with most somewhere in between. On the eve of the invasion, the top 120 Western companies in Russia had $147 billion in sales there and employed 493,000 thousand people. Yet they accounted for only a small fraction of Russian GDP.[8] Their overall numerical significance for the Russian economy, in other words, was modest. But their departure has had a significant impact in several important sectors, notably IT and certain branches of industry, such as automobiles. Outside the top 120, most of the other Western businesses in Russia were medium to small companies, concentrated in retail, consumer goods and electronics, health and medical products, and professional services. Many of them remain in Russia, but their activities have generally been sharply reduced.

For the departing Western companies and those that have suspended their operations, the losses have been heavy, although there is no agreement on precisely how much they amount to. According to the Russian Institute for Strategic Studies (RISI), the aggregate losses of the large foreign companies in Russia ran between $200 billion and $240 billion in 2022, with the largest losses suffered by the United States. But the hit has also been severe in Europe. By mid-2023, a survey by the *Financial Times* reported that 176 departing European companies had written down over $100 billion in losses, of which more than half came from the energy and power sectors.[9] But a calculation by Reuters, based on company filings and statements, puts the loss at only $80 billion.[10] The exact numbers are difficult to pin down.

Western shareholders who had invested in Russian companies have increasingly found themselves blocked from selling their shares. In some cases the companies in which they took stakes have offered to buy them out, but at deep discounts.[11] Thus the Russian owners of Magnit, Russia's second-largest retailer with 28,000 food and home-goods stores all across Russia, bought out the shares of their foreign stakeholders, but via a bidding process that left the foreigners with heavy losses.[12]

The foreign companies that were the earliest to leave were those that had the smallest investments at stake, chiefly the "professionals," such as law firms, accountancies, advertisers, and consultancies, as well as Internet service providers. Many by this time were staffed by Russians, who took over the offices of the departed companies and hung out new shingles with new names. Thus, among the accountancies, PwC's former Moscow office was renamed Trust Technology Auditors and Consulting Group; Accenture became AKSTIM; and Ernst and Young turned into B1 Konsult.

Far more reluctant to leave were the companies that had either made major investments in joint projects and in retail networks or were making good profits in Russia, or both. Speed was crucial. The ones that left first were usually able to make a clean exit. But those that delayed have increasingly found themselves trapped by obstacles of all kinds. Over time, the attitude of the Kremlin has shifted from a stance of "more in sorrow than in anger," to one of punitive vengefulness, and with each passing month it has made it more and more difficult for the remaining Western companies to leave. Three years after the invasion, Russian policy toward the remaining Western companies has become increasingly one of thinly veiled expropriation, despite protestations by Putin that Western companies are still welcome (as discussed in Chapter 3).

As the Western companies leave, they are being replaced by well-placed Russians. In a handful of sectors, such as automobiles and consumer electronics, there is a growing Chinese presence, but for the time being that consists mainly of imports rather than investment in Chinese production inside Russia.

The departure of the Western companies is significant for several reasons. In several branches of industry they had brought new technologies, as well as people with skills and experience (as always the most efficient vehicles of technology transfer, via live example and training). Throughout the Russian economy, the Western companies had introduced new products and services, and whole new ways of doing business. Their exit symbolizes the dashed aspirations and illusions of an entire era.

Equally significant is the fate of the large number of Western companies that have so far remained in Russia, either by choice or under compulsion. The mounting pressure on them at all levels and in all forms, ranging from harassment to outright confiscation, is completing the destruction of Russia's image as a place for foreigners to do business. Even when a new generation of Russians comes to power and the Ukrainian war is settled—however and whenever that happens—it will be a long time before Western capital and businesses return to Russia.

The Shock of the Invasion, The Storm of Announcements

The Russian invasion caught nearly everyone by surprise, including most of the Russian leaders themselves. Despite the massing of Russian troops at the Ukrainian border in late 2021 and early 2022, life had gone on as usual, both in Russia and the West. Very few appeared to believe that war was imminent.

Among the foreign companies in Russia, and indeed among the Russian ones, there had been no preparations for such a cataclysmic event. The limited Western sanctions imposed following the occupation of Crimea, though they had brought a range of responses by the Russian government,[13] had changed practically none of the foreign companies' behavior. On the eve of the invasion, no foreign companies had exited. No investment projects had been suspended, with the sole exception of the oil industry, where sanctions had caused ExxonMobil to withdraw from a major offshore joint venture. No offices had closed, and no expatriates had left. Russians in Moscow and other major Russian cities lined up for cheeseburgers at McDonald's as usual, shopped at Auchan, fought traffic jams in their new Renault-made Ladas, and paid for their purchases with VISA and Mastercard. Russian companies continued to rely on foreign importers and partners for a wide range of essential goods and services (including many so-called dual-use ones) and resisted the government's half-hearted efforts to promote domestic

substitutions. Despite the darkening clouds over Russia's geopolitical relations with the West (a process that had already been underway for a decade
and a half, so that it had almost become background noise), business life was
unaffected.

Suddenly, on February 24, 2022, everything changed. Within days, the
first wave of expanded Western sanctions struck Russian companies, personalities, and products. Some Western companies had not waited for the
sanctions and had already begun to exit on their own. McDonald's, VISA and
Mastercard, Renault, and several others, announced their immediate departure. Hundreds more vowed that they would suspend new investments and
projects, begin closing their offices and withdrawing foreign personnel, and
selling off accumulated stocks of goods. To judge from the intense coverage
in the Western and Russian media, it looked like a stampede out the door.

Yet as the months went by, it was apparent that matters were not so simple.
Despite the early departures and the storm of corporate statements, most of
the Western companies were not actually leaving. Rather, they were strung
out along a continuum of indecision. There were many flavors of "leave,"
ranging from "I'm out of here" to "I'm thinking about it." Many companies
cut back or suspended their operations, while debating what to do. An early
Russian study, mentioned earlier, concluded that although 87% of them had
stopped working, either wholly or partially, few had left, mostly in "soft"
services such as legal advice, accounting, or investment consulting.[14] But
the immediate impact on Russian employment was minor; although some
workers had been placed on leave and others moved to part-time work, few
had been laid off, and most kept right on working. The immediate hit was
greatest in the consumer sector, especially food and retailing, where the supply of imported goods had been interrupted (although only temporarily, as
we have seen), but insignificant in other branches.

Only a handful of regions were touched, notably Kaluga, a province near
Moscow with a substantial concentration of foreign companies, which the
local governor had actively campaigned to bring in. But even there only some
11% of the workforce in the foreign firms had stopped work. In Russia as a
whole, only a handful of industrial sectors were hit by the foreign stoppages,
and in most cases, after a few initial months of confusion, work resumed—
for the most part with the same foreign companies continuing to provide
components and maintenance.[15]

The great exception was the automotive sector, and in particular the joint
venture of Renault and AvtoVAZ, described above, which on the eve of the

invasion had become the largest producer of automobiles in Russia. It was one of the first to leave, and to date Renault is the third-largest Western investor to have done so.[16] Of all the Western manufacturing ventures in Russia, it was the most vulnerable. That was no surprise, since Renault's project at AvtoVAZ had been built deliberately around a business model that made it largely dependent on the supply of imported parts, especially digital components.

But Renault was not the only Western automaker in Russia. Practically all the major Western automakers had set up assembly plants there, either in partnership with Russian automakers or on their own. This too was the result of a systematic policy by the Putin government, which in 2005 established a special "industrial assembly regime" to attract foreign investment and participation into the auto industry, by providing preferential customs duties for imported auto components, and subsidies for foreign companies that built assembly plants.[17]

Within weeks of the invasion most of the other Western automakers had also stopped work and were preparing to leave.[18] Their Russian partners were suddenly under sanctions, and like Renault, they were no longer able to import digital components to support their assembly plants.[19]

The initial impact of their departure was devastating.[20] By June 2022, Russian passenger car production was down nearly 90% from June 2021, as the entire logistical chain disintegrated. Russian consumers stopped buying, and unsold cars piled up in dealerships. AvtoVAZ itself stopped production altogether for much of the winter and spring. When it finally resumed in early June, the best it could do was a dumbed-down version of the Lada Granta, without automatic transmission or automatic braking systems (ABS) or airbags—much to the hilarity of Russian drivers, who had already grown to expect "smart" cars.[21]

It was in the automotive sector that Western manufacturing companies had made the largest investment and played the greatest role. In addition to Renault's partnership with AvtoVAZ, Volkswagen had partnered with GAZ, Daimler with KAMAZ, and Mazda with Sollers; there were also several other partnerships with smaller Russian manufacturers. A dozen other foreign automotive companies opened assembly lines on their own, such as Nissan in Saint Petersburg. In addition, several created networks of dealerships, and some, such as the truck makers MAN and Scania (both part of the VW group), did a thriving business importing finished vehicles. Scania and MAN alone sold over 100,000 trucks in Russia in 2021, 12% of the Russian truck market.[22] European companies were especially active; at their height in 2021, Europe's top sixteen automakers accounted for nearly one-third of all the cars and trucks sold in Russia.

In the first six months following the invasion, all four of Russia's major automakers were sanctioned, forcing their Western partners to suspend operations and look for the exit. It took them over a year to fully dispose of their assets—in some cases with considerable difficulty, as we shall see in a moment—but by the end of 2023 they too were gone. The sanctions inflicted a heavy blow on the entire Russian auto industry, not just AvtoVAZ. In 2022, Russia's overall production of automobiles dropped by two-thirds.[23] Production of trucks was similarly hard-hit. Imports of cars briefly plummeted as well. Even where sanctions had not been imposed, the leading Western importers, Scania and MAN among them, closed their dealerships and sold out to Russian dealers.[24] By the end of 2022, out of the more than sixty foreign brands previously selling cars in Russia, there were only eleven left—all Chinese.[25]

The Impact on the Regions—The Case of Kaluga

The impact on several regions was sizable. The second-largest Western investor in the Russian automotive sector was VW, which built a large assembly plant in the western province of Kaluga, 150 km northwest of Moscow. Kaluga's economy had been largely dependent on military production, and when military orders stopped at the end of the Soviet period, Kaluga's economy nosedived. But in 2000 Kaluga elected a new governor, Anatolii Artamonov. A well-known personality there, having worked his way up through local government, Artamonov ran on a promise to revive the province's economy by attracting foreign investment.

He proved remarkably successful. He was a born promoter, and over the following twenty years he attracted dozens of foreign companies.[26] But his most spectacular coup came in 2005, when VW concluded an agreement with the Kaluga province government to build an assembly plant to make VWs and Skodas. The new factory, which cost €774 million to build, had a capacity of 225,000 vehicles a year. It began operation in 2007, and two years later, Vladimir Putin flew in by helicopter to preside over its official inauguration, a sign not only of his high regard for German industry, but also his personal commitment to the modernization of the Russian auto industry.

But following VW's exit from Russia, the Kaluga plant was left idle, as its new owner, a Russian auto-dealer group called Avilon, was unable to resume production on its own.[27] One year later, it negotiated a partnership with Chinese automaker GAC, under which the Chinese would supply imported "semi-knocked down" (SKD) modules for a Chinese-made VW model, to be assembled in Kaluga. Under this arrangement, many local operations, such as painting, will remain unused. Russian consumers mockingly refer to this as "screwdriver assembly" (*otvertochnaia sborka*).[28]

As we have seen, cars and everything connected with them, including spare parts, are banned by the EU as "luxury goods." As an illustration of the baffling complexity of the sanctions, Does the ban apply to tires, or only if they contain rubber, which is banned? Different tire companies have interpreted this differently, some deciding to leave, others to remain. The largest and best-known leaver was the French tire-maker, Michelin, which sold its plant in Davydovo to its distributor, Power International Tires, which has sales outlets all over Russia. Michelin, which had been in Russia since 1997, had stopped production in March 2022.[29] The Finnish tiremaker Nokian, which had been lured by the prospect of cheap natural gas in Russia (a source material for synthetic rubber) and made 80% of its car tires there, also decided to leave. By October 2022 it had sold its entire operation to the Russian oil company Tatneft for €285 million—"a fraction of its total value," lamented Nokian's CEO and president Jukka Moisio.[30] The two other main Western tire-makers, Continental and Bridgestone, likewise decided to exit, after selling their Russian assets to a well-connected Russian-Armenian entrepreneur.

By 2023, the automotive sector had stabilized somewhat, as Russian consumers resumed buying, thanks partly to a discount scheme (*util'sbor*), under which consumers choosing to scrap their old cars get a discount on their new one. AvtoVAZ reported a 70% increase in production over 2022, an all-time record, and an 87% increase in sales.

The Arrival of the Chinese

Even as the Europeans were leaving, the market began to shift toward Chinese sources. Once practically unknown, Chinese brands made a massive appearance, as Haval, Geely, Changan, and Great Wall all began selling cars in Russia.[31] By 2023 they had captured 80% of the Russian market in money terms, focusing on upscale models, leaving the Russian producers with the lower-priced end, such as the "simplified" Lada Granta and Niva.[32] But so far the Chinese automakers have shown no enthusiasm for replacing the departed Western automakers with assembly plants of their own.[33]

A similar trend can be seen in heavy vehicles for construction, such as frontloaders and excavators for road building and housing construction. In 2023, imports of such machinery, mainly from China, were five times larger than domestic Russian production and were growing five times faster, helped by well-placed banks, such as Gazprombank and VTB, which finance these imports from China and then lease them to Russian contractors.[34]

These trends pose acute dilemmas for Russian automakers. One response is to assemble Chinese cars under Russian brands, as VW's former joint venture in Kaluga has begun to do under its new Russian owner Avilon. Similarly, Nissan's former joint venture in Saint Petersburg, which has been taken over by AvtoVAZ and renamed the Saint Petersburg Automobile Plant, is producing a Chinese SUV from FAW under the Russian name Lada X-Cross 5, with a new Russian logo featuring an appropriately enigmatic X inside an oval.[35] But the Chinese are ambivalent about such arrangements, since they do not wish to create competition for themselves in the Russian market.

Meanwhile, the flood of Chinese auto imports continues. Chinese companies have acquired idled dealerships and showrooms and are marketing their brands actively—at prices below cost, claim some Russian politicians, who accuse the Chinese of "dumping." In the latest twist, the Chinese are selling cars on the Russian Internet, with great success. Russian automakers, increasingly at a loss, are appealing to the government to limit government contracts to Russian brands only, in order to save the industry. But Russian consumers are flocking to the Chinese brands, attracted by their lower prices, and Chinese imports are expected to reach 1.2 million cars in 2024.[36]

We return now to the central question of this chapter: How much of the pattern of exits and non-exits of Western companies is due to the direct or indirect effects of sanctions?

Self-Sanctioning, Over-Sanctioning, De-Risking, Pre-Emptive exits

Many of the Western companies that have left Russia were not dealing in sanctioned goods or working with sanctioned companies or persons. Instead, they "self-sanctioned," that is, they exited out of concern for their reputations, or fear of possible secondary sanctions by the United States, or to avoid legal trouble or damage to their brands.[37] McDonald's is the best example: no part of its Russian business was under sanctions, but it quickly exited anyway. However, it was the exception. Most of those that have publicly committed to staying deal in products that are unsanctioned—food and beverages, pharmaceuticals, health-related products, and items of "humanitarian assistance."[38] Imports of these items are broadly allowed (although exporting the proceeds is another matter, as we saw in the last chapter). In addition, there are so-called derogations that may exempt certain Russian companies and banks from restrictions where such items are involved, subject to the EU Commission's case-by-case approval. The boundary between "sanctions" and "self-sanctions" is often unclear. Some Western companies have stopped doing business simply because they are confused about the rules.

The most widely publicized example of this is shipments of Russian grain and fertilizers to developing countries. Starting shortly after the invasion, European port operators and shippers refused to allow cargoes of Russian fertilizer to sail on to their destinations. Banks cut off export credits, and insurance companies denied insurance (without which the ships could not leave port). Fertilizers began piling up in warehouses, notably in Rotterdam and Antwerp and in Estonia. Confusingly, the principal Russian fertilizer producers were under sanctions, and imports of fertilizers into the EU itself were banned, but exports outside the EU, notably to developing countries, were not. US and EU officials issued multiple public appeals to allow the fertilizers to proceed, but to no avail. This presented President Putin with a golden public-relations opportunity: in September he grandly announced that 260,000 tons of Russian fertilizer that had been blocked in European ports would be donated free to developing countries such as Mozambique and Angola. In late 2022, the EU, clearly embarrassed by the scandal, granted derogations for Russian exports related to food intended for developing countries.

Yet shippers and port operators, confused by the shifting rules, continued to block the Russian cargoes, and pile-ups mounted.[39] The biggest foreign operator of container vessels in and out of Russia, Moller-Maersk, closed its depots and warehouses in Russia and left the Russian market,[40] as did several other European operators.[41] On the other hand, MSC, the world's largest container shipping line, continued to operate in Russia, but only for "food, medical, and humanitarian cargoes."[42] Several other Western shipping companies, even those who had no actual assets in Russia, have refused to ship Russian goods, even unsanctioned ones, partly because of delays in Russian ports caused by lengthy inspections.

A more straightforward case of self-sanctioning is the pharmaceutical sector.[43] Over the previous two decades, all the major western "Big Pharma" companies, such as Pfizer, GlaxoSmithKline, and Eli Lilly, had set up operations in Russia, mostly in the form of "contract manufacturing," under which they made drugs for Russian partner companies. This was a rapidly growing business, with ambitious plans. Thus, Pfizer had partnered with a large Russian company, Pharmstandard, to start making cancer treatments in 2024 at a joint facility in Bashkortostan.[44] But after February 2022 the project was abruptly terminated, and there are no new investments planned, even though pharmaceutical products benefit from a "carve-out," under which they are not sanctioned. Yet at this writing, the activity of the Western pharmaceutical companies in Russia is limited to "arm's length" imports of essential drugs.

Why Some Companies Choose to Stay: Food and Cosmetics—and Alcohol

In the category of food and beverages, about half of the roughly 130 foreign companies that were in Russia on the eve of the invasion have chosen to stay.[45] The four largest and most profitable "remainers" are Nestle from Switzerland, Mars and Mondelez from the United States, and Ferrero from Italy. Nestle is first, with seven plants in Russia, 7,000 employees, and $2.95 billion in 2021 revenues. Right behind is Mars, with $2.6 billion in revenues in 2021. Mars, though, is a whole story unto itself. With only one large plant but 6,000 employees, its main product, a candy bar called Snickers, became iconic in Russia as the very symbol of the penetration of Western capitalism into Russia. It was singled out for attack by Russian nationalists, who decried the destruction of traditional Russian brands of chocolate at the hands of the invader. [46]

All four of these companies had established their brands in Russia after decades of effort, producing in local plants with Russian personnel, and they were highly profitable. It is no wonder that they elected to stay. Some sixty others in the food and beverages category have also stayed, but they are nearly all under $300 million in revenues, and no major brand names are among them. Still, many of them have established local niches, and they appear likely to endure, unless geopolitics take a sharp turn for the worse.

For the well-known French retail chain Auchan, the decision to stay brought some unwelcome publicity, when US right-wing commentator Tucker Carlson held a scandalously supportive interview with Putin in the Kremlin, which created a worldwide furor in early 2024. While he was in Moscow, Carlson made a side trip to Auchan's vast *hypermarché* in Moscow's Gagarin mall; with camera crew in tow, he marveled at its well-stocked aisles, and praised Russia's "resilience."[47] In actual fact, it was Auchan, not Russia, that was resilient: together with its sister company Leroy Merlin, Auchan had been in Russia for twenty years, and had 235 stores with 90,000 employees. Auchan continues to do business in Russia, but since the invasion, it has been unable to withdraw its profits from the country.[48]

A special case in the category of foods and beverages is Coca-Cola, which has long been popular in Russia. It was mostly produced there by a Swiss subsidiary, Coca-Cola HBC,[49] which operated ten soft-drink and juice plants in Russia, while its local Coke drink was produced with imported concentrate. In August 2022, Coca-Cola HBC announced that it had transferred its Russian operations to a Russian company Multon Partners. However, Multon had actually been acquired by Coca-Cola in 2005, to provide a sales outlet throughout the FSU.[50] In other words, Coca-Cola HBC continues to operate, but as a Russian company. It no longer produces Coca-Cola under its own name, but makes a Coke look-alike called *Dobryi Cola*, or "Kind Cola."[51] In parallel, the original Coca-Cola continues to arrive via parallel imports and countries like Kazakhstan. It can be still found throughout Russia, mostly at street stands and in underground metro passages.

Alcohol is a different matter. Alcohol imports into Russia are explicitly banned by the EU as luxury goods, and presumably by extension, Western companies are no longer allowed to brew or distil alcoholic drinks inside Russia. Yet, when the sanctions were imposed, the three biggest brewers in Russia—Heineken, ABInBev, and Carlsberg, were all foreign. The company most affected was the Danish brewer Carlsberg, which brewed the second-most popular beer in Russia, Baltika, as well as fifty other brands, and employed 8,400 people in eight breweries.[52]

Carlsberg's case illustrates in extreme form all the problems we have been discussing. Having declared early on that it would leave, Carlsberg had to spend a year searching and negotiating before it finally reached agreement with a Russian buyer, Arnest, a manufacturer of metal packaging and aerosols. However, it could still not exit until it received permission from the approvals committee. The year had not been totally wasted: Carlsberg's revenues from Baltika had increased by 20%, and its net profit had nearly doubled, since many of its competitors had left the market (although getting its profits out of the country was another matter).[53] But this only made Baltika an increasingly attractive target, and in July 2023, the Kremlin suddenly placed it under the "temporary management" of a Russian oligarch, a move tantamount to expropriation. Carlsberg's CEO angrily claimed that its Russian operation had been stolen and terminated the license agreement under which Baltika sold Carlsberg's brands inside Russia and the FSU. In retaliation, Russia arrested two of Baltika's former Russian managers, evidently meaning to hold them hostage to force Carlsberg to back down.[54]

Another foreign brewer, Heineken, was slightly more fortunate. In August 2023, it succeeded in selling its Russian operation of seven breweries and 1,800 employees, also to Arnest, which from modest local origins in the southern province of Stavropol had suddenly grown to be one of the largest brewers in Russia. As with Carlsberg, it had taken over a year for Heineken to obtain permission from the Russian government's approvals committee for this transaction. Heineken handed over its business for a grand total of €1, without an option to return, but with a promise from the buyer to guarantee its Russian employees for three years, and it declared a loss of €300 million. But Heineken at least was able to close the books on its Russian venture, following a storm of public criticism over its continued production of its lead brand, Amstel.[55]

Tobacco, and the case of Philip Morris, is another variation on the same theme of mixed decisions. Imports into Russia of tobacco goods such as cigars and cigarillos were banned by the EU, but not cigarettes, nor the manufacture of them inside Russia. Before the invasion, Philip Morris International (PMI) was one of the largest foreign companies in Russia, having been there since 1977 and invested over $2.5 billion. It had a factory in Saint Petersburg to make Marlboros, and another in Krasnodar, with a total of 3,200 employees and sales offices in more than 100 cities. In 2022 Russia accounted for $2.6 billion billion in revenues, 8% of Philip Morris's global revenues.[56] By early 2023, PMI announced that it had decided to stay on. But there was a catch: although the tobacco business in Russia is highly profitable, thanks to a strong and growing domestic market, the foreign companies are unable to move their profits out of the country. Other tobacco groups run the gamut from "exit" to "stay": Davidoff is gone; BAT has sold its Russian assets to a group of members of its Russian management team; only Japan Tobacco International is staying.[57]

What Does "Leave" Mean?

Why have so many Western companies announced their intention to leave—but not actually done so? The word "leave" turns out to have multiple meanings, reflecting the widely different histories, circumstances, and perceptions of the companies involved, as well as the countries they come from. Each case is unique. But there are four broad patterns.

- *New versus old*: Many companies have drawn the line at new investments and new projects, while continuing to operate or supply existing stores and factories, to make or sell existing products, or to honor existing licenses.
- *No more supplies or services*: A more restrictive definition of "leave" is the refusal of Western companies to continue supplying goods and services to their former Russian partners, or conversely to accept exports from them. In that case, the foreign company stays temporarily, while it draws down existing inventory.
- *"We'll be back"*: One common form of "leave" is a "temporary exit," under which the departing company negotiates some provision for an eventual return, such as a buy-back clause, stipulating that assets sold to a Russian buyer can be re-acquired at a later date, if circumstances change.[58]
- *"Part of me leaves; part of me stays"*: Some companies have multiple projects with different Russian partners, some of which may be under sanctions and others not. In such cases the Western company may shut down the sanctioned part but carry on with the others.

Companies that decide to remain, or have been slow to leave, likewise invoke a variety of reasons:

- *Difficulties in finding an eligible Russian buyer*: The preferred option for departing companies would logically have been to find a "third party" that would buy them out for a reasonable sum. But in actual fact three-quarters of them sold instead to their local partners or their local managers; in contrast, only 5% (by revenue) sold to third parties.

- *Procedural difficulties; slow approval process*: The early leavers had the smoothest exits. The more time went by, the more obstacles the Russian government raised to discourage the departure of companies from "unfriendly countries." Russian policy on this point was divided, with the Kremlin taking a hard line, while the RCB, and especially RCB chair Elvira Nabiullina, favored a more pragmatic approach.

- *Concern for Russian employees and communities*: Foreign companies that remain in Russia often cite concern for their Russian personnel as their chief reason for staying. Similarly, a number of Western companies have justified staying on the grounds that their products and services are essential to the Russian public's health and welfare, as in the case of life-saving drugs not otherwise available in Russia. These may be useful public-relations arguments, but they are probably not the main factors in their decision to stay or leave.

- *New opportunities opening up for the remainers*: In a handful of instances, the decision to remain has led to an increase in business. The leading example is that of Raiffeisenbank, which, because it is now one of only three unsanctioned large banks in Russia, has handled a growing share of the remaining capital exports and financial settlements in and out of the country—but has been blocked from exporting its own profits. This has placed the Austrian bank in an increasingly awkward position, and the anomaly will likely prove temporary. (See the discussion of Raiffeisenbank later in the chapter.)

The choice of "staying" or "leaving was particularly painful for German companies, which had the largest investments and commercial ties with Russia of any of the European countries. For many in the German business world, the exit from Russia was highly emotional. Michael Harms, who had been the head of the German-Russian Chamber of Commerce in Moscow and subsequently of Germany's *Ostausschuss* (the Committee on East European Economic Relations), spoke for many German businessmen when he said in early 2022, "I dedicated almost my whole life to these relationships. When you see this effort was somehow all in vain, you feel strongly, personally affected."[59] German middle-sized companies, many of them family-owned, were especially bitter. "The Russian state only wants to pay pig prices (*Schweinepreise*) for our plants . . . . We don't feel comfortable giving away our assets," said another, "just to make some Russian manager a millionaire overnight."[60] One of the biggest losers was the German gas giant Wintershall, a subsidiary of BASF, which had developed a close relationship with Gazprom, in both Russia and Germany, over a period of thirty years (described in Chapter 2). "We all greatly underestimated what Putin's Russia is capable of," lamented Wintershall's CEO Mario Mehren, "That was a mistake."[61]

Gazprom's exit from Germany also hurt its other major partner, Uniper, the former Ruhrgas, which had been taken over by the power giant E.On. When Gazprom stopped its gas deliveries to Germany, Uniper was forced to buy gas on the open market at prohibitive prices to fulfill its contracts with German gas buyers. It went bankrupt and was taken over by the German government.[62] Uniper brought suit against Gazprom for its failure to deliver. The Kremlin retaliated by taking over the assets of Uniper's Russian power subsidiary, Unipro (see below). Thus, Uniper's previously strong relationship with Russia was destroyed.

"Dual-Bottomed" Russian Companies

Whether or not to "leave Russia" also poses dilemmas for Russian companies that had expanded abroad.[63] One of the biggest success stories of the "Great Opening" was the creation of Yandex, a highly successful search engine and Internet platform that was sometimes called the Russian Google. (Indeed, it was so effective a competitor that it had largely held off Google's efforts to penetrate the Russian Internet market.) Yandex had developed so many sidelines outside Russia that it registered in the Netherlands as a Dutch company. But was it now a Russian company or not? This became an issue in 2022 when the Nasdaq Stock Exchange suspended trading in its shares shortly after the invasion, even though Yandex had not been sanctioned by any of the Western governments.[64] Faced with a decision, Yandex decided to split itself in two: in early 2024, after a lengthy search, it sold off its Russian assets to a consortium of Russian buyers, thus effectively exiting from Russia, and retaining only its Dutch-based unit.[65] This was enough to convince Nasdaq that the Dutch-based Yandex (now renamed Nebius) was no longer "Russian," and it retained its listing, while the Russia-based original remained delisted.[66] (For more on the story of Yandex, see Chapter 7.)

But that maneuver is not playing well among conservatives inside Russia. At SPIEF 2023, Andrei Kostin, the chairman of VTB, denounced what he called "dual-bottomed" companies that are Russian but have their headquarters outside the country. His main target was Yandex.[67] But there are others, such as Ekoniva, a Russian company that makes dairy products in Russia, but which has its home office in Germany.[68] Russian policy toward such hybrid companies has been inconsistent. Another leading company, Vympelcom, one of Russia's earliest telecoms and the creator of the highly successful BeeLine telecom system, had re-registered as a Dutch company and changed its name to Veon, to accommodate its growing activities outside Russia. In February 2023 the government approved its sale of its Russian assets to its Russian management team for a reported $2.1 billion, thus allowing it to sever its ties to Russia.[69] So far, Vympelcom has been spared from attack, perhaps thanks to its early origins in the military-industrial sector.[70]

Another dual-bottomed company leaving Russia is the Anglo-Russian gold producer Polymetal. In May 2023, the United States imposed sanctions on Russian gold exports, putting Russia's two top gold producers and exporters, Polymetal and Polyus, in the line of fire.[71] Polymetal International, the parent holding company of Polymetal, had eight gold and silver mines in Russia and two more in Kazakhstan. In response to the US sanctions, its CEO Vitaly Nesis moved the company's headquarters from Cyprus to Kazakhstan and began looking for a buyer for its Russian assets. It was not easy. As Nesis said, the pool of eligible buyers kept shrinking as the United States and the UK imposed more and more sanctions. One year later, it finally reached a deal with a small gold miner in eastern Siberia, Mangazeya, for a $3.7 billion non-cash deal, only a little more than five time its earnings—a considerable loss. "We probably had three or four offers," Nesis said, "only one of which was actionable." But Nesis, who had declared confidently six months earlier that nationalization was unlikely, now felt under growing threat. "Now it is more important to complete a satisfactory deal quickly than to continue striving for a good deal." The deal was finally closed in March 2023, without objections from the Russian government, which may have wanted to maintain good relations with Kazakhstan.[72]

Lastly, one highly visible case of a Russian exit is that of Telegram, which was founded in 2013 by Russian entrepreneur Pavel Durov, who had previously created VKontakte, a highly successful social-media platform, in Saint Petersburg in 2007. At the time, Durov was hailed in the media as the "Russian Mark Zuckerberg," after the US creator of Facebook. But Durov fled

Russia in 2014, after he refused to share data on Ukrainian subscribers to VKontakte and was forced to sell his shares in the company to a group of well-placed Russian oligarchs. Now based in Dubai, he remains the sole owner of Telegram. Oddly, Telegram, along with VKontakte, remains widely used in Russia (it is the second most popular platform after VKontakte), apparently without interference from Russian officials. (Telegram was briefly blocked by the Russian government in 2018, then unblocked again in 2020, after a loud outcry.[73]) One explanation for this is that Russian elites routinely use Telegram themselves, to spread Kremlin messages and disinformation, as well as compromising leaks about one another, among other reasons.[74] Telegram has gained a dubious reputation outside Russia for tolerating use by criminal and extremist groups, as well as crypto traders. (In September 2024, this led to Durov's arrest by the French authorities.) But Telegram is not considered a "Russian app"; it has spread worldwide, and reports over 900 million users.[75]

The Tightening Noose: The Evolving Russian Responses

Initially, the flurry of announcements of Western withdrawals took the Russian government and companies by surprise. Rosneft's CEO Igor Sechin, for example, stated at SPIEF 2022 that BP's announcement of withdrawal was "unexpected for Rosneft."[76]

Yet from an early date there was a clear divide between hawkish "politicians," such as deputies in the Duma and the United Russia Party, and the more cautious reactions of government technocrats and Russian companies.[77] The hawks fumed over exit announcements and called for retaliation. As early as March 2022 a group of Duma deputies drafted legislation mandating "external management" (effectively a takeover) of companies that had announced their departure or suspended operations. But this was opposed by both the government and the RSPP, the principal representative of Russian industry, and several leading industrialists spoke out against it. The government and the companies' main concern at this stage was to limit the impact of departures and suspensions, and to encourage the foreigners to keep operating and to keep supplying critical goods and parts, especially in such sectors as pharmaceuticals. They introduced a gentler measure, which failed to win over the hawks, and the result was stalemate.[78] In the end, the parliament put off debating the measure.[79]

But as the months went by, the Kremlin's tone became more hawkish. As the wave of exits expanded, the government responded by making it more and more difficult to leave. Those companies that had decided to depart early and had found willing buyers near at hand were the lucky ones. The government, taken by surprise, had not yet imposed restrictions. But as the war has ground on, the Kremlin has made it steadily harder for the foreign companies to find buyers, conclude deals, and gain permission to exit the country. Those who waited are finding the way out more costly and the waiting lines far longer. In a growing number of cases, the door has squeezed shut altogether. The cumulative restrictions and obstacles increasingly amount to an undeclared policy of expropriation.

Early on, companies contemplating a suspension of operations were warned that they would face bankruptcy proceedings. Local Russian managers were threatened with penalties ranging from fines to ten years in prison. Under this kind of pressure, many companies, such as the German tire-maker Continental, after a brief pause in the spring of 2022, resumed production.[80]

The pressure on the foreign companies grew by stages. In September 2022, Putin signed a decree mandating that they would be allowed to leave only if this was approved by a special commission on foreign investments, set up under the Ministry of Finance,[81] and that Russian buyers must be allowed to pay in installments. In December 2022, Western companies applying to leave were required to give Russian buyers a discount of at least 50% (now raised to 60%) of the asset's value.[82] Those that do sell their assets to a Russian buyer are not allowed to export the proceeds.[83]

The next step came in early 2023, when Putin imposed an additional "voluntary exit tax" of 5% of the assessed value of the foreign company as a condition for obtaining permission to leave. Putin seemed uncertain at first over what to do with the proceeds. He initially announced that the money would be used to fund tourist infrastructure in Crimea.[84] Then he changed his mind and ordered the government to use it to fund the Industry Development Fund and support R&D projects for "priority industrial goods."[85] Since then, the "voluntary" exit tax has been increased several times, first to 15% of the exiting company's "fair value," then to 20%, and in October 2024 to 35%. It has turned into a major contribution to the Russian federal budget.[86]

In April 2023, Putin signed a decree authorizing "temporary external management" of designated foreign-owned assets in response to actions by "unfriendly" states.[87] Even before the decree was issued, the procedure had already been applied to the Russian subsidiaries of Unipro and Fortum, which were seized and transferred to Rosneftegaz, a conglomerate mainly owned by Putin's long-time associate Igor Sechin.[88] The following month, Fortum made its final exit, having written down its assets and reported an "impairment" of €1.7 billion.[89] Fortum is receiving no compensation for what amounts to the seizure of its Russian assets; the government's position is that no compensation is due because this is not a confiscation, but only a temporary measure. Yet the government's statement makes clear that this move is a retaliation: "Russia is facing the expropriation of its assets abroad . . . No one should expect Russia to leave this without a response."

In July 2023, Putin broadened the category of "temporary external management" to include two more Western companies, Danone, the leading French producer of dairy products and of the mineral water Evian, and the Danish brewer Carlsberg, mentioned earlier.[90] Danone had been in Russia since 1994 and in the intervening thirty years had become the largest producer of dairy products there,[91] with 8,000 employees working at a dozen sites producing various products, including the popular Prostokvashino, named after a well-known cartoon character. Danone's annual revenues in Russia were about €24 billion a year, or 6% of the company's total in 2021, making it the most exposed of all the foreign consumer groups in Russia. It had initially declared it would not leave, but by October 2022, Danone's management had changed its mind and began looking for a Russian buyer.[92]

Danone ended up paying a high price for its delay. Putin justified the actions against Danone and Carlsberg as a retaliation for the blocking by the EU of Russia's foreign-exchange assets in Europe, but his actual motives were evidently mixed: When, after a year-long search, Danone finally found a buyer, it turned out to be a group of associates of Chechen strongman and Putin protégé Ramzan Kadyrov.[93] Once the deal was closed to the Kremlin's liking, Putin canceled his external management decree. Meanwhile, the "temporary" external manager of Carlsberg Russia is former partner Taimuraz Bolloev, reportedly a business ally of two Putin-era oligarchs, Iurii Koval'chuk and Arkadii Rotenberg.[94] The official approvals committee had earlier made a different choice but was overruled by a direct decision from Putin himself. Thus, Putin's latest moves herald a new phase in the takeover of the remaining foreign companies, to the benefit of the president's close associates.[95]

So far the external management decree has not been applied against the remaining foreign banks. RCB chair Nabiullina, who has been consistently careful not to shut down Russia's remaining financial ties with the West, has opposed using it. Nabiullina has been a cautious voice throughout and appears mindful of the likelihood of Western retaliation, which would ultimately be more harmful to Russian businesses than to Western ones. As she said in a speech to the Duma, it was essential for Russia to minimize restrictions on movements of foreign currency, "in order not to create obstacles for our companies, which need to rapidly, radically rebuild their foreign economic activity, the system of international settlements, and these restrictions would interfere with our companies building their foreign economic activity." [96]

Even when a foreign company is finally able to find a buyer and obtain official permission to leave, there remains the question of repatriating its assets. In May 2023, Putin instructed the government to impose a monthly limit of US$1 billion on foreign currency purchases by Russians if they intend to use that currency for buying assets from foreigners.[97] Consequently, when departing Western companies find a Russian buyer, the sale usually takes the form of a "non-cash" transaction, consisting of dividends and debt swaps.[98]

Adding to the pressure on Western companies in the spring of 2023 was a proposal from a hawkish Russian Duma deputy that companies wanting to exit from Russia be compensated for their stakes with special bonds tied to Russia's frozen assets abroad, thus creating a lever to force Western governments to release them. RCB chair Nabiullina reacted with caution, saying that the idea "could be considered in principle," but cited the likely obstacles.[99] At the time of writing this proposal is still being debated.

Thus, foreign companies that are trying to leave increasingly find themselves in a kind of no man's land, caught between the excruciatingly slow pace of the government's approvals commission, which performs a valuation of their business, and the steadily mounting pressure from the latest Western sanctions. According to Deputy Finance Minister Aleksey Moiseev (who oversees the review process), the review body (a special subcommission of the Commission on Foreign Investments) meets three or four times a week and considers twenty applications at a time. But there are hundreds of applications pending, and the line stretches out the door. In the spring of 2023, according to the *Financial Times*, over 2,000 foreign companies that wanted to leave were waiting for permission from the subcommission.[100] Moiseev is unsympathetic: "Foreigners should not be let off at full price," he says. "It should be hard for them."[101] Indeed, the RCB acknowledges that there is a deliberate policy of limiting the monthly volume of approvals by the commission, in order to minimize the risks of destabilizing the Russian companies and banks involved.[102]

The remaining foreign companies from so-called unfriendly countries are barred from exporting their profits and dividends outside the country, except for any additional investment aimed at expanding their business or creating new employment, or to pay for imports of goods and services used in their business. But the rules governing foreign profits and dividends are complex. Dividends to foreign shareholders must be kept in special so-called C-type accounts maintained by the RCB, where they are held in escrow.[103] The same applies to interest or repayments on Russian government debt or on bonds issued by a Russian entity, such as Gazprom.[104] Non-dividend profits are kept by the foreign companies in their own bank accounts in Russia and in their own name. The bottom line is that the foreign companies from unfriendly countries are accumulating billions in profits that they are unable to move out of the country, and foreign holders of Russian debt are not being paid.[105]

Both the Ministry of Finance and the RCB insist that there is no intention to force foreign companies to leave, but that companies wishing to exit will be treated fairly. The Ministry of Finance claimed that 90% of asset sales had been approved by its committee on foreign investments,[106] and the RCB reported that between March 2022 and March 2023 over 200 foreign companies had sold their assets to Russian buyers and received permission to depart. However, there have been reports from market players that some foreign companies, especially the larger ones, are facing demands to sell their assets at deeper discounts than the officially required 60%, and questions have been raised about the valuations imposed by the supposedly independent appraisers.

In sum, there are divisions, ambivalence, and mixed motives within the Russian government over whether to seek to retain the remaining Western businesses, or to drive them out. Russian hawks are uniformly hostile. But Putin himself insists that there is no policy aimed against Western companies. His position is echoed by First Deputy Prime Minister Denis Manturov, formerly the minister of economy and trade, who stresses the continuing appeal of the Russian market for Western companies and emphasizes how many European and even US companies have chosen to remain or have taken options to return. As he said at the Russia Forum in February 2024, "Our market remains of interest."[107]

Likewise, the Russian business community, represented by the RSPP, speaks out in defense of the foreign companies. But the actual behavior of all of these actors, when it comes to specific cases, increasingly belies their positive phrases. The clearest evidence is a growing wave of nationalizations.

The Expanding Wave of Nationalizations

The treatment of the remaining Western companies, both those wishing to stay and those seeking to leave, is becoming steadily more hostile and predatory. Local players, sensing support from the top, are getting into the act. In the summer of 2023, local courts began nationalizing foreign companies, supposedly to forestall them from leaving, but in reality to take them over. In Saint Petersburg, for example, the Russian assets of a German cement maker registered in the Netherlands, Heidelberg Cement AG, were seized, and similar actions are occurring elsewhere. In such cases, the courts are claiming that the original purchase of Russian assets by foreigners was illegal. The overall effort is being coordinated by the Prosecutor General's Office, which is seeking the renationalization of foreign companies in so-called strategic sectors, a category that is being interpreted ever more broadly.[108] At the same time, some Russian owners with foreign citizenships have come under attack as well.[109]

The foreign companies are now being caught up in a widening battle over the future of private companies generally.[110] On one side is Prosecutor General Igor Krasnov, who has been leading a campaign to review the privatization of thousands of Soviet-era companies, which he claims were illegal. At Krasnov's direction, Russian arbitration courts have approved over 24,000 claims brought by the Procuracy on the grounds that they were illegally privatized, some of them as far back as thirty years ago. Russian media reports a growing number of criminal prosecutions, with some aimed at prominent oligarchs but others at Russians abroad who own companies inside Russia.[111]

Krasnov describes his campaign as part of the "de-offshorization" of the Russian economy, especially "releasing from foreign control a number of key strategic enterprises." Krasnov, who was formerly the deputy to Aleksandr Bastrykin, the hawkish head of the Investigative Committee, appears to reflect the views of parts of the security services.[112]

On the other side is the economic bloc of the government: this includes the *finansisty*, the Ministry of the Economy, and the RSPP, which represents the large companies. These have strongly condemned the Prosecutor General's campaign and the courts' actions. Alexander Shokhin, one of the early market reformers and the veteran head of the RSPP, spoke out against seizing assets from the current owners, adding, "Nobody knows who is next."[113] He was joined by the pro-business Minister of Economic Development Maksim Reshetnikov, who declared that such renationalizations "call into question the inviolability of property rights" and were "a path to nowhere."[114] Shortly afterward, Putin intervened, declaring (in the presence of the head of the General Procuracy, Igor Krasnov) that "there will be no deprivatization in Russia." The next day, the seizure of a German cement-maker was rescinded.[115] But despite Putin's reassurances, the wave of seizures, which according to Krasnov totaled over 180 companies and a trillion rubles in assets in the first two years after the invasion, is still growing.[116] In March 2024, Putin felt moved to repeat the point in even stronger terms at a meeting of the collegium of the General Procuracy: "I want to underscore my position: there is no deprivatization or return to state property, nor can there be." Yet, as if in defiance of his words, literally two days later, a lawsuit was filed before the General Procuracy, aimed at nationalizing Russia's largest pasta maker, Makfa.[117]

Not all of the lawsuits against the foreign companies are attempts at takeovers; some are related to the companies' stopping of their Russian operations. It is often hard to tell the difference. Thus, if a foreign company is unable to deliver on its commitments because of sanctions, or if it is attempting to close its business and leave Russia, its local clients or partners will sue to freeze its assets. As one example among many, the Moscow Arbitration Court has frozen the Russian assets of Adidas, the sporting-goods chain, following a suit by the Moscow amusement park Island of Dreams, where Adidas had closed a leased retail outlet.[118] The number of cases being brought is astounding: in 2023 alone there have been over 30,000,[119] although apparently only a handful have led to actual freezes. Similarly, foreign investors may find their stakes frozen if they fail to fulfill agreements on the grounds that their Russian partners have been sanctioned. Thus, Goldman Sachs has been blocked from unwinding its 5% stake in the Russian retailer Detskii Mir.[120]

The nationalization campaign continues to expand, and now includes some purely Russian-owned companies. In early 2024, three manufacturers of ferroalloys in the Urals heartland city of Cheliabinsk and two other Siberian cities had their assets frozen by a local arbitration court, on the grounds that their initial privatization in 1992 was illegal and that they were cooperating with partners from unfriendly countries in exporting materials of military significance to the United States and Europe. The local court reportedly acted at the orders of the General Procuracy in Moscow.[121] The three plants, grouped into a private holding group called Etalon, under the ownership of a local entrepreneur named Yurii Antipov, supply some 90% of the ferroalloys used in Russian industry.[122] Antipov rejected the charges, arguing that his company's only foreign "partners" were external commodity traders, acting as middlemen for exports but having no role in the company.[123] Nevertheless, its assets were seized,[124] and there is a growing wave of similar nationalizations of Russian companies taking place elsewhere in the country.[125]

Yet there is also pushback: some leading policymakers are actually arguing for re-privatization, on the grounds that state ownership has gone too far. This was first espoused in April 2023 by VTB chairman Andrei Kostin, who is not known for his liberal views.[126] Speaking on Rossiia 24, Russia's main TV station, Kostin suggested that Transneft (the oil transmission company), the Russian Railroads (RZhD), and the post office would all be good candidates for privatization.[127] At SPIEF 2023 all the major economic policymakers chimed in.[128] For some conservatives, such privatization would be a quick way to raise money from the private sector to support the state budget, while for liberals, it would protect the market economy against the present tendency to state-ify everything. There was criticism, however, from the *silovik* wing of the government, notably from Aleksandr Bastrykin, head of the Investigative Committee, who called instead for more nationalization.

The future course of the battle over de-privatization will depend in large part on what course Putin himself chooses to take. So far, as noted, he has opposed "deprivatization," at least in public, and he has promised not to revisit the past by challenging the privatizations of the 1990s. But he leaves a zone of deliberate uncertainty by insisting that private ownership is conditional on performance and loyalty,[129] and his actions in specific cases are, to say the least, ambiguous.

The foreign companies are being caught up in this turbulence. The most striking example of the resulting purgatory in which the remaining foreign companies in Russia find themselves is the venerable Austrian bank Raiffeisenbank, one of the oldest banks in Europe.

Trapped in a Gilded Cage: The Case of Austria's Raiffeisenbank

Raiffeisenbank was one of the first foreign banks to arrive in Russia, in 1996. Despite the Russian default in 1998 and the general chaos of the Russian banking sector at that time, Raiffeisenbank stayed on and prospered. In 2006 it acquired a large Russian bank, Impeksbank, which brought with it a network of local branches, and Raiffeisenbank continued to grow rapidly. On the eve of the invasion, Raiffeisenbank was the seventh-largest bank in Russia, operating a network of ATMs and online banking offices in over 300 cities, with more than 9,000 employees.[130] All told, the four largest foreign banks in Russia (Société Générale, Raiffeisenbank, UniCredit, and Citibank) had a combined exposure of over $57 billion, and more than 30,000 staff in 417 branches, with almost 10 million customers. While Unicredit had focused primarily on corporate customers, with three-quarters of its loans going to over 1,500 industrial companies and multinationals,[131] the other three conducted a wide range of banking operations through retail branches and virtual offices throughout Russia.

Then came the Russian attack on Ukraine on February 24, 2022. Some of the foreign banks resolved to make a fast exit and escaped cleanly. Citibank sold its portfolio of installment loans and credit card balances to a Russian bank, Uralsib. Some left a few feathers behind. France's Société Générale, which had bought a Russian bank, Rosbank, from billionaire Vladimir Potanin, quickly sold it back to him—although at a loss of over €3 billion—and departed.

But most of the other foreign banks hesitated, and in particular Austria's Raiffeisenbank and Italy's Unicredit. Why didn't they leave? The answer is that since the invasion they had suddenly become very profitable. Whereas the leading Russian banks were under Western sanctions, the foreign banks were not, and consequently they became the main remaining conduits for moving foreign exchange in and out of Russia and conducting settlements, especially since they remained part of the SWIFT international messaging system, while the leading Russian banks had been "de-SWIFTed." Russian companies and individuals, as well as the Western companies still in Russia, rushed to transfer their money to the two largest remaining foreign banks, Unicredit, and above all Raiffeisenbank.[132]

Raiffeisen, because of its extensive network of virtual branches throughout Russia, benefited spectacularly. By the beginning of 2023, Raiffeisen alone was handling up to half of the money flows between Russia and the out-side world, as both Russian savers and companies turned to Raiffeisenbank to handle their foreign transactions. Italy's Unicredit was in a distant sec-ond place. The business was hugely profitable. In 2022 Raiffeisenbank alone made 141 billion rubles in profits (roughly $2 billion), triple the average of earlier years; Unicredit came far behind at about 57 billion rubles; all the other foreign banks totaled only 13 billion. Meanwhile, the Russian banks as a group lost money.[133]

But there was a catch. In early 2022, Putin signed a decree barring foreign banks from transferring dividends back to their parent companies abroad. For those who now wished to leave, Putin had further bad news. Foreign companies from unfriendly countries were welcome to depart, but only with his permission. And getting that permission would require the approval of the subcommission mentioned earlier, plus submitting to the haircut and the special "donation" to the state of described earlier.[134] The review board slow-walked the whole approvals procedure, forcing the foreign companies to wait for months for the green light to leave. Meanwhile, well-connected Russian players circled about them, looking to pick up their assets on the cheap. Pressures were mounting on all sides. When in late April, Putin's decree authorizing "temporary external management" was announced, the new procedure was immediately applied to the Russian subsidiaries of Uniper and Fortum, which have been taken over by managers from Rosneft.

Would the foreign banks be next? On this point there appears to be dis-agreement between the hawks in the government and the RCB. Nabiullina, chair of the RCB, has spoken out against using the decree to take over foreign banks, since they are the last remaining conduit for moving dollars and euros in and out of the country. As the RCB points out, of the thirteen banks on its list of "institutionally strategic" banks, only the two foreign banks, Raif-feisenbank and Unicredit, are unsanctioned. But if they were taken over by Russian managers, the United States and the EU would undoubtedly quickly sanction them too. So, for the time being, the foreign banks have not been targeted. They are simply too useful.[135]

But it may be just a matter of time. As the hostility between Russia and the West grows, the foreign banks become more exposed. In April 2023, as mentioned earlier, a deputy in the Russian Duma proposed compensat-ing companies exiting the Russian market with bonds tied to Russia's frozen assets, in particular the $300 billion in RCB foreign exchange reserves that are marooned in the West. The logic of the plan was that it would give the exiting companies a strong incentive to lobby their home governments for the unfreezing of those reserves. RCB chair Nabiullina, who was present, did not dismiss the idea out of hand,[136] although it has not yet been adopted.

Meanwhile, pressures are mounting from outside Russia as well, as the United States and the EU urge the foreign banks to leave. In February 2024, the US Treasury's OFAC sent Raiffeisenbank a "request for clarification" of its operations in Russia, although it refrained from threatening to sanction the Austrian bank.[137] In May, it followed up with a direct ultimatum to Raiffeisenbank to drop a plan to take a stake in a construction company with ties to a Russian oligarch. (Raiffeisenbank complied within twenty-four hours.) The European Central Bank, for its part, has stated that "the window to quit is closing," and it has demanded that Raiffeisenbank submit regular reports on its exit plans. Raiffeisenbank is clearly feeling the heat. Johann Strobl, the CEO of Raiffeisen International, in response to a reporter's question, snapped, "The bank is not a sausage stand that can be closed overnight."[138]

Raiffeisenbank's Russian operation is making a fortune inside Russia— in 2022 its profits amounted to 60% of the parent corporation's total—but it was effectively trapped in a gilded cage, since it cannot export them. Yet as the months go by, the damage to Raiffeisenbank's reputation and that of the other foreign banks only grows. In September 2023, the Russian government created a "payment holiday" system, which grants loan payment holidays to soldiers serving in Ukraine and writes off any debts they may owe if they are maimed or killed. All told, Russian banks restructured 800 million rubles (or about $12 million) in loans to soldiers in the first three months of the program. The foreign banks had no choice but to also comply with the arrangement. In response to criticism, Raiffeisen acknowledged that 0.2% of its loans were affected, an amount that it called "negligible"; but this amounts to about $7 million in outstanding loans to Russian soldiers, a potential liability that will only grow as Russian battlefield casualties mount.[139]

Raiffeisenbank has been casting about for buyers for its Russian operation. Eligible candidates are scarce, since any Russian bank large enough to do a deal is likely to be under sanctions. Raiffeisenbank initially turned to Rosbank, which had earlier reacquired Société Générale's Russian assets, but the deal fell through after Raiffeisenbank's shareholders objected and the European Central Bank signaled disapproval. (Rosbank and its owner

Vladimir Potanin are under US and EU sanctions.[140]) It then began talking to Sberbank, Russia's largest bank, about a possible "prisoners' exchange." Sberbank, which is also under sanctions, has had its assets frozen in Europe. Under the plan, Raiffeisenbank would have traded its Russian assets against Sberbank's frozen ones in Europe. But this plan too collapsed when it was vetoed by the European Central Bank. In any case, any plan would have required Putin's permission, which because of the foreign banks' usefulness might not have been forthcoming.[141]

Consequently, for the moment Raiffeisenbank and Unicredit have been gradually cutting back on foreign-exchange operations and shedding their corporate customers while accepting no new ones. Raiffeisenbank claims it has reduced its lending in Russia by 85% since the invasion and has cut ties with three dozen sanctioned individuals and businesses. Back in Vienna, Raiffeisenbank International has shut down all its correspondent accounts with Russian banks, with the sole exception of its own Russia-based subsidiary.[142] The two banks have also taken a few symbolic steps to lower their profile. Raiffeisenbank recently removed its logo from its retail branches, and Unicredit has begun closing its remaining Russian locations.[143] But Raiffeisenbank, despite somewhat lower profits from Russia in 2023, is continuing to add Russian clients and is actively advertising for new personnel.[144] Its dilemma is that it is making big money but it remains trapped, unable to export its profits, and its cage is shrinking.[145]

Good Deals: "New Russians" Pick Up the Pieces

For some enterprising Russians, the departure of the Western companies has been a golden opportunity to pick up valuable assets on the cheap.[146] Some are well-known entrepreneurs, such as Ivan Tavrin, one of the three co-founders of the Russian internet provider Megafon, who reportedly spent over $2.3 billion acquiring departing Western assets during the first year after the invasion, the largest of which is Avito, an online classified ads business bought from the Japanese conglomerate Naspers. Tavrin evidently got a good deal, since Avito had been valued at three times as more than his purchase price just before the invasion. In some accounts Tavrin is seen as a stalking horse for Putin's close ally Iurii Koval'chuk.[147] Others are relative unknowns, such as Armen Sarkisyan, founder of a company called

S8 Capital, who has gone on a buying spree, scooping up the Russian assets of Otis (elevators), Bosch (sparkplugs), and two tire-makers, the German-based Continental and Japanese Bridgestone.

Another newly prominent beneficiary of the buy outs is Aleksandr Govor, a Siberian billionaire who had previously made a fortune in the coal business but had long been a McDonald's franchisee. Govor and McDonald's reached a deal quickly, and Govor acquired McDonald's entire Russian chain of over 800 restaurants with 62,000 employees, taking over McDonald's liabilities to landlords and suppliers. Russians continue to enjoy hamburgers and fries, but under the name *Vkusno—i tochka*, meaning "Delicious—full stop." Other fast-food chains hesitated and soon found themselves in difficulty.

Local figures such as Govor are frequently stand-ins for more powerful personalities, who prefer to remain in the shadows. Govor's senior partner is Arsen Kanokov, the former governor of the province of Kabardino-Balkaria and a member of the Russian Senate. Kanokov heads a group of investors called Sindika, which has been one of the biggest winners in the race to pick up the assets of departing foreign businesses. In addition to McDonald's, Sindika has also acquired the former Starbucks, Domino's Pizza, and Obi, a German supermarket chain, as well as hotels, retail outlets, and restaurants. Significantly, Sindika's minority investors include figures from the entourage of Chechen strongman Ramzan Kadyrov.[148]

The best-known beneficiary of the Western sell offs is the oligarch Vladimir Potanin, the majority owner of Nornikel', who bought back Rosbank from the departing Société Générale for a symbolic €1, after selling it to the French bank when it first entered Russia. Potanin is disadvantaged in the competition for foreign assets, however, since he is under sanctions from the United States and the UK, whereas most of the emerging cohort of Russian buyers are not—at least not yet.

What Has Been the Impact on the Russian Economy?

The impact of the ongoing exodus of Western businesses on the Russian economy depends on the sector, the size of the company, the amount of its stake in Russia, and the time frame. Here we look separately at the consumer, financial, IT, and industrial sectors.

The impact has been least on the consumer sector. While hundreds of foreign retail outlets closed their doors and thousands ceased sales, they are being quickly replaced by Russian firms and substitute products, many arriving by roundabout routes. Franchise networks like McDonald's soon found Russian buyers. French fashions and perfumes began arriving via third countries, as did high-end foods (assisted by a government measure authorizing "parallel imports," bypassing foreign intellectual property rights). Western smartphones and consumer electronics remain widely available. Familiar Western brands can be found everywhere, or have been quickly replaced with Russian, or increasingly Chinese, equivalents. Of the hundreds of Western companies in the consumer sector, most were small, and have faded without much of a trace; only a handful of the larger ones, most notably the French chains Auchan and Leroy Merlin, and the British (actually Brazilian-owned) Avon, are still visible on the Russian scene.[149] In commercial real estate, the impact of the Western departures was only temporary. Foreign companies accounted for 30% of the occupancy of Moscow commercial space on the eve of the invasion, and their mass exit initially caused the real-estate market to plummet, but it has since largely recovered, as Russian companies have moved in.[150] In Moscow and in the major cities, despite a few boarded-up stores in the high-rent districts, life has gone on as usual.

The impact of the exodus on the financial sector is growing. On the eve of the invasion, foreign banks represented only about 2% of the assets of the Russian banking sector. Four major Western banks, Citigroup, Unicredit, Raiffeisen, and Société Générale, had developed networks of retail banks, but these had only a minor share of total deposits (where the Russian giant Sberbank dominated), and they played a minor role in such fast-growing sectors as consumer credit and mortgages. Of the sixty-odd other foreign banks, most served the foreign community. However, as the sanctions have blocked the access of the Russian banks to the West, business has flowed toward the two main remaining foreign banks, Austrian Raiffeisenbank and Italian Unicredit, as we have seen. Thus, in addition to Gazprombank, Russia now depends on two foreign banks for a large share of its international settlements, and these are understandably under growing European pressure to leave.

The impact on Russian industry is concentrated in only a handful of sectors. The most severely affected sector is transportation, especially the automotive industry, and AvtoVAZ most of all, following the departure of Renault. All the Western automakers have left. Other parts of the transportation sector, including shipbuilding, railroad cars and high-speed locomotives, and aviation, have also been held back by the Western exits. Joint industrial projects, ranging from LNG liquefaction and transportation, gas turbines in the power sector, equipment for advanced fracking and horizontal drilling in the oil industry, leading-edge computer chips, and more, have been similarly affected.

In the oil industry, the immediate impact of the departure of the foreign companies has been small. Shell and ExxonMobil have left Sakhalin; BP and Total have been reduced to the role of passive stakeholders; and the oil-service companies, chiefly Schlumberger and Halliburton, have severed all but current field services. To date, their departure has left hardly a trace. It is only over the longer term that their absence will be felt, as the Russian oil industry is obliged to suspend work on the next frontier, for example, in offshore exploration or tight oil.

The exit of the Western companies has been especially noticeable in IT, where it has affected all sectors of the Russian economy. Different Western IT companies have responded in different ways. SAP, Oracle, Dell, and HP suspended all new sales and services in Russia immediately after the invasion. SAP and Microsoft continued to serve existing unsanctioned Russian clients, including schools and hospitals. SAP, Microsoft, and IBM all kept their Russian staffs on salary—about 1,000 apiece in the case of IBM and SAP. Dell broke off all technical support. But IBM angered its Russian customers when it abruptly stopped all access to its cloud services, without giving its Russian clients time to make copies of their files and data.[151] The immediate impact of the Western exit on the Russian IT sphere was cushioned by the fact that a Russian "systems integrator" called IBS, which was previously the Russian partner of SAP, was able to service existing contracts. But over time, it will be unable to support subsequent software editions and provide corrections, especially those that affect security.[152]

Conclusions

The arrival of the foreign companies in Russia was the prime symbol of what was hailed as a new era in Russian Western relations. But there is no similarly clear symbol to be drawn from the mixed pattern of their leaving. Only about 10% of them have actually left. But equally few have declared unambiguously that they intend to stay. The rest are strung out on a continuum ranging from scaling back and suspending operations to continuing business while they wait for permission to exit. Overall, three years into the Ukrainian war, the rate of departures has slowed to a crawl. For some, Western pressure to leave has faded. The CEO of Mondelez, a Chicago-based chocolate maker, put it bluntly, saying that investors "did not morally care" whether companies stayed in Russia, and that his own shareholders were not pressuring him to do so.[153]

Yet the foreign companies still in Russia are increasingly caught in a vise, as pressure mounts on them from all sides—from the Kremlin but also from organizations representing the security bloc, such as the General Procuracy and its Investigative Committee, as well as local courts and opportunistic Russian businessmen. Western businesses that have elected to stay are barred from exporting their profits,[154] and the ones that wish to leave cannot do so without official permission, which is increasingly difficult to obtain.

This chapter argues that the exit of Western businesses will have enduring and wide-ranging consequences beyond the direct impact on the sectors and regions they have left. In industry, the arrival of new foreign-mediated investment has stopped. The flow into Russia of skilled and experienced personnel—the key to efficient technology transfer—has reversed, as the Westerners depart, but also a fair number of the Russians they had trained. The supply of spare parts and components has become slower, more costly, and less reliable. Maintenance and product support are no longer available from former foreign partners. In the consumer and service sectors, the long-term impact of the Western departures will be less critical, because many of the niches they occupied are already being filled by Russian entrepreneurs.

The greatest loss is symbolic. Above all, the reputation of Russia as a promising market, as a place where foreign businesses were welcome and risks could be managed, as an exciting place where careers and profits could be made—all of that has disappeared. Above all, trust and confidence have been shattered, and that will not soon be repaired.[155] The opening of Russia was a single lifetime event; and so is the exodus.

Chapter 7
The Balance Sheet

In early 2020, just as the COVID-19 virus set in, a remarkable three-hour documentary went viral on the Russian Internet. In it a well-known YouTube personality named Iurii Dud' traveled to Silicon Valley and interviewed a dozen young Russians who had left Russia and made it in California. The documentary's message at the end was sobering: "The high-tech future of the world is Russian, but not in Russia."[1] By late April, a month after its release, it had drawn over 17 million Russian viewers. A few years ago, a liberal economist named Andrei Klepach, deputy minister of economic development at the time, famously voiced the same thought when he exclaimed, "Russia has become a country that exports oil, girls, and future Nobel Prize laureates."[2]

Russia also exports IT entrepreneurs. Perhaps the most famous example is Andrei Doronichev, who grew up in the poor Moscow neighborhood of Medvedkovo and is today one of the top executives of Google. He spent his childhood playing on the Internet, partly because the neighborhood was too dangerous to venture outside. Inspired by early programs such as Crazy Frog, he became entranced with the potential of YouTube. If only the software could be written to put it on the world's billions of personal phones, he thought. So he wrote a letter to Sergey Brin, the co-founder of Google, asking for a job. Remarkably, Google hired him. For the next fourteen years Doronichev was vice-president for product development at Google in Mountain View, California, before departing in 2021 to found his own start-up in the field of AI.[3]

Today there are thousands of Russians in Silicon Valley. When asked why they have left Russia, they cite the many obstacles that entrepreneurs face back in Russia.[4] For example, Dmitrii Dumik, who founded a successful company in California called ChatFuel, explains, "There's a constant uncertainty ... You wonder, Will I get a surprise inspection today? Once you reach a certain level, they start to get interested in you ... As soon as you become someone, they'll come to collect."[5] Crime and extortion in Russia, often by official bodies, figure high on their list, but also bureaucratic obstruction and inflexible rules.

The Russians of Silicon Valley reject the name *émigrés*. Though many of those who left in the 1990s were driven by hardship, the latest generation is different. The Russians in California insist that they were not trying to *get away* from something, but to *get toward* something—like Doronichev—to realize a vision, "to change the world." Though many have made their fortunes in California and have become US citizens, they travel freely about the world, including to Moscow—at least until recently. Maksim Mikheenko, for example, who has created well-known computer games such as *Call of Duty* and *Fallout* in his company 5518 Studios, describes himself as a conduit of Russian talent to the United States, and before the invasion he shuttled between Los Angeles and Moscow,[6] outsourcing art and designs from 3D artists inside Russia. Another example is Nikolai Davydov, who ran a successful venture capital company in Silicon Valley. On the eve of the invasion, he said, "I pay taxes in Russia. I employ several hundred people there. I come and go freely."[7] Today, these talented people are essentially lost to Russia.

The story of the mass emigration of Russians following the 2022 invasion, and the success that many of them have found in Silicon Valley, symbolizes the two key themes of this book—the failed opening of Russia to the West and the impact of its reclosing as a result of war and sanctions. Let us pause to take stock of the argument developed so far.

Summary of the Argument to This Point

The story of Russia's economic opening to the West since the end of the Soviet Union can be summed up in three phases: the two-way opening (roughly mid-1980s through mid-2010s), followed by the waves of Western sanctions (2014–the present), and finally the continuing exodus on both sides and the growing isolation of the Russian economy from the West since the Russian invasion of Ukraine in 2022. Together these make up a unique period of history, the unprecedented reopening of a previously locked society, followed thirty years later by its dramatic reclosing to the West, accompanied by a reorientation toward the East, especially China. It is a story of Russia, but also of the world at an equally unique time, at the apogee of Western power and neoliberal globalization, and the ways the two stories interacted.

The aim of this chapter is to draw up a balance sheet of the successes and failures of Russia's opening, and of the impact of the war, the sanctions, and the exodus, as recounted in the preceding chapters, and to appraise Russia's assets and liabilities as they will stand by the end of the present decade. This will form the basis of the scenario for "Russia 203X," the book's final chapter.

Part I, "Russia's Failed Opening," argues that the negative legacy of the two-way opening outweigh the positives in three key respects. First, Russia's version of a market economy is deeply flawed. It is dominated by large state-owned companies, with only a relatively weak private sector; it is geographically unbalanced, with deep inequalities between the leading cities, above all Moscow, and the outlying regions, particularly east of the Urals; and it is unbalanced by sector, with overdeveloped commodities groups concentrated in high-cost locations, such as the Russian Arctic coast. Above all, Russia's market economy is hobbled by a deeply corrupt state and leadership. Second, Russia's opening led to an excessive dependence on foreign capital and financial ties, on imported technologies, and on vulnerable supply chains, and especially on an Internet infrastructure largely based in the United States.[8] Third, the experience of the opening created resentments, suspicions, and disappointments, among both Russians and Westerners, which contributed to the overall deterioration of Russian–Western geopolitical relations after the mid-2000s.

Part II, "Perfect Storm: Sanctions and Responses," analyzes the impact of sanctions on the economy and argues that the Russians' responses to them, although effective in the near term, will be increasingly unable to overcome their long-term debilitating effects. Three aspects are especially significant. First, Russia's access to global finance and investment has been disrupted, while at the same time private capital continues to leave the country. Second, Russia has been forced by the sanctions to turn to higher-cost trade routes and payment arrangements, diminishing its margins from exports and increasing its dependence on non-Western partners, chiefly China. Third, there has been a loss of human capital and know-how, as well as of channels for people-based transfer of skills and technology, as a result of the mass emigration of skilled Russians and the exit of Western companies and personnel. The overall result is a slow degradation of Russia's potential for innovation, profit, and growth. Over time, these effects will be compounded by the war, which has aggravated long-standing distortions and weaknesses throughout the economy, by drawing labor, money, and resources into the military-industrial sector, to the detriment of the civilian economy.

Russia's Achievements

In drawing up the balance sheet of Russia's opening, however, one must begin by recognizing Russia's considerable achievements during this period. Beginning under Boris Yeltsin, and then through the late 2000s, Russia laid down many of the economic and institutional foundations of a modern market economy. Despite the growing intrusion of the state and the partial remilitarization of the economy under Putin since the mid-2010s, these accomplishments have not been reversed.

As a result, since the end of the Soviet Union, Russia's economy and society have fundamentally changed. The consumer sector and many services are now private, as is most Russian housing. Modern telephony and the Internet have revolutionized the ways Russians communicate, shop, trade, bank, entertain themselves, and travel. The long lines and chronic shortages of the Soviet period have disappeared. Money and credit are now at the center of the economy. Russian professionals and entrepreneurs have acquired the skills and experience needed to run a market-based system. These changes are here to stay.

There have also been far-reaching changes in Russian industry and the commodities sector. Metallurgy has been modernized, especially steel and aluminum, as well as some branches of manufacturing. Up-to-date production techniques are now widespread in the oil and gas industries. The rise of export-oriented corporate farming has reversed the abysmal productivity of Soviet-era agriculture. There have been improvements in transportation. Whole cities have been rebuilt, especially Moscow, which is unrecognizable from its Soviet days.

Credit for these achievements belongs both to private enterprise and to the Russian state. The latter deserves more recognition than it usually gets. Much of the progress, to be sure, was achieved in the period from 2000 to 2008, when oil prices were high and money was plentiful, and the Putin government actively promoted reforms. Above all, credit belongs to the highly professional and conservative team of fiscal and financial experts—the *finansisty*—who have run the Russian Central Bank and the Ministry of Finance for much of the last twenty years. They have managed to keep the Russian economy afloat through three major economic crises, as well as the sanctions of the last decade.[9]

Weaknesses and Vulnerabilities on the Eve of the War and Sanctions

Despite these positives, Russia's opening left Russia with serious vulnerabilities. These were the product of weaknesses inherited from Soviet times, combined with policy mistakes, missed opportunities, and neglected needs in the Putin era. Russia emerged from the Soviet period with a misshapen economy and infrastructure, but with an immense potential for modernization, thanks to its endowment of natural resources and its highly educated population. Russia's state and political elites could have used these assets to greater advantage to lay the basis for a diversified and modern post-industrial economy and a trade profile better positioned to be competitive in the new century. But they largely failed to do so. Instead, after a brief period of reform, they concentrated their efforts and resources on the development of exportable commodities, especially hydrocarbons, while neglecting the rest.

That failure was ultimately political, and it had two faces. The first was the massive misallocation of Russia's wealth to state-owned corporations run by politically favored elites. The second was the failure to encourage and protect private enterprise, especially in the service and high-tech sectors. The state systematically discriminated against small and medium businesses, preying upon them to feed the state bureaucracy and to fill privileged pockets, above all those of the security services. The energy of the private sector was sapped by political corruption at all levels. Thus, the opportunity to build an independent entrepreneurial class, based on a diversified economy, was missed.

Corruption and neglect are also at the root of the continuing deterioration of Russia's Soviet-era infrastructure. Basic urban services such as centralized heating, electrical grids, and streets and roads, have been allowed to decay. Water management systems, both for reclamation and flood control, have received little investment or maintenance. The only exceptions are large new projects backed by influential industrial interests, such as hydropower in East Siberia, or oil and gas development along the Arctic coastline. The result of these lopsided priorities has been a spate of breakdowns of older infrastructure in many places around the country.[10]

Both of these failures preceded the Ukrainian war. After the mid-2010s, economic reform and modernization increasingly gave way to the delusional dream of rebuilding a Russian empire. The war and the sanctions have aggravated the country's underlying weaknesses, while diminishing the long-term effectiveness of the responses to them. "Russia's economy," concludes economist Elena Ribakova, "was already in decline before the Ukraine invasion and Western sanctions."[11]

The Impact of Sanctions and the Russian Responses

The second part of the book also deals with the Western sanctions and Russia's responses to them since the 2022 invasion.

Despite the unprecedented scale of the Western sanctions, the conservative fiscal and monetary team headed by Prime Minister Mikhail Mishustin, Finance Minister Anton Siluanov, and the chair of the Russian Central Bank, Elvira Nabiullina, has been largely successful in keeping the Russian economy stable. So far Putin has given it steady support.

The big question ahead is whether he will continue to do so. Following Putin's re-election in the spring of 2024, all of the leading financial technocrats were reappointed to their positions under Prime Minister Mishustin,[12] underscoring Putin's continuing stress on stability. However, the promotion of several "statist" technocrats shows Putin's growing focus on the economic and industrial support for the war machine, as indicated by his appointment of a civilian economist, Andrei Belousov, as minister of defense.[13] Belousov has long argued for a stronger state role in promoting innovation, and his views have frequently put him at odds with the pro-market *finansisty*.[14] His promotion may augur a shift in economic policy away from market solutions.

Despite the efforts of the pro-market financial team, economic growth has slowed sharply over the past decade, compared to the early Putin years.[15] Real GDP growth and disposable incomes have been stagnant since 2013. During that time, global GDP has increased by 31.5%, but that of Russia by only 11.5%, and Russia remains stuck in fifty-eighth place in global rankings of GDP per capita, far behind the world's leaders. More ominously for the long term, ever since the 2008–9 financial crisis Russia has underinvested in new technology and infrastructure.

An added factor in the slowdown has been persistent inflation, despite the Central Bank's anti-inflationary policy. This has contributed to a three-fold decline in the value of the ruble against the dollar over the past decade, and although this has stimulated Russian exports and helped the Russian budget to remain solvent (since exporters must pay their taxes to the government in rubles), the overall result has been a relative decline in popular living standards compared to the West.

These effects are not due solely to the sanctions, but rather primarily to the slowdown in the growth of oil prices over the last decade, to the COVID-19 pandemic, and above all to the government's attempt to fight a war while simultaneously preserving civilian consumption. This policy is causing increasing strain, especially in the form of runaway wage increases, which are encouraging Russian consumers to borrow more. The simultaneous growth of civilian credit and military spending, without a corresponding increase in productive capacity or productivity or increased imports, is making the economy overheat.[16] German Gref, whom we met earlier as the CEO of Sberbank, warns that the economy has reached its limits. There are no reserves left: unemployment, at 2.6%, is at an all-time low; capacity utilization, at 81% of capacity, is at an all-time high. Gref concludes, "Our present growth model has reached exhaustion."[17]

Manpower shortages have become acute. The Ukrainian war, and the large-scale increase in military spending and production since the invasion, have aggravated shortages of manpower in skilled categories. Arms producers, who pay higher wages, are drawing workers away from civilian sectors. Many civilian companies, including small and medium enterprises, report that workers are quitting and moving to regions with large military plants, leaving them short-handed. The problem is aggravated by the low level of automation typical of Russian industry. Elvira Nabiullina, chair of the Russian Central Bank, describes the shortage of labor as "the main problem" facing the Russian economy, calling the situation "very acute." "Enterprises are saying their top problem is not lack of credit, or demand, but manpower."[18] From the conservative side, Nikolai Patrushev, until recently the secretary of Russia's Security Council and one of Putin's closest associates, agrees. Criticizing the continued dependence of Russian industry on foreign suppliers, Patrushev said, "The main obstacle is the shortage of scientific and engineering specialists."[19]

In appraising the impact of the Western sanctions, one must take into account aggravating factors such as Russia's pre-existing infrastructural weaknesses, its declining population, and its lopsided trade profile, with its heavy weighting on exports of commodities, coupled with imports of technology, on which it still depends heavily. It is claimed that the chief effect of sanctions has been to isolate Russia. But the theme of isolation requires some elaboration, because it is a mixed picture. By some measures, Russia is not isolated at all. Russian exports of commodities are back to all-time highs. Russia's foreign trade has been rerouted to the east and the south, but it is nearly as large as it was before the sanctions. Russians still travel abroad for their holidays, although to different countries than formerly. Russians continue to surf the Internet for business and entertainment. In all these ways, Russia remains very much in touch with the outside world.

But Russia is indeed isolated in more fundamental ways—from the channels and flows that create efficient investment and innovation, from human transfers of technology and know-how, from the most efficient trade routes and patterns, and from a global communications web that remains largely centered in the United States. These are still concentrated in the West. The pivot to the East is slow and costly, and it locks Russia into a less efficient relationship than with the West. Moreover, it is not an "opening," in the same sense as the period from 1992 to 2022. It is more limited and superficial, more of a relationship of political convenience, rather than the mutual interaction that was briefly the case between Russia and the West. It is also one in which Russia becomes ever more dependent on an unequal relationship with China.

This is a deep change. If it is not reversed, it will mark a fateful new chapter in Russian history, and by and large an unfavorable one. Indeed, it is already doing so.

The rest of this chapter expands on these points, by looking at four illustrative cases. The first is the impact of the reclosing of Russia on Russia's three leading banks, Gazprombank, VTB, and Sberbank, and on the banking sector generally. The second is the fate of Russia's most innovative Internet company, Yandex. The third is the impact of increased military spending on civilian innovation and infrastructural investment, using the example of the lagging modernization of Russia's transportation infrastructure, chiefly its railroads. Lastly, the fourth is the evolution of Russia's economic ties with China, and particularly the growth of the Russian–Chinese energy trade in the wake of Putin's destruction of Russia's pipeline gas business in Europe and the rerouting of Russia's oil trade under the pressure of sanctions.

All four cases speak to the same point: that the Western sanctions and the war, if maintained over time, will have long-term debilitating effects on the Russian economy, increasing its economic backwardness and isolation from the Western world, at a time of accelerating technological change in the leading economies. On its present course, Russia will be left behind.

A Tale of Three Banks: The Long-Term Impact of Sanctions on the Banking Sector

In February 2018, the flower of Russia's economic and political elite gathered at the eighteenth Russian Investment Forum in the southern resort town of Sochi, near Crimea. It was not a joyous occasion. By that year, the euphoria from Russia's long oil-fueled boom had faded. The sanctions imposed by the West four years before, in response to the Russian occupation of Crimea, had constrained Russia's access to foreign capital; instead, domestic capital was leaving the country. Investment as a share of GDP, which had long been low by international standards, had fallen even farther, as domestic savings were unable to fill the gap.[20] Meanwhile, global oil prices had dropped by over half between 2012 and 2017, cutting deeply into Russia's export revenues and its economic growth, and driving the Russian state budget into deficit. The mood at the Forum was somber, in sharp contrast to the festive atmosphere of earlier gatherings.

At the main session, three men sat together on the stage, the heads of the three most powerful banks in Russia—Andrei Akimov of Gazprombank, Andrei Kostin of VTB, and German Gref of Sberbank. The three were a study in contrasts. Akimov and Kostin were both in their mid-60s. They had come from privileged Soviet families; they had lived for many years abroad as members of the Soviet elite; and they had had long careers in investment banking. But there the resemblance ended. Kostin had built his early career as a Soviet diplomat, serving in embassies and consulates all over the world, before turning to banking in Russia when the Soviet Union fell.[21] Akimov, by contrast, was a professional banker, who had worked abroad for seventeen years in Russian banks and investment companies in Switzerland and Austria. However, they both occupied positions that were typically held by intelligence officers; Akimov, in particular was reputed to hold the rank of general in the security services.[22] Both Kostin and Akimov, in short, were classic products of the last Soviet *nomenklatura* generation, and would be considered statist conservatives.

German Gref, the head of Sberbank, was different. Born into a modest family of German exiles in Kazakhstan, he had made his way up through local schools and provincial universities to a law degree at Saint Petersburg State University. A decade younger than the other two,[23] Gref in the early 1990s had been one of the leading liberal reformers in the mayoralty of Saint Petersburg, serving as legal advisor to the city's property committee, before rising to deputy mayor and head of the property committee. It was in that capacity that he had first met Vladimir Putin, and from that point on worked closely with him. In 1998, Gref moved to Moscow, as part of the second wave of economic reform that included the future finance minister, Aleksey Kudrin (as told in Chapter 1). Thus, unlike Kostin and Akimov, he had been a consistent voice for liberal reform. However, what all three men had in common was close ties to Putin.

All three banks had profited handsomely from Russia's opening to the West, establishing subsidiaries and banking and investment operations throughout Europe. Sberbank, Russia's largest savings bank, had acquired a large retail network in Eastern Europe, with 800,000 customers, 3,900 employees, and assets of €13 billion. VTB had opened investment offices in Frankfurt and London to manage corporate borrowing and investment on behalf of Russia's largest companies and some well-placed oligarchs (discretely referred to as "special state projects"). VTB also handled most of Russia's corporate debt, which in 2020 stood at more than $700 billion. Gazprombank, through local offices throughout Europe, served as the conduit for payments by European gas buyers.

But by 2018 the political atmosphere in Europe had begun to turn against the Russian presence, and the three bankers in Sochi could sense that the heyday of expansion had ended. All three were already under sanctions, as a result of the Crimean occupation, as were two of their three banks (only Gazprombank was as yet exempt, for reasons already discussed). The subsequent invasion and the blizzard of Western sanctions was a game-changer for all three. VTB and Sberbank have now been forced out of Europe, with considerable losses. Only Gazprombank is still spared, but it has lost its traditional function as the channel for Europe's gas payments. For the time being, it remains a member of SWIFT, and is able to process settlements for third parties via Euroclear and Eurostream, but that privileged position may not last much longer.

The contrast between the three banks' vigorous expansion over the preceding twenty years and their situation after the invasion, illustrates the many-sided impact of the sanctions on Russia's financial system. On the one hand, the three banks have been forced to "reshore" to Russia and the FSU.[24] Sberbank has turned back to the domestic market in Russia, and lately it has specialized mainly in property loans. VTB has expanded its operations in the FSU (except for Ukraine, where it was previously strongly present) and China. Gazprombank is the only one of the three to have retained a limited foreign presence for the time being.

But paradoxically, all three banks, after sharp drops in revenues in 2022, are now reporting record profits. Gazprombank, in particular, is enjoying a resurgence in Europe despite Gazprom's much-diminished gas revenues, thanks to an expanded list of Russian clients of all sorts, who have switched to Gazprombank because it is as yet unsanctioned.[25] In short, all three of Russia's three leading banks, like the rest of the Russian economy, have adapted to sanctions, and for the present they are doing well.

Yet all three face mounting constraints in the longer term. Sberbank's pioneering efforts to expand into digital banking and data storage on the cloud have been stymied by the withdrawal of its Western IT partners and managers (as described in Chapter 6). Gazprombank's new role as a middleman is hardly a replacement for its previous business servicing Russia's gas trade in Europe, and European pressure against it is mounting. VTB has made only limited progress in diversifying away from Western currencies, and Chinese banks have been cautious lenders. The main long-term effect of the Western financial sanctions, in sum, is a drastic curtailment of all three banks' access to foreign investment capital, credit, settlements, and leading-edge technologies. In these respects, they mirror similar problems in the Russian IT sector, to which we turn now, with the story of Yandex.

The Rise and Fate of Yandex: Russia's Answer to Google

The greatest success story of the Russian IT opening was unquestionably the creation and remarkable growth of Yandex, often described as Russia's answer to Google.[26] On the eve of the invasion, it was Russia's largest technology company, and its search engine was the third largest in the world. Inside Russia, Yandex controlled over half of the search market and nearly two-thirds of online advertising, and its numerous sites, which included taxis, online shopping, real-time traffic mapping, payments, music, and education, and much more, drew over 60 million Russian visitors each month.[27] Today, despite war and sanctions, Yandex continues to prosper, but the withdrawal of its foreign partners, the suspension of its foreign activities, and the emigration of IT talent, will likely spell stagnation ahead, and may even lead to the company's absorption by the state. In all of these aspects, Yandex stands as a prime symbol of the thirty-year opening of Russia and its subsequent reclosing.

Yandex was created in the early 1990s by two school friends, Arkady Volozh and Ilya Segalovich, who even before the founding of Google got the idea of developing a Russian-language search engine.[28] They first unveiled it in 1997, and it was an immediate hit. The following year, Yandex launched an on-line advertising service. These two features, on-line search and advertising, have been its main sources of revenue ever since, providing a steady flow of cash to invest in Yandex's diversification at home and its expansion overseas. (Ironically, one of its first foreign ventures was in Ukraine, where it launched a Ukrainian-language search engine in 2007.)

From 2000 through the mid-2010s, Yandex rode the wave of economic prosperity and political stabilization that brought laptops and smart phones to Russia's expanding middle class, and it was the chief driver—and beneficiary—of Russian citizens' enthusiastic adoption of the Internet. Every year brought an expansion of Yandex's activities, as it acquired one start-up after another. By the end of the 2010s, in addition to its core search engine, Yandex offered over fifty different on-line services and products, ranging from weather forecasting and maps to music and movies. In many ways, Yandex *was* the Russian Internet, and the Russian Internet was Yandex.

From 2015 on, however, life became more complicated, both for Russia and for Yandex. The decline in oil prices brought an economic slowdown, just as the first Western sanctions were imposed following Russia's occupation of Crimea. Competitors began to challenge Yandex's domination. Google's share of the Russian search-engine market grew steadily, and by 2018 it appeared on the verge of overtaking Yandex. Uber made its appearance in Russia and launched a fierce challenge to Yandex for the growing ride-hailing market. Sberbank began building data centers, aiming to dominate Russia's emerging "cloud." Above all, the COVID-19 pandemic hit Yandex hard. As Russians stayed home and cut back on their purchases, its ride-hailing business collapsed, and advertising revenues plummeted.

But Yandex responded creatively, by expanding its e-commerce services and mobilizing its fleet of taxi-drivers to deliver food and other consumer services, through which stay-at-homes could purchase online from a new line of Yandex retail stores, called Yandex.Market and Yandex.Lavka. It offered a new search engine, streaming video, and blog platforms, and launched a new e-commerce site that it called Russia's Amazon. It even developed Alisa, a Russian-speaking Alexa-like virtual assistant. A fierce turf battle with Uber for control of the ride-hailing market ended in an alliance, thanks to which Yandex gained access to Uber's software and international market. Yandex emerged from the pandemic stronger and more profitable than ever. Its management was chuffed. As its COO said at the time, "We potentially have an opportunity to build a FedEx in a matter of a few months."[29]

Then came the invasion. In some ways, Yandex actually benefited. Google exited Russia, leaving Yandex in control of the domestic search-engine market. Uber terminated the two companies' alliance and left Russia as well.[30] After an initial sharp decline in 2022, Yandex reported record profits in 2023, and as the Russian economy has recovered, Yandex has continued to prosper. Yandex's taxi service remains very popular: in the month of December 2022 alone, over 40 million people used it. Just as the Internet remains fundamental to Russian life and business, Yandex remains fundamental to the Russian Internet.

But over the longer term Yandex faces three fundamental threats. The first is brain drain. Over the years, Yandex had built a formidable team, consisting of young Russian IT specialists. These are now leaving en masse for jobs abroad.

The second threat is a split-up of the company and the loss of Yandex's international operations. From an early date, Volozh had ambitions to expand abroad. But his international ventures were never very successful; for example, an attempt to create a Turkish-language search engine in Turkey ended in failure, and its forays into food delivery in Paris and London likewise went nowhere, as Yandex lost out to local competitors. Yandex's twenty-odd overseas offices ended up mainly serving foreign companies seeking to sell their products inside Russia. All told, 95% of Yandex's revenues remained Russian.[31] But Volozh kept trying to give

Yandex an international face. In 2007, he moved the company's corporate headquarters to the Netherlands.

The ironic result was that Yandex was viewed with suspicion by both the Russian government and the Western sanctioners. In the West, Volozh was seen as close to the Kremlin (which he was not), and following the invasion both the New York Stock Exchange and NASDAQ suspended trading in Yandex's shares. Volozh and his top deputy were sanctioned by the EU, although Yandex itself remained untouched, being officially a Dutch company.[32] In Moscow, Putin had long expressed misgivings about Yandex.[33] The company came under growing pressure as it tried to limit access to its databases by the security services.[34] In 2022 it was compelled to transfer its news service to VKontakte, a rival platform favored by the Kremlin.[35] Following the invasion, Volozh resigned from the company and moved to Israel, where he became an outspoken critic of the war.[36] In March 2024, the EU Commission lifted the sanctions on him.

Under pressure from both the West and the Putin regime, Yandex announced in November 2022 that it would split the company in two.[37] The smaller part, which includes Yandex's international ventures, would stay in the Netherlands, under a new name, but its Russian assets would remain in Russia under new Russian owners. The split took fifteen months of negotiations to complete. For a heavily discounted price of $5 billion (payable partly in shares and partly—interesting detail—in renmimbi), a consortium consisting of Yandex's Russian managers and several Russian investors (among whom the main figure is said to be Putin's close ally Iurii Koval'chuk) took over 95% of the company, while 5% remained in the Netherlands in the former corporate headquarters. Yandex's most profitable businesses—such as its web browser and its taxi-hailing and food delivery services—will continue to operate in Russia as Yandex, while the Dutch rump, now called Nebius, will focus on artificial intelligence.[38]

The split leaves the "Russian Yandex" as an exclusively domestic company, focused on its existing services. Like the rest of the Russian IT sector, Yandex will find it difficult to move on to the next generation of services, such as cloud-for-hire. Russia's increasing isolation effectively condemns Yandex, Russia's most successful Internet company, to relative—if still highly profitable—stagnation.

Beyond the IT sector, the long-term impact of sanctions and the Western exodus will likewise be severe throughout industry. As an illustration, we turn to the case of the modernization of the Russian railroads.

In Russia, Freight Moves by Rail

In the United States, freight moves by truck; in Russia, it moves mostly by rail. In the 1990s, along with the rest of the Soviet economy, the industry that built trains and railcars had stopped. For some fifteen years following the Soviet fall, there was no investment in it. By the mid-2000s Russia's rolling stock, consisting of hundreds of thousands of cars, was worn out and obsolete, and was not being replaced.

But in 2015, the Russian government (which at the time was still enjoying growing oil revenues and had money to spend) decided on an ambitious program to modernize the entire rolling stock.[39] At the center of attention was an obscure but crucial component, called bearings, which enable the wheel of a truck or a train to turn smoothly on its axle. No bearing—no wheel—no modern railcar. It's that simple.

Outside Russia, a new generation of high-performance bearings was transforming the economics of rail transportation. The technology had evolved from spherical "ball" bearings and first-generation cylindrical bearings to cone-shaped "tapered roller" bearings, enclosed in conveniently mounted "cassettes." This was a game-changer, because such tapered roller bearings (called TBUs) enable train wheels to support much heavier loads, and they last up to three times longer, thus requiring less frequent substitution and repairs.[40]

But Russia had mostly (you might say) missed the train. By the mid-2010s the Russian builders of bearings and railcars had fallen a generation behind: Russian trains were still rolling on ball bearings, while the rest of the world had moved on to cassette-mounted TBUs. Russia turned to Western companies for help. In 2014, a long-established US firm, Timken, signed a joint-venture agreement with Russia's United Wagon Company, to make modern TBUs at a new assembly plant at Tikhvin, near Saint Petersburg.[41] A second US company, Brenco (a division of Amsted Rail), set up a joint venture with another Russian bearing producer, EPK.[42] The two joint ventures between them were projected to take a 70% share of the Russian TBU market for Russian freight cars.

Under both arrangements, components were supplied from the United States and assembled in Russia under license. The two deals were criticized in the United States from the start, since they came shortly after the Obama Administration had announced sanctions against Russia following its seizure of Crimea. But bearings were not sanctioned goods, and Timken and Brenco's partners were not under sanctions. Therefore, the deal was legal.

In parallel, the German bearing producer Schaeffler opened a plant in Ulyanovsk in 2014 to produce advanced bearings for use in the Sapsan and Lastochka high-speed electric passenger trains that were being developed jointly by the German engineering company Siemens and a Russian partner called Ural Locomotives, and which was set to begin production at the end of 2024.[43]

The program to convert to cassette-mounted roller bearings became mandatory in 2019. From 2020 on, all new railcars would require cassette-mounted roller bearings. Railcar builders complained that the cassette models were two or three times more costly and would require expensive adaptation to fit on existing cars. But the ministry of transportation held firm, and by 2021 the modernization program was in full swing.[44]

The Russian invasion of Ukraine changed everything. On February 27, 2022, three days after the start of the invasion, Russian Railways (RZhD), the monopoly owner of the Russian rail system, was sanctioned by the EU, and the next month by the UK. Also in March, the United States banned the export of bearings to Russia. That same month, Timken announced that it was suspending sales and operations in Russia; Brenco, SKF, and Schaeffler quickly followed suit.[45] Not only bearings, but also essential materials for them such as lubricants and sealants, could no longer be supplied to Russia, and the licenses under which production took place were also terminated. Timken's former joint venture came to an abrupt halt, and although the others managed to keep producing, their production slowed sharply.[46] Railcar manufacturers, lacking bearings, stopped production. Freight car operators, receiving fewer new cars, were forced to cannibalize existing stock for spare parts.

To rescue production, Russian railcar manufacturers turned to Chinese producers of bearings. The Chinese had plenty of spare capacity; they had been producing modern cassette bearings for the previous fifteen years, and their production had reached 23.3 billion sets in 2021, of which 7.804 billion were exports, and their output was growing fast.[47] Russia levied a 41.5% tariff on Chinese bearings as an "antidumping" measure, but the Russian railcar makers were desperate. In the first quarter of 2023, China shipped between 87,000 and 120,000 bearings (estimates vary) to Russia—roughly equal to the entirety of normal Russian production.[48] Most of the Chinese cassettes were used for substitutions on existing rolling stock, so the railroads were able to keep running, despite the interruption of manufacturing.[49]

For the Russian government, however, this was too much of a good thing, because at about the same time, Russia's own production recovered, as its three main bearing producers resumed work. By this time, they were able to "localize" most of their own production, despite the fact that the departing foreign partners had taken their licenses with them. They reported that the only parts they still needed to import were rollers, sealants, and lubricants, which they were able to obtain from China and Kazakhstan.[50]

Thus, the immediate crisis has passed, and the Russian bearing industry is once again producing full tilt, as are the railcar manufacturers.[51] But they are not yet out of the woods. The prices of the Russian-made bearings have doubled, owing mainly to higher interest rates, but also to growing labor shortages.[52] Consequently, the railcar producers, not surprisingly, have held back their purchases of Russian bearings,[53] and have lobbied the Eurasian Economic Commission to rescind the high "antidumping" tariff on Chinese bearings. The commission has rejected their request, however, and the 41.5% tariff remains in force. As a result, Chinese imports of bearings into Russia have almost ceased, much to the relief of the Russian bearing manufacturers. But this may be only a respite.

These problems have slowed the Russian government modernization program. Railcar production recovered sharply in 2023, thanks mainly to a strong resumption at Tikhvin, which had shut down almost entirely in 2022. However, the increase is primarily in the older models (for which prices have actually declined), whereas the number of the higher-priced "innovative" models is still small.[54] The operators are clamoring for a suspension of the modernization program, which mandates that the freight car stock must be completely updated by 2030.[55] The Ministry of Transportation is holding back, fearful that suspending the program would lead to a massive cancellation of orders and a flood of re-imports of used Russian freight cars from neighboring FSU countries. But something will have to give. The number of freight cars in operation is now above 1.3 million—an all-time record. But most of those are older models. At present rates, it will be long past the 2030 deadline before the modernization is complete.

In short, the problems with the modernization of Russia's rolling stock, which is essential for its war effort, show the long-term impact of the withdrawal of Russia's Western partners and the dilemmas resulting from Russia's dependence on Chinese suppliers, In Russia's long-term adaptation to sanctions, China is a potentially decisive force, whether as an investor or a trading partner. In this final section we look at China's multiple roles.

The "Pivot to the East": Is China Coming to Russia's Rescue?

Russia's "pivot to the east" aims to cut Russian dependence on Western markets and money, chiefly by turning to China. But China remains a question mark. Despite repeated proclamations of friendship by Putin and Xi Jinping, and their assertion that the partnership between Russia and China "has no limits," the underlying reality is that China has been a cautious partner, and is likely to remain so. China condemns the Western sanctions, but in several respects, notably financial relations, it has been careful not to cross them.

The centerpiece of Russia's pivot policy to China is gas, both by pipeline and liquefied natural gas, or LNG. First, a little background. Russia's gas-export business in Europe was for half a century the very symbol of Russian–European détente and collaboration, both during the Cold War and after. After the fall of the Soviet Union, it became the prime example of the confident belief, which dominated Russian–European relations from the 1990s through the mid-2010s, that good business would build good relations.[56]

The Russians had long prized the gas relationship with Europe. Putin spoke frequently on gas issues, calling natural gas the cleanest of all energy sources. In the mid-2000s, as the Soviet-era fields in West Siberia began to decline, Putin launched one of the largest investment projects of his presidency, pouring over $200 billion into developing the next generation of gas, on the remote Yamal Peninsula in the north of West Siberia. In parallel, he built four major new export pipelines to Europe, aimed at modernizing the inefficient Soviet-era transmission system, but also at lessening Russia's dependence on Ukrainian transit. The ill-fated Nord Stream 2 pipeline was meant to be the final capstone of that project.

As a result, Russia's gas position in Europe appeared to be assured for another generation. The delivered cost of Russia's pipeline gas was by far the lowest in Europe, well below that of its nearest competitor, LNG from Qatar and the United States. Russia's gas exports grew steadily; by 2020–21 they were breaking new records, and Russia's share of the European market reached 45%. Yet in the space of a few months all that was thrown overboard.

Today, Russian gas exports to Europe are a mere 16% of their peak on the eve of the invasion, and they are likely to go lower still. It is the end of an era.

Even before the invasion, however, Russia had begun developing gas exports to China. By the mid-2000s, gas was becoming a major priority of the Chinese government. But Chinese gas demand far exceeded domestic production. Accordingly, as early as 2006, China began turning to imports. Its first LNG terminal was built in its booming Guangdong Province, supported by supplies from Qatar, Australia, and Southeast Asia. This was then followed by a major pipeline project, the West-to-East line, which brought gas from Turkmenistan to the populous eastern coast.

At about the same time, China began negotiating with Russia about building a gas pipeline from East Siberia to China's northeast, to be called "Power of Siberia." It took over fifteen years to reach agreement. China was in a strong bargaining position, since the Russia's East Siberian gas had no other ready outlet, and it got a good deal. According to Sergey Vakulenko, a leading expert on Russian energy, under the current pricing formula China pays about $285 per 1,000 cubic meters, while the same gas, if shipped to Europe, would have fetched a price nearly twice as high. Russian gas is priced even lower at its destination in northeastern China than imported Turkmen gas, even though it has greater value.[57] Power of Siberia, at least from the Russian perspective, has been a disappointment.

A second proposed pipeline project to China initially appeared more promising. Called Power of Siberia 2, it would run from Russia's gas powerhouse, the Yamal Peninsula in the far north, through Siberia and Mongolia to China's central coastal region. At the time it was first proposed, Russia's European market was still going strong, and the new pipeline to China would have given the Russians the ability to swing between the two markets, thus playing the Chinese against the Europeans. However, with the demise of Russia's gas exports to Europe, the swing strategy has disappeared. As a result, the Russians now find themselves in essentially the same position with Power of Siberia 2 as with Power of Siberia 1—with overabundant reserves, a monopsonist buyer, and the prospect of lower prices.

Nevertheless, the Kremlin continues to promote the second pipeline, repeatedly announcing that the deal is done, but the Chinese have been in no hurry to close. As Elena Burmistrova, until recently the deputy chair of Gazprom and the head of Gazprom Export (and now a deputy head of Gazprombank), said philosophically: "Negotiations on the first Power of Siberia project did in fact last around 10–15 years . . . With the Chinese, all plans are made for a century, as you know."[58] There have been similar issues with Russian LNG exports to China (discussed in Chapter 1).

Russian exports of oil and coal to China also face long-term uncertainties. Coal exports, although they have recovered somewhat since 2022,[59] face lukewarm interest from the Chinese side, owing to China's own rapid expansion of coal capacity. In addition, rail capacity remains a bottleneck, as China is tying up Russia's rail transit routes for the highly profitable trade in non-energy goods.[60] Oil exports continue to grow strongly: they topped 107 million tons (2.14 million barrels a day) in 2023, and now represent 19% of Chinese oil imports.[61] But they are threatened over the longer term by the strong growth of electric vehicles in China, which will likely bring a peak in Chinese oil demand, perhaps as early as 2030.[62] And lastly, over everything looms the specter of a prolonged slowdown of the Chinese economy. In sum, Russian energy exports, although they are the centerpiece of Russian–Chinese economic relations, and have increased steadily since the invasion, will likely not be able to play that role in the longer term.

There remains nuclear power. Russia has been trying to export civilian nuclear technology to China, but with little success, apart from one project in Liaoning Province, as China has a vigorous nuclear program of its own, which is entirely independent of Russia; it ranks first in the world in the number of units under construction and is moving quickly toward next-generation designs. China's first Gen IV reactor recently reached full power. It uses a modular design, with each module having 100 MWe of output. The commercial unit will have six modules arranged in circular fashion for 600 MWe of total output. At this moment neither Russia nor any Western country has anything similar at a comparably advanced stage of deployment. So far, the Chinese civilian nuclear program is focused on its domestic market, and its only international project is in Pakistan. But the Chinese have ambitious plans to expand overseas, and if past experience is any guide, they will soon be dangerous competitors for Rosatom, Russia's nuclear-power monopoly.

In other sectors as well, China is more likely to be a competitor than a partner. A striking example is steel. China has over 500 steel mills, which previously did a lively business supplying China's property boom. But with the collapse of the property sector, Chinese steel producers now suffer from overcapacity, and inventories are piling up. The Chinese government is encouraging them to find buyers abroad. Chinese steel exports already grew strongly in 2023 and 2024, and this trend is likely to continue in the future.[63]

The Russian steelmakers will find it increasingly difficult to compete on foreign markets, especially since the Chinese producers do not shrink from exporting at a loss.[64]

Chinese–Russian economic cooperation outside the energy sphere often shows a sharp contrast between bullish press releases and slower or no implementation in practice. Finance and investment are the biggest issues. China in principle strongly supports Russia's policy of "de-dollarization," that is, transitioning its foreign trade away from "toxic" currencies, mainly toward the renminbi. But progress has been slowed by technical obstacles, plus growing caution on the part of Chinese banks and companies, in response to the threat of secondary sanctions by the United States and the EU.[65] Initially Russia did not have ready access to adequate supplies of the Chinese currency to pay for its imports from China. To help out, China's top four banks opened special lines of credit for Russian companies: by late 2023 these totaled $9.6 billion. Despite that, of the two countries' total $185 billion in trade in 2022, only 16% was in renminbi,[66] and since early 2024, even these facilities have been closed.

A full shift away from the dollar and euro to the renminbi would have major disadvantages from the Russian perspective. First, the renminbi is not fully convertible. Second, it is subject to unpredictable fluctuations, as China combats its own internal economic slowdown since the pandemic. In short, it is not suitable as a reserve currency. Yet, as a result of Russia's rejection of the dollar and the euro, it may have no alternative to the renminbi, but it is a second-best arrangement from the standpoint of Russia's future competitiveness and growth.

Lending by China to Russia has been modest, amounting to only about $170 billion between 2000 and 2021.[67] Investment is similarly small, and was declining even before the invasion. China has shown little interest in Russia's showcase projects, such as the proposed "Eurasia" high-speed railroad line from Beijing to Berlin.[68] The biggest single Chinese stake in a Russian project is for Novatek's LNG project, Yamal LNG (discussed in Chapter 1). Russia has received only a minor share of Chinese commitments under China's Belt and Road Initiative (BRI). From the inception of the BRI program in 2013, Russia has received only about $36 billion in pledged BRI investment and loans, representing about 3% of China's total of $932 billion in BRI engagements worldwide. But the key words here are "commitments" and "engagements." According to China's Chun'ian Institute for Financial Research at the People's University in Beijing, in 2022 actual Chinese capital spending (FDI) in Russia accounted for only 0.36% of total Chinese overseas investment.[69] The main obstacle is the US threat to apply secondary sanctions. China's two biggest BRI lenders, the China Development Bank and the Chinese Eximbank, have been careful not to risk breaching the Western sanctions, and since the invasion no new BRI projects have been approved in Russia.[70]

Chinese objectives in foreign investment mesh poorly with Russia's. Aleksey Maslov, the head of the Asia and Africa Institute at Moscow State University and a leading expert, puts it succinctly: "China is interested in supplying machines that are produced in China, not producing them in Russia . . . China invests in well-known international brands, which don't exist in Russia . . . China only invests where it can retain control." As another example of conflicting aims, Maslov adds, "Russia wants [Chinese] investments to serve the reindustrialization of the Russian Far East, but China is absolutely not interested."[71] China's stake in Novatek, in other words, is the exception, not the rule.

Russia had hoped for better. In July 2022, the Russian minister for the Far East and Arctic, Aleksey Chekunkov, voiced the feelings of many policymakers, when he said, "If you count those projects in Russia where large Chinese investors actually participated, then the fingers of one hand will suffice. For an economy with a market capitalisation of $20 trillion and banking system assets of $50 trillion, this is not enough."[72]

For the time being the fastest-growing Chinese presence in Russia consists mainly of imported goods and components rather than investment in Chinese production inside Russia. Despite the difficulties in processing payments, Chinese imports into Russia are expanding rapidly across the entire consumer sector and increasingly include basic capital goods such as construction machinery. We have already noted the penetration of Chinese automobiles into the Russian market, as well as the growing share of Chinese utility trucks for road building and construction of housing. In the case of machinery, there are powerful interests (such as Gazprombank and VTB) that manage the leasing of imported equipment to construction companies, and thus have an interest in promoting Chinese products. So far, the Russian government, despite the rhetoric of import displacement, has not made serious efforts to stem the Chinese tide.

Finally, the most sensitive aspect of Russian–Chinese cooperation is military. China has refrained from providing weapons directly, but it is a major source of dual-use technology, mostly supplied through third-country middlemen.[73] A larger partnership has been held back so far by Chinese caution, as well as by the fact that both China and Russia depend on imported

next-generation technology themselves. Some current-generation components do go to Russia from China, primarily by way of middlemen in Hong
Kong, for example, by way of Iran, for the manufacture of drones that end
up in Russia.[74]

The pivot to the East has been controversial in Russia, with some leading figures warning against the dangers of excessive dependence on China.
In October 2023, on the eve of a Putin trip to China, the influential mayor
of Moscow, Sergei Sobianin, advised against relying on Asian countries—
meaning China—for advanced technologies. "Nobody wants to donate technology," he says, "either in the field of mechanical engineering, or in the field
of aircraft manufacturing, or the field of microelectronics . . . [the Chinese]
openly tell us: 'if you want to get some technology, buy the product as a
whole,' whereas what Russia needs is components. Whereupon the Chinese
reply, 'We understand this, so we are not going to do it, at least at normal
prices. Here's double the price, please.'" Sobianin concludes, "Eastern markets, we must understand that they are even tougher than Western ones.
There is already a serious war going on with us there, an economic war."[75]

Russia's relations with China are a blend of cautious complementarity
and wary competitiveness. Which of the two will ultimately prevail? For
the Russians, it is a difficult choice. Expanding the relationship beyond its
present boundaries implies increasingly accepting a subordinate role—in
energy trade, in investment, and in policy priorities. It often means dancing to China's tune, in such matters as the pricing of gas, the openness of
Russia's domestic market to Chinese imports, access to the Arctic, or technology transfer in space.[76] Putin appears increasingly willing to pay the
price, for the sake of gaining Chinese support for his war and cementing
a geopolitical relationship based on a common rejection of America. But
how far will China be willing to go? What price are Chinese manufacturers
and banks willing to pay, if the cost is secondary sanctions by the United
States? As China strives to expand its own leading-edge technologies and to
develop its export markets, increasingly in competition with Russia's, how
much does Russia have to offer, compared to its liabilities?

Conclusions: The Balance Sheet of War and Sanctions

All four of the cases in this chapter tell the same story: with the invasion
of Ukraine, Russia has cut itself off from its main future sources of wealth
and progress, which are still mostly located in the West. Whether it is the

interruption of access to Western capital and financial operations, or the expansion of Russian Internet entrepreneurs outside of Russia, or the self-imposition of obstacles to the modernization of its civilian industry and infrastructure, or Russia's growing dependence on an ambivalent China that is as much competitor as partner—in all of these respects Russia has closed the door on its own future.

But can it reverse course? Will it do so? Under what circumstances? These are the subjects of Part III.

PART III
LOOKING INTO THE FUTURE

Chapter 8
Around the Corners of History

Toward a Second Opening of Russia?

As we peer through the present fog of war and sanctions, we may be sure of one thing: Someday, under circumstances we cannot yet foresee, Russia will seek to reopen to the West. A country that extends across eleven time zones, with an educated society and an advanced industrial economy, not to mention formidable weaponry, will not remain an international pariah indefinitely. But we may also be sure that a second opening of Russia will not be like the first. Both Russia and the world will have changed. The result will be a different opening.

A reopening of Russia to the West can take two possible paths—good or bad. A "good" reopening would be based on the reaffirmation and recodification of mutual interests between Russia and the West, based on negotiation and concessions on both sides. A "bad" reopening is one in which Russia re-enters the world "through the back door," because of Western fatigue, inattention, attrition, and erosion of will and unity, which Russia exploits through evasion, manipulation, and subversion. In a good reopening, the Ukrainian war is settled by negotiation, fighting stops, and the sanctions are gradually removed, while in a bad reopening, there is no negotiation, the Ukrainian war grinds on, the sanctions remain in place, and Russia works around the West, while seeking to weaken and undermine it.

The bad path is the one we are on today. It is harmful and dangerous for both Russia and the West. It locks Russia and the West into a new Cold War, less stable and even more dangerous than the first one. Quite apart from geopolitical instability, the economic consequences are enormous. For Russia, the present path deprives it of investment and credit, locks it into costly trade workarounds, and handicaps its technological progress. For the West, it endangers the status of the dollar and the euro, weakens the self-governing institutions that underpin the global economy, distracts attention from the increasingly urgent tasks of green energy transition, and alienates much of the developing world. The bad path is a dead end for both sides. But is a good reopening possible? That is the subject of this final chapter.

Heraclitus Revisited: Why It's Not the Same Man, and Not the Same River

Let us first look back to the early 1990s, after the Soviet Union collapsed. Russia is vastly changed from the traumatized country it was then. The abrupt demise of the Soviet Union had left an ideological void and caused economic chaos and political upheaval. Despite widespread disaffection with the Soviet command economy, there was as yet no clue what might replace it, and the Russian people still clung to the mindset of state socialism: for most the word *rynok* (market) had no meaning other than corruption and crime. All institutions were shaken to their core—including the Communist Party apparatus, which was itself the foundation of the entire system—and there was a pervasive sense of shock and disbelief. Those days are long gone.

In the outside world, it was widely hoped—and believed—that Russia would progress toward a peaceful democracy and a market economy, and that it would be welcomed as a partner into the US-European security system, as well as global economic organizations such as the Organisation for Economic Co-operation and Development (OECD). The United States was then at the height of its strength and self-confidence; neoliberal globalization was at its optimistic peak; and the "born-again" market was supreme in global affairs. The West believed it could "re-form" Russia along Western lines. That world is also long past. New players and driving forces have appeared; the playing field has been altered by events along the way; the global balance of economic and political power has shifted; and the war in Ukraine has changed the strategic landscape in Europe, notably with the increase in European military spending and the accession of new members to NATO.

In the outside world, as in Russia, there will be no repeat of the explosion of hope and illusion that accompanied the end of the Soviet Union. The store of goodwill that briefly prevailed under Gorbachev and the early Yeltsin and Putin years has been replaced by a deep skepticism. In key respects, Russian–Western relations are now well behind the starting line of the late 1980s and lie closer to the low point of 1982–3.[1] The bilateral structure of arms control and strategic communication, which despite periodic tensions had continued to evolve over a half-century, as well as the financial and trade ties that had gradually grown from the 1970s, have now both been largely dismantled. Even in the best case, these connections will take a long time to rebuild.

Inside Russia, the Putin regime's legacy of anti-Western bile and corrupt expropriation complicates the task of rejoining the world, and this too guarantees that Russia's second opening will not be like the first. Western investors, having been forced to sell at a loss to well-placed businesses in Putin's entourage, will not soon re-enter. Russia's business class, both inside the country and outside, will continue to be viewed with suspicion. The reintegration of Russian banks into SWIFT and other international financial systems will be slowed by memories of Russia's widespread abuse of them for money laundering and other criminal transactions. Putin's successors, rightly or wrongly, will be perceived as the products of his corrupt system. Russia's image in the West, far more than in 1992, will long remain that of a country unfit for polite company. And image is of the essence, since more than anything else it is the key to progress in negotiations and in particular, to removing the sanctions.

Nevertheless, there are reasons for a guarded optimism. A second opening of Russia to the West will arguably not bring the same disorientation and upheavals as the first. The initial conditions that made the 1990s so traumatic for much of the Russian population have disappeared. The foundations of a market economy have been laid. A centralized administrative state has been rebuilt, with an effective fiscal and monetary system. Two generations of Russian elites have come of age and have acquired modern skills and international experience. The Russian population remains largely open to the outside world through the Internet and foreign travel, even if not to most of the West. The extreme range of scenarios that seemed possible in the early 1990s has narrowed. Whatever the future may bring, it is unlikely to feature a collapse or a disintegration of the country—or the sudden rise of a democracy. Russia will remain statist and capitalist—Russian-style.

What might a reopening of Russia to the West look like? Government planners and corporate strategists routinely build scenarios as a tool to help them to imagine possible futures. In the early 1990s, Daniel Yergin and I published a book called *Russia 2010 and What It Means for the World*, based on a scenario exercise, to attempt "to peer around the corners of history." In many ways, it turned out to be prescient. The present moment calls for a new generation of Russia scenarios. Here is one.

"The Meeting in Saint Catherine's Hall"

In the mid-2030s, a cardinal event takes place. Suddenly, Putin is gone. Let us try to imagine what might happen then.

Putin stepped down unexpectedly during his sixth term, a visibly aged and exhausted man. Two months later, he was dead, apparently of natural causes. For the next few months, the country was absorbed in the elaborate commemoration of the man who had ruled Russia longer than any of his modern predecessors, including Joseph Stalin. During that time, political life was suspended, as though the country was holding its breath.

But politics soon returned, in the form of a loud public settling of scores among the Moscow elites, together with less visible maneuvers behind the scenes. Anyone who had held a leading position in Putin's entourage magically discovered that he had actually been a hidden dissident all along, an opponent of the war, and a lover of democracy.[2] But those "deathbed conversions" were so obviously fake that they failed to save Putin's discredited team, and they were quickly swept off the stage, all the more easily since most of them were well past retirement age. Putin's chosen heir, a technocrat whom he had groomed for the job and installed as prime minister, was pushed aside.

In the resulting vacuum, an interim Governing Council, largely self-appointed from among second-tier officials from the Presidential Administration and assorted government ministries, was assembled to decide on a successor. It quickly reached agreement that the Constitution would remain in force, and especially Article 92, which mandates that a new president must be elected within three months of the death or disability of the old one. The group settled on a respected elder figure, who had not been a member of Putin's inner circle, as its candidate. With the support of the elite (and some boost from the Kremlin's usual "administrative resource"), the Governing Council's candidate was duly elected, apparently with broad popular support. A new cabinet of ministers was quickly approved.

Following his inauguration, the new president meets his new cabinet. On a cold winter's day, they are seated around the same ornate twenty-foot, Italian-made table in the Kremlin where Putin used to meet with their predecessors. But this time none of the faces are familiar. In particular, the last remaining *Pitertsy*, Putin's cohort of friends and relations from Saint Petersburg, are nowhere to be seen. (The various children of Putin "securocrats," who were heads of banks and companies, quickly lost their positions following their parents' departures, and they are missing as well.) Since Putin's death a few months earlier, there has been a near-complete turnover at the top. The new group includes the principal economic and political officials, and the security services and the military are naturally also present.

Who are they? They are all in their fifties, born around 1980, one or two a little younger. Not one, but two generations have passed since the end of the Soviet Union. Only the older members of the group have childhood memories of the Soviet flag and the hammer and sickle; the others know the Soviet past only from family stories told around the kitchen table. Most of them come from Moscow families well-placed in the intelligentsia and the managerial world. Most went to university in the capital, mainly MGIMO, the prestigious Moscow State Institute of International Relations, and some to VShE, the Higher School of Economics. A handful are graduates of the respective academies of the FSB and the General Staff. When they were in their late teens and twenties, many spent years in the West, the younger ones in British or Swiss secondary schools, others in British and US universities, and several have degrees from the West, in fields such as economics, finance, or management science. A few worked for Western banks or private equity firms before joining the government. Unlike their Soviet grandparents, none of them is an engineer.

This generation is wholly at home in the world of the Internet. They all owned Nokia cellphones in their teens and, like all Russians, switched to Apple smartphones after about 2007. They use Telegram and VKontakte, the two leading social-media platforms, as a matter of course, and they all discretely maintain virtual personal network (VPN) connections, despite the attempts of the late Putin regime to ban them. Neither they, nor for that matter their parents, would think of getting their news from official television. In short, this generation of Russian leaders is more knowledgeable about the world outside Russia, and in closer daily touch with it, than any preceding generation.

Yet they are all Russians. And like every previous generation of Russians, they share a common belief in the greatness of Russia, and a common faith in its future as a strong and united power. Despite their different life paths, they share a common concern: to restore their country as a global leader, led by a strong state. Above all, they want to avoid a repeat of the flawed opening of the 1990s, the missed opportunities of the 2000s, and the long descent into the self-defeating authoritarianism and isolation of the later Putin period.

The dominant experience of their lives, and the most formative influence on their careers, was the invasion of Ukraine in February 2022. Ever since the 2010s, they had risen through the Putin networks of power. Some worked in the Presidential Administration, on occasion serving tours as governors in the provinces, and more recently in the occupied eastern provinces of Ukraine. Those who are military officers have experienced the war at first hand, as have many of those who come from the security services. One or two worked in Russian embassies abroad, perhaps under diplomatic cover. The technocrats in the group came up through the Ministry of Finance and the RCB, as the students and proteges of the *finansisty* who ran the economy under Putin. The latter are highly experienced, and they have managed to keep the Russian economy on a more or less even keel, albeit with mounting difficulty, as the war and the sanctions have taken their toll. As a group, they all chose to remain at their posts and keep their private views to themselves. Until now.

The new president has called this meeting to debate what actions to take to end the war and to relieve Russia's extreme alienation from the West, which reached a low point in Putin's final years. Time is pressing. The war is increasingly unpopular. The group is uneasily aware that the present surface calm in the regions is deceptive. History stops for no one, and all too soon the brief lull will give way to new contests for power and battles over property and rents, between warring factions with warring beliefs. Uncertainties threaten everywhere. One or two of those around the table have brought well-thumbed copies of the one-time best-seller *Rossiia: Dvadtsat' let spustia* (*Russia: Twenty Years After*), a scenario exercise written in the United States in the mid-1990s and published there under the title, *Russia 2010.*[3] They all read it at university. No less today than then, it remains a cautionary tale.

The president takes the floor and addresses the group.

The President's Question

Ladies and gentlemen, we all share much the same life experience that has brought us here today. We came of age in the Time of Troubles of the 1990s. We all rejoiced in the reconsolidation of the Motherland under President Putin during his first two terms, and we all benefited from the unprecedented good times that followed, thanks mainly to our oil and gas, but also to greater political stability. But beginning in the mid-2010s, things started go wrong. The relatively liberal Putin, whom we had welcomed in our early careers, gradually turned into an angry and vengeful autocrat. His seizure of Crimea marked a fateful turning point. From that time on, as relations with the West grew ever darker, Putin became an increasingly isolated figure, more and more obsessed by his dreams, his grievances, and his desire for revenge. We have lived for over a decade at war and under sanctions.

We now have a unique opportunity to decide on a new course. What have we learned, what has Russia learned, from the events since February 24, 2022? First, the news is far from all bad. We have learned that we are stronger and more resilient than we initially feared, when faced with the unremitting hostility of the West. Our economy has stood up to the test of sanctions. Our government has managed to function and maintain essential services. Our military has shown improved competence—if not exactly brilliance, let us be frank—compared to its early unpreparedness and poor organization. Above all, our people have demonstrated remarkable discipline and patience, if in a bad cause. Russia stands whole, and there has been no repeat of the chaos of the early 1990s.

But these positives are meager comfort. The situation we face today is fragile and untenable. War and sanctions have worn the country down and left it increasingly impoverished and isolated from the West, which is still the financial and technological center of the globe. Our position has been lowered in the eyes of much of the world. We are locked in a frozen conflict that has made us a pariah in the West without winning us more than superficial gains in the East, in particular from China, despite protestations of "no limits" friendship. Where do we go from here?

We have learned three painful lessons. The first is that the path of revanchist imperialism is a dead end. It has brought NATO and the EU up to the very borders of Russia, precisely the result that Putin sought to prevent. The second is that Ukraine is not within our grasp at any acceptable price. Ukraine with its Western allies is too strong to lose the war, and we are too weak to win. The third is that an alliance with China leads only to our becoming a junior partner, locked into dependence on Chinese technology and investment, which have not been forthcoming on any significant scale—in contrast to its massive exports of automobiles and consumer goods into Russia, and its exports of commodities like steel to the rest of the world, where they compete with our own. Chinese demand for our oil and gas has grown only slowly. The conclusion is inescapable: we must turn back to the

West, both to Europe and to the United States, and seek to develop a balanced economic relationship with all sides. But is a constructive reopening with the West possible?

I'm not talking about a return to political integration—joining NATO and the EU and so on. We will not repeat those illusions. We are a great power, and we have no need of burdensome alliances. But a great power requires a strong and competitive economy. And like it or not, the only way to get there is through *economic* reintegration with the West, which remains the center of world financial power. The United States continues to control the physical infrastructure—the "pipes and plumbing"—of global finance, communications, and technology.[4] Local or regional networks are inadequate substitutes; we are not North Korea, which is able to get by with subterranean financial networks and illicit marketplace traders. We must regain access to advanced Western infrastructure, even as we continue to develop our own.

There is extra urgency here. An end to the Ukrainian war means that our economy, which under Putin was on a wartime footing, must return to a civilian structure. This will be a time of crisis. Workers who have benefited for a decade from high employment and high wages in military industry will suddenly experience unemployment and lower pay, setting off a chain of repercussions throughout the economy and society. GDP and consumption will decline, as happened in the West after the First and Second World Wars, and in Russia after the end of the Soviet Union. The only way to avoid a catastrophic postwar recession is to reopen the country to Western credit and investment.

That means negotiating an end to the sanctions, through which the United States exploits its technological dominance—its "underground empire"—as a geopolitical lever over us. We must turn back to economic partnerships with Western private business—by rejoining SWIFT, regaining access to dollar- and euro-centered capital markets, reopening foreign markets for our goods, and attracting Western partners and technology back to Russia. Only in that way can we leapfrog into the future and realize Russia's true destiny.

The war has also distracted us from an increasingly serious danger, the accelerating climate crisis and the coming decline of hydrocarbons. Under Putin we were able to take advantage of the Soviet hydrocarbon legacy, and oil and gas revenues fueled our recovery during the early Putin years. But make no mistake: oil's days are numbered, and gas, though with some lag, will be right behind. We have no adequate substitutes—not coal, or grain, or weapons. We must diversify our role in the world economy, modernizing our exports with new commodities such as hydrogen, and upgrading our energy exports with LNG, advanced civilian nuclear power, and sustainable agriculture. We must move toward the technologies of the future, such as renewables and artificial intelligence. China will be of little help here, because China is a competitor. Once again, the only way forward points westward.

I'm choosing my words carefully, because I know that the group around this table represents different institutions with different concerns and interests. But the three key questions before all of us are: Can we reach a consensus among ourselves on the ways forward? Can we reach genuine agreements with the West? Will the country remain peaceful in the meantime?

At this point, we leave the group in Saint Catherine's Hall. Let us now examine the president's questions and try to answer them.

Is a Good Reopening Possible?

Putin's departure, and the accession of a new generation of leaders, will open new possibilities for dialogue. There will be a brief window of suspended judgments. There may be a basis for renewed understandings, if both sides seize the moment, and if realistic step-by-step concessions are made by both sides, on three fronts: Ukraine, sanctions, and strategic agreements.

However, the obstacles are enormous. A succession in Moscow and a truce in Ukraine will not by themselves bring peace or stability. Like a matryoshka doll, the Russian toy in which several dolls are nested together, each inside the next, the war is actually four conflicts in one. The innermost doll is the war itself and the battle over Ukraine's territory and future. The second is Russia's continuing effort, using the modern weapons of disinformation and cyberwarfare, to undermine the unity and coherence of the EU. The third is Russia's ever-deepening hostility to NATO and to the United States. And finally, the fourth is the war's contribution to the ongoing shift in the global balance of power and trade, as Russia "pivots to the East" in response to Western sanctions, deepening its alliance with China.

On all of these levels, Putin's war will leave a legacy that will complicate any effort to re-establish relations with the West. The war itself has devastated much of Ukraine's territory. It is leading to a massive rearming of Europe. NATO, as a result of the war, has now expanded its membership to the borders of Russia. And Russia's growing trade ties with China add to China's leverage, even as the center of great-power rivalry shifts to the Pacific. We are indeed no longer in the same river of world relations as we were in the 1990s; the river has become a raging torrent.

The chief victim of the war is trust. The West will not easily forgive Russia for its crimes in Ukraine, or its population for their passivity in the face of Putin's naked aggression and his remilitarization of their society. It could take a decade or more before the West is willing to accept Russian overtures, and rebuilding the treaties, relationships, and understandings that had been slowly constructed over the course of a half-century will take even longer.

We return now to the opening question: Is a good reopening of Russia to the West even possible? Let us take each of these layers of conflict one by one.

Ukraine

Ukraine is at the center of the challenges facing a reopening. Without a settlement of the Ukrainian conflict there can be no lifting of the sanctions and no rebuilding of Russian–Western relations. There will be three main issues: (1) the status of Crimea and the eastern provinces of Ukraine; (2) Ukrainian membership in the EU and NATO; and (3) the issues of reparations and reconstruction, and prosecution for war crimes. Any progress on these will require concessions on both sides, and the probability of deadlocks is high.

Nevertheless, there are possible first steps that could ease the way. The first is that Russia publicly reaffirms the legitimacy of Ukraine as an independent state. It removes all of its armed forces from the eastern provinces of Ukraine, as well as outside Russian administrators. A permanent cease-fire goes into effect, guaranteed by an international peacekeeping force. Donetsk and Luhansk are governed as semi-autonomous provinces. Open access to the Black Sea for both Russian and Ukrainian exports is restored. Inasmuch as these steps amount to reversing Putin's failed policies, they should not be beyond reach for his successors. However, the West must be prepared to make one fundamental concession in reply: Crimea remains part of Russia.[5]

Second, Ukraine continues down the path to joining the EU. EU membership will not be achieved overnight, or even, realistically speaking, in less than a decade. But each step forward will consolidate Ukraine's identity as a European power, and Russia must accept this. The likely quid pro quo, however, is that Russia will expect Ukraine to join the Russia-led Eurasian Economic Union (EAEU). But one result of the war is that its non-Russian members have grown more independent-minded and assertive than they were under Putin, when the EAEU was essentially a Russian club. A dual membership in both organizations might actually provide some advantages for Ukraine.

As for NATO, Putin's policies have achieved a far greater enlargement and strategic reinforcement of the alliance than could have been gained by Ukrainian membership. Given the new security map of Europe, Ukrainian membership in NATO is neither necessary nor beneficial. Moreover, even a post-Putin government can be expected to strenuously oppose NATO membership for Ukraine. Instead, Russia and the West might agree on a neutral status for Ukraine, similar to that of Finland and Sweden before the invasion. The hardest part will be to persuade Ukraine to accept it as well.

The third issue is reparations and reconstruction. This will be particularly difficult, since no Russian government is likely to accept the obligation of rebuilding Ukraine, or the use of the RCB's frozen funds for that purpose. Under a measure recently adopted by the EU, the profits from the RCB's frozen funds will be used to provide weapons to Ukraine, together with smaller amounts for Ukrainian recovery (as discussed in Chapter 4).[6] This in itself will be a lasting source of recriminations. An even tougher question will be the final disposition of the frozen principal.

Prosecution of war crimes will likely prove the most contested issue of all. There is no lack of documentary evidence of Russian guilt from the battlefield, but it only implicates lower-ranking personnel, despite the tacit complicity of their superiors. It is difficult to imagine that any Russian government will agree to accept guilt at any level. It is perhaps not impossible that some former members of Putin's inner circle could be sent to the International Criminal Court in The Hague to face charges (leaving aside the awkward fact that the United States is not a member of this court). But it is more likely that war crimes will remain an unresolved bone of contention.

This agenda will entail years of negotiation to agree on and implement. But if the first steps can be taken, and in particular the cessation of hostilities in eastern Ukraine, they will start the all-important process of building confidence and enable the lifting of sanctions to begin.

Lifting the Sanctions

Removing the Western sanctions, which now consist of over 15,000 documents and counting, may seem an impossible task. But as described in Chapter 4, many of the sanctions are either self-extinguishing (as in the case of the EU) or can be removed by rescinding executive decrees (as with many of the post-invasion US sanctions). The sanctions cannot be lifted all at once—nor should they be, since they will be needed as bargaining chips—but they can be removed layer by layer, as the Ukrainian agenda moves forward.

The first layer is the sanctions on consumer goods. This is the simplest part. Bans on trade in consumer goods, including luxury items, can easily be removed. On the Russian side, protection for foreign trademarks and intellectual property will need to be restored.

The next layer is the financial sanctions. These are the most important, yet they too are relatively straightforward to address. Russian banks can rejoin SWIFT, and their access to international settlement and messaging channels, such as Euroclear, can be quickly restored, as well as access to Western credit cards and online payment systems. Russian banks can be allowed to reopen correspondent accounts in the United States and the EU, to conduct trade in dollars and euros with Western entities, and to access international credit markets. Frozen "non-sovereign" assets can be released on both sides, while in parallel, talks over frozen sovereign assets proceed. Treaties barring double taxation can be restored.

Russia will seek to reopen to Western business, but it will have to face a wall of mistrust, owing to the abuses of the late Putin period. Forced "renationalizations" of Western businesses in favor of well-placed political interests must be halted, and arbitrary reductions in capital value must cease. Previous tax treaties must be restored on both sides, and arbitrary taxes must end.

On the energy front, the oil embargo will need to end and the oil price cap will need to be removed. Insurance and related services must be allowed to operate, together with unrestricted access to mainstream shippers. Russian gas exports to Europe by pipeline should once again be permitted, provided that the total share of Russian gas to Europe does not exceed a ceiling fixed by the EU. Western investment in Russian energy should be reopened, where consistent with climate-related restrictions on fossil fuels.

In technology trade, the list of items subject to export controls can be reduced and limited to those items with clear dual-use applications to military purposes. Restrictions on Russian imports of non-military IT technology (including chips and equipment for their fabrication) should be lifted, as well as controls on Russian imports of energy-related technologies (such as optics for oil exploration or materials for LNG cryogenics).

Finally, sanctions on persons and personalities can be lifted. Visa restrictions should be rescinded, and Russian citizens allowed to move across borders under prewar rules. Sanctions aimed specifically at "pre-Putin oligarchs" and their foreign property should be abolished.[7] (The Putin-era oligarchs, however, are a different matter, and will need to be addressed case-by-case.) At the same time, international measures to control illicit flows of capital and hidden investments should be strengthened, and the Russian government should be encouraged to rejoin international bodies such as FATForce, as well as joining in efforts to control cyber-crime.

In parallel, negotiations to rebuild the framework for arms control, strategic communication, and associated confidence-building measures, should be pursued with the highest priority. But since these lie outside the scope of this book, I do not examine them further here.

This is a long list, which amounts to rebuilding the entirety of the accomplishments of both détente and the post-Soviet opening over a half-century. The temptation will be for Russia to continue down the bad path, by banking on the declining commitment of the West to Ukraine's defense. On the Western side, "Ukraine fatigue" is already evident, and it will no doubt increase. Washington will be increasingly focused on China and the Pacific, as well as the Middle East, and US support for Ukraine's defense will be hampered by domestic disagreements. Europe will likewise be divided.

In the best case, Russia will never be an easy neighbor or partner, any more tomorrow than in the past. By its geography it is present on every border, as well as along 11,000 miles of strategic Arctic coastline. More than ever, it is poised between Europe and Asia, part of both yet not fully in either. It will remain a frustrated rival to the United States, an ambivalent partner to China, and an uncomfortable neighbor for Europe. Even under a good reopening, dealing with Russia will always be a challenge.

Yet over the coming decade, the costs and dangers of the present path will become increasingly evident. Putin's departure and the advent of a new leadership will bring the opportunity to attempt a cautious but constructive reopening, beginning with the reestablishment of working commercial and financial relationships, which will bring benefits to both sides. The time to begin thinking about this is now.

Conclusion—and a Personal Note

This book closes with a message of guarded hope, and a personal note. I have spent my adult life as an observer of Russia, and I have seen both thick and thin, from the Cuban Missile Crisis of 1962 to détente in the 1970s, then back again to the near outbreak of war in Europe in the early 1980s, followed by the resumption of détente at Reykjavik with Gorbachev and Reagan. The present low point in Russian–Western relations represents the latest phase. But this too will eventually pass, as everything does in this world, to be succeeded by the next crisis. We have been here before.

It is often argued, particularly by historians and specialists on Russian culture, that Russia remains eternally the same. I respectfully disagree. No less than other countries, Russia is shaped by long-term trends in its economy, its demographics, and its circumstances. The Putin era has served as a great "revealer," of both Russia's genuine interests and the emptiness of its illusions. Russia will always aspire to be a great power, but the ways in which it defines and seeks greatness will evolve as the world moves on, and as new generations of Russians come of age.

I too have come of age—literally—but I hope to live to see that meeting in Saint Catherine's Hall. May this book make a useful contribution to a deeper understanding of a unique period of history, one that has shaped my entire generation and will continue to shape the next ones. And with any luck, this will not be our last word on Russia, or Russia's on the West.

Endnotes

Introduction

1. Throughout this book I use "liberal" in the European sense of "market-oriented," not the American sense of someone who is culturally liberal. Thus, European "liberals" can be conservative on cultural issues. This is also the Russian usage. I use the term "liberal" with reference to the Russian "pro-market technocrats" and the "pro-market *finansisty*." Thus the term covers both market reformers such as former ministers Anatoliyii Chubais and Aleksey Kudrin, as well as Elvira Nabiullina, the chair of the Russian Central Bank, and Finance Minister Anton Siluanov, as opposed to a pure technocrat such as Prime Minister Mikhail Mishustin, who came out of the Federal Tax Service and is an expert on fiscal systems. They might better be called "technocrats" and "*finansisty*," rather than liberals, which can be misleading, especially to an American reader. The nomenclature is admittedly unsatisfactory.
2. I am borrowing here from Samuel P. Huntington's prophetic book, *The Clash of Civilizations and the Remaking of World Order* (New York: Simon and Schuster, 1996).
3. Throughout this book, I use the term "oligarch" to designate wealthy Russians whose fortunes derive from close ties to the state. Russians, who use the term freely, distinguish between "white" oligarchs, who are associated with Putin, and the earlier "black oligarchs," whose fortunes predate the Putin era. In both cases, however, the term is awkward, because many "oligarchs" are also talented entrepreneurs, who in some respects resemble the "robber barons" of nineteenth-century US history. However, in the Russian case the connection to the state is fundamental.
4. Three books summarize these contrasting narratives. Thomas Graham's history of post-Soviet US–Russian relations, *Getting Russia Right* (Hoboken, NJ: Polity Press, 2023) focuses on the geopolitical trends from the 1990s to the present. Daniel Satinsky's *Creating the Post-Soviet Russian Economy* (Abingdon, UK: Routledge: 2024) is the most comprehensive telling of the economic story. Henry Farrell and Abraham Newman's *Underground Empire* (New York: Henry Holt, 2023), in an original and challenging approach, takes the economic narrative and turns it into a central part of the geopolitical story. In the classic three-model framework of international relations theory, Graham's book represents the realist model of great-power interaction; Satinsky's is the constructivist/liberal model of economic relations, while Farrell/Newman is a synthesis of the two.
5. The "pivot to the East" is part of an overall policy aimed at shifting Russia's trade corridors away from Europe. It includes the Northern Sea Route and planned southern routes through Turkey and Iran. For a valuable overview, which includes an analysis of the roles of Putin and major interest groups in promoting and implementing the eastward shift, see Stephen Fortescue, "The Reorientation of Russia's Trade Corridors since the Invasion of Ukraine," *Post-Communist Economies*, 36, no. 4 (March 2024), https://www.tandfonline.com/doi/full/10.1080/14631377.2024.2324223.
6. On the partial but nevertheless far-reaching reforms of the judicial system through the early 2020s, see the path-breaking work of Kathryn Hendley, for example (among her many publications), her summary chapter, "The Rule of Law," in *Putin's Russia*, ed. Darrell Slider and Stephen K. Wegren (Lanham, MD: Rowman and Littlefield, 2023), pp. 85–110.
7. It should not be forgotten, of course, that money laundering and corrupt finance were hardly Russian inventions, and they existed in the West long before the Russians arrived and took advantage of them. In this as in other fields, the West was often long on condemnation but short on introspection.
8. For a thoughtful and well-reasoned dissenting view, which argues that containment will remain both feasible and necessary after Putin's departure, see Max Bergmann et al., "America's New Twilight Struggle with Russia: To Prevail, American Must Revive Containment," *Foreign Affairs*, March 6, 2024, https://www.foreignaffairs.com/russian-federation/americas-new-twilight-struggle-russia.

Chapter 1

1. See George Cohon's entertaining autobiography (with David MacFarlane), *To Russia with Fries* (Toronto, Ontario: McLelland and Stewart, 1997), p. 218.
2. Louis Uchitelle, "Moscow Journal: That's Funny, Those Pickles Don't Look Russian," *The New York Times*, February 27, 1992, https://www.nytimes.com/1992/02/27/world/moscow-journal-that-s-funny-those-pickles-don-t-look-russian.html.
3. Andrew Kramer, "Russia's Evolution, Seen through Golden Arches," *The New York Times*, February 1, 2010, https://www.nytimes.com/2010/02/02/business/global/02mcdonalds.html.
4. Cohon, *To Russia with Fries*.
5. Zbigniew Brzezinski, "The Cold War and Its Aftermath," *Foreign Affairs* (Fall 1992), www.foreignaffairs.com/articles/russia-fsu/1992-09-01/cold-war-and-its-aftermath.
6. Satinsky, *Creating the Post-Soviet Russian Economy*, p. 94.
7. Strobe Talbott, *The Russia Hand: A Memoir of Presidential Diplomacy* (New York: Random House, 2003), p. 83. At the time, Larry Summers had just joined the Clinton Administration, fresh from two years as chief economist of the World Bank.
8. Satinsky, *Creating the Post-Soviet Russian Economy*, p. 130.
9. Satinsky, *Creating the Post-Soviet Russian Economy*, p. 130.
10. For the conflicts over fracking, see my *Wheel of Fortune: The Battle for Oil and Power in Russia* (Cambridge, MA: Harvard University Press, 2012), especially Chapters 5 and 7.
11. For a post mortem on the exit of Carlsberg from Russia, see Madeleine Speed et al., "Blood in the Water," *Financial Times*, November 10, 2023, https://www.ft.com/content/af2fa231-881e-4241-9b37-ab772bf376a2.
12. Satinsky, *Creating the Post-Soviet Russian Economy*, p. 203.
13. In a handful of cities there were resident Western diplomats in ones and twos, for example, in Ekaterinburg, where the US representative worked closely with Russian officials on defense conversion.
14. Anne Garrels, *Putin Country: A Journey into the Real Russia* (New York: Picador, 2016). Chelyabinsk, with a population of 1.24 million in 2022, had been a closed defense-industry city up to the end of the Soviet Union, but it was typical of many of the dozens of run-down industrial *millionniki* that populate the map of Russia. Garrels's memoir, based on hundreds of interviews over a decade, is one of the few Western portraits of Russian life outside Moscow and Saint Petersburg in the 1990s and 2000s.
15. Gregory Grossman, "Scarce Capital and Soviet Doctrine," *The Quarterly Journal of Economics*, 67, no. 3 (August 1953): 311–343, https://www.jstor.org/stable/1881692.
16. Yegor Gaidar, *Days of Defeat and Victory* (Seattle: University of Washington Press, 1996), Chapters 1 and 2.
17. For a self-critical account of the IMF's role in advising the Russian government in the lead-up to the Russian default of 1998, see Martin Gilman, *No Precedent, No Plan: Inside Russia's 1998 Default* (Cambridge, MA: MIT Press, 2010). Revealingly, Michel Camdessus writes in his foreword to the book (p. x), "In retrospect, I wish that the World Bank had been able to play a more effective role at an earlier stage. In a sense, the IMF became the main focus of external efforts to assist Russia in its transformation more or less by default." See also a defense of the IMF's role in the memoirs of John Odling-Smee, who headed the department for the former Soviet economies at the IMF for a decade from 1992 to 2003, *Towards Market Economies* (Lanham, MD: Hamilton Books, 2022).
18. The OECD, while it had no offices or permanent staff in Russia, maintained close relations with the Russian government and also played an important role in advising on more technical matters, such as converting Soviet statistics to standard Western methodologies. Several Russians who hold important positions today spent time training in Paris, such as Aleksey Lavrov, now deputy minister of finance for budget policy. I am grateful to Silvana Malle, who headed the OECD's department for non-member countries and led its work on Russia, and to Julian Cooper, for this information.
19. The recollections of the various participants differ on this point. Boris Jordan, who worked in the Privatization Committee, recalls joint working sessions with the reformers to draw up the privatization program. The Russians, on the other hand, created their own think tank with the same mission. It is fair to say that it was a joint creation. For Jordan's recollections, see Satinsky, *Creating the Post-Soviet Russian Economy*, pp. 94ff.

20. Odling-Smee, *Towards Market Economies*.
21. For a gripping blow-by-blow account of the events leading up to the 1998 default, see Evgeniia Albats's interview with Anatoliy Chubais, "Anatolii Chubais: Nas zhdut ochen' tiazhelye poltora-dva goda," *Kommersant*, September 8, 1998, https://www.kommersant.ru/doc/204695?ysclid=lwjbx8uisa746073897. I am grateful to Bob Otto for calling this source to my attention.
22. The weakening of the Soviet command economy had actually begun under Gorbachev, whose policy of *perestroika* weakened the central controls of the Party apparatus and the planning system over the enterprise managers. Gorbachev notably abolished the central monopoly over foreign trade and allowed enterprises to create joint ventures outside of the Soviet Union.
23. See Anders Aslund, *Russia's Capitalist Revolution: Why Market Reforms Succeeded and Democracy Failed* (Washington, DC: Peterson Institute for International Economics, 2007), as well as his brief but fascinating first-person account of the final days leading up to the Russian default, in his Anders Aslund, *Russia's Crony Capitalism* (New Haven, CT: Yale University Press, 2019), pp. 72–73.
24. Aslund, *Russia's Crony Capitalism*, p. 73. Camdessus, along with the IMF, became the special target of the reformers' bitterness. Boris Fedorov, the reformist minister of the economy at the time, wrote angrily in 2000, "Even in the most obscure village in Smolensk Province ordinary peasants pepper me with questions about the IMF and Camdessus, who spoiled our entire lives." Boris Fedorov, *Pytaias' poniat' Rossiiu* (Saint Petersburg: Limbus Press, 2000), p. 98.
25. "Kudrin pervym predupredil Putina o posledstviiakh voiny s Ukrainy," *Radio Svoboda*, June 21, 2022, https://www.svoboda.org/a/agentstvo-kudrin-pervym-predupredil-putina-o-posledstviyah-voyny-/31908208.html.
26. For a discussion of the Gref Program and its subsequent implementation during Putin's first term, see Chris Miller, *Putinomics: Power and Money in Resurgent Russia* (Chapel Hill, NC: University of North Carolina Press, 2018), pp. 27–34; and Anders Aslund, *How Russia became a Market Economy* (Washington, DC: Brookings, 1995). For a Russian commentary, see Sergei Kochetov, "Moda na malen'kie nalogi," *Vedomosti*, May 11, 2000, http://www.vedomosti.ru/newspaper/articles/2000/05/11/moda-na-malenkie-nalogi.
27. See Gilman, *No Precedent*, especially Chapter 7.
28. Gilman, *No Precedent*, p. 230.
29. For a detailed account of the founding and evolution of the new generation of Russian research institutes in economics, and their divergent fates since the invasion, see the interview with the former pro-rector of the Higher School of Economics, Andrei Yakovlev, "Po linii FSB Vyshku peredali iz vedeniia sluzhby ekonomicheskoi bezopasnosti," *T-Invariant*, October 2023, https://www.t-invariant.org/2023/10/andrej-yakovlev-po-linii-fsb-vyshku-peredali/. The European Commission until 2000 played an important role with grants to the new institutions.

    The Higher School of Economics was founded by Evgenii Yasin, one of the leading early reformers, co-author (together with reform economists Leonid Abalkin and Stanislav Shatalin) of the very first market reform program, and subsequently the "500 Days" privatization program under Gorbachev (which was never implemented). Yasin was then minister of economy under Chernomyrdin from 1994 to 1997. He died in September 2023, bringing a chorus of eulogies from liberals such as Akeksey Kudrin and RCB chair Elvira Nabiullina (who had been one of his students). For a biography and useful links, see https://www.rbc.ru/photoreport/25/09/2023/64f1e33f9a7947941de87a6d?from=article_body.
30. The Bell, Telegram, October 3, 2023, https://t.me/thebell_io/24692. For background on Yudaeva, see https://tass.ru/encyclopedia/person/yudaeva-kseniya-valentinovna.
31. In 2001, the Russian government publicly admitted the existence of forty-two secret cities, (Government Decree of 5 June 2001, https://web.archive.org/web/20080213062055/http://npa-gov.garweb.ru:8080/public/default.asp?no=83489). Most of the previously closed cities are officially open today, but some closed cities, now called "closed administrative-territorial formations," (or ZATO), still remain. See Kaichao Chang and Charles Becker, "The Fates of Soviet Secret Cities," Working Paper #75, (University of Central Asia, Graduate School of Development, Institute of Public Policy and Administration, 2022), https://ucentralasia.org/media/l2ffkgw2/uca-ippa-wp75eng.pdf.
32. https://data.worldbank.org/indicator/BX.KLT.DINV.CD.WD.
33. Aslund, *Russia's Crony Capitalism*, p. 178.

34. "The Reminiscences of Peter A. Charow," November 22, 2016, Harriman Institute Oral History project, Columbia University, https://oralhistory.harriman.columbia.edu/interview/3. I am grateful to Peter Charow for many good conversations over the years.

35. Thomas Pickering, oral history interview, 2003, Association for Diplomatic Studies and Training, https://adst.org/2015/10/kopeks-and-big-macs-russias-move-to-a-market-economy/.

36. "Reminiscences of Peter A. Charow."

37. See Aslund, *How Russia Became a Market Economy*. For a personal account of how the sale of vouchers enabled some Russian friends to acquire shares in Gazprom, see my *Capitalism Russian-Style* (Cambridge, UK: Cambridge University Press, 1999), pp. 41–42.

38. See Bill Browder's two memoirs, *Red Notice* (New York: Simon and Schuster, 2015) and *Freezing Order* (New York: Simon and Schuster, 2022). *Red Notice* is a lively account of the more lurid aspects of Moscow life in the 1990s.

39. https://www.firehousecapital.com/investments/.

40. Browder, *Red Notice*, p. 126. According to Browder, Freeland's story was picked up by Reuters, Bloomberg, the *Wall Street Journal*, and the *Moscow Times*.

41. Anna Levinskaia and Vladislav Gordeev, "Kopaiut pod IKEA," *RBC*, September 15, 2014.

42. In 2022, the headquarters of the *Moscow Times* was relocated to Amsterdam in the Netherlands in response to restrictive media laws enacted in Russia. In 2023 the Ministry of Justice of Russia designated the paper as a "foreign agent."

43. Quoted in Satinsky, *Creating the Post-Soviet Russian Economy*, p. 177.

44. https://www.themoscowtimes.com/2023/03/24/baring-vostok-investors-leave-russia-after-fraud-sentences-expire-a80603.

45. Satinsky, *Creating the Post-Soviet Russian Economy*, pp. 123–124.

46. Satinsky, *Creating the Post-Soviet Russian Economy*, pp. 122–123. On Kirill Dmitriev, see John Hyatt, "How Putin Used Russia's Sovereign Wealth Fund to Create a State-Sponsored Oligarchy," *Forbes*, March 8, 2022, https://www.forbes.com/sites/johnhyatt/2022/03/08/sanctions-on-russian-fund-show-dashed-hope-of-moscows-cooperation-with-democracies/?sh=26171682a431. Further background on Dmitriev is in Wikipedia, https://en.wikipedia.org/wiki/Kirill_Dmitriev.

47. https://home.treasury.gov/news/press-releases/jy0612.

48. Juliet Johnson describes the campaign against the foreign banks in her admirable book, *For a Fistful of Rubles* (Ithaca NY: Cornell University Press, 2000), which describes the rise of the new Russian banks in the 1990s. See esp. pp. 139ff.

49. Juliet Johnson, *Priests of Prosperity* (Ithaca, NY: Cornell University Press, 2016), Table 7.3, p. 224.

50. Johnson, *Priests of Prosperity*, p. 93.

51. On the contributions of the IMF to the strengthening of the RCB, see Johnson, *Priests of Prosperity*, pp. 99ff.

52. Juliet Johnson's book on the consolidation of the central banks in the Former Soviet Union describes the evolution of the RCB through the mid-2010s. See *Priests of Prosperity*, esp. pp. 94, 180–184, 269ff.

53. Johnson, *Priests of Prosperity*, pp. 91 ff. TACIS, created in 1991, stands for Technical Assistance for the Commonwealth of Independent States.

54. The role of Valmet (Valeurs et Métaux) in the rise of the "first generation" Russian oligarchs is described in a three-part series by Catherine Belton, then of the *Moscow Times*. See in particular "Banking Lessons for Future Oligarchs," *Moscow Times*, May 17, 2005, https://www.themoscowtimes.com/archive/banking-lessons-for-future-oligarchs.

55. Gref was notably a strong advocate for Russia's joining the World Trade Organization.

56. Tat'iana Voronova, "Vo chto German Gref prevratil Sberbank za 10 let," *Vedomosti*, December 4, 2017, https://www.vedomosti.ru/finance/articles/2017/12/04/743989-gref-sberbank.

57. Elena Pashutinskaia, "Sberbank sdaet plokhie dolgi Germanu Grefu," *Kommersant*, June 26, 2009. In the wake of the financial crisis of 2008–9, Gref created a kind of "bad bank" division, into which he grouped all of Sberbank's problem loans and placed them under his direct supervision, in a unit headed by Svetlana Sagaidak, a specialist on loan insurance and restructuring.

58. Savelii Vezhin, "Sberbank podrastil dividendy," *Nezavisimaia gazeta*, June 8, 2011.

59. In 2020, the RCB, which was the majority owner of Sberbank (with 50% plus one share), sold its stake to the National Welfare Fund (the rainy-day fund that is managed by MinFin). See "Problema Sberbanka reshena," *Ekspert*, February 17, 2020.

60. Voronova, "Vo chto German Gref prevratil Sberbank za 10 let."

61. "SberCloud budet razvivat' iskusstvennyi intellekt s amerikanskoi Nvidia," *RBC*, June 6, 2019, https://www.rbc.ru/technology_and_media/06/06/2019/5cf8314a9a79477dce6c5bb6.

62. Ul'ianov.

63. A year later, Rafalovsky was named CEO of California-based digital bank Oxygen.

64. Timofei Konev, "Baikal ne serveruetsia," *Kommersant*, June 16, 2022, https://www.kommer sant.ru/doc/5412025. See also Lara Williams, "Taiwan's Semiconductor Ban Could Spell Catastrophe for Russia," *Investor Monitor*, March 3, 2022, https://www.investmentmonitor. ai/special-focus/ukraine-crisis/taiwan-semiconductor-ban-russia-catastrophe. Russia had to suspend development of its Russian-made "Baikal-S" servers (by "Baikal Electronics") for such domestic clients as Sberbank, for lack of imported processors.

65. Ksenia Zubachev, "How Credit Cards Took Over Post-Soviet Russia," *Russia Beyond*, January 27, 2020, https://www.rbth.com/business/331600-first-credit-cards. I am grateful to Julian Cooper for calling my attention to this early history.

66. We will meet Maslov again in Chapter 5, on the Russian responses to the Western financial sanctions.

67. Video presentation by RAEK general director Sergei Blagodarenko at the Annual Russian Internet Forum, May 2021, https://www.youtube.com/watch?v=mNQE9ILl0uw. (This appears to be the twenty-fifth annual forum.)

68. For an account of the origins of the first country-wide Soviet e-mail network, see Andrei Soldatov and Irina Borogan, *Red Web: The Kremlin's War on the Internet* (New York: Public Affairs, 2015). According to this source, which is based on personal testimonies by the participants (beginning with Soldatov's own father), the "server" at the center of Relcom was actually an early personal computer, an IBM 386. But the designation 386, strictly speaking, refers to a microprocessor, which was developed by Intel in 1985, and was first incorporated into a personal computer (what we would refer to today as a small desktop) only in 1991 by Compaq. IBM, which had introduced the first PC a few years earlier, based on the 286 microprocessor, did not incorporate the 386 until a few years later. Consequently, the PC that anchored the Relcom network was presumably an IBM 286.

69. These microcalculators were produced in large numbers by the government. Soviet engineers and scientists put them to all kinds of uses, both at work and at home. See Polina Kolozaridi, *Neprikosnovennyi Zapas*, No. 2 (2020), and Kolozaridi's interview with Kseniia Tatarchenko in the same publication, https://magazines.gorky.media/nz/2020/2/kak-zhe-sluchilos-chto-vy-tak-lyubite-eti-kalkulyatory.html.

70. Although he was viewed as a technocrat (variously called a tekhnar' or an otraslevik, someone from industry), he also proved to be a radical liberal. As minister, he presided over a voucher privatization of Rostelekom, in which all employees were given 4,000 shares at a face value of 2.5 rubles each. Soon after, the same shares were worth 20,000 rubles apiece. As a result, each voucher became worth 80 million rubles, about the price of two Volga cars at the time. In 1991, Bulgak's first trip as deputy prime minister took him to the Hannover Fair in Germany, to which he led a delegation of 250 Russian enterprises. The trip was an eye-opener for Bulgak, who realized to his dismay that Russian products were nowhere to be seen. See Valentin Nikolaenko, *Rossiiskie vesti*, no. 73, April 18, 1997.

71. Soldatov and Borogan, *Red Web*, pp. 46–47.

72. Soldatov and Borogan, *Red Web*, pp. 62–63.

73. Satinsky, op. cit., Chapter 4, describes US West's role in the Russian telecoms sector.

74. For MegaFon, see https://en.wikipedia.org/wiki/MegaFon. MegaFon was the first Russian company to deploy 2G, in 1995, and then 3G service, in 2007.

75. Forbes publishes an annual ranking of the top 200 private-sector companies in Russia. For the 2020 ranking, see: https://www.forbes.ru/rating/409143-200-krupneyshih-chastnyh-kompaniy-rossii-2020-reyting-forbes; also the summary in *Vedomosti*, https://www.vedomosti.ru/business/news/2020/09/17/840236-forbes-nazval-200. The top IT-related company was Vympelkom at about $8 billion profit, followed by MTC and Megafon. For comparison, the *vyruchka* (profit) of LUKoil, the leader, was about $100 billion in 2019. The largest IT company was, in fiftieth place, NKK (National Computer Company) (about $2.5 billion). Yandex was ranked at fifty-six (about $2.2 billion); with LANIT at seventy-four, Mail.ru Group at 133, and Softline at 133. All told, five companies.

76. IDC, M.Video-Eldorado, from RIForum video, minute 37.

77. Mark Halper, "Siemens Steps on the Gas in Russia," *ZDNet*, December 7, 2011, https://www.zdnet.com/article/siemens-steps-on-the-gas-in-russia/. Siemens, formerly a major player in

German nuclear power, also had a JV with Rosatom to work on civilian reactors, but this was disbanded after Germany downgraded nuclear power following the Fukushima disaster.

78. Following the exit of Siemens after the 2022 invasion, its former Russian partner took over the manufacture of the Lastochka, but shortly afterward changed its name to Finist. This was hailed as a bright example of successful import substitution (Dmitri Skvortsov, "Kliuchevye proekty rossiiskogo transporta obreli nezavisitmost' ot Zapada," *Vzgliad*, December 31, 2023, https://vz.ru/economy/2023/12/31/1246342.html). But more recent news accounts suggest that both the Russian-made Lastochka and the Finist are having severe reliability problems, leading to several accidents (https://newizv.ru/news/2024-01-04/tretiy-za-den-eshche-odin-lokomotiv-zastryal-v-pole-na-6-chasov-v-chelyabinskoy-oblasti-425851).

79. I am grateful to Pete Charow, who served on the board of MMK, Russia's third-largest steel company, for several helpful conversations about MMK and its head, Viktor Rashnikov.

80. Referred to herein as Total, as it was known at the time. Today it is known as TotalEnergies.

81. Gustafson, *Wheel of Fortune*, p. 145.

82. Gustafson, *Wheel of Fortune*, p. 145.

83. Conversation with T. Don Stacy, head of Amoco Eurasia in the mid-1990s. Cited in Gustafson, *Wheel of Fortune*, p. 153.

84. The Sakhalin II Project, Russia's first LNG project, was initially developed by Shell, Mitsui, and Mitsubishi under a production sharing contract. Gazprom subsequently joined the project during its construction phase, by taking over a 50% + 1 share of the project's equity. Following Russia's invasion of Ukraine, Shell exited the project completely.

85. https://www.forbes.ru/news/271259-gendirektor-total-pogib-v-aviakatastrofe-vo-vnukovo.

86. The shareholding of the Yamal LNG is Novatek (50.1%), Total (20%), CNPC of China (205), and the Silk Road Fund of China (9.9%).

87. "LNG Carrier's Homage to Man with the Moustache," *Trade Winds*, https://www.tradewindsnews.com/gas/lng-carrier-s-homage-to-man-with-the-moustache/2-1-233912.

88. The following paragraphs are based on a detailed report by Tat'iana Diatel, "Szhizhenie v okruzhenii," *Kommersant*, March 15, 2024, https://www.kommersant.ru/doc/6564364. See also the perceptive summary by Vitalii Yermakov, who is currently with the Higher School of Economics, "*Tsena voprosa*," *Kommersant*, March 15, 2024, https://www.kommersant.ru/doc/6552201. Yermakov, a long-time expert on the Russian energy sector, is also a regular contributor to the Oxford Institute for Energy Studies.

89. Arctic-LNG 2 is Russia's third major LNG project and Novatek's second. Its shareholders included Novatek (60%), Total (10%), CNPC (10%), CNOOC (10%), and Japan Arctic LNG (10%), the latter being a 75/25 JV between JOGMEC and Mitsui of Japan. The project has a planned nameplate capacity of 19.8 mpta from three LNG trains, but only one train has been completed with the other two indefinitely on hold due to sanctions.

90. "Russia Faces Mighty Obstacle in Western LNG Sanctions," *Euractiv* (co-published with Reuters), December 28, 2023, https://www.euractiv.com/section/global-europe/news/russia-faces-mighty-obstacle-in-western-lng-sanctions/.

91. Vera Zelendinova, "Iuzhnokoreiskie miny pod proekt 'Arktik SPG-2," *Oktagon Media*, March 6, 2024, https://octagon.media/ekonomika/yuzhnokorejskie_miny_pod_proekt_arktik_spg_2_.html.

92. Cited in Kateryna Serohina, "Russia Lacks Arctic Tankers for Gas Delivery," *RBC-Ukraine*, December 23, 2023, https://newsukraine.rbc.ua/news/russia-lacks-arctic-tankers-for-gas-delivery-1703284984.html.

93. The story of BP's multiple wars with the Russian oligarchs is told in the remarkable first-person account of the history of TNK-BP by Alastair Ferguson, the long-time head of gas at TNK-BP, and the follow-up conversation between Ferguson and James Henderson, in their book, *International Partnership in Russia: Conclusions from the Oil and Gas Industry* (Houndmills, Basingstoke UK: Palgrave Macmillan, 2014), Chapter 6, pp. 206–238. For further background, see Gustafson, *Wheel of Fortune*, pp. 419–429. Bob Dudley went on to serve as the CEO of BP from 2010 to 2020.

94. Interview with SLB CEO Olivier Le Peuch, *Financial Times*, March 25, 2024, https://www.ft.com/content/8741411f-9d0c-4295-949a-2345fc87730c.

95. This account of Schlumberger's history in Russia is recounted my 2012 book, *Wheel of Fortune*, and is based on interviews with SLB leadership.

96. https://www.rosatom.ru/en/about-us/.

97. https://report.rosatom.ru/go_eng/go_rosatom_eng_2022/rosatom_2022_2_eng.pdf.

98. World Nuclear Association, https://world-nuclear.org/information-library/nuclear-fuel-cycle/conversion-enrichment-and-fabrication/uranium-enrichment.
99. "US Nuclear Industry Clamors for Waiver Process Details," *S&P Global Commodity Insights*, May10, 2024, https://www.spglobal.com/commodityinsights/en/market-insights/latest-news/electric-power/051024-us-nuclear-industry-clamors-for-waiver-process-details-as-russian-uranium-ban-looms. At the time the law was passed, Russia accounted for nearly one-quarter of the US supply of enriched uranium.
100. Sergei Kirienko's name has long been linked to that of Yurii Koval'chuk, one of Putin's closest associates and the chairman of the Rossiya Bank. Koval'chuk was reportedly instrumental in the revival of Kirienko's career and his success at Rosatom. The two men's families appear to be close. Kirienko's son Vladimir heads the *VKontakte* social media group, while Kovalchuk's great-nephew Stepan is head of the *VKontakte* social network and its other media content divisions. See the report by Philipp Dietrich, "Russia Purports to Build a Fully-Controlled, State-Run IT Ecosystem," German Council on Foreign Relations External Publications, November 17, 2023, https://dgap.org/en/research/publications/russia-purports-build-fully-controlled-state-run-it-ecosystem.
101. https://www.rbc.ru/politics/05/07/2018/5b3de1389a7947e911764450.
102. The nuclear weapons division is hardly secret; it is featured on Rosatom's public website, https://www.rosatom.ru/production/nuclear-weapons-complex/.
103. See https://www.atomic-energy.ru/news/2023/01/12/131918. The security services also maintain close ties with Rosatom. The first deputy director of the FSB (Federal Security Service, the successor to the Soviet-era KGB), Sergey Korolev, sits on the board of Rosatom and is responsible for security policy on Rosatom's military programs, as was his predecessor Yurii Yakovlev (https://lenta.ru/news/2017/01/23/rosatom_nabsovet/?ysclid=lsdawf3eku929543230.transparency).
104. Dmitrii Gorchakov, "Rosatom teriaet vnutrennuiu energiiu," *Novaia gazeta (Evropa)*, February 25, 2024, https://novayagazeta.eu/articles/2024/02/25/rosatom-teriaet-vnutrenniuiu-energiiu.
105. "Rosatom's Output Dropped over the Last Year. We Look at Three Reasons Why," *Bellona*, March 13 2024 (https://bellona.org/news/nuclear-issues/2024-03-rosatoms-output-dropped-over-the-last-year-we-look-at-three-reasons-why).
106. Gorchakov, "Rosatom teriaet vnutrennuiu energiiu."
107. Javier Blas and Jack Farchy, *The World for Sale* (Oxford, UK: Oxford University Press, 2021), p. 134.
108. On these points, see Alena Ledeneva, *How Russia Really Works* (Ithaca, NY: Cornell University Press, 2006).
109. Petr Aven, quoted in Petr Aven and Alfred Kokh, *Gaidar's Revolution: The Inside Account of the Economic Transformation of Russia* (London: Tauris, 2015), p. 236.
110. See the memoir of Glenn Schweitzer, who led the International Science and Technology Center in Moscow in the 1990s, *Moscow DMZ: The Story of the International Effort to Convert Russian Weapons Science to Peaceful Purposes* (New York: Routledge, 2015).
111. On the importance of the physical "pipes and plumbing" for the digitalized global economy, and the potential political leverage that goes with it, see Henry Farrell and Abraham Newman, *Underground Empire: How America Weaponized the World Economy* (New York: Holt, 2023).

Chapter 2

1. Harley Balzer, "Russia and China in the Global Economy," *Demokratizatsiya*, 16, no. 1 (2008): 37–48.
2. Catherine Belton, *Putin's People* (London: William Collins, 2020).
3. Natalya Gevorkian et al., Vladimir Putin, *First Person: An Astonishingly Frank Self-Portrait* (New York: Public Affairs, 2000).
4. For a magisterial overview of Soviet technology and its relations with the West in the 1970s, see Ronald Amann et al., *The Technological Level of Soviet Industry* (New Haven, CT: Yale University Press, 1977). On the Germans working on Soviet-era pipelines, see my 2020 book, *The Bridge: Russian Natural Gas in a Redivided Europe* (Cambridge, MA: Harvard University Press, 2020), pp. 158–159.

5. Throughout these years the Soviet Union and the West carried on an elaborate game of cat-and-mouse over the acquisition and control of "dual-use" technologies, i.e., technologies of both civilian and military significance. The Soviets built an elaborate network to identify and capture key technologies, to which the West responded with an equally elaborate system of export controls. For an overview and critique, see Thane Gustafson, *Selling the Russians the Rope? Soviet Technology and U.S. Export Controls* (Santa Monica, CA: The RAND Corporation, 1981). See also Bruce Parrott (ed.), *Trade, Technology and Soviet-American Relations* (Bloomington IN: Indiana University Press, 1985).

6. https://www.nytimes.com/1972/08/17/archives/soviets-losses-in-grain-continue-72-crop-estimated-to-come-in-at-10.html.

7. Javier Blas and Jack Farchy, *The World for Sale: Money, Power, and the Traders Who Barter the Earth's Resources* (Oxford, UK: Oxford University Press, 2021), esp. pp. 31 and 38–42. For a blow-by-blow reconstruction of the wheat deal, see John Fialka, "The Big Soviet Wheat Deal," *Washington Star*, October 29, 1972, https://web.archive.org/web/20170123160330/https://www.cia.gov/library/readingroom/docs/CIA-RDP80-01601R000300340010-4.pdf. This is the first article in a four-part series.

8. See the 2008 oral memoir of Evgenii Bannikov, Foreign Affairs Oral History Project, Association for Diplomatic Affairs and Training, 2020, https://adst.org/OH%20TOCs/Bannikov.Eugene.pdf.

9. Sam Jones, Wirecard Fugitive Faces Superspy Allegations," *Financial Times*, April 6, 2024, https://www.ft.com/content/c3b50060-aa53-40fd-a698-579e8e1ae67d.

10. Dan McCrum, "Wirecard Fugitive Accused of Spying for Russia," *Financial Times*, March 2, 2024, https://www.ft.com/content/f15610a0-e94d-4672-bc73-f2e5e364f2d1. Listen also to the podcast by *Der Spiegel*, "Der Österreicher, der für Moskau spionierte," March 2, 2024, https://www.spiegel.de/ausland/jan-marsalek-der-oesterreicher-der-fuer-moskau-spionierte-podcast-a-11b7b1f5-c665-42c6-86ab-a1a7f9eb436f. *Der Spiegel* was a participant, along with the *Financial Times*, in the investigation that revealed Marsalek's double identity. Finally, for a detailed account of Marsalek's career, see—with caution—a lengthy reportage based on joint research by *Der Spiegel*, *ZDF*, and *Der Standard*, published in *The Insider*, March 1, 2024, https://theins.ru/en/politics/269612.

11. For two post-invasion reports, see John Paul Rathbone et al., "Europe Kicked out Vladimir Putin's Spies. Now They're Back, "*Financial Times*, March 6, 2024, https://www.ft.com/content/f066d653-70e2-42e9-baac-c342417c8ef3, and "The Return of Russia's Spies," *The Economist*, February 24, 2024.

12. For a useful primer on SWIFT, see Marco Cipriani et al., "Financial Sanctions, SWIFT, and the Architecture of the International Payment System," *Journal of Economic Perspectives*, 37, no. 1 (Winter 2023): 31–52. SWIFT is often described in the media as a "payment" system, but it is not a bank, and it does not manage accounts on behalf of its customers; its primary role is as a message carrier. Actual settlements are conducted between correspondent banks or through international settlement systems such as Euroclear.

13. For a description of the various European settlement systems, including Euroclear, ClearStream, and Target2, see https://www.bis.org/cpmi/publ/d105_eu.pdf. Euroclear Bank joined the Target2 platform in December 2021. See also an explainer on Target2 from the ECB: https://www.ecb.europa.eu/ecb/educational/explainers/tell-me/html/target2.en.html.

14. Richard Connolly, *Russia's Response to Sanctions* (Cambridge, UK: Cambridge University Press, 2018), pp. 162–168.

15. Laura Dubois and Philip Stafford, "EU Discusses Plan to Send Profits," *Financial Times*, May 25, 2023 (https://www.ft.com/content/68af1b50-2088-4128-a2fd-f35cde914eaf).

16. The lengthy negotiations leading up to Russia's accession were conducted by Putin's close ally, Viktor Zubkov, with a high-level envoy from the US Department of Justice. For an eyewitness account, see Juan Zarate, *Treasury's War: The Unleashing of a New Era of Financial Warfare* (Philadelphia, PA: Public Affairs Press, 2013), pp. 159–163.

17. With the end of the Soviet Union, Vneshekonombank was abolished, to be replaced by a new Russian entity, Vneshtorgbank, which then evolved into today's VTB.

18. https://techmonitor.ai/technology/sovam_teleport_sole_swift_electronic_funds_transfer_node_in_russia.

19. Aleksey Maslov, *Rossiia i SWIFT*, https://www.rosswift.ru/doc/ROSSWIFT_MASLOV_ONLINE_VERSION.pdf Maslov's book appeared on the eve of the invasion, and describes the history of Russia's relations with SWIFT, and the situation up to the end of 2021.

20. Sberbank Europe website, which is no longer operating.

21. Following the Russian invasion in 2022, VTB Bank (Europe) was cut off from the parent company by the German regulatory authority; its IT services (previously provided from Russia) were switched to Western providers; and it was barred from taking instructions from Russia. While the parent company VTB in Russia was sanctioned, VTB (Europe) was not, pending its complete liquidation. See, https://www.vtb.eu/en/news-blog/news/situation-vtb-bank-europe-se-has-stabilized/, unfortunately no longer accessible. VTB Europe is "in liquidation," and its business is being wound down. It is not allowed to accept new deposits or grant new loans (for more on this, see Chapter 7.)

22. VTB concentrated instead on expanding into the FSU, notably into Ukraine, where on the eve of the Crimean occupation it was one of the biggest banks. See, https://www.vtb.eu/en/about-us/, unfortunately no longer accessible.

23. Connolly, *Russia's Response to Sanctions*, Chapter 7.

24. See World Bank World Development Indicators. The total refers to so-called private non-guaranteed debt (PNG). In contrast, the volume of initial public offerings (IPOs), under which Russian companies raised capital on foreign capital markets such as the London or New York stock exchanges, remained modest, reaching only $12.6 billion in 2007. But it too was growing fast, having developed from nothing in 1999. On IPOs by Russian companies, see Ia. Sh. Pappe and Ia. S. Galukhina, *Rossiiskii krupnyi biznes: pervye 15 let* (Moscow: GU-VShE, 2009).

25. For a thorough review, see M. A. Baeva and O. D. Ismagilova, "Mirovoi rynok aviatsionnogo lizinga i uchastie v nem rossiiskikh kompanii," *Ekonomicheskoe razvitie Rossii* (Gaidar Institute for Economic Policy), 30, no. 2 (February 2023), https://cyberleninka.ru/article/n/mirovoy-rynok-aviatsionnogo-lizinga-i-uchastie-v-nem-rossiyskih-kompaniy. Today, Pobeda is part of the Aeroflot Group, having been reabsorbed by Aeroflot in the wave of reconsolidation that has taken place under Putin.

26. *Ch-aviation*, https://www.ch-aviation.com/ (the Swiss aviation industry portal).

27. *The Insurer*, "Russian Aviation Lessor Disputes Now Exceed $10 Billion," July 31, 2023, (https://www.theinsurer.com/news/russian-aviation-lessor-disputes-now-exceed-10bn-as-aircastle-files-102-4mn-claim/.)

28. I am indebted to Julian Cooper for his perceptive observations on the leasing dispute in civil aviation. See also the interview with Steven E. Harris, *The Russia File*, Kennan Institute, podcast, June 11, 2024, https://www.wilsoncenter.org/audio/russian-aviation-industry-two-years-after-sanctions?emci=57266651-b029-ef11-86d2-6045bdd9e096&emdi=797431b8-b129-ef11-86d2-6045bdd9e096&ceid=387415.

29. A path-breaking study of the Russian new rich, written by a Austrian-British sociologist who brings a comparative perspective to the subject, and based on numerous interviews with the top "0.1 percent," is Elisabeth Schimpfössl, *Rich Russians: From Oligarchs to Bourgeoisie* (Oxford, UK: Oxford University Press, 2018).

30. Deripaska interview with Eric Reguly, "At Home with Russian Oligarch Oleg Deripaska," *The Globe and Mail*, February 11, 2011, https://www.theglobeandmail.com/report-on-business/careers/careers-leadership/at-home-with-russian-oligarch-oleg-deripaska/article573998. For a list of additional sources, see Wikipedia, https://en.wikipedia.org/wiki/Oleg_Deripaska.

31. Deripaska interview with Luke Harding, "How Metals and a Ruthless Streak Put Russian Patriot at Top of the Rich List," *The Guardian*, February 24, 2007, https://www.theguardian.com/world/2007/feb/24/business.russia.

32. The story that follows is based on Stephen Fortescue, "The Russian Aluminum Industry in Transition," *Eurasian Geography and Economics*, 47, no. 1 (2006): 76–94. I am grateful to Stephen Fortescue for several enlightening conversations on the origins of Deripaska and RusAl.

33. https://www.nytimes.com/2005/04/22/business/worldbusiness/briefly-forbes-rates-abramovich-as-richest-russian.html.

34. Derek Saul, "A Colossal Mistake," *Forbes*, June 28, 2022, https://www.forbes.com/sites/dereksaul/2022/06/28/a-colossal-mistake-russian-billionaire-deripaska-doubles-down-on-ukraine-war-criticism/?sh=1098fb263368.

35. Fortescue, "The Russian Aluminum Industry in Transition," p. 260.

36. Iuliia Fedorinova, "Aleksey Mordashov verit v Ameriku," *Vedomosti*, March 10, 2010, https://www.vedomosti.ru/business/articles/2010/03/10/alexej-mordashov-verit-v-ameriku.

37. Iuliia Fedorinova, Bloomberg, https://www.bloomberg.com/news/articles/2014-07-21/mordashov-s-severstal-to-sell-u-s-steel-plants-for-2-3-billion. The deterioration in US–Russian relations between 2010 and 2014 no doubt played a role as well, although Mordashov and Severstal at that time were not under US sanctions.

38. Luke Donnelly, "Fyning Hill: The £18 million South Downs Estate Once Owned by Chelsea's Roman Abramovich," *Sussex Live*, March 2, 2022, https://www.sussexlive.co.uk/news/sussex-news/fyning-hill-18m-south-downs-6731466. In 2007 Abramovich turned over the estate to his estranged second wife Irina Maladina, as part of a divorce settlement. As of 2022, she still lives on the estate with her grown children.

39. He did so with Putin's apparent blessing, as his reward for having agreed to perform loyal service as the governor of remote Chukotka from 2000 to 2008, in parallel to his other activities, and to invest in the economy of the province. In 2022, after the invasion, Abramovich sold Chelsea and since then has been living mainly in Istanbul.

40. Wendy Leigh, "Welcome to Londongrad," *Mail on Sunday*, November 2, 2003, https://www.proquest.com/central/docview/328812114/402686CD6E54421CPQ/1.

41. Over the years, *The Economist* has devoted many articles to the rise of "Londongrad," or, more recently, to its decline. See among others, "Londongrad Is Falling Down," https://www.economist.com/1843/2022/05/05/londongrad-is-falling-down.

42. See also Nick Leader, "From Red Square to Berkeley Square," *Financial Times*, November 29, 2003, https://www.proquest.com/central/docview/249672957/673AE07B7072478CPQ/2.

43. The Russian business daily *Kommersant* publishes a British edition in Russian, aimed at the Russian community in the UK (https://www.kommersant.uk/).

44. For the context of Abramovich's rise and the origins of the first private Russian oil companies, see my "Riding Chaos," in *Wheel of Fortune*, Chapter 2, pp. 63–97. For an account of Abramovich's beginnings, see Dominic Midgley and Chris Hutchins, *Abramovich: The Billionaire from Nowhere* (London: HarperCollins, 2005). Russian sources include Vladimir Sumarokov, "Chernoe zoloto Romana Abramovicha," *Tribuna*, no. 24 (June 11, 1999), and A. Lazarev and S. Sorokin, "Roman Abramovich i ego sledy v Komi," *Molodezh' severa*, June 10, 1999, both cited in *Lentapedia*, http://lenta.ru/lib/14161457/full.htm.

45. Dominic Kennedy, "Chelsea Owner Admits He Paid Out Billions in Bribes," *The Independent* (Ireland), https://www.independent.ie/world-news/europe/chelsea-owner-admits-he-paid-out-billions-in-bribes/26459423.html.

46. For an excellent portrayal of Russians and offshore havens, see Aslund, *Russia's Crony Capitalism*, Chapter 6.

47. Giacomo Tognini, "Inside the 150 Frozen Homes, Yachts, and Jets of Sanctioned Russian Oligarchs, *Forbes*, April 14, 2023, https://www.forbes.com/sites/giacomotognini/2023/04/14/inside-the-150-frozen-homes-yachts-and-jets-of-sanctioned-russian-oligarchs/?sh=5edf2d544baf. As of April 2023, $9 billion worth of yachts and private jets belonging to sanctioned Russians had been seized by Western authorities, including fifteen superyachts. But this is likely only an underestimate of the actual size of the "luxury navy" accumulated by wealthy Russians in the West.

48. "13 prichin pochemu na Kipre tak mnogo russkikh," *Astons*, https://www.astons.com/ru/news/raiskii-ugolok-v-sredizemnom-more-pochemu-na-kipre-tak-mnogo-russkih/. Astons is a real-estate agency specializing in "citizenship investment" in Europe and the UK.

49. https://apnews.com/article/cyprus-government-business-europe-31fe716d5e0d71016a96c256b4330670 and https://www.residency-bond.eu/blog/cyprus-golden-visa.html.

50. Personal communication with a Russian resident of Cyprus.

51. Estimate from the Central Bank of Cyprus, in "Cyprus Counts the Cost of Weaker Russian Ties," *Financial Times*, April 17, 2022, https://www.ft.com/content/4e537bec-514f-4f03-8337-2f4777ffa53c.

52. Max Seddon, "Panama Papers: Russian Cellist at Centre of $2bn Offshore Web," *Financial Times*, April 4, 2016, https://www.ft.com/content/31d99184-fa66-11e5-8f41-df5bda8beb40.

53. Even before the invasion, the Russians in Cyprus were vulnerable to the periodic financial upheavals that swept both Russia and Europe, such as the Russian default of 1998 and the global financial crisis of 2008–9. The Greek crisis of 2021 also hit the Russians hard, when the Greek government sold bonds to the Cypriot banks, which subsequently turned out to be worthless.

54. "Na Kipre obratili vnimanie na massovyi ukhod rossiiskikh kompanii iz strany," *Kommersant*, January 17, 2024, https://www.kommersant.ru/doc/6454820.

55. "Nederland liet Russische miljarden ongemoeid" ("The Netherlands Left Russian Billions Untouched"), *NRC Handelsblad*, April 16, 2022. See also an op-ed piece by Dutch MP Paul Tang, "Raak Poetin waar het pijn doet; richt de pijlen op de Zuidas," *NRC Handelsblad*,

February 17, 2022. One of the reasons for the selective attention of the Dutch financial authorities was that Amsterdam, in the wake of Brexit (the UK's exit from the EU), was rapidly growing into the leading financial center of Europe.

56. Ironically, the end of ATB came just as Amsterdam had taken over from London as Europe's top financial hub, following Brexit (https://www.ft.com/content/3dad4ef3-59e8-437e-8f63-f629a5b7d0aa).

57. For a valuable source on Gazprom in Amsterdam, see the report *Enabling Putin's War: The Ties between Amsterdam's Financial Centre and Gazprom*, SOMO (Amsterdam: International Center for Research on Multinational Corporations, March 2022), https://www.somo.nl/enabling-putins-war/.

58. See Henk Villen Smits and Hugo Rasch, "Een van Ruslands grootste bedrijven zit op de Zuidas," *Follow the Money*, July 7, 2023, https://www.ftm.nl/artikelen/veon-vimpelcom-groot-russisch-bedrijf-zuidas?share=mhIwSVMFBL0HPFjQTQM0xUQZqY47IrkrRsQpyhg U6E9N5X1Ryf0XWyeoiXDMyoM%3D.

59. Henk Villen Smits and Hugo Rasch, "De brievenbussen van gesanctioneerde Russen," *Follow the Money*, February 14, 2023, https://www.ftm.nl/artikelen/corrupte-kremlin-oligarchen?share=ByUI54afPxU8Pw%2F8eunWUaxFk9W%2Bfsb0v6wP2YSr8E4FHum9RU dWn0leiDRWZUw%3D.

60. See Aslund, *Russia's Crony Capitalism*, esp. Chapter 7. Aslund, on the basis of a careful comparison of various estimates, concludes that over $800 billion in private Russian money is held abroad (p. 178).

61. Sam Jones and Owen Walker, "Swiss Sanctions Alarm Chinese Depositors," *Financial Times*, March 9, 2023. This number is undoubtedly a considerable underestimate, since the ultimate beneficiaries of most of these accounts are unknown. On Roldugin, see Nick Cumming-Bruce, "Swiss Bankers Are Charged with Aiding Putin Ally," *The New York Times*, March 9, 2023.

62. Brooke Harrington, *Capital without Borders: Wealth Managers and the One Percent* (Cambridge, MA: Harvard University Press, 2016). See also Ho-Chun Herbert Chang, "Complex Systems of Secrecy: The Offshore Networks of Oligrchs," *PNAS Nexus*, 2023, 2, no. 3, (2003): 1–12, https://academic.oup.com/pnasnexus/article/2/3/pgad051/7059318. For a valuable update, listen to the interview with Brooke Harrington, *MindScape*, podcast, May 22, 2023, https://www.preposterousuniverse.com/podcast/2023/05/22/237-brooke-harrington-on-offshore-wealth-as-a-complex-system/. A transcript is also available.

63. For a portrait of Fridman and Aven and their background, see https://www.ft.com/content/2797a5ec-9c02-47dc-ad13-b4348edb51e7. Aven had been spending most of his time in the Hamptons, in the United States, but he has now moved to Latvia (https://www.washingtonpost.com/world/2023/08/11/russia-sanctions-fridman-aven-alfa/.)

64. For example, LetterOne owns shares in Spain's Dia supermarket chain, the German oil company Wintershall Dea, and the British retailer Holland and Barrett (https://www.ft.com/stream/2f2a79d9-3e51-4a22-847a-bf452ab92d28).

65. According to a company statement, "They have no role in L1, no access to premises, infrastructure, people and funds or benefits of any description." LetterOne's activities have been hampered, however, by the fact that up to $5 billion of its funds are tied up inside a former partner, Pamplona, which is trying to cut all Russia-related business. Pamplona, which used to invest in Western companies on behalf of LetterOne, bought such companies as Perlsis, a Yorkshire-based pest-control company, and Signature Foods, a Dutch snack foods company (https://www.ft.com/content/6545e2a0-2b4d-4067-9ce8-8bbcdfee41b0). A third founding partner, German Khan, returned to live in Moscow in the summer of 2022 (https://www.forbes.com/profile/german-khan/?sh=2a8a84a56dbd).

66. "Countering America's Adversaries through Sanctions Act," Public Law 115-44, Section 252, August 2, 2017, https://congress.gov/115/plaws/publ44/PLAW-115publ44.pdf.

67. Daniel Thomas, "Mikhail Fridman and Petr Aven: Oligarchs Caught between Putin and the West, *Financial* Times, March, 4 2022 (https://www.ft.com/content/2797a5ec-9c02-47dc-ad13-b4348edb51e7.) Fridman first moved to Israel after he was sanctioned by the United States in August 2023, then moved on to Moscow. German Khan returned to Russia in 2022. Petr Aven, who now lives in Latvia, is the only one of the three main partners in LetterOne still in the West (*Financial Times*, October 10, 2023). Aleksey Kuzmichev, who was one of the founders of the Alfa-Group and its top oil specialist, moved to France after divesting himself of

his shares in LetterOne. In October 2023 he was placed under investigation by French authorities, on suspicion of tax evasion and money laundering (Abdelhak El Idrissi, "L'oligarque russe Alexeï Kouzmitchev placé en garde à vue," *Le Monde*, October 30, 2023, (https://www.lemonde.fr/les-decodeurs/article/2023/10/30/l-oligarque-russe-alexei-kouzmitchev-place-en-garde-a-vue-par-la-justice-francaise-dans-une-affaire-de-blanchiment_6197379_4355770.html).

68. Javier Espinoza et al., "EU Court Rules in Favor of Russian Oligarchs Fridman and Aven in Blow to Sanctions Regime," *Financial Times*, April 10, 2024, https://www.ft.com/content/722d0e1e-6bf2-4cb7-a290-518dacb5899f. Following the EU's ruling, Fridman is seeking compensation from the Duchy of Luxembourg for damages caused by the sanctions and may bring suit before the Stockholm arbitration court.

69. Henry Foy and Max Seddon, "EU Sanctions Regime in Turmoil," *Financial Times*, April 11, 2024, https://www.ft.com/content/722d0e1e-6bf2-4cb7-a290-518dacb5899f.

70. On the handful of Russian oligarchs who have taken positions in publicly listed companies, see https://www.businessinsider.com/russian-oligarchs-that-own-western-companies-2015-2.

71. These few examples do not even begin to cover the breadth and detail of the Rotenberg files. See https://www.occrp.org/en/rotenberg-files/.

72. The OCCRP is a global network of investigative journalists, specializing in investigations of organized crime and corruption (https://www.occrp.org/en). For the OCCRP's reporting on the Rotenbergs and their advisors in the West, see https://www.occrp.org/en/rotenberg-files/.

73. See, for example, a series of articles in *The Guardian* on the international management of Roman Abramovich's overseas assets, https://www.theguardian.com/world/2023/jan/06/roman-abramovich-trusts-transfer-leak-russia-sanctions and https://www.theguardian.com/world/2023/apr/17/roman-abramovich-chelsea-world-beaters. On his Cyprus connections and the impact of sanctions on Cyprus, see https://www.theguardian.com/world/2023/apr/22/cyprus-russia-sanctions-us-uk and https://www.theguardian.com/world/2023/apr/18/the-cyprus-connection-the-family-firm-that-helped-pour-abramovichs-millions-into-chelsea.

74. Strictly speaking, *vory* means the "thieves in the law," that is, criminals who have taken an oath of loyalty to the fraternity of thieves inside prison. Other thieves, including those originating from "sports clubs" and other backgrounds, are technically not *vory*.

75. Semyon Mogilevich, a noted Russian-Ukrainian crime boss, reputedly worked closely with Ukraine's gas kingpin Dmitro Firtash. As Firtash told former US ambassador William Taylor, "In the 1990s one needed Mogilevich's support to do business," from WikiLeaks, as related by Glenn R. Simpson, "U.S. Probes Possible Crime Links to Russian Natural-Gas Deals," *The New York Times*, December 22, 2006. For background on Firtash's role, see my *The Bridge*, pp. 336–338. Semyon Mogilevich controlled Rosukrenergo, the main channel for exporting pipeline gas through Ukraine, and also owned one of Russia's largest private banks of the day, Inkombank. Like the other Russian crime bosses, Mogilevich needed a respectable foreign face for his operations. He was the mastermind behind the notorious Philadelphia-based YBM Magnex Corporation, which from 1992 up to its unmasking and collapse in 1998 served as a money-laundering front for Russian mobsters. YBM had impeccable public credentials: it boasted a blue-ribbon board, it was audited by the best accounting companies, and was listed on the Canadian stock exchange (*The New York Times*, July 25, 1999). See also Douglas Century, *The Last Boss of Brighton: Boris "Biba" Nayfeld and the Rise of the Russian Mob in America* (New York: Morrow, 2022).

76. Mark Galeotti, *The Vory: Russia's Super Mafia* (New Haven, CT: Yale University Press, 2018).

77. For an overview of "Russian" organized crime in the United States, see James O. Finckenauer, *Russian Organized Crime in the United States* (Washington, DC: US Dept. of Justice, National Institute of Justice, 2007), https://www.ojp.gov/pdffiles1/nij/218560.pdf, and James O. Finckenauer, and Elin J. Waring, *Russian Mafia in America* (Boston, MA: Northeastern University Press, 1998).

78. Presentation to the US-Russian Business Council, Washington DC, January 27 1999 (author's notes).

79. Galeotti, *The Vory*, especially Chapter 12, "The Gangster-Internationalist," pp. 181–206.
80. One of the "middleman" activities of the new generation of Russia criminals was arranging protection, or *kryshi*, for more traditional criminal activities. The older *vory* sometime found the new generation disconcerting. One of the "old school," "Biba" Nayfeld, relates that when he asked one of the most famous *vory* of the day, Vyacheslav "Yaponchik" Ivankov, to organize a *krysha* for him, Ivankov referred him to his son. The son turned out to be, in Nayfeld's words, "young and polite and spoke in a quiet manner. He didn't have the face of a criminal." Nayfeld at first could not believe that the young man would be able to do the job, but he proved highly professional (Century, *The Last Boss of Brighton*, p. 303).
81. Finckenauer and Waring, *Russian Mafia in America*.
82. For background on Viktor Bout, see Wikipedia, https://en.wikipedia.org/wiki/Viktor_Bout. Bout, following his return to Russia, ran for a seat in a provincial legislature on the ticket of the Liberal Democratic Party of Russia (LDPR) (*Kommersant*, July 4, 2023).
83. For a good summary of Prigozhin's origins and rise, and the murky origins of his private army, see "Chastnaia armiia dlia prezidenta: Istoriia samogo delikatnogo porucheniia Evgeniia Prigozhina," *The Bell*, January 29, 2019, https://thebell.io/41889-2.
84. I am grateful to my former student Tina Dolbaia, now with the Center for Strategic and International Studies (CSIS), for her prescient early work on Prigozhin and the Wagner group in Africa in my Georgetown seminar. See her two excellent follow-up reports for CSIS, Tina Dolbaia and Mathieu Droin, *Russia Is Still Progressing in Africa: What's the Limit?* (Washington, DC: CSIS, August 2023), https://www.csis.org/analysis/russia-still-progressing-africa-whats-limit, and Tina Dolbaia and Mathieu Droin, *Post-Prigozhin Russia in Africa: Regaining or Losing Control?* (Washington, DC: CSIS, September 2023), https://www.csis.org/analysis/post-prigozhin-russia-africa-regaining-or-losing-control.
85. For the story of the absorption of Soiuzgazeksport by Gazprom, see my *The Bridge*, p. 249. Gazeksport, in its previous identity as a Soviet foreign-trade specialist, had a longer history than Gazprom itself, since it had been the Soviets' monopoly gas exporter since the early 1970s. As Gazeksport people liked to joke, "We may be a daughter company, but we are the only daughter that is older than its mother." Down through the years, it retained a distinct corporate culture, more commercial-minded and entrepreneurial than the legacy engineering culture of Gazprom itself.
86. Gustafson, *The Bridge*, Chapter 8.
87. Gazprom Marketing & Trading set up a successful LNG trading office in Singapore, initially based on volumes Gazprom lifted as part of its 50% share of the Sakhalin II Project. Today, Novatek also has a trading office in Singapore. I am grateful to Andrew Seck for his valuable insights into Russian LNG.
88. The goal was to produce 200 bcma of gas and 40 mtpa of liquids (i.e., "condensate"). Natal'ia Skorlygina, "'Achimgaz' nachnet dobychy v blizhaishie dni," *Kommersant*, March 29, 2006, https://www.kommersant.ru/doc/661859.
89. Under the arrangement between the two companies, all the gas would be sold to Gazprom, two-thirds of it at the local price in Yamal-Nenetsk and one-third at the German border price, minus transportation costs. Dmitrii Butrin, "Dobycha gaza. Wintershall burit vse glubzhe," *Kommersant*, July 18, 2003, https://www.kommersant.ru/doc/397251. Later reports put the split at three-quarters to one-quarter. Russian independent gas producers reportedly greeted the price deal with envy.
90. The transit through Ukraine is scheduled to end on December 31, 2024, and it will not be renewed.
91. In April 2024 Gazprom reported that it lost money in 2023, for the first time since 1999 (https://www.kommersant.ru/doc/6680326). According to an internal report commissioned by Gazprom, the company's exports to Europe will not recover to their pre-war levels before the mid-2030s, if then. See Max Seddon et al., "Gazprom Badly Hurt by Ukraine War, Says Company-Commissioned Report," *Financial Times*, June 5, 2024, https://www.ft.com/content/21f8f63f-80d6-455f-abf8-fce269d70319.

Coda

1. Both the Levada Center in Moscow and the Pew Research Center in the United States have conducted multiple surveys of public opinion on the opening of Russia. According to the Levada Center, Russian public opinion toward the United States and the EU was on the whole positive from 1997 through 2013, following which it turned predominantly negative (https://www.levada.ru/indikatory/otnoshenie-k-stranam/). According to the Pew Research Center, the views of Russians toward the United States, and those of Americans toward Russia, have declined in tandem since about 2010 (https://www.pewresearch.org/short-reads/2018/10/04/6-charts-on-how-russians-and-americans-see-each-other/).

Chapter 3

1. In contrast to the rich Western literature on Putin's geopolitics and broader domestic politics, his views and roles in the economic opening of Russia and foreign investment have received less attention among his Western biographers. The best analysis, which integrates every aspect of Putin's complex personality and public persona, is Fiona Hill and Clifford G. Gaddy, *Mr. Putin: Operative in the Kremlin* (Washington, DC: Brookings Institution, 2015), especially Chapter 7, "The Free Marketeer," pp. 132–152. Here and elsewhere, I have benefited from many fruitful conversations with Anders Aslund, whose views on Putin's approach to economic reform and foreign investment are distilled in his book, *Russia's Crony Capitalism.*
2. These words are borrowed from the equally excellent biography by Philip Short, *Putin* (New York: Henry Holt and Company, 2022), p. 233, apparently based on a conversation between Putin and the French consul general in Saint Petersburg, Roland Blatmann.
3. Putin had lived in East Germany for five years where he witnessed its mixed economy, although he was not directly involved in economic affairs. While in Saint Petersburg, he developed a relationship with the Saint Petersburg Mining Institute and its rector V. Litvinenko and wrote a *kandidat* dissertation (roughly the equivalent of a PhD thesis), mainly devoted to local economic issues, which he later defended shortly after moving to Moscow. For a discussion of the thesis (which is not publicly available) and Putin's associated writings and statements at this time, see Harley Balzer, "Vladimir Putin's Academic Writings and Russian Natural Resource Policy," *Problems of Post-Communism* (January/February 2006): 48–54, as well as Short, *Putin*, pp. 233–234.
4. For background and an update through early 2022 see Oleg Dilimbetov, "Avtoritetnomu biznesmenu doraboltali obvinenie," *Kommersant*, February 20, 2022, https://www.kommersant.ru/doc/5227753.
5. Materials from Putin's first two terms, and in particular his *poslaniia*, could still be found on the Kremlin website until recently, but as of late 2024 they are apparently no longer available. Most of the presidential *poslaniia* from 2008 to 2024 (including the four by Medvedev between 2009 and 2012, as well as several statements by Putin as prime minister) can be found (in English) at http://en.kremlin.ru/events/president/transcripts/messages, and (in Russian) at http://kremlin.ru/events/president/transcripts/messages.
6. See especially the many fine writings of Kathryn Hendley on the Russian legal system and judiciary, for example, Hendley, "The Rule of Law."
7. Jordan Gans-Morse, *Property Rights in Post-Soviet Russia: Violence, Corruption, and the Demand for Law* (Cambridge, UK: Cambridge University Press, 2017), p. 79, see also especially Chapter 4.
8. On this point, see Aslund, *Russia's Crony Capitalism*, pp. 185–188.
9. Transcript of Putin's November 2008 *Poslanie*, kremlin.ru/events/president/transcripts/messages/1968.
10. Address by Putin to members of the RSPP (Russian Union of Industrialists and Entrepreneurs), April 21, 2011. His remarks were formerly available on the government's website at http://government.ru/docs/14934/, with an English-language text at http://government.ru/eng/docs/14934/, but they are no longer accessible. This excerpt is quoted in Hill and Gaddy, *Mr. Putin*, p. 136.

11. See Clifford G. Gaddy and Barry W. Ickes, "Resource Rents and the Russian Economy," *Eurasian Geography and Economics*, 46, no. 8 (2005): 559–583.

12. For a description of the origins and structure of state corporations, see Vadim Volkov, *Russia's New "State Corporations": Locomotives of Modernization or Covert Privatization Schemes?* Policy Memo No. 25 (Washington, DC: PONARS Eurasia, August 2008).

13. http://kremlin.ru/events/president/transcripts/24329.

14. The best book on the roles of the CPSU apparatus at the regional and local levels remains Jerry Hough, *The Soviet Prefects* (Cambridge, MA: Harvard University Press, 1969).

15. See especially Peter Reddaway, *Russia's Domestic Security Wars: Putin's Use of Divide and Rule against His Hardline Allies* (Cham, Switzerland: Palgrave Pivot, 2018).

16. The five governors were those of Kaliningrad (Anton Alikhanov to minister of energy and trade), Kursk (Roman Starovoit to minister of transportation), Kemerovo (Sergey Tsivilev to minister of energy), Tula (Aleksey Dyumin to presidential aide), and Khabarovsk (Mikhail Degtyarev to minister of sports). See *TASS*, May 15, 2024, https://tass.com/politics/1788285. A useful source of analysis to follow on elite appointments is the Mikhail Zygar, "The Last Pioneer" Substack series, https://zygaro.substack.com/.

17. I am indebted to Bob Otto for his invaluable help in documenting Putin's public responses to the problem of predation by the security services.

18. "Poslanie Prezidenta Federal'nomu Sobraniiu," December 3, 2015, www.kremlin.ru/events/president/news/50864. The only concrete measure taken to defend private business was the creation of a Federal Corporation for the Development of Medium and Small Business. But as Putin acknowledged, it didn't have much of an impact.

19. "Bol'shaia press-konferentsiia Vladimira Putina," December 14, 2017,www.kremlin.ru/events/president/news/56378

20. www.kremlin.ru/events/president/news/59863.

21. http://kremlin.ru/events/president/news/73585.

22. There has been abundant coverage of this issue in the Russian media. See, for example, Konstantin Shaprov, "Pravitel'stvo reshilo ne vypolniat' porucheniia Putin. V chem prichina?" *Pravda.ru*, November 4, 2020, https://www.pravda.ru/news/politics/1547799-proval/. Shortly before the invasion, Prime Minister Mishustin vowed to address the problem, but there is little evidence that it has improved. See, for example, E. Pashkovskaia, "'Dvoenniki' Mishustina. Kto iz ministrov chashche vsego 'zabivaet' na porucheniia prezidenta" [Mishustin's "Delinquents." Which Ministers Most Often "Blow Off" Presidential Assignments], *Baza*, November 3, 2020, https://baza.io/posts/139fdeb5-89db-436c-854f-fd8320fe14aa.

23. Vladimir Putin, "Poslanie Prezidenta Federal'nomu Sobraniiu," February 29, 2024 (http://kremlin.ru/events/president/news/73585).

24. For a detailed account of Putin's roles in the Saint Petersburg energy sector in the 1990s, see my *Wheel of Fortune*, especially Chapter 7. See also Catherine Belton, *Putin's People* (New York: Farrar, Straus and Giroux, 2020), especially Chapter 3, pp. 84–114.

25. On Putin's dealings with foreign businesses in Saint Petersburg, and especially the "resources for food" scandal, see Hill and Gaddy, *Mr. Putin*, Chapters 5 and 7.

26. V. V. Putin, *Sankt-Peterburgskie vedomosti*, January 31, 1996, cited in Short, *Putin*, p. 233.

27. Belton, *Putin's People*, p. 236. Raymond has never confirmed the content of his words to Putin, and Belton's account of it is based on a conversation with an anonymous "Yukos shareholder." But indirect confirmation comes from an article published at the same time by Andrew Jack and Carola Hoyos, "ExxonMobil May Offer $25 Billion for 40 Percent of Yukos," *ft.com*, reprinted in *The New York Times*, October 2, 2003, https://www.nytimes.com/2003/10/02/business/ExxonMobil-may-offer-25-billion-for-40-of-yukos.html, which reported that ExxonMobil was discussing acquiring "possibly more than 50 percent."

28. Belton, *Putin's People*, p. 237.

29. For blow-by-blow accounts of the Yukos Affair and the events leading up to it, see Short, *Putin*, pp. 354–362, and Belton, *Putin's People*, pp. 219–240, as well as my *Wheel of Fortune*, Chapter 7, pp. 272–318.

30. Patrick Pouyanné, the CEO of Total, has acknowledged that it has not received a dividend from Yamal LNG since 2023, as sanctions on financial transactions with Russia have made it difficult to get money out of the country. "TotalEnergies Chief Calls Potential

EU Sanctions on Russian LNG a Financial Boon," *Reuters*, April 26, 2024, https://www.reuters.com/business/energy/totalenergies-chief-calls-potential-eu-sanctions-russian-lng-financial-boon-2024-04-26/#:%7E:text=%22If%20the%20EU%20sanctions%20Yamal,quite%20limited%2C%22%20he%20added. Pouyanné believes that if the EU sanctions Russian LNG from being delivered to Europe, Total's overall LNG portfolio will benefit, as the price of LNG in the market will rise.

31. Joint press conference in Lipetsk: http://kremlin.ru/events/president/transcripts/22434. In 2014 Merloni was absorbed by Whirlpool, a US company. In June 2022, Whirlpool sold its Russian assets to Arçelik, a Turkish company, which continues to operate in Russia.

32. On the eve of the Ukrainian invasion, there were 130 Italian companies in Russia. In aviation and space, the main Italian player was Superjet; in automotive, Pirelli. Of these, 102 still remained as of mid-2024, mostly smaller business in food and beverages, consumer goods, and clothing (Kyiv School of Economics, https://leave-russia.org).

33. Presidential website, http://kremlin.ru/events/president/transcripts/24922.

34. Kyiv School of Economics website, https://leave-russia.org.

35. For the beginning of the story, see Chapter 2.

36. Aleksey Grivach and Iurii Shpakov, "Ot 'vzaimoponimaniia' k 'vzaimoproniknoveniiu': Gazprom budet meniat'sia energeticheskimi aktivami s BASF," *Vremia novostei*, April 12, 2002.

37. Aleksey Grivach and Iurii Shpakov, "Biznes-Finansy. Etalon dlia Evropy," *Vremia-Novostei*, April 28, 2006.

38. Vladimir Putin, "Shell Distinguished Lecture Series: Speech," November 14, 2001, https://www.bakerinstitute.org/event/shell-distinguished-lecture-series-russian-president-vladimir-putin. However, unlike Dmitry Medvedev, who made a much-noted visit to Silicon Valley, Putin never visited any US companies on-site during his seven visits to the country between 2000 and 2015. His one personal meeting with a US CEO in the United States was with Lee Raymond of ExxonMobil (which had the dramatic sequel already recounted).

39. http://kremlin.ru/events/president/transcripts/24329.

40. The story of Boeing's activities in Russia from 1992 to 2022 was told in Chapter 1.

41. Putin speech at the 2023 Saint Petersburg Economic Forum, http://kremlin.ru/events/president/news/71445.

42. Oleg Osipov, "Vladimir Putin prizval pravitel'stvo i predprinimatelei sozdat' blagopriiatel'nye usloviia dlia vozvrashcheniia v Rossiiu kapitala iz-za rubezha," *RIA Novosti*, June 19, 2002, https://ria.ru/20020619/176912.html.

43. Putin speech at the 2023 *poslanie* (http://kremlin.ru/events/president/transcripts/messages/70565).

44. Putin, "Shell Distinguished Lecture Series: Speech."

45. For a list of Putin's travels outside Russia, by year, country, and occasion, see Wikipedia, https://en.wikipedia.org/wiki/List_of_international_presidential_trips_made_by_Vladimir_Putin.

46. The sole exception was Switzerland in June 2021, where Putin met with President Joe Biden for a summit meeting.

47. Kyiv School of Economics database, https://leave-russia.org/.

48. Xi Jinping has also made several visits to Russia. In addition, the two leaders have met frequently in virtual meetings. According to the *Economist*, the total of all meetings between the two leaders stood at forty-three by mid-2024. Joe Leahy et al., "Russia-China: An Economic Friendship That Could Rattle the World," *Financial Times*, May 15, 2024, (https://www.ft.com/content/19eb54ba-f6f7-48ba-a586-b8a113396955).

Chapter 4

1. https://www.youtube.com/watch?v=W4keR51qGBs.

2. Telegram is an instant messaging app founded in Russia in 2013 by the creators of VKontakte. For more on Telegram, see Chapter 5.

3. The leading academic writer on the history of economic sanctions is Nicholas Mulder, a professor at Cornell University. See Nicholas Mulder, *The Economic Weapon: The Rise of Sanctions as a Tool of Modern War* (New Haven, CT: Yale University Press, 2022). For his view on the 2022 sanctions, focusing on their possible impact on the world economy, see Nicholas Mulder, "The Sanctions Weapon," International Monetary Fund, FD (Finance and Development), June 2022. https://www.imf.org/en/Publications/fandd/issues/2022/06/the-sanctions-weapon-mulder.

4. Aleksandra Prokopenko, "Kreml' protiv rublia," *Carnegie Politika*, August 14, 2023, https://carnegieendowment.org/politika/90371. Prokopenko expanded on this point in early 2024 in two articles on the state of the Russian economy after two years of war. See Aleksandra Prokopenko et al., "Kak rossiiskaia ekonomika perezhila dva goda voiny," *The Bell*, February 23, 2024, https://thebell.io/kak-rossiyskaya-ekonomika-perezhila-dva-goda-voyny and Aleksandra Prokopenko et al., "Viazkaia stabil'nost': chto spasaset i chto gubit rossiiskuiu ekonomiku," *Carnegie Endowment for International Peace*, March 20, 2024, https://storage.googleapis.com/crng/pub_92016.html.

5. https://www.bloomberg.com/opinion/articles/2023-08-17/a-sickly-ruble-reveals-russian-economic-weakness-that-vladimir-putin-will-not.

6. Singh then qualified his initial language slightly by adding, "We're not cowboys and cowgirls, pressing buttons to destroy an economy." Still, the sweeping nature of his claim was clear. Daleep Singh, *60 Minutes*, March 21, 2022, https://www.youtube.com/watch?v=iu08uqap-WU. Singh had previously served at the Treasury as deputy assistant secretary for financial markets in the Obama Administration. An economist, he is primarily an expert on financial markets. In 2021–22, he was simultaneously advisor to the National Security Council and deputy director of the National Economic Council. He briefly left the government in 2022 but returned in February 2024 as deputy national security advisor for international economics. In that position he has played an active role in designing a policy to capture the frozen sovereign assets of the RCB held in the West (see discussion later in this chapter). On Singh's roles, see Stephanie Baker, *Punishing Putin: Inside the Global Economic War to Bring Down Russia* (New York NY: Simon and Schuster, 2024).

7. @POTUS, March 26, 2022, https://twitter.com/POTUS/status/1507842574865866763?ref_src=twsrc%5Etfw.

8. https://ec.europa.eu/commission/presscorner/detail/en/speech_22_1968. She used many of the same phrases when she spoke together with Biden in Brussels three weeks later.

9. Remarks by David O'Sullivan at the European Policy Center, October 2023, https://www.youtube.com/watch?v=YafhpiUXYCs.

10. The EU sanctions, however, have automatic sundown clauses, and must be renewed periodically, usually at intervals of six months. Thus if the European Council can no longer muster unanimous agreement for extensions, the EU sanctions will begin to atrophy, not because of shared policy, but simply because of the potential veto power of dissenting member-states. So far, however, the Council has been able to maintain unanimity, if at the cost of delays and compromises.

11. See, for example, the remarks by Secretary of State Antony Blinken in an interview on NPR, March 16, 2022, https://www.npr.org/2022/03/16/1086835380/blinken-sets-a-standard-for-lifting-sanctions-an-irreversible-russian-withdrawal.

12. Woodrow Wilson, *Woodrow Wilson's Case for the League of Nations* (Princeton, NJ: Princeton University Press, 1923), pp. 67–72, cited in Nicholas Mulder, *The Economic Weapon*, pp. 1–2 and 6.

13. A useful book on the sanctions against Iran, written by a seasoned practitioner, is Richard Nephew, *The Art of Sanctions: A View from the Field* (New York: Columbia University Press, 2017). One special quality of the book is that it places the Iran sanctions in the context of the evolution of sanctions policy throughout history. The common theme of all economic sanctions, however, is that they represent a contest between "the application of pain against resolve."

14. For an excellent overview of the 2014–17 post-Crimea sanctions and their impact, see Richard Connolly, *Russia's Response to Sanctions* (Cambridge, UK: Cambridge University Press, 2018).

15. Thus, imports of Russian aluminum, copper, and nickel, as well as the stocking of them on the London and Chicago Exchanges, were banned by the United States and the UK in April 2024.

In response, traders in these metals have begun shifting to the Shanghai Exchange (https:// www.kommersant.ru/doc/6648427).

16. The current detailed list of "luxury items" is contained in Annex XVIII of Regulation 833/2014, as amended by Regulation 2022/2474 of December 16, 2022 (https://eur-lex. europa.eu/legal-content/EN/TXT/?uri=uriserv%3AOJ.LI.2022.087.01.0013.01.ENG&toc=O J%3AL%3A2022%3A087I%3ATOC#:~:text=LIST%20OF%20LUXURY%20GOODS%20RE FERRED%20TO%20IN%20ARTICLE%C2%A03h).

17. https://www.bis.doc.gov/index.php/documents/regulation-docs/420-part-746-embargoes-and-other-special-controls/file, Supplement No. 5 to Part 746. Note that these are only "examples" of banned items.

18. Daniel Flatley, "Treasury Officials Warn Banks Over Sanctions Compliance Overkill," *Bloomberg*, January 6, 2023, https://www.bloomberg.com/news/articles/2023-01-06/ treasury-officials-warn-banks-against-sanctions-overcompliance.

19. The US system is underpinned by a series of enabling laws passed by Congress, for example, the Export Control Reform Act of 2018, which authorizes export controls on dual-use technologies. I do not discuss those further here, even though they provide the legislative authority for the sanctioning agencies and the actions of the president. For background on the legislative authority for the sanctions, see a report by Cory Welt, *US Sanctions on Russia: Legal Authorities and Related Actions*, R48052 (Washington DC: Congressional Research Service, April 26, 2024), https://crsreports.congress.gov/product/details?prodcode=R48052.

20. For a description of the export-control system as it was in the Cold War, see my *Selling the Russians the Rope? Soviet Technology Policy and U.S. Export Controls*, R-2649-ARPA (Santa Monica, CA: Rand Corporation, April 1981) https://www.rand.org/pubs/reports/R2649.html. The office responsible for the export-control system in Commerce was the Office of Export Administration, which worked closely with the Department of Defense. Together they maintained a Commodity Control List of items with potential military applications.

21. There is some overlap between the two categories. Export controls may also apply to end-uses and end-users. But products and processes subject to export controls require an export license, and thus tend to be specific, while sanctions apply to the entire range of transactions involving the banned person or entity.

22. The relevant office in the State Department is the Office of Economic Sanctions Policy and Implementation, located in the Bureau of Economic and Business Affairs. For a description of the shared duties of State and Treasury, see https://www.state.gov/promoting-accountability-and-imposing-costs-on-the-russian-federation-and-its-enablers-for-putins-aggression-against-ukraine/. In addition to SDNs, which are mainly the province of the State Department, there are also so-called SSI sanctions, which apply to particular types of transactions, such as debt or equity of equities of designated entities. These tend to be the province of OFAC.

23. https://www.justice.gov/opa/video/attorney-general-merrick-b-garland-announces-launch-task-force-kleptocapture. For the flavor of KleptoCapture's activity, see, for example, "Task Force KleptoCapture Announces Array of New Charges," US Department of Justice, Office of Public Affairs, February 22, 2024, https://www.justice.gov/opa/pr/task-force-kleptocapture-announces-array-new-charges-arrests-and-forfeiture-proceedings. Since its creation in 2022, KleptoCapture "has restrained, seized, and obtained judgments to forfeit nearly $700 million in assets from Russian enablers and charged more than 70 individuals."

24. Sanctions Explorer, https://sanctionsexplorer.org/search. See also, https://home.treasury.gov/ news/press-releases/jy1296.

25. See the webpage of OFAC at https://ofac.treasury.gov/. OFAC is also responsible for US sanctions on Cuba, Iran, and North Korea, among others. Treasury's remit is not limited to financial matters. Treasury officials also travel abroad to brief allies and third countries on Russian shadow trade, armed with detailed lists of dual-use technologies.

26. In July 2023 then-director Andrea Gacki and her then-deputy Bradley Smith (who has now succeeded her as head of OFAC) launched a series of videos to acquaint the public with OFAC and its activities. See the first installment, on the history of OFAC, at https://ofac.treasury.gov/ ofac-video-series.

27. Gina Raimondo, Secretary of Commerce, "The Department of Commerce Budget in Brief: Fiscal Year 2023," https://www.commerce.gov/sites/default/files/2022-03/Commerce-FY2023-BIB-Introduction.pdf, p. 67.

28. *Economic Sanctions: Treasury and State Have Received Increased Resources for Sanctions Implementation but Face Hiring Challenges* (Washington, DC: U.S. Government Accounting Office, October 2019), https://www.gao.gov/assets/710/701891.pdf. See also https://export compliancedaily.com/article/2020/11/02/us-sanctions-agency-is-losing-record-number-of-employees-2010290028#:~:text=%E2%80%9CTreasurys%20Office%20of%20Foreign%20Assets,goals%2C%E2%80%9D%20the%20spokesperson%20said. One major departure was that of Liz Rosenberg, who left her position as assistant secretary of the Treasury for terrorism and financial intelligence in February 2024 to move to the Bank of America, where she is managing director for global financial crimes. Another significant departure was that of Ben Harris, who as assistant to Undersecretary Wally Adeyemo and advisor to Treasury Secretary Janet Yellen was one of the main architects of the oil price cap (discussed later in this chapter). He left the government in March 2023 and is currently vice-president and director for economic studies at the Brookings Institution.
29. https://www.state.gov/promoting-accountability-and-imposing-costs-on-the-russian-federation-and-its-enablers-for-putins-aggression-against-ukraine/.
30. For example, a joint note on sanctions compliance was co-issued in March 2023 by Justice, Commerce, and Treasury (https://home.treasury.gov/policy-issues/financial-sanctions/recent-actions/20230302_33).
31. In the mid-1980s, when President Reagan first imposed sanctions on Libya, OFAC had just twenty-two employees, including clerks. Peter Kilborn, "Treasury Department: They Who Dig the Trenches for Economic War," *The New York Times*, January 15, 1986, https://www.nytimes.com/1986/01/15/us/treasury-department-they-who-dig-the-trenches-for-economic-war.html.
32. Zarate, *Treasury's War*, pp. 202–207.
33. For background on Zubkov and his relationship with Putin, see Hill and Gaddy, *Mr. Putin*, pp. 164–166 and 188.
34. Zarate, *Treasury's War*, pp. 160–163. As recently as 1999, Russia had been blacklisted by FATForce.
35. As described in Chapter 2, by this time, Russia had also joined the SWIFT international messaging system and become the second-largest user after the United States, with over 300 Russian banks participating. Russian National Swift Association, https://www.rosswift.ru/en/#:~:text=Russian%20National%20SWIFT%20Association%20(ROSSWIFT,behalf%20in%20the%20Russian%20Federation.
36. See in particular Elizabeth Rosenberg et al., *The New Tools of Economic Warfare: Effects and Effectiveness of Contemporary U.S. Financial Sanctions* (Washington, DC: CNAS, 2016), which laid out the doctrine of "smart sanctions" and features a helpful bibliography. See also Zachary Goldman and Elizabeth Rosenberg, "American Economic Power and the New Face of Financial Warfare" (Center for a New American Security, June 2015).
37. Serving directly under Treasury Secretary Janet Yellen, Brian Nelson, as undersecretary, had formal authority for six offices responsible for financial intelligence, terrorism, and sanctions. Reporting to Nelson was Bradley Smith (who has succeeded Liz Rosenberg), the assistant secretary, who currently oversees three of those offices—OFAC, FINCEN, and the Division of Intelligence and Analysis. In September 2024 Nelson left the Treasury to serve as an advisor to Kamala's Harris's presidential campaign.
38. https://home.treasury.gov/news/press-releases/jy1731.
39. "On Second Anniversary of Russia's Further Invasion of Ukraine and Following the Death of Aleksey Navalny, Treasury Sanctions Hundreds of Targets in Russia and Globally," U.S. Department of the Treasury, Press Release, https://home.treasury.gov/news/press-releases/jy2117.
40. "U.S. Continues to Degrade Russia's Military-Industrial Base and Target Third-Country Support with Nearly 300 New Sanctions," U.S. Department of the Treasury, May 1, 2024, https://home.treasury.gov/news/press-releases/jy2318.
41. Chris Cook and Max Seddon, "US Extends Bank Sanctions to Target Kremlin War Economy," *Financial Times*, June 12, 2024, https://www.ft.com/content/1ba434bb-e579-4819-977b-cff6b6b98ecc.
42. Wally Adeyemo, "The US Is Ready to Impose Sanctions on Foreign Financial Institutions When Others Don't," *Financial Times*, Op-Ed, December 22, 2023, https://www.ft.com/content/f1fe5ece-323c-401f-870b-cd45c92bf84a.

43. A valuable historical overview of the evolution of the European system is Luuk van Middelaar, *The Passage to Europe: How a Continent Became a Union* (New Haven, CT: Yale University Press, 2013).

44. As one striking illustration, the Commission's guidance on the Russia sanctions currently runs to 365 pages (https://finance.ec.europa.eu/system/files/2023-06/faqs-sanctions-russia-consolidated_en.pdf).

45. Josep Borrell was replaced by Kaja Kallas, an Estonian politician, at the end of 2024.

46. RELEX also plays a role in sanctions implementation, collecting information on alleged circumventions, and meeting periodically with experts from the member states to discuss implementation and exchange experiences.

47. FISMA's staff is about half the size of that of DG-TRADE. https://epthinktank.eu/2021/02/09/european-commission-facts-and-figures-2/number_staff/.

48. "Paying It Forward," *Politico Europe*, Interview with Mairead McGuinness, March 2023 https://www.youtube.com/watch?v=3O47AJiEAfQ.

49. It is perhaps no coincidence that there is a phalanx of Irish nationals in FISMA, and Commissioner Mairead Guinness happened to be Irish. This may have partly reflected the fact that there had been a vigorous development of the financial industry in Ireland in the previous twenty years, of which Russian companies and banks took advantage (https://www.irishtimes.com/business/economy/on-a-dublin-backstreet-a-once-thriving-hub-of-russian-finance-is-falling-apart-1.4882925).

50. The current head of trade sanctions in DG-Trade is a career Commission official named Denis Redonnet, whose first training was in economics and finance in France and Belgium. Redonnet has also served in the World Trade Organization.

51. https://www.eeas.europa.eu/eeas/creation-european-external-action-service_en.

52. Borrell was simultaneously vice-chairman of the EU Commission.

53. https://ireland.representation.ec.europa.eu/news-and-events/news/eu-appoints-david-osullivan-international-special-envoy-implementation-eu-sanctions-2022-12-13_en. O'Sullivan remains the director of the Institute of International and European Affairs, although presumably in absentia.

54. Speech by David O'Sullivan at the Institute of International and European Affairs, January 14 2011, https://www.youtube.com/watch?v=JCJoq7DNQzk.

55. Ibid.

56. There are three separate bodies responsible for sanctions enforcement in the EU structure in Brussels, one in the Commission's DG-Trade, headed by Denis Redonnet, and another in the Directorate-General for Finance (FINCEN). The current head of the sanctions division in FINCEN is Alina Nedea, a lawyer by background. Finally, there is a sanctions division in the external-action service, the EEAS, until recently under Sandra DeWaele. The latter is in charge of the diplomatic aspects of the EU sanctions policy, while the first two oversee implementation and coordination with the sanctions offices of the member states.

57. https://www.youtube.com/watch?v=hBnIgcoZ5w4. https://www.youtube.com/watch?v=3O47AJiEAfQ. The sanctions are considered part of the EU's Common Foreign and Security Policy, and as such are coordinated by the EEAS sanctions team.

58. His first press conference since his appointment the previous month (FT, March 1 2023: https://www.politico.eu/article/eus-new-sanctions-envoy-set-to-fight-sanction-cirvumvention/).

59. In April 2023 O'Sullivan traveled to Turkey, the UAE, and Kyrgyzstan. He then went to Kazakhstan with Liz Rosenberg, then assistant secretary of the Treasury. In May he went to Uzbekistan, Serbia, Georgia, and Armenia. His current focus seems to be trade in dual-use goods rather than financial flows. O'Sullivan maintains close coordination with US officials: thus, he stopped off in Washington after his April travels and briefed reporters there (https://www.ft.com/content/07da95be-909f-4fc5-89fb-7262b41a519e).

60. *Politico Europe*, Interview with Mary McGuinness, March 2023.

61. Stéphane Bonifassi and Julie Bastien, "EU Sanctions Enforcement," in *GIR Guide to Sanctions*, 4th ed., Chapter 2, pp. 27–40, https://globalinvestigationsreview.com/guide/the-guide-sanctions/fourth-edition.

62. On these points a valuable source is the periodic reports of the Global Investigations Review (GIR), produced and published by a group of law firms.

63. Sergey Panov, "False Colors: European Paint Companies Are Still Working in Russia Despite Claims of Withdrawal," *The Insider*, February 5, 2024, https://theins.press/en/society/268902. AkzoNobel, in a 2022 statement, announced it had stopped supplying coating to the Russian aviation industry and restricted its sales to household paints, but this has apparently not happened (Statement on the Business in Russia, AkzoNobel, https://www.akzonobel.com/en/statement-on-the-business-in-russia). Tikkurila pledged to donate its Russian profits to humanitarian organizations supporting Ukraine, but has so far failed to do so.

64. "Dutch Suspect Evaded Sanctions by Exporting Microchips to Russia through Third Countries," *NL Times*, February 13, 2023, https://nltimes.nl/2023/02/13/dutch-suspect-evaded-sanctions-exporting-microchips-russia-third-countries.

65. https://www.ft.com/content/2d9b41a9-c125-43fd-9037-1d471dcc0304.

66. Giles Thomson, YouTube, https://www.youtube.com/watch?v=sLiUbtED3j0, September 2022.

67. David Sheppard et al., "London Targets Insurer Protecting Moscow's Oil 'Shadow Fleet,'" *Financial Times*, June 14, 2024, https://www.ft.com/content/13d496bc-116c-460a-b490-fe2f352837b5.

68. Eleanor Myers, "UK Sanctions Watchdog Flops in Face of Russia's War," *Politico*, May 20, 2024, https://www.politico.eu/article/britain-ofsi-miss-opportunity-sanctions-watchdog-step-up-in-face-russia-war/.

69. There is a noticeable difference between the language used by OFSI and that of its US and EU counterparts. OFSI's director speaks of serving its "customers" and "clients," and his overall stress is on speed and efficiency of service in processing license applications. Indeed, he almost sounds apologetic that OFSI, because of the press of business and shortness of staff, is not able to process them faster.

70. Canadian House of Commons, Report No. 23: "Canada's Sanctions Regime," January 31, 2024, https://www.ourcommons.ca/documentviewer/en/44-1/FAAE/report-23/page-69#15.

71. Given the shortages of staff and resources in government agencies, some private companies have stepped into the breach, such as Euromonitor International in Europe (which does a broad range of market research) and Silverado Compliance Solutions in the United States.

72. As an example of the subtleties involved, consider the question of whether a US investment fund can invest in a Russian banned entity, or SDN. Clearly the answer is no. But what if the investment fund already held equity in that SDN? Must it divest? OFAC uses a "50% rule," which states that the US fund will not be in violation if its stake in the Russian SDN represents less than 50% of its assets. So far, so good. But what if the US fund invests in a (hypothetical) "Europe Energy Fund," which in turn owns stocks of Russian SDN companies as part of a broader portfolio? Must that entire fund be blocked, and must the US investment fund divest? (The answer is no, at least in theory.) OFAC attempts to answer such questions through its online Frequently Asked Questions (FAQs) feature, which often reads like a running exercise in scriptural interpretation. (I am grateful to my Georgetown colleague Jeffrey Lord for his kind coaching on such questions.)

73. Extraterritorial sanctions are not new in the United States, but they have become standard practice since 1996, with the passage of the Helms-Burton Act, which dealt with US sanctions on Cuba. The concept was broadened in 2010 and after to include secondary sanctions. For a good discussion of the difference, together with concrete examples, see Agathe Demarais, *Backfire: How Sanctions Reshape the World against U.S. Interests* (New York: Columbia University Press, 2022), Chapter 5. For a European perspective, see Ellie Geranmayeh and Manuel Lafont Papnouil, "Meeting the Challenge of Secondary Sanctions," Policy Brief, European Council on Foreign Relations, June 25, 2019, https://ecfr.eu/publication/meeting_the_challenge_of_secondary_sanctions/.

74. See Thane Gustafson, *Soviet Negotiating Strategy: The East-West Gas Pipeline Deal, 1980–1984* (Santa Monica, CA: RAND Corporation, 1985).

75. Sandra De Waele, "Russia's War on Ukraine," Presentation at the European Parliamentary Research Service, June 2022, from Minute 23, https://www.youtube.com/watch?v=hBnIgcoZ5w4. (In September 2023, Sandra De Waele was named the EU ambassador to Lebanon. She was replaced as EEAS head of sanctions by Brice de Schietere. For an interview with Schietere, see the EU Finance Podcast, https://euagenda.eu/videos/125604.) See also https://www.eeas.europa.eu/eeas/european-union-sanctions_en.

76. https://www.politico.eu/article/russia-ukraine-war-vladimir-putin-trade-partners-sanctions-loopholes-in-face-of-eu-pressure/.

77. Henry Foy, "EU Agrees Measures to Target Russian Sanctions Evaders," *Financial Times*, June 21, 2023, https://www.ft.com/content/4531e5da-7520-408f-8f58-0714a04a785a.

78. This was also note by De Waele: "In dealing with third countries, we need to rely on diplomatic tools," De Waele, June 2022. See also the neatly titled commentary following the adoption of the eleventh package of sanctions, "EU Gains New Sanctions Weapon but Will Probably Be Too Nice to Use It," *Politico*, June 2023, https://www.politico.eu/article/eu-new-sanction-weapon-russia-ukraine-war-trade-ban/.

79. There is considerably less flexibility when the US sanctions are mandated by legislative acts such as CAATSA (Countering America's Adversaries through Sanctions Act), adopted by Congress in 2017. The implementation of CAATSA also takes place through executive orders, but there is no clear, explicit provision for rescinding them. (The implementation of CAATSA is itself contained in a presidential executive order, signed by President Trump in September 2018, https://ofac.treasury.gov/media/8671/download?inline). Since CAATSA, however, there has been no comparable sanctions legislation by Congress. This may have the result of giving the president more freedom of action in modifying or rescinding sanctions by executive order, but this power is as yet untested.

80. Sam Fleming, "The True Faith of Ursula von der Leyen," *FT Spectrum*, April 22–23, 2023.

81. Andrea Gacki has since become assistant secretary in charge of FinCen. She has been replaced at the head of OFAC by Bradley Smith, an attorney who had been deputy director of OFAC since 2018, and chief counsel of OFAC since 2013.

82. https://ireland.representation.ec.europa.eu/news-and-events/news/eu-appoints-david-osullivan-international-special-envoy-implementation-eu-sanctions-2022-12-13_en.

83. US Treasury, "READOUT: REPO Deputies Meeting," https://home.treasury.gov/news/press-releases/jy1716#:~:text=Deputies%20emphasized%20that%20those%20profiting,to%20store%20and%20access%20wealth.

84. The fate of the blocked sovereign assets has been the subject of some controversy, first, because initially the sanctioning countries could not establish where they were held (hence the "mapping" effort) and second because the question of what to do with them once they have been identified remains a subject of continuing debate today, with some G7 members pressing to devote them to paying for damage done to Ukraine, or to buying weapons for Ukraine, and others objecting on grounds of international law. For the time being, REPO members have only committed themselves to "immobilizing" the sovereign assets until a joint decision is reached. (For further discussion see later in this chapter.)

85. In June 2024, Ursula von der Leyen was re-elected chair of the Commission by the heads of the EU governments. But as of mid-summer the selection of new commissioners was still ongoing. The head of the European Council, Charles Michel, has stepped down to take a seat in the EU Parliament and has been replaced by a Portuguese politician, former prime minister Antonio Costa. The High Representative for Foreign Affairs and Security Policy, Josep Borrell has yielded his post to Kaja Kallas, a politician from Estonia, https://www.consilium.europa.eu/en/press/press-releases/2024/06/28/remarks-by-president-charles-michel-following-the-european-council-meeting-of-27-june-2024/.

86. In the case of the United States, as mentioned earlier, the Biden Administration has been concerned about disrupting oil markets with an overly vigorous enforcement of the price cap. See Timothy Gardner and Laura Sanicola, "As Russian Oil Crosses G7's Price Cap, US Eyes Soft Enforcement," *Reuters*, July 27, 2023, https://www.reuters.com/business/energy/russian-oil-crosses-g7s-price-cap-us-eyes-soft-enforcement-2023-07-27/.

87. Tri-Seal Compliance Note: "Voluntary Self-Disclosure of Potential Violations," US Treasury, July 26, 2023, https://ofac.treasury.gov/media/932036/download?inline. The US system requires that companies maintain internal controls and keep records of suspected sanctions violations. Thus the burden of proof is on the companies, including third parties. See OFAC Tri-Seal Compliance Note: "Cracking Down on Third-Party Intermediaries," US Treasury, March 2 2023, https://ofac.treasury.gov/media/931471/download?inline.

88. The intent of the measure is to ensure uniformity in criminal prosecutions by the member states, which are responsible for sanctions implementation.

89. One of the few actual arrests of suspected violators to date was reported in July 2023, when the Dutch Fiscal Intelligence and Investigation Service arrested a Dutch citizen on suspicion

of exporting computers and computer parts to Russia (https://sanctionsnews.bakermckenzie. com/dutch-authorities-make-arrest-over-russia-sanctions-circumvention/).

90. Microsoft had voluntarily "self-disclosed" the violations, and even though the two agencies agreed that the violations had been "non-egregious," they imposed $3.3 million in civil penalties on Microsoft (https://home.treasury.gov/news/press-releases/jy1394).

91. https://www.rt.com/business/573088-german-firm-fined-russia-sanctions/?utm_source=rss &utm_medium=rss&utm_campaign=RSS. The original source is the German daily *Tageschau*.

92. https://www.theregister.com/2022/12/14/us_doj_disrupts_russian_smuggling/.   More recently, in August 2023, a Russian citizen was arrested in Cyprus at the request of the United States, for leading a smuggling ring that forwarded microelectronics to Russia (https://www. kommersant.ru/doc/6187222).

93. Baker McKenzie has a helpful blog series called Sanctions Enforcement around the World, with links to the specific countries covered (https://sanctionsnews.bakermckenzie.com/ new-blog-series-sanctions-enforcement-around-the-world/). For current updates, see https:// sanctionsnews.bakermckenzie.com/.

94. A number of NGOs such as Euromonitor International track trade data, and these are regularly reported in the media—including the Russian press. See, for example, "Ekspert Euromonitor nashel torgovye 'anomalii' v stranakh SNG," *RBC*, January 31, 2023, https://www.rbc.ru/ economics/31/01/2023/63d7d3fa9a79471e5c6228b8.

95. David O'Sullivan, Presentation at the European Policy Center (EPC), October 2023, https:// www.youtube.com/watch?v=YafhpiUXYCs.

96. Quoted in https://www.bloomberg.com/news/articles/2023-04-19/us-task-force-seeks-to-transfer-seized-assets-to-ukraine?srnd=premium.

97. I am grateful to Craig Kennedy for his valuable advice on the oil embargo and price cap, and especially on the complexities of the tanker fleet and the marine insurance system. Kennedy is the author of an important newsletter, *Navigating Russia*, on Substack. See notably his essay, "Measuring the Shadows: Moscow's Strategies for Evading Oil Sanctions and How to Stop Them from Succeeding," *Navigating Russia*, August 23, 2023 https://navigatingrussia.substack. com/p/measuring-the-shadows.

98. One of the principal architects of the US price cap plan was Ben Harris, an advisor to Deputy Treasury Secretary Wally Adeyemo. In March 2023 Harris left the Treasury Department and moved to the Brookings Institution, where he directs the economic studies program. Another important figure in the team that designed the price cap was Catherine Wolfram, who was deputy assistant secretary of the Treasury for Climate and Energy Economics while on leave from UC Berkeley. She is now the Sloan Professor at MIT. In May 2023 she co-authored an article with Simon Johnson on the "Design and Implementation of the Price Cap on Russian Oil Exports," which lays out the reasoning behind the price cap (https://mitsloan.mit.edu/ shared/ods/documents?PublicationDocumentID=9910).

99. The members of G7 are the United States, Canada, France, Germany, Italy, Japan, and the UK. Australia, though it participated in the G7 deliberations and is aligned with the others on sanctions policies, is not a member. In addition, Norway, though not a formal member of the G7, has joined the group as an active member of the price-cap coalition.

100. Insurance policies for maritime shippers must be renewed each February; if a shipper is not in compliance, its policy will be canceled at that time.

101. This combination of objectives in the price cap is clear from the statements from the US Treasury Department. See in particular an article by two key policymakers at Treasury, Elizabeth Rosenberg and Eric van Nostrand, "The Price Cap on Russian Oil: A Progress Report," May 18, 2023, https://home.treasury.gov/news/featured-stories/the-price-cap-on-russian-oil-a-progress-report. As mentioned above, Elizabeth Rosenberg was the assistant secretary of the Treasury for Terrorist Financing and Financial Crimes. Eric Van Nostrand is acting assistant secretary for Economic Policy.

102. For the first few weeks, Turkish officials blocked passage through the Turkish Straits to any tanker that did not provide proof of insurance coverage, and tankers piled up outside the Straits, trapping oil exports not only from Russia but also from Kazakhstan.

103. David Sheppard et al., "US Taps Big Trading Houses to Help Move Price-Capped Russian Oil," *Financial Times*, March 9, 2023, https://www.ft.com/content/36c5367b-06f9-48e7-9867-20671665c8a7.

104. Sheppard et al., "US Taps Commodity Traders to Shift Russian Oil." Notably, Elizabeth Rosenberg, then assistant secretary of the Treasury for Terrorist Financing and Financial Crimes, met with leading oil traders at CERA Week in Houston. Vitol, Gunvor, and Trafigura have resumed trading Russian oil products. However, their trades of Russian oil are dwarfed by those of other traders, chiefly Litasco (the trading arm of LUKoil), Bellatrix Energy (a previously unknown company based in Hong Kong that trades oil for Rosneft), and Nord Axis (also a new trader based in Hong Kong) (https://www.ft.com/content/ba9754e3-6f4e-4455-b6be-c6c6edf6b853). In July 2022, Trafigura sold its 10% stake in Vostok Oil to Nord Axis.

105. Provided one is prepared to pay the price. Driven by the Russian demand for tankers, the price of a fifteen-year-old tanker has risen to over $40 million since the Russian invasion, an increase of 129%. Oliver Telling, "Global Shipping Fleet Ages," *Financial Times*, January 7, 2024, https://www.ft.com/content/ca7736ab-35eb-4f87-a60a-d4279e8aecb7.

106. According to *Kommersant*, shipping costs for an Aframax or Suezmax tanker traveling from Novorossiisk to India over the summer of 2023 ran between $3.9 and $4.4 million per round trip. "Rossii ne podfrakhtilo," August 28, 2023, https://www.kommersant.ru/doc/6184351.

107. For a valuable update on the impact of the embargo and the price cap, see "The Price Cap on Russian Oil: Is It Working?" Brookings Institution, video, October 16, 2023, https://www.brookings.edu/events/the-price-cap-on-russian-oil-is-it-working/.

108. The only exception was Russian oil exported out of the Far Eastern port of Kozmino, which traded at prices in the high $70s per barrel, well above the price cap. The main buyers were Chinese and the main destination was China.

109. North Standard, https://www.standard-club.com/about/what-is-pi/#:~:text=Protection%20and%20Indemnity%20(P%26I)%20is,people%2C%20property%20and%20the%20enviro nment.

110. The owners of record of the Russian shadow tankers are typically small shell companies, often listing only one tanker and registered in various tax havens around the world. These are hired mainly through spot charters. The ultimate beneficiaries are difficult to pin down, but the footprints point to Russia. Indeed, over time, an increasing share of the shadow fleet belongs directly to Russian owners, who are seen as more reliable than small non-Russian ship owners, who are frequently reluctant to dedicate their vessels to the Russia trade (Kennedy, "Measuring the Shadows," Chapter 4).

111. One year after the invasion, some 60% of all vessels transporting Russian oil still used hull or cargo insurance from members of the IGP&I club, most of whom are based in London (https://www.bloomberg.com/news/articles/2023-03-30/russia-still-reliant-on-western-insurance-for-half-oil-shipments). According to CREA, a consultancy, the percentage on the eve of the invasion was 80%, but by March 2023 was down to 60%.

112. Deputy Treasury Secretary Wally Adeyemo, Remarks at the Center for a New American Security, US Treasury, June 15, 2023, https://home.treasury.gov/news/press-releases/jy1540. Other sources believe that the actual number may be only about half that, and most of it is for the Sovcomflot-owned portion of the fleet.

113. https://www.bloomberg.com/news/articles/2023-03-30/russia-still-reliant-on-western-insur ance-for-half-oil-shipments.

114. The Russian shadow fleet includes about seventy Aframax tankers that belong to Sovcomflot. Before the invasion, these were insured through the P&I system and were financed with Western bank loans. But in March 2022 Sovcomflot was sanctioned, and its IG insurance and Western bank loans were cancelled (Kennedy, "Measuring the Shadows,").

115. Tom Wilson, "Big Read: How Dubai Became 'the new Geneva' for Russian Oil Trade," *Financial Times*, July 19, 2023, https://www.ft.com/content/7ac92047-b306-49d0-9811-ddde5c916dd6.

116. https://www.bloomberg.com/news/articles/2023-03-21/new-kings-of-russian-oil-were-these -six-traders-in-december.

117. The European Central Bank has been steadily ratcheting up pressure on Raiffeisenbank. In May 2024 it instructed Raiffeisenbank to reduce its lending in Russia by two-thirds from its 2023 level by 2026, on pain of fines for non-compliance. Raiffeisenbank has reportedly already reduced its Russian loan book by 85% since the invasion began. Unicredit, meanwhile, has been given a June 1 deadline to provide a detailed breakdown of its Russian operations and plans. Source: Owen Walker et al., "ECB Presses Banks to Speed Up Russia Exits on Fear of

US Curbs," *Financial Times*, May 18, 2024, https://www.ft.com/content/77653edb-2951-4ee2-8953-60de359c2002.

118. Andrei Kostin, "Kostin rasskazal o roste otkazov v platezhakh ot druzhestvennykh bankov," *RBK*, April 11, 2024, https://www.rbc.ru/finances/11/04/2024/6617cbb19a7947c8c6001f9c. Kostin was speaking at the 2024 annual meeting of the Association of Banks of Russia.

119. Quoted in Anastasia Stognei and Joseph Cotterill, "Russia Halts Foreign Exchange Trading as US Sanctions Sow Confusion," *Financial Times*, June 13, 2024, https://www.ft.com/content/50d6bcd1-f1f6-41a1-bb26-a5482654883f. See also an analysis by Alexandra Prokpenko, "How the Latest Sanctions Will Impact Russia—and the World," *Carnegie Politika*, June 20, 2024, https://carnegieendowment.org/russia-eurasia/politika/2024/06/finance-sanctions-russia-currency?lang=en¢er=russia-eurasia.

120. As of November 2022, according to the RCB, the combined total of assets of the over 5 million Russian investors blocked in Euroclear and ClearStream was 5.7 trillion rubles (at 100 rubles to the dollar, that would be about $57 billion). Belgian authorities, who have jurisdiction over assets in Euroclear, have resisted unblocking them. Ivan Yakunin, "'Tsifra broker' pishet zhalobu," *Kommersant*, August 3, 2024, https://www.kommersant.ru/doc/6138235.

121. Laura Keffer, "Razrabotchik protsessorov 'El'brus' khochet perenesti proizvodstvo iz Taivania v Zelenograd," *Kommersant*, May 30, 2022, https://www.kommersant.ru/doc/5379687. In 2021, according to the Russian business daily *Vedomosti*, TSMC fabricated 130,000 chips designed by Baikal Electronics, but in 2022 it broke off the arrangement, with 300,000 processors still unshipped. Since that time, according to *Vedomosti*'s sources, Baikal has attempted to soldier on alone, but more than half of its chips have been defective (reported by "Meduza," t.me/meduzalive/103332).

122. The next two paragraphs are based largely on Julian Cooper, "The Machine Tool Industry of Russia at a Time of War and Sanctions," *Post-Soviet Economies*, March 2024, https://doi.org/10.1080/14631377.2024.2325787. I am grateful to Professor Cooper for the opportunity to read earlier drafts of this article and for his many kind suggestions and comments.

123. Toru Tsunashima et al., "Russia Scours China for Second-Hand Machine Tools," *Financial Times*, June 19, 2024, https://www.ft.com/content/944dfd76-eb9d-4746-9695-fe5b15230bd8, based on a report by the Center for Advanced Defense Studies (C4ADS), a Washington thin tank. See Allen Maggard, "War Machine: The Networks Supplying and Sustaining the Russian Precision Machine Tool Arsenal," C4ADS Report, June 18, 2024, https://c4ads.org/reports/war-machine/.

124. See his thoughtful testimony before the House Foreign Affairs Committee. Adam Szubin "Sanctions and Financial Pressure: Major National Security Tools," January 10, 2018, https://docs.house.gov/meetings/FA/FA00/20180110/106761/HHRG-115-FA00-Wstate-SzubinA-20180110.pdf.

125. See Alexander Libman, "Will the Strategy of Isolating Russia Ever Work?" *Russia.Post*, January 25, 2024 https://russiapost.info/global_south/isolating.

126. Excerpts of Treasury Secretary Jack Lew's speech to the Carnegie Endowment for International Peace, on March 30 2016, are still available on the Treasury Department website, https://home.treasury.gov/news/press-releases/jl0397.

127. At the beginning of 2024, the share of global central bank reserves held in dollars was about 58%, compared to 65% in 2016, with the euro at about 20% and the renminbi at 2.3%. The share of the renminbi is growing, but slowly, while that of the euro remains unchanged. See the Official Monetary and Financial Insitutions Forum (OMFIF), a think tank based in the UK omfif.org.

128. RCB internal assessment, as reported by Bloomberg, September 14, 2022, https://www.bloomberg.com/news/articles/2022-09-14/russia-quietly-adds-up-direct-losses-from-financial-sanction. (Unfortunately, this page is no longer available on the Bloomberg website.)

129. For a summary account of recent changes in Russian taxation, see "The Price Is Right," *Meduza*, April 1, 2024, https://meduza.io/en/feature/2024/04/15/the-price-is-right?utm_source=email&utm_medium=briefly&utm_campaign=2024-04-16.

130. Anastasia Stognei et al., "Russia's War Economy Leaves Businesses Starved for Labor," *Financial Times*, October 10, 2023, https://www.ft.com/content/dc76f0bb-cae2-4a3a-b704-903d2fc59a96.

131. See, for example, "Freezing Russians Plead for Help . . . ," https://www.abc.net.au/news/2024-01-21/freezing-russians-make-plea-to-vladimir-putin-after-heating-fail/103323062.

132. Anastasia Stognei, "Putin Focused on Defense as Pipes Burst and Flats Freeze in Russia," *Financial Times*, February 5, 2024, https://www.ft.com/content/81985842-e20a-4f2a-96b6-69aeddbe5109. See also Polina Iachmennikova et al., "Energetika ushla v minus," *Kommersant*, January 8, 2024, https://www.kommersant.ru/doc/6443034. The problems have become so widespread that *Kommersant* maintains a regular rubric on them (https://www.kommersant.ru/theme/3579), and the governor of Moscow Oblast', Andrei Vorobyov, runs a channel on *Telegram* reporting on breakdowns (https://t.me/vorobiev_live). Some two-thirds of communal heating, electricity, and water and sewage services are paid for directly by households and businesses, which makes them highly visible to the population. The payments system is managed by Bank Rossiya, which is owned by a close associate of Putin, Iurii Koval'chuk, a point that has not escaped public notice in Russia.

133. CAATSA (Countering America's Adversaries through Sanctions Act), Public Law 115-44. For the detailed content of the law, see https://www.govinfo.gov/app/details/PLAW-115publ44.

134. Richard Nephew: "The Hard Part: The Art of Sanctions Relief," *The Washington Quarterly*, 41, no. 2 (2018), pp. 63–77, https://www.tandfonline.com/doi/full/10.1080/0163660X.2018.1484225. See also Richard Nephew's 2022 update, which focuses specifically on the post-2022 Russia sanctions: "Beyond the Ukraine Crisis: The Future of Russian Sanctions," Columbia/SIPA, Center on Global Energy Policy, March 18, 2022, https://www.energypolicy.columbia.edu/publications/beyond-ukraine-crisis-future-russian-sanctions/. Richard Nephew is a seasoned practitioner who has also written about the sanctions against Iran, placing them in the context of the historical evolution of sanctions policy. The common theme of all economic sanctions, Nephew writes, is that they represent a contest between "the application of pain against resolve" (Nephew, *The Art of Sanctions*). Nephew was for over a decade a sanctions negotiator for the State Department, and a leading participant in the JCPOA negotiations with Iran. Since July 2022 he has been the Department of State's Coordinator on Global Anti-Corruption (https://www.state.gov/richard-nephew-named-as-coordinator-on-global-anti-corruption/).

135. In 2024 US authorities redoubled their efforts to block financial transfers between Russia and the FSU (with notable success against Kyrgyzstan), as well as Turkey and the UAE (Reuters, cited in t.me/agentstvonews/5801).

136. Steven Feldstein and Fiona Brauer, "Why Russia Has Been So Resilient to Western Export Controls," *Carnegie Endowment for International Peace*, March 11, 2024, https://carnegieendowment.org/2024/03/11/why-russia-has-been-so-resilient-to-western-export-controls-pub-91894.

Chapter 5

1. From an internal newsletter of the RCB, Aleksandr Morozov, "The New Life of the Economy: Four Stages," *ECONS: Economic Conversations*, May 18, 2022, https://econs.online/en/articles/opinions/the-new-life-of-the-economy-four-stages/.

2. For a lengthy, thoughtful, and well-informed essay on the leadership and policies of the RCB, see Svetlana Reiter and Margarita Liutova, "Kyshka groba zakryto i zakolochena," *Meduza*, June 27, 2022, https://meduza.io/feature/2022/06/27/kryshka-groba-zakryta-i-zakolochena. Co-author Margarita Liutova worked in the RCB from 2018 to 2021. She was the editor of Econs.online, a public newsletter of the RCB.

3. A partial exception is evasion of the oil price cap, which the Western sanctioning powers have stepped up efforts to control. For a report on Russian methods for evading the oil-price cap, see Oil Price Coalition (OPC), Oil Price Cap (OPC) Compliance and Enforcement Alert, February 1, 2024, OPC-Coalition-compliance-and-enforcement-alert-1-February-2024.pdf (mef.gov.it).

4. Max Seddon and Polina Ivanova, "How Putin's Technocrats Saved the Economy to Fight a War They Opposed," *Financial Times*, December 16, 2022, https://www.ft.com/content/fe5fe0ed-e5d4-474e-bb5a-10c9657285d2.

5. See, for example, the polls of consumer sentiment conducted by Russia's last remaining independent pollster, the Levada Center (https://www.levada.ru/en/).

6. Remarks by Andrei Kostin on Russia's TV24, quoted by Reuters, https://www.reuters.com/business/finance/russian-state-bank-vtb-blames-2022-losses-sanctions-ceo-2023-02-07/.

7. For a valuable analysis of the post-Crimean sanctions, see Richard Connolly, *Russia's Response to Sanctions* (Cambridge, UK: Cambridge University Press, 2018).
8. Levada Center, "Sanctions," June 10, 2022, https://www.levada.ru/en/2022/06/10/sanctions-6/.
9. Morozov, "The New Life of the Economy."
10. Elvira Nabiullina, "Plokhie vnesnie usloviia dlia rossiiskoi ekonomiki mogut sokhranit'sia navsegda," *Kommersant*, June 16, 2022, https://www.kommersant.ru/doc/5412935.
11. The price of Brent crude, in particular, had risen throughout 2021 and peaked in early 2022 at over $120 a barrel. It declined steadily thereafter, but still remained above $80 throughout the rest of 2022, before rising again in mid-2023. Source: International Energy Agency.
12. Russian exporters, though they earn revenues in dollars, must pay their taxes to the government in rubles; therefore, the higher the ruble, the fewer rubles the government receives from them.
13. Glaz'ev has been an increasingly virulent opponent of the liberal *finansisty*, and of Nabiullina in particular. He has called for the RCB to buy government bonds to finance infrastructural investment, which it would pay for by printing rubles, thus supplying the budget with additional ruble revenue, but of course at the cost of higher inflation. On other occasions, writing in nationalist-oriented media such as *Zavtra* and *Voenno-promyshlennyi kur'er* (now defunct), Glaz'ev charged that the CBR and the economic bloc of the government serve the interests of the Rothschilds, Rockefeller, Goldman-Sachs, et al. Ironically, Glaz'ev was once considered one of the liberal reformers in the Gaidar government in the 1990s. Glaz'ev is said to have good personal ties with Putin, having served on the academic board that awarded Putin his doctoral (*kandidat*) degree with high distinction.
14. Oreshkin represents a new generation of financial technocrats. Unlike the early liberal *finansisty*, Oreshkin does not come from Saint Petersburg (he is a graduate of Moscow's elite Higher Economics School, informally known as the *Vyshka*). He did not rise through the Finance Ministry (although he served a brief two years as deputy minister there) and was not a protégé of Aleksey Kudrin. Instead, at the young age of thirty-two, he was named minister of economic development in 2016, and in 2020 he became economic advisor to Putin in the Presidential Administration. In October 2024 Oreshkin was named Putin's special representative for relations with the "BRIC" states.
15. Dmitrii Grinkevich, "Kakovy prichiny deval'vatsii i chto budet s rublem?" ("What Are the Reasons for the Devaluation and What Will Happen with the Ruble?") *Vedomosti*, August 15, 2023, https://www.vedomosti.ru/economics/articles/2023/08/15/990114-kakovi-prichini-devalvatsii-i-chto-budet-s-rublem.
16. As early as mid-2022, Morozov had argued that the strong ruble would be temporary, and that in the event of a decline in export revenues ahead, the ruble would decline again, making it necessary to return to raising interest rates. Morozov's view was prescient, as that is precisely what happened. Morozov, "The New Life of the Economy."
17. "Elvira Nabiullina obiasnila padenie rublia," *Kommersant*, July 6, 2023, https://www.kommersant.ru/doc/6084557.
18. Interfax, September 12, 2023, https://www.interfax.ru/russia/918901.
19. In early September 2023, the conflict between Siluanov and Nabiullina made headlines in the Russian media. See *Interfax*, September 1, 2023, https://www.interfax.ru/business/918892.
20. *Interfax*, December 21, 2023, https://interfax.com/newsroom/top-stories/97869/. For background, see Max Seddon et al., "Moscow Sets Terms for Swap of Frozen Retail Assets," *Financial Times*, March 12, 2024, https://www.ft.com/content/a478c820-e796-4be4-b384-2c3982aa9dc0.
21. Out of the €260 billion in sovereign assets of the RCB frozen outside Russia, about €191 billion are held by Euroclear; the location of the remaining €70 billion is not publicly known.
22. For a vigorous defense of the idea of confiscation, see the article by a former president of the World Bank, Robert Zoellick, "Transferring Frozen Russian Reserves to Ukraine Is Elegant Justice," *Financial Times*, January 21, 2024, https://www.ft.com/content/7fc0334e-4c06-444d-9c90-01cb9e449f43.
23. Laura Dubois, "Russia's Frozen Assets Yield 4.4 billion Euros Interest for Euroclear," *Financial Times*, February 2, 2024, https://www.ft.com/content/f4c21b08-5f89-4abb-b72c-6f4b110c790b. In June 2024, the G7 powers agreed in principle to the creation of a loan fund backed by the profits from the frozen Russian sovereign reserves, but the proposal requires

the approval of the member states, and the details have yet to be worked out. See Henry Foy and James Politi, "G7 Countries Agree $50bn Ukraine Loan Backed by Frozen Russian Assets," *Financial Times*, June 13, 2024, https://www.ft.com/content/cd38dbad-0441-474d-8aea-bedd77dd4095.

24. For useful background on the debate over seizing Russia's frozen sovereign assets, see Paola Tamma et al., "The Heated Debate over Frozen Assets," *Financial Times*, May 3, 2024, https://www.ft.com/content/0d77f54b-af74-4186-9cae-237528ad7d69.

25. OFAC press release, February 24, 2023, https://home.treasury.gov/news/press-releases/jy1296.

26. I am grateful to Chris Weafer and his team at MacroAdvisory consultancy for his helpful coaching on this ever-changing picture. See also a June 2022 article in *Meduza* on the RCB: https://meduza.io/feature/2022/06/27/kryshka-groba-zakryta-i-zakolochena.

27. Russian Customs Service, http://customs.ru/folder/513. Unfortunately, its website is no longer accessible.

28. Russian Ministry of Finance year-end reports, https://minfin.gov.ru/ru/statistics/fedbud/execute?id_57=80041-kratkaya_ezhegodnaya_informatsiya_ob_ispolnenii_federalnogo_byudzheta_mlrd._rub. By 2022, the share of oil and gas exports in the federal budget had grown to 41.6%.

29. Connolly, *Russia's Response to Sanctions*.

30. Kennedy, "Measuring the Shadows." The ghost tankers tend to be old and in poor condition, and they are generally too small to be efficient over long distances. Kennedy, who has done an exhaustive investigation of the Russian tanker fleet, estimates that Russia would need the equivalent of nearly 640 Aframax tankers, of which it currently has only about one-third. The result, as he puts it, is a large "tanker gap," which at present rates will take years to fill.

31. See Kennedy's latest analysis on Substack, April 8, 2024, navigatingrussia@substack.com.

32. In April 2023, OFAC issued a warning to brokers and mainstream (i.e., IGP&I-registered) tanker owners, reminding them not to ship oil from Kozmino without an attestation of compliance with the price cap. Although there have been no prosecutions so far, the warning may have been effective in discouraging mainstream tanker owners from accepting Russian cargoes, forcing Russia to use shadow tankers instead.

33. The proposal to create a "white list" has been strongly urged by Craig Kennedy, the leading Western expert on the subject of the oil sanctions.

34. See Daniel Flatley and Alex Longley, "US Sanctions Traders of Russian Oil as It Tightens Price Cap," *Bloomberg*, December 20 2023 (https://www.bloomberg.com/news/articles/2023-12-20/us-sanctions-traders-of-russian-oil-as-it-tightens-price-cap). In February 2024, OFAC designated Sovcomflot and fourteen crude-oil tankers in which Sovcomflot had a stake as shadow traders. February 23, 2024, https://home.treasury.gov/news/press-releases/jy2121.

35. https://www.bloomberg.com/news/articles/2024-02-13/tankers-tied-to-the-russian-oil-trade-grind-to-a-halt-following-us-sanctions.

36. See https://www.bloomberg.com/news/articles/2024-02-05/greek-shipowners-are-stampeding-out-of-the-russian-oil-trade. Traders and shippers operating out of several locations with "flags of convenience," notably Liberia, the Marshall Islands, and Gabon (which was popular with Sovcomflot), interrupted their operations. But the halt is likely only temporary, while the shippers shop around for new flags. See Jonathan Saul and Timothy Gardner, "Russia Oil Fleet Shifts Away from Liberia, Marshall Island Flags amid US Sanctions Crackdown," *Reuters*, March 6, 2024, https://www.reuters.com/business/energy/russia-oil-fleet-shifts-away-liberia-marshall-island-flags-amid-us-sanctions-2024-03-06/.

37. "Oil Sanctions Are Deepening Russian Crude Discounts, Novak Says," *Bloomberg News*, January 31, 2024, https://www.bloomberg.com/news/articles/2024-01-31/oil-sanctions-are-deepening-russian-crude-discounts-novak-says.

38. For a short biography, see Aleksandr Borisov, "U piati ministerstv Rossii poiavilis' novye rukovoditeli," *Sankt-Peterburgskie vedomosti*, November 20, 2020, https://sanktpeterburg.bezformata.com/listnews/rossii-poyavilis-novie-rukovoditeli/88989259/.

39. On his recent interventions in defense of renewables, see Polina Smertina and Tat'iana Diatel, "Zelenaia energetika ne rezhetsia na glaz," *Kommersant*, January 20, 2021, accessed at https://www.kommersant.ru/doc/4653626.

40. I am grateful to Sergey Vakulenko for this account of Novak and Sorokin's diplomatic roles.

41. Shotaro Tani and Tom Wilson, "Saudis and Russians Lead OPEC+ Push on Oil Prices by Extending Output Cuts," *Financial Times*, March 4, 2023, https://www.ft.com/content/d6236674-75e5-4893-889a-b412501891fa.
42. For a detailed account of the evolving Russian–Saudi oil relationship, see Ibrahim Almuhanna, *Oil Leaders: An Insider's Account of Four Decades of Saudi Arabia and OPEC;s Global Energy Policy* (New York: Columbia University Press, 2022), Chapters 9–11.
43. In January 2024 the Saudis announced they would postpone any expansion of production. An earlier plan, to increase production from 12 to 13 million barrels per day by 2027, was canceled, on instructions from the Saudi government to Saudi Aramco. See Stanley Reed, "Saudi Aramco Drops Plan to Expand Oil Production," *The New York Times*, January 31, 2024, https://www.nytimes.com/2024/01/30/business/saudi-aramco-oil-production.html#:~:text=Aramco%2C%20the%20national%20oil%20company,plan%20announced%20several%20years%20ago.
44. Julian Lee, "Saudi Crude Exports Plummet to Pandemic-Era Levels," *Bloomberg*, July 5, 2024, https://www.bloomberg.com/news/newsletters/2024-07-05/saudi-oil-exports-plummet-to-pandemic-era-levels-with-benefits-for-russia.
45. David Sheppard and Ian Johnston, "OPEC+ Production Cuts Leave Oil Market Skeptical," *Financial Times*, November 30, 2023, https://www.ft.com/content/b809994d-6a1b-40e0-b75c-a659c46ffedd.
46. David Brower and David Sheppard, "The Unravelling Global Oil Market," *Financial Times*, November 29, 2022, https://www.ft.com/content/3c15dd27-9b7a-4905-aaa6-f6009b1aec50.
47. "Murtaza Lakhani: The Trading Tycoon Steering Russia's Global Oil Business," *Bloomberg*, October 14, 2023, as reprinted by *The Times of India*, https://timesofindia.indiatimes.com/business/international-business/who-is-murtaza-lakhani-karachi-native-steering-russias-global-oil-business/articleshow/104426281.cms.
48. Anna Hirtenstein, "U.S. Probe of Russia-Sanctions Busting Focuses on Major Oil Trader," *Wall Street Journal*, October 9, 2023, https://www.wsj.com/economy/trade/u-s-probe-of-russia-sanctions-busting-focuses-on-major-oil-trader-fac754da.
49. Tom Wilson, "Dubai Is 'the New Geneva' for Russian Oil Traders," *Financial Times*, July 20, 2023, https://www.ft.com/content/7ac92047-b306-49d0-9811-ddde5c916dd6.
50. For an account of the negotiations leading up to Russia's accession, and of Putin's fluctuating motives for wishing to join it, see Aslund, *How Russia Became a Market Economy*, pp. 183 and 185–187. Russia is also a signatory of related international agreements such as the Paris Convention on Industry Property and the Madrid Convention on the Registration of Trademarks. These remain in effect for all imports not covered by the March 2022 decree on parallel imports.
51. https://www.kommersant.ru/doc/5282995 and https://www.kommersant.ru/doc/5327638.
52. See an analysis of the implications for intellectual-property rights in "Has Russia Legalized Intellectual Property Theft," *The Economist*, June 2, 2022 (https://www.economist.com/business/2022/06/14/has-russia-legalised-intellectual-property-theft).
53. https://www.kommersant.ru/doc/5341117.
54. Evgeniia Kriuchkova, "S novym vvozom!" *Kommersant*, May 6, 2022, https://www.kommersant.ru/doc/5346439. For an update on the application of the parallel imports decree, see Polina Makarova "Parallel'noe ischerpanie," *Kommersant*, June 15, 2023, https://www.kommersant.ru/doc/6042006.
55. https://www.linkedin.com/feed/update/urn:li:activity:7036709552435691520/.
56. https://public-inspection.federalregister.gov/2023-17643.pdf.
57. https://www.kommersant.ru/doc/5864186.
58. On Turkey and the MIR card, see my Substack piece, "Peace and the World—All on One Convenient Russian Debit Card," *Substack*, April 20, 2023, https://thanegustafson.substack.com/p/peace-and-the-world-all-on-one-convenient. Russians now living outside Russia, including in the FSU, have been increasingly unable to draw on their own assets from home via the MIR card. See interview with Oleg Buklemishev, director of the Center for Research on Economic Policy of Moscow State University, *Republic*, April 12, 2024, https://republic.ru/posts/112082.
59. Ol'ga Sherunkova et al., "Lira pobudila nedobroe," *Kommersant*, January 17, 2024, https://www.kommersant.ru/doc/6454712.
60. https://www.kommersant.ru/doc/6480776.
61. Interview with Denis Manturov, *Kommersant*, https://www.kommersant.ru/doc/5410216.

62. See Timofei Kornev, "V Rossii rastet populiarnost' braka," *Kommersant*, October 17, 2022, https://www.kommersant.ru/doc/5619160.
63. Steve Stecklow et al., "The Supply Chain That Keeps Tech Flowing to Russia," *Reuters Special Report*, December 13, 2022, https://www.reuters.com/investigates/special-report/ukraine-crisis-russia-tech-middlemen/. The original RUSI report, "Silicon Lifeline," is available at https://static.rusi.org/RUSI-Silicon-Lifeline-final-web.pdf.
64. For example, the online journal *The Insider* has published several reports on Russia's continued access to dual-use technologies from Western manufacturers. See, for example, Michael Weiss, "Short Circuit. How Europe Turns a Blind Eye to Russia Smuggling Dual-Use Microchips," *The Insider*, August 21, 2023, https://theins.press/en/politics/264419, and Sergei Ezhov, "Killjoy Alert: Europe Keeps Supplying Equipment and Components to Russian Missile Manufacturers," *The Insider*, October 25, 2023, https://theins.press/en/politics/266147. For a video based on the Ezhov article, see Simon Ostrovsky, "Faster than the Speed of Sanctions," *The Insider*, October 2023, https://www.youtube.com/watch?v=5AWex38_12Y. A 2024 exposé by *The Insider* features the Labin family, who work from their home base in Brussels to purchase Western components with military applications and distribute them through their company, Sonatek, in Moscow. The father, Viktor Labin, is a graduate of the GRU Academy in Moscow. See Sergei Ezhov, "Svoi chelovek v Briussele," *The Insider*, January 27, 2024, https://theins.ru/politika/267297.
65. See, for example, Maria Snegovaya et al., "Back in Stock? The State of Russia's Defense Industry after Two Years of the War," Center for Strategic and International Studies (CSIS), April 2024, https://csis-website-prod.s3.amazonaws.com/s3fs-public/2024-04/240419_Snegovaya_Backin_Stock.pdf?VersionId=R.2JNVf7ECi8Jyk_9QVWuP8_g5KLkbCe.
66. On this point, see Chris Miller, *Chip War: The Fight for the World's Most Critical Technology* (New York: Simon and Schuster, 2022), https://www.simonandschuster.com/books/Chip-War/Chris-Miller/9781982172008, Chapters 7 and 8.
67. Miller, *Chip War*, Parts 5 and 6.
68. For an overview of the TSMC story, see Nikita Korolev and Evgenii Khvostok, "Protsessory v izoliatsii," *Kommersant*, April 6, 2022, https://www.kommersant.ru/doc/5294238.
69. Nikita Korolev,"Pravitel'stvo snatsproektirovalo elektroniku," *Kommersant*, April 15, 2022, https://www.kommersant.ru/doc/5306920.
70. I am grateful to Julian Cooper for these points, which are covered in his article, "Military Production in Russia before and after the Start of the War with Ukraine," *The RUSI Journal*, August 29, 2024 (https://doi.prg/10.1080/03071847.2024.2392990).
71. On the history of Mikron, see https://55.mikron.ru/story.
72. Nikita Korolev, "Karty podchipuiut," *Kommersant*, October 4, 2022, https://www.kommersant.ru/doc/5594632.
73. Deanna Ritchie, "Apple Said to Be First in Line for TSMC's 2nm Chip Supply," *Readwrite*, January 25, 2024, https://readwrite.com/apple-said-to-be-first-in-line-for-tsmcs-2nm-chip-supply/#:~:text=Apple%20began%20using%203%2Dnanometer,series%20chips%20found%20in%20Macs.
74. Steve Stecklow et al., "The Supply Chain That Keeps Tech Flowing to Russia," *Reuters*, December 13, 2022, https://www.reuters.com/investigates/special-report/ukraine-crisis-russia-tech-middlemen/.
75. Chris Cook, "Moscow Imports a Third of Battlefield Tech from Western Companies," *Financial Times*, January 11, 2024, https://www.ft.com/content/96c4f3f8-bd7b-41a3-9e76-7280490a3dbb, based on data from the Kyiv School of Economics.
76. Valuable insight into this supply chain comes from intercepted internal e-mail traffic from e-commerce intermediaries with names like "Nag" and "OCS Distribution." Many of these existed long before the invasion but have adapted their operations to work around sanctions. See Paul Mozur et al., "Chinese Traders and Moroccan Ports: How Russia Flouts Global Tech Bans," *The New York Times*, December19, 2023, https://www.nytimes.com/2023/12/19/technology/russia-flouts-global-tech-bans.html.
77. Michael Weiss, "Short Circuit. How Europe Turns a Blind Eye to Russia Smuggling Dual-Use Microchips," *The Insider*, August 21, 2023, https://theins.press/en/politics/264419.
78. Thus Kyrgyzstan, not previously known for its IT industry, increased its imports of integrated circuits and semiconductors from the EU from €62,000 in 2021 to €3.7 million in 2023. *Verstka*, reported in Telegram, February 20, 2024, https://t.me/svobodnieslova/4086.

79. Adam Samson et al., "Turkey's Exports of Military-Linked Goods to Russia Soar," *Financial Times*, November 27, 2023, https://www.ft.com/content/1cef6628-32eb-49c9-a7f1-2aef9bce4239.

80. https://www.rusi.org/explore-our-research/publications/commentary/risky-business-south east-asias-continued-trade-russia.

81. https://www.reuters.com/investigates/special-report/ukraine-crisis-russia-tech-middlemen/. There is apparently no connection between Pixel Devices and the Pixel smartphone.

82. Aleksandr Atasuntsev, "Sanktsionnaia dyra," Verstka, July 31, 2023, https://verstka.media/rassledovanie-kak-v-rossiyu-popadayut-lyubye-sankcionnie-tovary.

83. https://www.bloomberg.com/news/articles/2023-09-07/eu-chief-set-to-press-uae-president-on-russia-sanctions-evasion#xj4y7vzkg.

84. *The Wall Street Journal*, September 4, 2023, https://www.wsj.com/world/middle-east/western-officials-plan-to-warn-u-a-e-over-trade-with-russia-686ab06c.

85. Timofei Kornev, "V Rossii rastet populiarnost' braka," *Kommersant*, October 17, 2022, https://www.kommersant.ru/doc/5619160.

86. Timofei Kornev, "V Rossii rastet populiarnost' braka."

87. Cooper, "The Machine Tool Industry of Russia," op. cit.

88. https://re-russia.net/review/304/, based on a survey of over 1,000 enterprises by the NIU/VShE, the Institute of Statistical Research and the Economics of Knowledge, which is part of the Higher School of Economics. For the Bank of Finland's overview, see a report by Heli Simola, "Recent Trends in Russia's Import Substitution of Technology Products," Bank of Finland, BOFIT Policy Brief No. 5, June 5, 2024, https://publications.bof.fi/handle/10024/53402. See also https://www.hse.ru/data/2023/06/06/2020599676/Digital_industry_06_06_2023.pdf, published as I. S. Lola et al., *Trends in Import Substitution in Industry in 2022–23* (Moscow: NIU/VShE, June 2023), p. 9.

89. Statement by Brad Smith, "Microsoft Suspends New Sales in Russia," Microsoft Blog, https://blogs.microsoft.com/on-the-issues/2022/03/04/microsoft-suspends-russia-sales-ukraine-co nflict/.

90. On the anticipated consequences of Microsoft's withdrawal from Russia, via Eastview, see Anna Sokolova and Valeriia Borodina, "Chem kompanii zameshchaiut zapadnoe ofisnoe PO," *Vedomosti*, July 22, 2022, https://www.vedomosti.ru/management/articles/2022/07/26/933196-kompanii-zameschayut-zapadnoe-po

91. Evgenii Cherkesov, "Rossiian otluchili ot obnovlenii Windows," *CNEWS*, September 27, 2022, https://www.cnews.ru/news/top/2022-09-27_rossiyan_otluchili_ot_obnovlenij.

92. Gennadii Efremov, "Microsoft otmenil sanktsii protiv Rossii," *CNEWS*, May 13, 2024, https://www.cnews.ru/news/top/2024-05-13_microsoft_ne_mozhet_bez_rossii.

93. Microsoft also announced plans to close its Moscow office, but two years on, the office remained open. Efremov, "Microsoft otmenil sanktsii protiv Rossii."

94. The speaker was the general director of a leading defense plant, the Sergei Factory. He made the remark at the Tatarstan Machine-Building Forum and was reported in "Govorim, chto importozameshchenie, a tashchim iz Kitaia! Eto ne importozameshchenie, nichego podobnogo," *Biznes Online*, December 7, 2022, https://www.business-gazeta.ru/article/575046,%207%20December%202022. A variant on "pseudo-substitution" can be seen in the automotive industry, where Russian automakers have replaced former Western partners with Chinese companies that provide imported components for assembly in Russia. So far, the Russian government, concerned to promote "Russian" production, has not seriously opposed this trend. See Efim Rozkin, "Sdalis' bez boia: chinovniki okonchatel'no reshili otdat' rossiis-skii avtorynok na otkup Kitaiu," *Avtovzgliad*, reprinted in *Moskovskii komsomolets*, January 17, 2024. Efim Rozkin is a frequent Russian commentator on the Russian automobile industry. I am indebted to Stephen Fortescue for calling my attention to this anecdote.

95. See Vitaly Yermakov, "Russian Oil Output Increases in 2022 amid unprecedented Western sanctions. What's Next?" Oxford Institute for Energy Studies, July 2023, https://www.oxfordenergy.org/publications/russian-oil-output-increases-in-2022-amid-unprecedented-western-sanctions-whats-next/. For background on these points, see my *Wheel of Fortune*, as updated in my *Klimat: Russia in the Age of Climate Change* (Cambridge, MA: Harvard University Press, 2021).

96. https://special.kommersant.ru/import/industry-1.php. The record of company-by-company efforts to substitute for SAP, Oracle, and Microsoft imports consists largely of hopes and plans.

No home-grown substitutes are currently available. The campaign predates the invasion; it was instituted by a Putin decree in 2018 and is overseen by the Ministry of Digital Technology (Mintsifry). Thus, for example, last October, the Ministry of Finance canceled the state purchase of Microsoft software for Transneft for 600.9 million rubles. Rosatom structures, after another controversial tender for 776 million rubles, were ordered to implement Russian solutions by 2023, moving away from the enterprise management systems of German SAP.

97. Anna Balashova and Ekaterina Shokurova, "Krupnyi biznes priznal otsutstvie polnotsennoi al'ternativy produktam SAP," *RBC*, May 21, 2024, https://www.rbc.ru/technology_and_media/21/05/2024/664cba4b9a794749ae245e18.

98. This section has benefited greatly from two excellent works, Richard Connolly, *The Russian Response to Sanctions*, op. cit., and Daniel McDowell, *Bucking the Buck: U.S. Financial Sanctions and the International Backlash against the Dollar* (Oxford, UK: Oxford University Press, 2023).

99. Unfortunately, the RCB does not publish a breakdown of Russian reserves by currency. Total international reserves, including all foreign currencies and gold, stood at about $400 billion in 2017. Source: Russian Central Bank.

100. The Chinese currency is called the renminbi, but specific number amounts are referred to as yuan.

101. See *Obzor riskov finansovykh rynkov* (Moscow: Russian Central Bank, January 2024), pp. 13–14 (https://www.cbr.ru/collection/collection/file/48852/orfr_2024-01.pdf).

102. The Indian rupee is only partially convertible. The first settlement of foreign trade in rupees with Russia took place in December 2022. For helpful details, see M. Jadayev, "The Indian Rupee as an International Currency," *International Banker*, September 18, 2023, https://internationalbanker.com/banking/the-indian-rupee-as-international-currency/.

103. Purchases of so-called dim sum bonds, denominated in renminbi and sold out of Hong Kong, have proven unpopular with Russian banks, despite high initial expectations, because of their high interest costs and limited liquidity. See "Russia's Chinese Yuan Funding Lifeline Is Getting Too Expensive," *Bloomberg News*, March 5, 2024, https://www.bloomberg.com/news/articles/2024-03-05/russia-s-chinese-yuan-funding-lifeline-is-getting-too-expensive.

104. Maria Zholobova, ed., "Tainyi pokupatel'," *Vazhnye istorii*, September 1, 2022, https://storage.googleapis.com/istories/investigations/2022/09/01/tainii-pokupatel/index.html.

105. From an investigation by the *Financial Times*, reported in Chris Cook et al., "The Smuggling Trail Keeping Russian Passenger Jets in the Air," *Financial Times*, May 10, 2024, https://www.ft.com/content/f8d61a5d-708f-47c4-8dbd-0e80452dea5a.

106. Kremlin website, http://kremlin.ru/events/president/transcripts/71993.

107. See blog post by Steven E. Harris, "Sanctions Are Spoiling Russia's Plans to Make Its Own Airplanes," *The Russia File*, April 9, 2024, https://www.wilsoncenter.org/blog-post/sanctions-are-spoiling-russias-plans-make-its-own-airplanes.

108. Significantly, the phrase "no limits" has not been used in official pronouncements since the start of the invasion of Ukraine. See Chapter 7 for further discussion of the Russian–Chinese relationship.

109. Angus Berwick and Ben Foldy, "Inside the Russian Shadow Trade for Weapons Parts: Fueled by Crypto," *Wall Street Journal*, April 1, 2024, https://www.wsj.com/finance/currencies/crypto-fuelsrussian-shadow-trade-for-weapons-parts-1bfdc1a1. Wally Adeyemo, Testimony before the House Committee on Banking, Housing, and Urban Affairs, April 9, 2024, https://www.banking.senate.gov/imo/media/doc/adeyemo_testimony_4-9-241.pdf.

110. Richard Connolly, *Russia's Response to Sanctions*. McDowell, *Bucking the Buck*, particularly pp. 42–49, 84–95.

111. "Glava TsB zaiavila o riske restavratsii planovoi ekonomiki," *Kommersant*, June 15, 2023, https://www.kommersant.ru/doc/6044169.

112. https://www.cbr.ru/Collection/Collection/File/46328/forecast_230915.pdf.

113. http://static.government.ru/media/files/xvETAZEiRAjIRmO5DsH3S2ZbwIwBA0Ts.pdf. This measure was pushed by Putin personally, despite the RCB's objections.

Chapter 6

1. Source: *Leave Russia*, a website maintained by the Ukrainian KSE Institute (https://leave-russia.org/companies-that-exited, last checked in October 2024). An early Russian study, by the Center for Strategic Studies, based on a sample of the 600 largest Western companies actually engaged in production, came up with comparable numbers, concluding that 87% of them had stopped working, either wholly or partially. But only about 13% of them at that stage had actually left Russia, mostly in "soft" services such as legal advice, accounting, or investment consulting. The Center for Strategic Studies is a Moscow-based think tank, originally founded in 1999 by German Gref and a group of "in-system liberals." *A Picture of Foreign Business under the New Economic Conditions* (Moscow: Center for Strategic Studies, Tsentr strategicheskikh razrabotok, TsSR, June 2022), 2xnbgwcbkvr541808y8uzd6qbez2iywv.pdf (csr.ru). The study is summarized in "Kak inostrannyi biznes ogranichivaet rabotu v Rossii," *Kommersant*, June 10, 2022, https://www.kommersant.ru/doc/5405633. *Kommersant* also keeps a scorecard on the exodus of Western companies.
2. On Renault's "spoke and wheel" business model, see https://www.automotivelogistics.media/renault-a-new-direction-for-parts-supply/14071.article.
3. For an account of Putin's visit to Paris and the origins of the strategic alliance with Renault, see Julian Dupont-Calbo, "Renault: Quinze Années Sauvages au Pays des Oligarques," *Les Echos*, March 24, 2022, https://www.lesechos.fr/industrie-services/automobile/renault-quinze-annees-sauvages-au-pays-des-soviets-1395914.
4. Anne Feitz, "A Togliatti, l'Usine des Lada en Pleine Mutation," *Les Echos*, September 25, 2017 (https://www.lesechos.fr/2017/09/a-togliatti-lusine-des-lada-en-pleine-mutation-183182).
5. Anne Feitz and Benjamin Quénalle, "Renault: Vers une Reprise de Renault par un Institut Scientifique de l'Etat Russe," *Les Echos*, April 27, 2022, https://www.lesechos.fr/industrie-services/automobile/renault-vers-une-vente-de-lada-a-un-institut-scientifique-de-letat-russe-1403288. One reason that Renault exited so quickly was that it was undergoing financial difficulties back in its home market, accompanied by an internal change of leadership.
6. The bottom line on Renault in Russia: "Quinze ans d'efforts et d'investissements, 2,2 milliards d'euros de pertes nettes. Le pays représentait 18 % des ventes du groupe, 10 % de son chiffre d'affaires et 12 % de sa marge opérationnelle." Anne Feitz, "Renault peut-il s'en sortir?," *Les Echos*, July 11, 2022, https://www.lesechos.fr/idees-debats/editos-analyses/renault-peut-il-sen-sortir-1775835.
7. Anne Feitz, ""La Retraite Russe ou La fin de la stratégie internationale de Carlos Ghosn," *Les Echos*, May 17, 2022, https://www.lesechos.fr/industrie-services/automobile/renault-la-retraite-russe-ou-la-fin-de-la-strategie-internationale-de-carlos-ghosn-1407278.
8. Sources: Forbes and Macro-Advisory. Macro-Advisory Eurasia Strategic Consulting is a consultancy specializing in economic and business developments in Eurasia. I am grateful to its chairman, Chris Weafer, for his kind permission to access his analysis. Forbes's numbers come from the Russian Tax Service and from SPARK-Interfax and can be found in a Forbes report published in July 2022, https://www.forbes.ru/biznes/472197-prodazi-50-krupnejsih-inostrannyh-kompanij-v-rossii-dostigli-9-trln-rublej. The Tax Ministry data include basic tax and profit information, but not the value of assets.
9. Peggy Hollinger et al., "European Companies Suffer 100 Billion Euro Hit from Russia Operations," *Financial Times*, August 6, 2023, https://www.ft.com/content/c4ea72b4-4b02-4ee9-b34c-0fac4a4033f5, assembled from an FT survey of annual reports from 600 European companies. Estimates vary, however. An analysis by Reuters as of the end of 2023 came up with an estimate of only $107 billion for all foreign companies (https://www.reuters.com/markets/europe/foreign-firms-losses-exiting-russia-top-107-billion-2024-03-28/#:%7E:text=March%2028%20(Reuters)%20%2D%20The,company%20filings%20and%20statements%20showed).
10. https://www.reuters.com/markets/europe/moscow-demands-bigger-discounts-foreign-companies-exiting-russia-sources-2023-08-25/.

11. https://www.reuters.com/business/finance/jp-morgan-says-client-shares-russias-magnit-may-be-missing-2023-07-13/.
12. "Magnit zakryl sdelku po vykupu 21.5% aktsii u zarubezhnykh investorov," *Kommersant*, September 14, 2023, https://www.kommersant.ru/doc/6212777.
13. Connolly, *Russia's Response to Sanctions*.
14. *A Picture of Foreign Business under the New Economic Conditions*.
15. Several groups track the status of the Western businesses in Russia. The most comprehensive, and the one that I have relied on most in this chapter, is that of the KSE, which can be accessed at https://leave-russia.org/. It is organized by country, by category of business, and by size and is continuously updated, with detailed references to each company, keyed to company websites.
16. Two other Western companies that have exited, British-American Tobacco (BAT) and Veon, the Dutch base of Russian mobile operator Vimpelcom, were actually larger than Renault in capital invested (https://leave-russia.org/companies-that-exited). Veon/Vimpelcom is a special case, described in Chapter 7 (#LeaveRussia: VEON Closed Its Business in Russia, leave-russia.org).
17. For a useful overview, including many helpful links to Russia sources, see Vakhtang Partsvania, "A Bumpy Ride for Russia's Car Industry," *Riddle Russia*, May 30, 2023, ridl.io. Partsvania was formerly an economist and associate professor in the Department of Public Administration and Public Policy in Moscow (RANEPA). Prior to that, he was in charge of "sustainability policy" for the Scania (a Swedish truck manufacturer, part of the VW Group) operation in Russia. He has since left Russia, relocated to the University of the Caucasus in Georgia, and is a frequent contributor to *Riddle*.
18. For example, Toyota, which had been the seventh-largest Western company in Russia, https://www.rbc.ru/spb_sz/30/11/2022/638771db9a7947a58404bad6. In March 2023 Toyota transferred ownership of its Saint Petersburg manufacturing operations to a Russian institute, NAMI (Central Scientific Research Automobile and Automotive Engines Institute) (Source: Toyota Europe newsroom, https://newsroom.toyota.eu/).
19. On KamAZ (partnered with Daimler), see Olga Nikitina, "KamAZ nagruzilsia sanktsiami," *Kommersant*, June 29, 2022, https://www.kommersant.ru/doc/5435457. On GAZ (VW's partner), see "GAZu lokalizovali sanktsii," *Kommersant*, May 26, 2022, https://www.kommersant.ru/doc/5368505. On Ural, see *Kommersant*, December 17, 2022, https://www.kommersant.ru/doc/5732737.
20. Partsvania, "A Bumpy Ride for Russia's Car Industry."
21. Andrei Sazonov, "AvtoVAZ vozobnovil vypusk Lada Granta," *Kommersant*, June 8, 2022, https://www.kommersant.ru/doc/5394460. See also Aleksandr Astapov and Aleksey Grammatchikov, "AVTOVAZ snova russkii," *Ekspert*, May 9, 2022, https://kiozk.ru/article/ekspert/avtovaz-snova-russkij.
22. https://interfax.com/newsroom/top-stories/86167/.
23. "Proizvodstvo legkovykh avtomobilei v Rossii v 2022 godu upalo vtroe" (Production of Passenger Automobiles in Russia Fell by Two-Thirds in 2022.") *Interfax*, February 1, 2023, Производство легковых автомобилей в России в 2022 году упало втрое interfax.ru.
24. Vakhtang Partsvania, "A Bumpy Ride for Russia's Car Industry," *Riddle*, May 30, 2023, https://ridl.io/a-bumpy-ride-for-russia-s-car-industry/.
25. Ben Aris, "Only 11 Foreign Car Brands Left in Russia out of 60 before the War," *bne Intellinews*, December 15, 2022, https://intellinews.com/only-11-foreign-car-brands-left-in-russia-out-of-60-before-the-war-265282/.
26. Anton Severov, "Anatolii Artamonov—kaluzhskii eksperimentator," *Rossiiskie vesti*, June 20, 2007. (*Rossiiskie vesti* ceased publication in November 2019 and its website is no longer available. This copy was obtained through Georgetown University's subscription to *East-View*, at https://dlib-eastview-com.proxy.library.georgetown.edu/browse/doc/12175928.) For background on Artamonov and Kaluga, see Chris Miller, *Putinomics: Power and Money in Resurgent Russia* (Chapel Hill: University of North Carolina Press, 2018), pp. 87–90. Artamonov is presently a senator in the national Duma in Moscow.
27. Gleb Stolyarov, "Six Months after Volkswagen Exit, Idle Russian Car Plant Offers Workers Redundance," *Reuters*, November 29, 2023, https://www.reuters.com/business/autos-transportation/six-months-after-volkswagen-exit-idle-russian-car-plant-offers-workers-2023-11-29/.

28. Kirill Sazonov and Denis Budenkov, "Poslednie shtrikhi: v Kaluge rasskazali o sud'be zavoda VW," *Izvestiia*, January 16, 2024,https://iz.ru/1634613/kirill-sazonov-denis-budenkov/poslednie-shtrikhi-v-kaluge-rasskazali-o-sudbe-zavoda-vw. In parallel, another plant in Kaluga, Peugeot-Citroen Rus (PSMA Rus), which previously assembled Stallantis's Citroen's C5 crossover, has resumed production after a two-year pause, using imported parts from Stellantis's joint venture in China with Dongfeng. There is no suggestion that Stellantis is involved. Ol'ga Nikitina, "Citroen vernulsia v Rossiiu cherez Kitai," *Kommersant*, March 27, 2024, https://www.kommersant.ru/doc/6595862.

29. Anne Feitz, "Michelin Suspend ses Activités en Russie," *Les Echos*, March 15, 2022, https://www.lesechos.fr/industrie-services/automobile/michelin-suspend-ses-activites-en-russie-1393737. (https://www.rbc.ru/business/26/05/2023/647095209a794781195c9dc5).

30. Source: Kyiv School of Economics. In retrospect, Nokian considers its decision to concentrate production in Russia to have been a mistake, and it is now seeking to diversify its global production base. See Patricia Cohen, "Political Security Is a New Corporate Priority," *The New York Times*, July 7, 2023, p. B1, https://www.nytimes.com/2023/07/05/business/economy/nokian-tyres-finland-romania.html.

31. https://avtostat-info.com/News/11515. Geely is an interesting case, since the parent company, Geely Holding, owns Geely Auto, but also Volvo, Mercedes, and several other well-known Western brands. While Geely's Western brands quickly suspended sales into Russia, Geely Auto increased its sales of Chinese cars. See https://www.ft.com/content/b77603d9-5a10-4e33-852e-2d31bea4161a.

32. Ol'ga Nikitina, "AvtoVAZ na 70% uvelichil proizvodtsvo v 2023 godu," *Kommersant*, January 11, 2024, https://www.kommersant.ru/doc/6444631. Apart from AvtoVAZ, much of the "Russian" production chiefly consists of assembling imported Chinese components.

33. https://www.ft.com/content/b77603d9-5a10-4e33-852e-2d31bea4161a.

34. Ol'ga Nikitina, "Apgreider dorozhnoi tekhniki: Kitaiskie proizvoditeli tesniat rossiiskikh," *Kommersant*, January 24, 2024, https://www.kommersant.ru/doc/6466069.

35. Mikhail Belyi, "Rossiiskii avtoprom poedet po kitaiskomu puti," *Octagon*, January 30, 2024, https://octagon.media/ekonomika/rossijskij_avtoprom_poedet_po_kitajskomu_puti.html.

36. Belyi, "Rossiiskii avtoprom poedet po kitaiskomu puti."

37. As explained later in this chapter, the United States is the only sanctioning power that explicitly imposes secondary sanctions. The EU traditionally considers them contrary to international law.

38. A catalog of the EU's sanctions against Russia, organized by categories, can be found at https://www.sanctionsmap.eu/#/main/details/26/lists?search=%7B%22value%22:%22%22,%22searchType%22:%7B%7D%7D.

39. See my Substack piece, "Russian-European Fertility Rites," thane.gustafson@substack.com.

40. It took Moller-Maersk another year to find a buyer for its main facilities in Russia, including a depot in Novorossiisk with a capacity of 1,500 containers. *Reuters*, February 20, 2023, https://www.reuters.com/business/maersk-divests-logistics-sites-russia-2023-02-20/. Moller-Maersk had begun divesting in August 2022, with the sale of a one-third stake in a Russian port to Russia's largest container operator, Delo.

41. However, MSC, a Swiss-owned company—and the second-largest foreign operator in Russia—has continued operating (after initially announcing suspension), and several new shippers from other countries have appeared to fill the void. *PortNews*, March 1, 2023, https://en.portnews.ru/news/343672/.

42. Like other Western companies that have chosen to stay, MSC has been in Russia for a long time, having begun operations there in 1998. https://www.msc.com/en/local-information/europe/russia.

43. Jamie Smyth and Hannah Kuchler, "Western Drugmakers Walk Ethical Tightrope over Russian Ties." *Financial Times*, March 18 2022 (https://www.ft.com/content/43378dea-3a7d-40e9-8be7-bafea1afaa1f).

44. https://pharmstd.com/archivedetails_64_2791.html.

45. Sources for this paragraph are from the KSE database, https://leave-russia.org/?flt%5B108%5D%5Beq%5D%5B5%5D=53957. There is some ambiguity in the database's classifications. For example, it classifies Nestle and Danone as "fast-moving consumer goods" (FMCG) instead of "food and beverages."

46. Figures are from the KSE database, with 2023 numbers when available or with 2022 if not.

47. See https://tuckercarlson.com/tc-shorts-moscow-grocery-story/?utm_medium=social&utm_source=TCNYT. Carlson's visit to Auchan is recounted in Anne-Sylvaine Chassany, "Western Groups Stay Put in Russia," *Financial Times*, March 1, 2024, https://www.ft.com/content/d0a51a3e-72b3-4f08-b2d9-eb3db508b262.

48. Together with Leroy Merlin, a seller of household goods owned by the same family, the French group had over 130,000 employees in Russia, and Russia was its third-largest market. Bertrand Philippe, "Auchan, Leroy Merlin, Decathlon: Les magasins Mulliez restent ouverts en Russie," *Les Echos*, March 10, 2022, https://www.lesechos.fr/industrie-services/conso-distribution/auchan-leroy-merlin-decathlon-les-magasins-mulliez-restent-ouverts-en-russie-1392548.

49. Coca-Cola HBC was originally founded in Greece in 1969 and subsequently relocated to Switzerland. It is 23.2% owned by the parent Coca-Cola company.

50. https://uk.practicallaw.thomsonreuters.com/1-200-6189?transitionType=Default&contextData=(sc.Default)&firstPage=true.

51. https://thedeepdive.ca/did-coca-cola-ever-really-leave-russia/.

52. "Gendirektor Carlsberg: rossiiskie vlasti ukrali nash biznes," *Kommersant*, October 31, 2023, https://www.kommersant.ru/doc/6311551. In October 2023 the new Russian owner won the right to continue using Carlsberg's brands inside Russia. (https://www.kommersant.ru/doc/6295080).

53. https://www.ft.com/content/85be4c75-996a-46ef-833a-67ef18fbbda6.

54. On the takeover of Baltika by Bolloev, see Madeleine Speed et al., "Blood in the Water," *Financial Times*, November 10, 2023, https://www.ft.com/content/af2fa231-881e-4241-9b37-ab772bf376a2, and Madeleine Speed and Courtney Weaver, "Ex-Carlsberg Executives Detained in Russia on Fraud Claims," *Financial Times*, November 16, 2023, https://www.ft.com/content/145f2310-7222-4df9-9976-f268ed1f1eb2.

55. Daniel Thomas, "Heineken Exits Russia at a Loss of 300 Million Euros," *Financial Times*, August 26, 2023, https://www.ft.com/content/31fe848b-1b66-4dce-8a9b-72f6dbf4af38. The Arnest Group has had considerable success in picking up the assets of foreign companies departing Russia. Another recent acquisition is the Russian assets of the Ball Company, a Colorado-based manufacturers of aluminum cans for beer and soft drinks.

56. https://www.pmi.com/resources/docs/default-source/investor_relation/pmi_2022_annualreport.pdf?sfvrsn=cb21d3b6_2.

57. Japan Tobacco International, which owns four plants in Russia making Winston and Camel as well as many other brands including Russian ones, is actually incorporated in Switzerland. According to the KSE database, it earns more than a third of its revenues in Russia (https://leave-russia.org/japan-tobacco-international).

58. "Obzor finansovoi stabil'nosti," No. 1 (Russian Central Bank, 2023), p. 23. In its report, the RCB notes that "most firms in which foreign owners have sold their ownership stakes have kept the necessary product licenses and patents and have continued to receive the materials, components, and services they need."

59. "Germans Steel Themselves to Sever Links with Russia," *Financial Times*, March 14, 2022.

60. Michel Scheppe et al., "Neun von zehn deutschen Unternehmen weiter in Russland aktiv," *Handelsblatt Online*, February 24, 2023, https://www.handelsblatt.com/unternehmen/handel-konsumgueter/krieg-in-der-ukraine-neun-von-zehn-deutschen-unternehmen-sind-weiter-in-russland-aktiv/29000354.html.

61. Quoted in Scheppe et al., "Neun von zehn deutschen Unternehmen weiter in Russland aktiv." For a detailed account of the relationship between BASF/Wintershall and Gazprom, see my *The Bridge*. The impact of the end of the partnership on Wintershall has been severe. See Florian Güßgen, "Sparkurs bei Wintershall Dea; Das harte Ende der Russland-Connection," *WirtschaftsWoche Online*, September 6, 2023, https://www.wiwo.de/my/unternehmen/energie/sparkurs-bei-wintershall-dea-die-alte-russland-connection-kommt-wintershall-dea-teuer-zu-stehen/29375716.html.

62. Uniper also suffered losses when it exited from its stakes in the Russian power sector.

63. A variation on this theme is EPAM, a software company founded in Belarus in 1993, but which had moved its global headquarters to the United States and had operations in forty different countries. In August 2023 EPAM completed the sale of its Russia-based assets to a Russian software company called Reksoft, partly owned by Vladimir Potanin (https://www.kommersant.ru/doc/6138263). But the bulk of its activity is still in Belarus, leaving its future uncertain.

64. However, Tigran Khudaverdian, one of its senior officers, had been sanctioned by the EU as a designated individual, following which he promptly resigned. In June 2022, the CEO and co-founder of Yandex, Arkadii Volozh, was placed under EU sanctions; he then divested himself from his stake in Yandex and left Russia. In March 2024, the EU Commission lifted the sanctions on Volozh, after he had condemned the Russian invasion of Ukraine.

65. See a report published by *Reuters*, https://www.reuters.com/markets/deals/after-months-negotiation-rare-russian-compromise-yandex-changes-hands-2024-02-09/?taid=65c6243276 567b0001ef1b0b&utm_campaign=trueAnthem:+Trending+Content&utm_medium=trueAn them&utm_source=twitter.

66. Other Russian companies, without similar "hybrid" structures that could be divided in this way, have not been so fortunate; thus Ozon, a fast-growing e-commerce firm, has been expelled from Nasdaq, which means that Ozon's shares in the US market (so-called depositary receipts, or ADRs) can no longer be traded, a major blow to the company. Alexander Marrow, "Yandex Granted Nasdaq Lifeline," *Reuters*, June 8, 2023. On the final split, see *Interfax*, https://www.interfax.ru/business/944509 and Anatoloy Kurmanaev, "Yandex Reaches $5 Billion Deal to Quit Russia," *The New York Times*, February 6, 2024, https://www.nytimes.com/2024/02/05/world/europe/yandex-russia-sale.html. That said, some of Russia's largest commodities and technology companies are still registered in Europe. These include the Switzerland-based fertilizer producer EuroChem Group AG and the agricultural company Ros Agro PLC, which is domiciled in Cyprus. Bloomberg, September 15, 2023.

67. https://newizv.ru/news/2023-06-21/kompanii-s-golovnymi-strukturami-za-rubezhom-mogut-popast-pod-vneshnee-gosupravlenie-410,860.

68. Ekoniva, incorporated in Germany under the name, Ekosem-Agrar AG, had been in financial difficulty and is in de facto default on loans from Rosselkhozbank. Construction of a major new dairy and cheese factory in Novosibirsk has been stopped.

69. https://www.reuters.com/markets/deals/russia-approves-veons-sale-vimpelcom-management-rbc-cites-sources-2023-02-01/.

70. Less fortunate has been the X5 Group, Russia's largest retailer, which is incorporated in the Netherlands but is owned primarily by Mikhail Fridman and his partners. In March 2024 the Ministry of Industry and Trade sued to deprive the Dutch head office of any control over its Russian subsidiary. (*Kommersant*, March 29, 2024, https://www.kommersant.ru/doc/6607994).

71. https://www.reuters.com/markets/commodities/polymetals-senior-managers-resign-after-us-sanctions-company-2023-06-05/.

72. For a detailed account, see Olga Tonkonog, "Polymetal Closes Deal to Sell Its Business in Russia," *Kursiv*, March 11, 2024, https://kz.kursiv.media/en/2024-03-11/polymetal-closes-deal-to-sell-its-business-in-russia/.

73. For background, see Anastasiia Rodionova, "Telegram: Zapreshchen i svoboden," *Moskovskii komsomolets*, April 17, 2018, https://www.mk.ru/social/2018/04/16/blokirovka-telegram-razvyazala-ruki-terroristam.html and Il'ia Titov, "Telegram Nash!" *Zavtra*, July 8, 2020, https://zavtra.ru/blogs/telegram_nash.

74. For example, Prime Minister Mikhail Mishustin is said to be a "fanatical" reader of Telegram. Farid Rustamova et al., "Piar-ministr Rossii: Mikhail Mishustin fanatichno ozabochen svoei reputatsei," *Meduza*, May 29, 2020, https://meduza.io/feature/2020/05/29/piar-ministr-rossii.

75. Hannah Murphy, "Telegram Hits 900 Million Users," *Financial Times*, March 12, 2024, https://www.ft.com/content/8d6ceb0d-4cdb-4165-bdfa-4b95b3e07b2a.

76. Sechin remarks at SPIEF 2022, as reported in "BP prodolzhaet ostavat'sia vladel'tsem doli v Rosnefti," *Infotek*, itek.ru.

77. Dmitri Butrin, "Tol'ko ne vtoroi front," *Kommersant*, March 10, 2023, https://www.kommersant.ru/doc/5251298.

78. Dmitrii Butrin and Diana Galieva, "Administratsiia nerezidenta," *Kommersant*, April 12, 2022, https://www.kommersant.ru/doc/5304847.

79. https://www.kommersant.ru/doc/5457535.

80. Scheppe et al., "Neun von zehn deutschen Unternehmen weiter in Russland aktiv."

81. https://www.kommersant.ru/doc/6028873.

82. https://www.ft.com/content/cd627211-68f6-4dfa-8a04-3344deee2e85.

83. Dmitrii Grinkevich et al., "Vlasti sformirovali 10 uslovii dlia vykhoda inostrantsev ot rossi-iskovo biznesa," *RBK*, July 14, 2023, https://www.vedomosti.ru/economics/articles/2023/07/14/985254-vlasti-sformirovali-10-uslovii.

84. http://kremlin.ru/acts/assignments/orders/70,890

85. https://www.interfax.ru/russia/905090. The tax was set at 5% of the asset's market value for assets that are sold at a discount of 90% or less, and 10% for assets sold at a greater discount. The first foreign company to pay the tax was the Norwegian hotel chain Wenaas, which sold its Russian assets to a well-connected conglomerate, Sistema, for about €203 million, which included the 10% "contribution" (https://www.ft.com/content/77368014-1397-4a08-901d-1f996e66d627).

86. Irina Degot'kova, "Bezvozmezdnye vznosy biznesa v biudzhet prevysili plan v 17 raz," *RBK*, March 20, 2024, https://www.rbc.ru/economics/20/03/2024/65f966329a7947885432dea1.

87. https://www.rbc.ru/finances/28/04/2023/644bc8b59a79471ce0d7ce34.

88. Petr Mironenko, "Promyshlennost' vyrosla na voine," *The Bell*, April 26, 2023, https://thebell.io/promyshlennost-vyrosla-na-vojne-ruka-sechina-v-natsionalizatsii-aktivov-fortum-i-uniper-novoe-delo-navalnogo-i-zdorove-erdogana. See also "Pochemu Putin vvel vneshnee upravlenie v energoaktivakh Fortum i Uniper," *RBC*, April 26, 2023, https://www.rbc.ru/business/26/04/2023/6448df6a9a79475b85691e6e.

89. https://www.fortum.com/media/2023/05/inside-information-fortum-fully-write-down-its-russian-assets-and-deconsolidate-russia-segment-publishes-restated-comparison-figures. Over the years since it first entered Russia in 2008, Fortum had invested a total of €6 billion, but had earned more than €4 billion, including the Russian operations of its German subsidiary Uniper.

90. Max Seddon et al., "Kremlin Oligarchs Eye Carlsberg Assets as Kadyrov Ally Takes Over Danone Unit," *Financial Times*, July 18, 2023, https://www.ft.com/content/d5234953-cddf-4b64-8a55-dc749843ab5c.

91. Danone first produced dairy products under its own brand in Russian factories; in 2000 it acquired (jointly with PepsiCo) an early Russian private producer, Vimm-Bill-Dan. See *The Bell*, July 16, 2023, https://t.me/thebell_io/23741.

92. Anatolii Kostyrev, "Iogurtam staviat srok vosvrata," *Kommersant*, February 3, 2023, https://www.kommersant.ru/doc/5799193.

93. Courtney Weaver and Adrienne Klasa, "Danone Plans Sale to Kadyrov-Linked Chechen," *Financial Times*, February 22, 2024. Danone's former business will continue operating under a new name, Life and Nutrition, under the ownership of a recently created company located in Kazan, Vamin Tatarstan.

94. Taimuraz Bolloev was the original founder and owner of the Baltika brand. He remained the president of Baltika after Carlsberg took it over in a fierce battle with its former joint venture partner Scottish and Newcastle. See Jenny Wiggins, "Carlsberg Thirsts for a Beer-Drinking Russia," *Financial Times*, June 10, 2008, https://www.ft.com/content/36299afe-3705-11dd-bc1c-0000779fd2ac.

95. Petr Mironenko, "Danone otdali Kadyrovu, Baltiku—piterskim," *The Bell*, July 18, 2023, https://thebell.io/danone-otdali-kadyrovu-baltiku-piterskim-kreml-nachal-peredavat-aktivy-zapadnyh-kompanij-svoim-bez-lishnih-tseremonij. According to the *Financial Times*, the transfer was engineered by Dmitrii Patrushev, who blocked the planned sale of Danone and Carlsberg to the two candidates that had already been found, in favor of Putin's cronies. Patrushev is Russia's deputy prime minister for agriculture and son of Nikolai Patrushev, who was at that time secretary of the Security Council. Well-placed Chechen favorites also recently acquired Stars Coffee, previously owned by Starbucks in Russia.

96. "Statement by Bank of Russia Governor Elvira Nabiullina," Bank of Russia website, April 28, 2023 (https://www.cbr.ru/press/event/?id=14742).

97. http://www.kremlin.ru/acts/assignments/orders/71178, Item 2.

98. One possible alternative is to settle in renminbi, in a transaction conducted outside of Russia. This was reportedly the method used by a Russian consortium, which includes an investment fund owned by LUKoil, that bought the Russian assets of Yandex for $5.2 billion in shares and cash, including a portion in renminbi. See Anatoly Kurmanaev, "Russian Tech Giant Reaches $5 Billion Deal to Quit Russia," *The New York Times*, February 4, 2024, https://www.nytimes.com/2024/02/05/world/europe/yandex-russia-sale.html.

99. "Nabiullina: Russian Central Bank Ready to Discuss Idea of Paying Foreigners with Special Bonds," *Interfax*, April 20, 2023 (https://interfax.com/newsroom/top-stories/89821/).

100. "Polina Ivanova and Anastasia Stognei, "Western Groups Leaving Russia Face Obligatory Donation to Moscow," *Financial Times*, March 27 2023 (https://www.ft.com/content/77368014-1397-4a08-901d-1f996e66d627).

101. Quoted in Alexander Marrow, "Remaining Western Firms Face Tricky Russian Exits," *Reuters*, June 1, 2023, https://www.reuters.com/business/remaining-western-firms-face-tricky-russian-exits-2023-06-01/.

102. "Obzor finansovoi stabil'nosti," p. 22. Moiseev is an interesting figure: he worked for fifteen years for PNP Paribas in London and subsequently for Renaissance Capital.

103. Not surprisingly, no foreign company has declared a dividend since the start of the invasion, with the exception of two Western banks, Italy's Unicredit and Hungary's OTP, which have been granted special permission to export up to half of their Russian profits in quarterly payments, so long as they have paid their local taxes.

104. This means that no Russian entity has technically ever defaulted, since the interest on Russian foreign debts to unfriendly countries is being kept in the C-type accounts.

105. I am grateful to Chris Weafer of Macro-Advisory for his kind coaching on the rules of the game governing foreign profits and dividends.

106. More precisely, the specialized subcommittee specifically charged with reviewing the asset sales of foreign companies. See the ministry communique on Telegram, https://t.me/minfin/3428.

107. "Manturov otsenil interes evropeiskogo biznesa k rynku Rossii," *Praim*, February 14, 2024, https://1prime.ru/business/20240214/843065815.html.

108. Olesia Pavlenko and Aleksey Kislov, "Sud po isku Genprokuratury arestoval tri zavoda nemetskogo miliardera Merkle," *Kommersant*, August 25, 2023, https://www.kommersant.ru/doc/6174178.

109. *Kommersant*, August 25, 2023, https://www.kommersant.ru/doc/6183473. See also https://www.interfax.ru/russia/917785.

110. For an overview of the battle over "deprivatization," see Nikolai Petrov, "The State Machine Redistributing Property into the Right Hands," *Russia.Post*, October 24, 2023, https://russiapost.info/politics/redistributing.

111. On newspaper coverage of major criminal cases, see https://www.kommersant.ru/theme/2342. One prominent target was Andrei Melnichenko, owner of coal-and-power giant SUEK, and reputed at that time to be Russia's richest man. However, the case against Melnichenko was later dropped (https://ngs24.ru/text/business/2023/10/06/72783752/).

112. "Bastrykin predlozhil natsionalizirovat' osnovnye otrasli ekonomiki Rossii," *Kommersant*, May 13, 2023, https://www.kommersant.ru/doc/5985380. Liberal commentator Andrei Kolesnikov, writing in *Kommersant*, claimed that Krasnov has "close ties" to the FSB, https://www.kommersant.ru/doc/4225870.

113. "Shokhin ob iz'iatii chastnykh aktivov," *RBC*, September 11, 2023, https://www.rbc.ru/economics/11/09/2023/64fedbc59a7947a77bae1aac. See also the full text of the RBC interview with Shokhin, https://www.rbc.ru/interview/economics/11/09/2023/64feca2f9a794776cbef70a1.

114. Interview with Reshetnikov, *RBC*, September 12, 2023, https://www.rbc.ru/business/12/09/2023/64ffd9cf9a794791f970b76d.

115. *Kommersant*, September 13, 2023, https://www.kommersant.ru/doc/6211782. There are some signs that Putin may have decided to soften his attitude toward foreign companies that are trying to leave. In November 2023, for example, he approved the sale of Caterpillar's Russian assets to a group of ex-Sberbank executives, clearing the way Caterpillar to exit from Russia (https://www.reuters.com/markets/deals/putin-clears-acquisition-caterpillars-russian-assets-2023-11-27/).

116. Statement by Igor Krasnov, speaking at the same conference as Putin, *Agentstvo*, March 26, 2024, t.me/agentstvonews/5730. Two other sources, *Novaia gazeta Evropa* and Transparency International, confirmed Krasnov's numbers. One might note in passing that the government continues to privatize state-owned assets as an additional means of balancing the budget. For 2024 the Finance Ministry set a target of $1 billion in sell-offs of state-owned assets.

117. Ivan Zhilin, "Spetsoperatsiia po deprivatizatsii," *Novaia gazeta*, April 4, 2024, https://novayagazeta.ru/articles/2024/04/04/spetsoperatsiia-po-deprivatizatsii.

118. The court imposed a penalty payment to the plaintiff of 3.5 billion rubles. Adidas, which operated 153 leased outlets on the eve of the invasion, announced in March 2022 that it was stopping operations in Russia and it started looking for a buyer (https://www.interfax.ru/moscow/925220). By 2023 it had sold its brand in Russia to a Turkish company, FLO, which had earlier acquired the Russian operation of Reebok.

119. "V Rossii za 1.5 goda nalozhili 93 aresta na aktivy inostrannogo biznesa," *RBC*, November 8, 2023, https://www.rbc.ru/economics/08/11/2023/654a2f429a7947e5f7db4495.

120. "Sud arestoval aktsii "Detskogo mira," prinadlezhashchie Goldman Sachs, *RBC*, August 7, 2023, https://www.rbc.ru/business/07/08/2023/64d0c3699a7947b565a133c3.

121. "U milliardera iz spiska Forbes khotiat zabrat' zavod v Sibiri," *NGS-RU (Novosibirsk Onlain)*, February 9, 2024, https://ngs.ru/text/business/2024/02/09/73208594/. See also "Genprokuratua potrebovala zabrat' u vladel'tsa ChEMK" *74-RU (Cheliabinsk Onlain)*, February 7, 2024, https://74.ru/text/business/2024/02/07/73203764/.

122. Antipov is an interesting example of a self-made regional entrepreneur. For a brief biography, see Zhilin, "Spetsoperatsiia po deprivatizatsii."

123. In actual fact, there is apparently more of a connection than the Russian owners claim. The main importer of the Russian company's ferroalloys, up to the time of the invasion, was a US company, Russian Ferro Alloys, owned by the son of Yurii Antipov.

124. Antipov never stood a chance. At about the same time, Putin stopped off in Cheliabinsk on a campaign tour and heard the complaint of the governor, Aleksey Teksler, that one of Antipov's plants, the Cheliabinsk Electrometal Combine, was a dangerous source of air pollution. Putin ordered its immediate nationalization. See Zhilin, "Spetsoperatsiia po deprivatizatsii."

125. Artur Iakushko and Nikolai Sergeev, "Vchera vashi, a teper' nashi," *Kommersant*, February 13, 2024, https://www.kommersant.ru/doc/6508794. For a commentary, see Tat'iana Rybakova, "Otniat' biznes v Rossii ne prosto. A ochen' prosto," *Republic.ru*, February 13, 2024, https://republic.ru/posts/111455. See also Denis Morokhin and Mariia Erlikh, "Iz"iato dlia SVOikh: v Rossii—novyi peredel sobstvennosti," *Novaia gazeta*, March 5, 2024, https://novayagazeta.eu/articles/2024/03/05/iziato-dlia-svoikh. Revealingly, the latter source notes that only one-quarter of the renationalizations in 2023 were in the military industry and the machine-building sectors (and could therefore be rationalized as motivated by the needs of military production); the other three-quarters concerned food and fishing, port facilities, and real estate—all highly attractive to well-placed claimants.

126. Andrei Kostin, "Tri otveta na odin vopros—kak vernut' den'gi v ekonomiku," *RBC*, April 11, 2023, https://www.rbc.ru/opinions/economics/11/04/2023/6434286c9a79475768678434.

127. "Kostin predlozhil aktivy-kandidaty na privatizatsiiu," *RBC*, April 24, 2023, https://www.rbc.ru/finances/24/04/2023/6446489d9a7947d3fdc14b09.

128. Excerpts from speeches at SPIEF 2023, published in *RBC*, June 15, 2023, https://www.rbc.ru/finances/15/06/2023/648ac0899a794751142cdd89.

129. Putin remarks at the April 2024 plenary session of the RSPP. "Plenarnoe zasedanie s"ezda RSPP," April 25, 2024, http://kremlin.ru/events/president/news/73940.

130. Since then, Raiffeisenbank's Russian operations have grown even larger. As of July 2023, it reported over 10,000 employees, 2,600 corporate customers, and 4 million individual customers.

131. https://www.ft.com/content/ecb4bccf-5cb2-49a7-ba36-61354ad8ad72. Unicredit's exposure to the Russian market was much smaller than that of Raiffeisenbank. In 2022 Russia accounted for only €1 billion out of Unicredit's total revenues of €20 billion. In contrast, Raiffeisenbank had by far the largest exposure to Russia of any foreign bank. (https://www.ft.com/content/ec5ad958-101c-4185-a56b-09234d2c9d36).

132. In 2022, retail depositors pulled out money, mostly in the form of foreign exchange, but corporate clients increased their deposits (more than offsetting the outflow from the departure of foreign companies), to take advantage of the fact that the foreign banks (especially Raiffeisenbank and Unicredit), being unsanctioned, could still handle international transfers, whereas the sanctioned Russian banks could not. (See https://www.kommersant.ru/doc/5695721 on the losses of the Russian banks.) This response by depositors was not new. Following the Crimean occupation too, Russians had responded to the first round of Western sanctions by moving their foreign exchange into the foreign banks, especially Raiffeisenbank, which they viewed as at lower risk of sanctions.

133. According to *Kommersant*, the remaining foreign banks in Russia made bigger total profits in 2022 than the entire Russian banking sector: 211 billion rubles vs. 203 billion rubles. That means that the rest of the sector actually lost money. According to the RCB, at the beginning of 2023 there were sixty-five foreign-controlled banks; all told there were 108 banks with foreign capital (https://www.kommersant.ru/doc/5902834). Their core business in Russia consisted of interest on loans and commissions. (Their ATM business collapsed, and those foreign banks that were engaged in it lost money.) Raiffeisenbank alone accounted for 141 billion rubles in profits, Unicredit for 57 billion rubles, and all the remaining sixty-three banks for only 13 billion rubles (which, however, they are barred from exporting out of Russia). The combined assets of banks "with foreign beneficiaries" accounted for 12.6 trillion rubles, or 9.4% of total assets in the Russian banking system in 2022.

134. Polina Ivanova and Anastasia Stognei, "Western Groups Leaving Russia Face Obligatory Donation to Moscow, *Financial Times*, March 27, 2023, https://www.ft.com/content/77368014-1397-4a08-901d-1f996e66d627.

135. "TsB ne odobril peredachu 'dochek' inostrannykh bankov pod vneshnee upravlenie," *RCB*, April 28, 2023, https://www.rbc.ru/finances/28/04/2023/644bc8b59a79471ce0d7ce34.

136. *Interfax*, April 20, 2023, https://interfax.com/newsroom/top-stories/89821/.

137. The request was sent to Raiffeisen International, which negotiated a delay and promised to answer OFAC's questions in tranches in April, May, and June (https://www.reuters.com/business/us-sanctions-authority-asks-raiffeisen-about-business-related-russia-2023-02-17/).

138. https://www.reuters.com/business/us-sanctions-authority-asks-raiffeisen-about-business-related-russia-2023-02-17/.

139. https://www.reuters.com/world/europe/loans-russian-soldiers-fuel-calls-european-banks-quit-2023-02-13/.

140. https://www.boersen-zeitung.de/banken-finanzen/est-220z-raiffeisen-russland-tochter?issue=99740db3-d165-424d-a550-dafd41419b7b.

141. https://www.ft.com/content/22acf30f-4ff5-4997-8f26-be582662194a.

142. *Forbes Russia*, May 5, 2023, https://www.forbes.ru/finansy/488889-raiffeisen-zaavil-o-priostanovke-vseh-korscetov-bankov-rossii-krome-svoej-docki.

143. Kseniia Dement'eva, "Inostrantsy zastriali v Rossii," *Kommersant*, April 20, 2023 (https://www.kommersant.ru/doc/5940988).

144. Ksenia Dement'eva and Ol'ga Sherunkova, "RBI snizhaet pribyl' ot Rossii," *Kommersant*, February 1, 2024, https://www.kommersant.ru/doc/6480354.

145. In June 2023, Raiffeisenbank's home office in Vienna announced that it will no longer make transfers in euros to Russia (https://www.raiffeisen.ru/about/press/news/201902/). It may be only a matter of time before it stops handling transfers of foreign exchange out of Russia.

146. See "Russia's New Elite Emerges to Fill Void after Multinationals Flee," *Bloomberg News*, November 9, 2023, https://www.bloomberg.com/news/articles/2023-11-09/russia-after-mcdonalds-henkel-and-others-flee-new-local-elite-fills-void#xj4y7vzkg.

147. https://thebell.io/kremlevskiy-kasting-kak-sergey-kirienko-ishchet-pokupateley-dlya-yandeksa.

148. For an extensive report on the "new Russians" acquiring departing foreign businesses, see Irina Pankratova, "Novye russkie: Reiting pokupatelei aktivov ushedshikh iz Rossii inostrannykh kompanii," *The Bell*, March 12, 2024, https://thebell.io/novye-russkie-reyting-pokupateley-aktivov-ushedshikh-iz-rossii-inostrannykh-kompaniy. For background on Kanokov, see Vitalii Soldatskikh "Kruto i tochka," https://www.proekt.media/investigation/kanokov-mcdonalds/.

149. Avon arrived in Russia in the early 1990s and built a successful business with locally produced perfumes (including the best-selling perfume in Russia) and its trademark army of door-to-door sales agents recruited from the local population ("Avon Calling!"). Avon has come under criticism since the invasion for continuing to recruit sales agents on Russian social media and for continuing production at its local Russian plant near Moscow. See Lora Jones, "Beauty Giant Avon under Fire over Russia Links," *BBC* News, January 27, 2024, https://www.bbc.com/news/business-67425366.

150. https://www.kommersant.ru/doc/5393453.

151. Iuliana Verbitskaia et al., "Inostrannye postavshchiki IT ukhodiat iz Rossii. Chto delat'?" *Vedomosti*, April 6, 2022, https://www.vedomosti.ru/management/articles/2022/04/05/916797-inostrannie-postavschiki-uhodyat.

152. https://www.reuters.com/article/us-ibs-group-ipo/russian-it-services-company-ibs-considers-ipo-in-2018-sources-idUSKBN1EE1VY. IBS was the creation of Russian entrepreneur Anatolii Karachinsky. It grew quickly both inside and outside Russia, and in 2013 Karachinsky spun off the international business under the name Luxoft, which held an international public offering in 2013. IBS from that point on focused on the domestic market, becoming known as the Russian SAP. It serves both the private sector and municipal governments, helping them to put their records on the cloud, and has introduced an online tax collection system for Russia's new VAT. Interview with IBS CEO Svetlana Balanova, *BNE Intellinews*, https://www.intellinews.com/interview-ibs-at-the-heart-of-russia-s-digital-transformation-135895/.

153. "Mondelez Chief Defends Decision to Stay in Russia," *Financial Times*, February 23, 2024, https://www.ft.com/content/10621358-55f2-4152-90a4-4cb4fea5116a.

154. Under current rules, foreign companies are only allowed to transfer up to 10 million rubles a month (currently about $125,000) to accounts in the West.

155. One of the strongest warnings, strikingly, comes from one of Putin's most loyal oligarchs, Vladimir Potanin, the head of Interros, who spoke out against any radical nationalization. "It will take us back a hundred years to 1917," he said, "and we will experience the consequences of such a step–global distrust of Russia on the part of investors–for many decades to come" (Potanin statement on Telegram, https://t.me/nornickel_official/1059).

Chapter 7

1. Andrei Doronichev quoted in *Kremnievaia Dolina*, video, Iurii Dud' webpage, https://www.youtube.com/watch?v=9lO06Zxhu88.

2. Cited in Elena Kukol, "Ne podelili dokhody ot nefti," *Rossiiskaia gazeta*, December 13, 2010, p. 2. Since 2014, Klepach has been the chief economist of VEB, the state-owned descendant of *Vneshekonombank*, the Soviet-era Foreign Trade Bank.

3. *Kremnievaia Dolina*, minutes 7–16. Doronichev also tells his story on the website immigrantsareus.org.

4. For a fascinating account of the world of small-scale high-tech entrepreneurship in Russia, see the interview with Dmitrii Dumik by online blogger Andrew Warner, at https://mixergy.com/interviews/chatfuel-with-dmitrii-dumik/.

5. *Kremnievaia Dolina*, minutes 2:46–2:28. In February 2018, Ovchinnikov was questioned after an anonymous tip claimed that his pizza chain was a foil for a distribution network of Latin American drugs; he said that this was an attempt to frame him.

6. See the interview with Maksim Mikheenko, "Eto bylo ne iavnaia, khrupkaia, no vseo-zhe mechta, s samogo detstva," *Cosmopolitan Russia*, January 20, 2020, https://www.cosmo.ru/lifestyle/stil-zhizni/maksim-miheenko-eto-byla-ne-yavnaya-hrupkaya-no-vse-zhe-mechta-s-samogo-detstva/.

7. *Kremnievaia dolina*, minute 2:47.

8. On the latter point, see the provocative book by Henry Farrell and Abraham Newman, *Underground Empire: How America Weaponized the World Economy* (New York: Henry Holt, 2023), especially pp. 26–37, 217–221.

9. See the thoughtful historical overview of Russia's repeated economic crises by Aleksandra Prokopenko, formerly with the Russian Central Bank and the Higher School of Economics, and presently a nonresident scholar at the Carnegie Russia Eurasia Center. *Permanent Crisis Mode: Why Russia's Economy Has Been So Resilient to Sanctions*, ZOIS Report, No. 4 (Berlin: Centre for East European and International Studies, November 2023), https://en.zois-berlin. de/fileadmin/media/Dateien/3-Publikationen/ZOiS_Reports/2023/ZOiS_Report_4_2023.pdf.

10. These disasters have received wide coverage in the Russian media (both inside Russia and offshore), especially from *Novye izvestiia*, which has devoted several hard-hitting articles to the problem of urban flooding. See in particular https://newizv.ru/news/2024-04-08/rossiya-uhodit-pod-vodu-srazu-neskolko-rossiyskih-regionov-ohvatil-pavodok-429039.

11. Elena Ribakova, "Sanctions against Russia Will Worsen Its Already Poor Economic Prospects," Peterson Institute for International Economics, April 18, 2023, https://www.piie.com/blogs/realtime-economics/sanctions-against-russia-will-worsen-its-already-poor-economic-prospects.

12. Oleg Sapozhkov and Aigul' Abdullina, "Perestanovka v kabinete," *Kommersant*, May 11, 2024, https://www.kommersant.ru/doc/6690240.

13. Andrei Belousov was an academic researcher in economics until he entered state service in 2006 as deputy minister of economic development and trade; from 2008 to 2012, he was director of the finance and economics department of the prime minister's office. It is during that period that he is said to have come to Putin's notice, and thereafter his rise was swift. In 2013, after a brief one-year tour as minister of economic development, he became Putin's special assistant for economic affairs, and then in 2020, he was named first deputy prime minister in Mikhail Mishustin's first cabinet. Belousov has consistently taken a more statist position than the "liberal" *finansisty*. For a useful review of his past public statements, see *Agentstvo*, May 11, 2024, https://t.me/agentstvonews/6092.

14. For a summary portrait of Belousov and his positions on economic policy over the years, especially in contrast to the "shock therapy" reformers, see Yakov Feygin, "Andrei Belousov and the Tragedy of Soviet Economics," *Riddle*, June 20, 2024, https://ridl.io/andrei-belousov-and-the-tragedy-of-soviet-economics/.

15. The next three paragraphs are based on numbers from Rosstat and Russian Central Bank. For an analysis and commentary, see "Novyi zastoi. Kak Rossiia prospala desiat' let," *Vazhnye istorii*, April 10, 2024, https://istories.media/opinions/2024/04/10/novii-zastoi-kak-rossiya-prospala-desyat-let/.

16. For a thoughtful analysis, see Vladislav Inozemtsev, "Will Russia's Central Bank Be Able to Stop the Economy from Overheating?" *Riddle*, August 2, 2024, https://ridl.io/will-russia-s-central-bank-be-able-to-stop-the-economy-from-overheating/.

17. "Gref: Model' rosta rossiiskoi ekonomiki chrezvychaino prosta, no uiazvima," *Kommersant*, June 7, 2024, https://www.kommersant.ru/doc/6748228. For the full video version of Gref's remarks, made at a breakfast meeting on the sidelines of the Saint Petersburg Economic Forum in May 2024, see https://roscongress.org/sessions/spief-2024-delovaya-programma-rossiya-2030-kak-priyti-k-finishu-chetvyertymi/translation/.

18. "Nabiullina nazvala osnovnuiu problemu ekonomiki Rossii," *RBC*, November 9, 2023, https://www.rbc.ru/economics/09/11/2023/654c8ef89a7947166afec281.

19. https://tass.ru/politika/19910859.

20. For background on the state of the Russian economy and the financial sector following the 2014 sanctions, see Connolly, *Russia's Response to Sanctions*, pp. 151–161.

21. https://en.wikipedia.org/wiki/Andrey_Kostin.

22. https://en.wikipedia.org/wiki/Andrey_Akimov.

23. https://en.wikipedia.org/wiki/German_Gref.

24. The same is true of the smaller Russian banks, many of which had also expanded into Europe, notably into Ireland.

25. In addition, Gazprombank International, located in Luxembourg, remains a major holder of Russian "shadow reserves," that is, foreign exchange retained abroad.

26. Yandex was actually founded one year before Google.

27. "Yandex, Russia's Biggest Technology Company, Celebrates 20 Years," *The Economist*, September 30, 2017, https://www.economist.com/business/2017/09/30/yandex-russias-biggest-technology-company-celebrates-20-years.

28. Of the two, Volozh went on to become the leader of Yandex for the next twenty-five years, and was the true creator of the company, while Segalovich faded from view. Volozh originally came from Kazakhstan, but was a student in Moscow.

29. Max Seddon, "In Lockdown, Yandex Evolves from Russia's Google to Its Amazon," *Financial Times*, May 10, 2020, https://www.ft.com/content/ee68326e-7be4-41c5-8180-74e805f1aef1.

30. In April 2023, Uber exited Russia and sold its 29% stake in Yandex-Taxi to Yandex for $702.5 million (a 60% discount to the 2021 valuation). Earlier, Yandex had "already bought back from Uber its share in Yandex-Eda, Yandex-Lavka, and Yandex-Dostavka, as well as its activity and robot delivery vehicles." The joint venture, which covered activities in Russia but also in other

countries, was formed in 2018. Uber had invested $225 million and Yandex $100 million. It had been registered in the Netherlands. Yandex gained access to Uber's technology, which it now retains for its taxi business (https://www.kommersant.ru/doc/5951622).

31. For a useful overview of Yandex's growth and evolution, including its frustrating experiences in international business, see Aleksey Grammatchikov, "'Yandeks': Umnozhenie deleniem," *Ekspert*, December 5, 2022, https://expert.ru/expert/2022/49/yandeks-umnozheniye-deleniyem/.

32. A year later, in March 2023, NASDAQ delisted Yandex and Ozon among others (https://www.kommersant.ru/doc/5875625). Yandex appealed the delisting, following NASDAQ rules (https://www.nasdaq.com/press-release/yandex-n.v.-notified-of-anticipated-delisting-from-the-nasdaq-stock-market-2023-03-15). NASDAQ granted the appeal, given the company's plans to split its Russian and foreign businesses. At this writing, however, the suspension of US trading remains in effect.

33. See the path-breaking dissertation by Jaclyn A. Kerr, "Authoritarian Management of (Cyber-) Society: Internet Regulation and the New Political Protest Movements" (PhD diss., Georgetown University, 2016). At a forum in Saint Petersburg in 2014, Putin stated that the Internet had first appeared as a CIA special project and charged that Yandex from its inception had been under Western influence or control (p. 247, fn. 308). See also Jaclyn A. Kerr, "Runet's Critical Juncture: The Ukraine War and the Battle for the Soul of the Russian Internet," *SAIS Review of International Affairs*, 42, no. 2 (Summer–Fall 2022): 63–84, https://muse.jhu.edu/article/892250.

34. In June 2023 a Moscow court fined Yandex for refusing to provide information about its user base to the FSB (https://www.reuters.com/technology/russias-yandex-fined-refusing-share-user-information-with-security-services-2023-06-18/).

35. Aleksey Grammatchikov, "'Zheltye' i 'sinie' raskhodiatsia po raznym uglam," *Monokl'*, December 5, 2022, https://monocle.ru/expert/2022/49/yandeks-umnozheniye-deleniyem/.

36. The 45.3% voting share held by Volozh and his family's trust (although only 8.65% of the capital) in Yandex was transferred to the board of directors after Volozh and his COO Tigran Khudaverdian were sanctioned by the EU as part of its sixth package. A golden share in the company, which had been held by Sberbank, was transferred to the Russian "Public Interest Fund" (https://www.kommersant.ru/doc/5391260).

37. https://www.kommersant.ru/doc/5691973 and https://www.bloomberg.com/news/articles/2023-11-14/yandex-to-fully-divest-russian-assets-and-distribute-proceeds?embedded-checkout=true.

38. The transaction, one of the largest corporate exits to date, was closely monitored by the Kremlin. In December 2022, Yandex hired former finance minister Aleksey Kudrin, relying on his long-standing ties to Putin, to help manage the negotiations, reportedly working through Sergei Kirienko, the first deputy head of the Presidential Administration. See https://www.kommersant.ru/doc/6493340 and Max Seddon, "Search Engine Yandex to Sell Russian Operations for $5 Billion, *Financial Times*, February 6, 2024, https://www.ft.com/content/2d7b3a64-f462-49c6-9583-11e339366eb4#post-cd66a047-f2a0-4f2c-a814-37224b73669c. But when the final deal was announced, Kudrin had evidently no place in it.

39. Natal'ia Skorlygina, "Starym vagonam perekryli puti," *Kommersant*, January 10, 2016, https://www.kommersant.ru/doc/2889220. Russia set a goal of one million new freight cars by 2030.

40. A TBU is an enclosed bearing permanently lubricated with grease and carefully sealed on the inside, and mounted as a unit. It thus avoids the expensive work involved in opening bearing boxes.

41. https://news.timken.com/2014-03-24-Timken-Signs-Joint-Venture-Agreement-With-United-Wagon-Company-UWC-to-Strengthen-Presence-in-Key-Rail-Market.

42. https://www.bearing-news.com/bearing-industry-updates-related-to-ukraine-russia-conflict-april-2022/. In addition, EPK signed an agreement with Uralvagonzavod under which it would satisfy 100% of UVZ's need for tapered bearings (https://www.lily-bearing.com/blog/european-bearing-corporation-and-uralvagonzavod-will-cooperate/).

43. https://www.bearing-news.com/schaeffler-opens-first-manufacturing-facility-russia/.   The Sapsan, a Siemens Velaro model, is a ten-car train, adapted for the Russian wide-gauge rails. A first contract, for eight trains, was signed in 2006; a second contract, for twenty more trains, was signed in 2011.

44. Natal'ia Skorlygina, "Shariki za roliki," *Kommersant*, September 13, 2019, https://www.kommersant.ru/doc/4089891.

45. *Bearing News*, April 27, 2022, https://www.bearing-news.com/bearing-industry-updates-related-to-ukraine-russia-conflict-april-2022/.

46. Natal'ia Skorlygina, "Vagony bol'she ne innovatsionnye," *Kommersant*, March 14, 2022, https://dlib-eastview-com.proxy.library.georgetown.edu/browse/doc/74889547.

47. https://www.zmsbearing.com/chinas-bearing-trend-in-future-3-years/.

48. Natal'ia Skorlygina, "Kitaiskim podshipnikam vnov' pokatilo," *Kommersant*, October 24, 2023, https://www.kommersant.ru/doc/6295770.

49. "Russian Bearings Have Strategically Defeated Imported Bearings," *VGudok*, November 13, 2023, https://vgudok.com/lenta/rossiyskie-podshipniki-strategicheski-pobedili-importnye-kitaycy-smogut-postavlyat-na-set-rzhd.

50. For example, after SKF left, the plant in Tver' continued producing under the name TEK.KOM. By 2023 it was the primary producer in Russia, with nearly 100% localized production, except for the rollers and lubricants. It has a capacity of 150,000 cassettes a year. Reportedly over 82% of the resumed output in 2023 has consisted of Russian-made bearings (the rest was made up partly of imports from Belarus, as well as re-imports of older Russian bearings that had previously been exported to Kazakhstan and other FSU countries) (https://railway.tek-kom.ru/).

51. One major exception, however, is Uralvagonzavod (UVZ), which produces both railcars and tanks. Starting in 2023, UVZ has switched to tank production, under an *oboronzakaz*, and it has had to move its labor force, and consequently its output of railcars has declined by one-third in 2023. Since it was the main producer of "open cars" and platform cars, there is now a shortage, especially of platform cars, output of which has declined sharply (https://rosstat.gov.ru/enterprise_industrial#, Proizvodstvo osnovnykh vidov produktsii v narutal'nom vyrazhenii v dekabre, 2023 god).

52. As a result, many operators are holding off buying newly produced railcars. Leasing costs have also become prohibitive, because of higher interest rates (Natal'ia Skorlygina, "Vagony nepod"emno podorozhali," *Kommersant*, September 4 2023 (https://www.kommersant.ru/doc/6196899).

53. "Platformy ot"ezzhaiut ot rynka," https://www.kommersant.ru/doc/6320540.

54. Natal'ia Skorlygina, "Novye vagony ne uspevaiut za starymi," *Kommersant*, August 9, 2023, https://www.kommersant.ru/doc/6148692.

55. This is controversial, however, and at this writing the request for suspension has not yet been granted by the Ministry of Transportation. For a background history of the modernization decree, see https://www.kommersant.ru/doc/6210679.

56. For background on the history of the Russian–European gas relationship, see my book *The Bridge: Russian Gas in a Redivided Europe* (Cambridge, MA: Harvard University Press, 2020).

57. Sergey Vakulenko, "What Russia's First Pipeline Reveals about a Planned Second One," Carnegie Politika, Carnegie Endowment for International Peace, April 18, 2023, https://carnegieendowment.org/politika/89552.

58. Quoted in "Gazprom raz'iasnil vyskazyvanie o peregovorah s Kitaem iz-za koronavirusa," *Interfaks*, February 13, 2020, https://www.interfax.ru/business/695245.

59. https://www.ft.com/content/ef9f2c78-a066-4557-acf2-9ca983447c6b.

60. For a detailed analysis of the outlook for Russian coal production and exports, see Irina Mironova, " Russia's Coal Sector: Between Sanctions and the Global Energy Transition" (Fairfax, VA: Energy Innovation Reform Project, March 2024), https://innovationreform.org/wp-content/uploads/2024/03/2024-02-Russias-coal-sector.pdf. Mironova is a leading Russian expert on the Russian coal industry. As for rail capacity, there are other bottlenecks on the East Siberian rail system besides the Chinese; another is military deliveries (called *mobilizatsionnye gruzy*) to the Ukrainian front, which have first priority. On this point, see Natal'ia Skorlygina, "BAM obnaruzhil v sebe pustotu," *Kommersant*, February 28, 2024, https://www.kommersant.ru/doc/6534442.

61. Chinese customs statistics, as reproduced in Aleksey Chigadaev, "Neftianoi povorot na vostok," *Riddle*, April 16, 2024, https://ridl.io/ru/neftyanoj-povorot-na-vostok/.

62. China's energy transition is mainly of a rapid expansion of renewables, while continuing to invest in coal and limiting exposure to oil and gas. The rapid progress of electric vehicles in China presages a peak in Chinese oil demand, which is mainly for transportation, as early as the mid-2020s. This will mark the end of an era, since China's oil demand has driven half of the global increase since 2001, when China joined the World Trade Organization. See Greg McMillan, "China's Waning Oil Demand Spurs Wider Change," *Financial Times*, September 28, 2023, https://www.ft.com/content/6acfcbb4-0a29-4f4a-bf13-d0242072fdae.

63. Joe Leahy and Harry Dempsey, "Bumper Chinese Steel Exports Spur Concerns of Over-supply," *Financial Times*, March 22, 2024, https://www.ft.com/content/a875f0bb-7087-477b-a015-f9abec625b74.

64. See "Iron Ore Fall Bodes Ill for Steel Demand and China's Economy," *Financial Times*, March 5, 2024, https://www.ft.com/content/611b2037-41a0-4e72-9d9a-6d6d1e311567.

65. In February 2024, China's Zhejiang Chouzhou Commercial Bank, which was the largest processor of payments for Russian imports from China, barred all operations with Russian and Belarussian companies. At the same time, several Chinese payments systems stopped serving Russian customers (https://www.vedomosti.ru/economics/articles/2024/02/07/1018866-glavnii-dlya-rossiiskih-importerov-bank-kitaya-ostanovil-vse-rascheti-s-rf). In the same month, three of China's four largest banks, Industrial and Commercial Bank of China (ICBC), China Construction Bank (CCB), and Bank of China, likewise stopped accepting payments from Russia, even when made in renminbi (https://iz.ru/1653256/mariia-kolobova-milana-gadzhieva/komissiia-bez-perevoda-tri-krupneishikh-banka-knr-perestali-prinimat-platezhi-iz-rf). In addition, many Chinese banks and payment platforms have tightened compliance procedures across the board. These obstacles have not yet stopped Russian imports from China from growing, but Russian buyers report increasingly long delays. This is notably affecting Russian imports of Chinese electronic components and assembly kits, even those covered by long-term contracts (https://www.kommersant.ru/doc/6636979). A growing number of Russian importers and exporters complain that their operations are suffering as a result. See Iuliia Suntsova, "Rossiiane rasskazali, kak 'zavis' ikh biznes iz-za blokirovannykh v Kitae platezhei," *Novye izvestiia*, April 24, 2024, https://newizv.ru/news/2024-04-24/biznesmeny-rasskazali-kak-zavis-ih-biznes-iz-za-zablokirovannyh-v-kitae-platezhey-429578. At the same time, smaller Chinese banks, which are less visible on OFAC's radar screen, are already beginning to replace the larger ones, and this process will no doubt continue. For an excellent overview of the evolution of Russian-Chinese currency relations and its consequences, see Aleksandra Prokopenko, "Kitaizataiia by design: Kak razvorot Rossii na Vostok izmenil mirovye finansy," Carnegie Politika, Carnegie Endowment for International Peace, May 16, 2024, https://storage.googleapis.com/crng/china-russia-yuan.html?utm_source=carnegieemail&utm_medium=email&utm_campaing=email_weekly&mkt_tok=ODEzLVhZVS00MjIAAAGTOgETu3klI9xJqzWUP2_LkxwFxG5MnTyS6lBWjEYXkib5aO5SZiTif9ZMtvyEX6s7mwqvMfChtO5s0Gc0L-W2b1az7295YOvdyuE5QhCrVlw.

66. Owen Walker and Cheng Leng, "Russia's Banks Propped Up by Chinese Cash after Sanctions," *Financial Times*, September 3, 2023, https://www.ft.com/content/96349a26-d868-4bd1-948f-b17f87cc5c72. For a broader analysis of Russia's increasing use of the renminbi, see Maxim Chupilkin et al., "Exorbitant Privilege and Economic Sanctions," Working Paper No. 281, European Bank for Reconstruction and Development, September 2023, https://www.ebrd.com/publications/working-papers/exorbitant-privilege-and-economic-sanctions.

67. See Bradley Parks et al., "Belt and Road Reboot," AidData, November 2023, https://docs.aiddata.org/reports/belt-and-road-reboot/Belt_and_Road_Reboot_Full_Report.pdf. AidData is a research laboratory at the University of William and Mary.

68. According to the former Russian website *finanz.ru* (unfortunately no longer active), Chinese FDI in Russia declined by 2.5 times between 2014—the beginning of the pivot to the East—and 2020.

69. Cited in Elena Petrova and Tat'iana Sviridova, "Direktor ISAA Aleksey Maslov: 'Kitai ozhidaet okonchanie goriachei fazy SVO," *Novye Izvestiia*, May 17, 2024, https://newizv.ru/news/2024-05-17/direktor-isaa-aleksey-maslov-kitay-ozhidaet-okonchaniya-goryachey-fazy-svo-430192.

70. Edward White, "China's Belt and Road Spending in Russia Drops to Zero," *Financial Times*, July 24, 2022, https://www.ft.com/content/470e2518-410b-4e78-9106-cf881dd43028.

71. Maslov interview, quoted in Petrova and Sviridova, "Direktor ISAA Aleksey Maslov."

72. Interview with Aleksey Chekunkov, "Glavnyi vyzov—naiti vnutrennie resursy," *Kommersant*, July 13, 2022, https://www.kommersant.ru/doc/5458995.

73. See Maria Snegovaya et al., *Back in Stock? The State of Russia's Defense Industry after Two Years of War* (Washington, DC: Center for Strategic and International Studies, April 2024).

74. China's drone manufacturer DJI, based in Shenzhen, announced in 2022 that it was suspending all sales to Russia. But DJI drones continue to be sold in Russia and to find their way to military training centers and the battlefield (https://www.rferl.org/a/russia-ukraine-

chinese-drones-training-centers/32621432.html). DJI drones are widely available for sale in the United States. In Russia they can be purchased on the open market through specialized firms such as Skymec (https://skymec.ru/).

75. Evgenii Karasiuk, "Nikto ne khochet darit' tekhnologii," *Republic*, October 2, 2023, https://republic.ru/posts/109879.

76. For an analysis of the expanding Russian–Chinese space relationship, see Kevin Pollpeter et al., *China-Russia Space Cooperation*, China Aerospace Studies Institute (Montgomery, AL: Air University, May 2023).

Chapter 8

1. In September 1983, the downing of a Korean airliner by a Soviet interceptor was followed three months later by the Able Archer Incident, in which a NATO exercise nearly touched off a nuclear exchange. This incident strongly influenced President Reagan and led him, by 1985, to adopt a policy of rapprochement with the new Soviet leader, Mikhail Gorbachev, which opened the way to the 1987 Intermediate-Range Nuclear Forces Treaty and subsequent treaties.

2. For an entertaining but all-too-plausible account of this sudden self-discovery, see the opening chapter of the novel by Boris Akunin, *Advokat besa: Strashnaia Povest'* (Tel-Aviv: Babel, 2022).

3. Daniel Yergin and Thane Gustafson, *Russia 2010 and What It Means for the World* (New York: Random House, 1993). The Russian edition, *Dvadtsat' let spustia*, was published in Moscow in 1995, by Mezhdunarodnye Otnosheniia Publishing House. *Russia 2010*, which was written in 1993, described five scenarios, ranging from chaos and reaction ("The Long Good-Bye" and a military dictatorship called "The Russian Bear") to the full development of a market economy ("Chudo," Russian for miracle), underpinned by a liberal (although not necessarily democratic) political system. In addition, the book featured two political scenarios, a more chaotic one called "Muddling Down," and an authoritarian/nationalist one, "Two-Headed Eagle." Over the past thirty years, elements of all five scenarios have come to pass, together with various surprises along the way (Vladimir Putin, for obvious reasons, does not appear in the book, since it was published before his arrival in Moscow in 1996).

4. The phrases "pipes and plumbing" and "underground" are borrowed from the path-breaking book by Henry Farrell and Abraham Newman, *Underground Empire: How America Weaponized the World Economy* (New York: Henry Holt, 2023), esp. Chapter 1. As Farrell and Newman show, much of the physical infrastructure of the Internet is concentrated in the United States, notably in northern Virginia, and is connected via undersea cables to the rest of the world.

5. This is not the place to go into the tangled history of how Crimea was "given" to Ukraine by Soviet premier Nikita Khrushchev in 1954. Suffice it to say that there is only a minority of Ukrainians in Crimea. Ukraine has already made significant tacit concessions on its sovereignty over Crimea, in agreeing to a long-term lease of Sevastopol as the site of the Russian Black Sea fleet.

6. The Belgian government, which has been receiving a 25% corporate tax on the profits from the frozen assets held in Euroclear, has agreed to earmark part of the tax revenue for military aid to Ukraine.

7. Under this scenario, a fresh wave of Putin-era oligarchs will seek to relocate to the West, to protect both their lives and their assets. Since many of them were complicit in the crimes of the Putin regime, this will raise further complicated legal and moral issues that will bedevil the removal of sanctions. It will be difficult for Western governments to resist the temptation to go after the Putin oligarchs, since they will be both visible and vulnerable. However, since many of them will also be tainted in the eyes of the new Russian leadership, they may make convenient scapegoats, over whom the two sides may tacitly cooperate.

Index

For the benefit of digital users, indexed terms that span two pages (e.g., 52–53) may, on occasion, appear on only one of those pages.